Monle Lee
Carla Johnson

Principles of Advertising
A Global Perspective

*Pre-publication
REVIEWS,
COMMENTARIES,
EVALUATIONS...*

"The global perspective and emphasis on ethics make this book a unique and very welcome addition to the body of advertising knowledge. It is clearly written, entertaining to read, and wonderfully current in its examples. Bravo to Professors Lee and Johnson!"

Susan K. Jones, MSJ
*Professor of Marketing,
Ferris State University,
Big Rapids, MI*

"Bingo! The Lee and Johnson text has all the numbers—informative, readable, global perspective, new technologies. From the IC (integrated communication) perspective, they clearly describe advertising while demonstrating it working with other marketing processes to affect consumers' buying behavior and brand loyalty. Contemporary and carefully drawn examples provide the foundation for the description and demonstration.

I particularly like the integration of a global view of the industry into every chapter, rather than clustering it as a separate chapter tucked away near the end of the text. Advertising is global! Exemplifying the major concepts of advertising and IC with cases from around the world, the authors emphasize the interconnectedness of commerce as well as the opportunities and problems that interconnectedness poses to advertising clients and agencies.

The 30- and 60-second 'spots' concluding every chapter should appeal to student readers. New employees—recent graduates—have written each 'spot,' giving a view of the advertising business closer to what the reader will experience. A nice way to bring the reader into the text."

Dan Pyle Millar, PhD, APR
*Professor and Coordinator,
Public Relations Program,
Indiana State University,
Terre Haute, IN*

NOTES FOR PROFESSIONAL LIBRARIANS AND LIBRARY USERS

This is an original book title published by The Haworth Press, Inc. Unless otherwise noted in specific chapters with attribution, materials in this book have not been previously published elsewhere in any format or language.

CONSERVATION AND PRESERVATION NOTES

All books published by The Haworth Press, Inc. and its imprints are printed on certified pH neutral, acid free book grade paper. This paper meets the minimum requirements of American National Standard for Information Sciences-Permanence of Paper for Printed Material, ANSI Z39.48-1984.

Principles of Advertising
A Global Perspective

HAWORTH Marketing Resources
Innovations in Practice & Professional Services
William J. Winston, Senior Editor

New, Recent, and Forthcoming Titles:

Managing Sales Professionals: The Reality of Profitability by Joseph P. Vaccaro

Squeezing a New Service into a Crowded Market by Dennis J. Cahill

Publicity for Mental Health Clinicians: Using TV, Radio, and Print Media to Enhance Your Public Image by Douglas H. Ruben

Managing a Public Relations Firm for Growth and Profit by A. C. Croft

Utilizing the Strategic Marketing Organization: The Modernization of the Marketing Mindset by Joseph P. Stanco

Internal Marketing: Your Company's Next Stage of Growth by Dennis J. Cahill

The Clinician's Guide to Managed Behavioral Care by Norman Winegar

Marketing Health Care into the Twenty-First Century: The Changing Dynamic by Alan K. Vitberg

Fundamentals of Strategic Planning for Health-Care Organizations edited by Stan Williamson, Robert Stevens, David Loudon, and R. Henry Migliore

Risky Business: Managing Violence in the Workplace by Lynne Falkin McClure

Predicting Successful Hospital Mergers and Acquisitions: A Financial and Marketing Analytical Tool by David P. Angrisani and Robert L. Goldman

Marketing Research That Pays Off: Case Histories of Marketing Research Leading to Success in the Marketplace edited by Larry Percy

How Consumers Pick a Hotel: Strategic Segmentation and Target Marketing by Dennis Cahill

Applying Telecommunications and Technology from a Global Business Perspective by Jay Zajas and Olive Church

Strategic Planning for Private Higher Education by Carle M. Hunt, Kenneth W. Oosting, Robert Stevens, David Loudon, and R. Henry Migliore

Writing for Money in Mental Health by Douglas H. Ruben

The New Business Values for Success in the Twenty-First Century: Improvement, Innovation, Inclusion, Incentives, Information by John Persico and Patricia Rouner Morris

Marketing Planning Guide, Second Edition by Robert E. Stevens, David L. Loudon, Bruce Wrenn, and William E. Warren

Contemporary Sales Force Management by Tony Carter

4 × 4 Leadership and the Purpose of the Firm by H. H. Pete Bradshaw

Lessons in Leisure Business Success: The Recreation Professional's Business Transformation Primer by Jonathan T. Scott

Guidebook to Managed Care and Practice Management Terminology by Norman Winegar and Michelle L. Hayter

Medical Group Management in Turbulent Times: How Physician Leadership Can Optimize Health Plan, Hospital, and Medical Group Performance by Paul A. Sommers

Defining Your Market: Winning Strategies for High-Tech, Industrial, and Service Firms by Art Weinstein

Alignment: A Provider's Guide to Managing the Practice of Health Care by Paul A. Sommers

Consumer Satisfaction in Medical Practice by Paul A. Sommers

Using Public Relations Strategies to Promote Your Nonprofit Organization by Ruth Ellen Kinzey

The Aftermath of Reengineering: Downsizing and Corporate Performance by Tony Carter

Principles of Advertising: A Global Perspective by Monle Lee and Carla Johnson

Principles of Advertising
A Global Perspective

Monle Lee
Carla Johnson

The Haworth Press
New York • London • Oxford

© 1999 by The Haworth Press, Inc. All rights reserved. No part of this work may be reproduced or utilized in any form or by any means, electronic or mechanical, including photocopying, microfilm, and recording, or by any information storage and retrieval system, without permission in writing from the publisher. Printed in the United States of America.

The Haworth Press, Inc., 10 Alice Street, Binghamton, NY 13904-1580

Cover design by Jennifer M. Gaska.

Library of Congress Cataloging-in-Publication Data

Lee, Monle
   Principles of advertising : a global perspective / Monle Lee, Carla Johnson.
      p.   cm.
   Includes bibliographical references and index.
   ISBN 0-7890-0615-4 (alk. paper)
   1. Advertising. I. Johnson, Carla. II. Title.
HF5821.L35 1999
659.1—dc21   99-15065
                                                                                                                                 CIP

To the memory of our parents,
Mrs. Wuyao Hsu Lee
and
Mr. Harold P. Jackson,
in appreciation for their years of love and support

ABOUT THE AUTHORS

Monle Lee, DBA, is Professor of Marketing at Indiana University South Bend, South Bend, Indiana. Dr. Lee's first book, *Advertising: Strategy and Management*, a Mandarin language advertising textbook, was released in Taiwan in 1998 for Taiwanese college students. Her research interests center on international marketing, ethics marketing, advertising, and ethical issues in different cultures. Her research has appeared in book chapters, business journals, and various conference proceedings. Dr. Lee was previously an international marketer in Taiwan.

Carla Johnson, PhD, is Assistant Professor of Communication at Saint Mary's College in Notre Dame, Indiana. A member of the faculty for ten years, she currently oversees the advertising and public relations minors, and teaches courses in public relations, writing for advertising and public relations, and Integrated Communication campaigns. Dr. Johnson previously taught journalism, business communication, and technical writing at Lake Michigan College where she served as publicity director for the Niles campus. She has been a special assignment writer for *The South Bend Tribune* for twenty-five years.

CONTENTS

Foreword	xiii
Don E. Schultz	
Acknowledgments	xvii
Chapter 1. Introduction to Advertising	**1**
Advertising Defined	3
Advertising Classifications	4
Advertising Functions	8
Advertising and Marketing	10
The Evolution of Advertising	13
Summary	18
The Global Perspective: Global Brand Creation	18
Ethics Track: Deception in Advertising	19
:30 Spot: "Integrating an IMC Philosophy"	20
Chapter 2. The Advertising Environment: Economy, Society, and Technology	**21**
The Advertising Environment	23
Economic Forces and Advertising	23
Social Forces and Advertising	25
Technological Forces and Advertising	27
Summary	30
The Global Perspective: Considering Culture	31
Ethics Track: Media Responsibility in Running Ads	32
:60 Spot: "The Times They Are Changin'"	33
Chapter 3. Legal and Political Forces and Advertising	**35**
The Political and Legal Environments in the United States	38
The Political and Legal Environments in Other Selected Countries	42
Summary	48
The Global Perspective: The Impact of Advertising Environment on International Advertising	49
Ethics Track: Tobacco's Woes	49

Chapter 4. The Advertising Business and Advertising Agencies — 51

The Advertising Business	52
The Advertising Agency	55
Agency Compensation	58
Future Trends	60
Summary	63
The Global Perspective: Agency Shopping	63
Ethics Track: Agency Reviews	64
:60 Spot: "Writing the Road to Success"	65

Chapter 5. Market Segmentation, Target Marketing, and Product Positioning — 67

Market Segmentation	69
Target Marketing	74
Product Positioning	78
Summary	80
The Global Perspective: One Person's Horror, Another Person's Humor	80
Ethics Track: Targeting the Middleman	80
:30 Spot: "Paws-itively Hilarious"	82

Chapter 6. Consumer Behavior and Advertising — 83

The Buying Decision Process	85
Factors Influencing the Organizational Market	87
Factors Influencing the Consumer Market	88
Consumer Behavior: The Next Century	92
Summary	93
The Global Perspective: Generous Exposure	94
Ethics Track: Subliminal Messages	95
:60 Spot: "Marketing Professional Services"	96

Chapter 7. Marketing and Advertising Research — 99

Marketing Research	101
Advertising Research	104
Research Trends in the 1990s and Beyond	108
Summary	109

The Global Perspective: International Research Needs 110
Ethics Track: Watchdogs Research Too 110
:60 Spot: "Planning in Marketing: The Milk
  Mustache Story" 112

Chapter 8. The Marketing and Advertising Planning Process — 115

The Marketing Plan 117
The Advertising Plan 122
Making Budget Decisions 125
Summary 127
The Global Perspective: Selecting an International Agency 127
Ethics Track: Tobacco Companies—The Decision
  to Cut Ad Spending 128
:60 Spot: "A Day in the Life of an Evolving Brand" 129

Chapter 9. The Creative Aspect of Advertising — 131

Creative Concepts or Creativity in Advertising 133
Development in Creative Strategy 136
Summary 148
The Global Perspective: Hard Sell Is a Hard Sell Overseas 148
Ethics Track: Ethnic Groups in the Mainstream 149
:30 Spot: "The Key to Great Creative" 150

Chapter 10. Advertising Production — 151

Print Advertising Production 153
Broadcast Advertising Production 156
Internet Advertising Production 165
Summary 169
The Global Perspective: Developing the Big Idea Abroad 169
Ethics Track: Culture Jam 170
:60 Spot: "Vicki's Choice: Healthy Challenges" 171

Chapter 11. Advertising Media Planning and Selection — 173

Media Planning 175
Media Buying 179
Summary 182

The Global Perspective: The Optimizer and the British
    Invasion   182
Ethics Track: Green Marketing   183

Chapter 12. Print Media   **185**

Magazine Advertising   187
Newspaper Advertising   194
Summary   200
The Global Perspective: Avon Calling—
    With International Ads   201
Ethics Track: Covert Advertisements, Advertorials,
    and Other Puffing   201
:60 Spot: "First Day"   203

Chapter 13. Broadcast Media   **205**

Television Advertising   205
Radio Advertising   214
Summary   217
The Global Perspective: Kia Shuma's Culture Clash
    in South Korea   217
Ethics Track: Celebrity Endorsements
    and Other Deceptions   218

Chapter 14. Alternative Advertising Media   **221**

Out-of-Home Advertising   223
Other Alternative Advertising Media   225
Cross-Promotions   229
Summary   230
The Global Perspective: Cross-Training Across Borders   231
Ethics Track: The Squawk Over L'eggs' Eggs   231

Chapter 15. Direct Marketing/Direct Response
Advertising   **233**

Direct Marketing   235
Direct Response Advertising   236
Direct Marketing History   237
Direct Mail   239

Catalog Marketing	241
Direct Marketing and the Environment	244
Telemarketing	244
Nonprofit Direct Marketing	246
Privacy Issues	248
Business-to-Business Marketing	248
Marketing Without Borders	250
Summary	253
The Global Perspective: European Problems with Technology	253
Ethics Track: Out-of-House, Out-of-Country Telemarketing	254

Chapter 16. Sales Promotion — 257

The Role of Sales Promotion in Marketing	259
Sales Promotion, Publicity, and Advertising	259
Types of Sales Promotion	262
Summary	271
The Global Perspective: Puccini Attracts International Sponsors to China	271
Ethics Track: Selling Your Name—The PTA Profits with Office Depot	271
:60 Spot: "Olympic Sponsorship Ambushed"	273

Chapter 17. Public Relations, Publicity, and Corporate Advertising — 277

Public Relations	279
Publicity	292
Corporate Advertising	292
Summary	294
The Global Perspective: International Public Relations Firms	294
Another Global Perspective: How to Overcome International Communication Barriers	296
Ethics Track: Texaco—Calling Basic Values into Question	296
:60 Spot: "Defining Public Relations—What's Your Function?"	298

Chapter 18. Internet Advertising **301**

    The Internet   303
    Web Advertising   305
    Internet Directory Advertising   311
    Internet Customer Service   312
    Summary   313
    The Global Perspective: English Language
        in the Cyberfuture   313
    Ethics Track: The Dirty Little Search Engine Secret   314

Notes **317**

Index **337**

Foreword

Forewords are strange animals. Sometimes they enhance the text to follow. Sometimes they simply summarize what the authors have said. Sometimes they are repayment for previous debts or favors between or among authors. Sometimes they are personal statements by the foreword writer. To understand a foreword and the value of it, I believe it is important for the reader to know how the foreword came about and why that particular person asked or was asked to write the comments.

When Carla Johnson called me about the text she and Monle Lee were writing, it was initially to get my permission to use some materials I had developed over the years on Integrated Marketing Communication (IMC) which they planned to use in Chapter 1. Since some of my views of IMC have changed over the years, Carla wanted to be sure that what she was quoting was how I now viewed the process. After all, some of my early writings are now about ten years old.

After reading Chapter 1, I called Carla and told her she and Monle had indeed captured the essence of IMC and what I have observed around the world. In fact, they had extended some of my own thinking, particularly in the global arena. That led to more discussions, and that led to this foreword. I wholeheartedly agree with what you will find in the pages which follow on IMC and advertising principles.

So now, as Paul Harvey might say, "You know the rest of the story."

I'm pleased to write this foreword for I believe that the approach which Carla and Monle have developed really does capture the concepts, practice, and spirit of Integrated Marketing Communication as we enter the twenty-first century. It is, to me, a unique principles text. It mixes the proven theory base of the academic community with the actual practice of IMC around the world. It is highly readable and easy to follow. It presents concepts and approaches in a logical, easy-to-follow sequence. It is filled with examples and case illustrations. But, then, one could say the same thing about a number of advertising principles texts. The real question is "What makes this introductory text different?" In my view, there are four areas.

Integration. Integration and Integrated Marketing Communication (IMC) are "hot" topics in marketing and marketing communication today.

Yet, many advertising and marketing text authors in the development of their approaches have treated IMC as a "bolt on" or "add-on" to their manuscripts. They've added a chapter or some time-worn examples here and there in the string of chapters and said, "Now, our text is integrated." That's not the case here. Lee and Johnson take a truly integrated approach to the development of advertising programs. IMC permeates this book. It is the basis for the entire approach to communication which they have developed. It is "integrated" in the best sense of the word. So, if you want to see an IMC process in action, this text personifies the process and the approach.

Global perspective. Communication traditionally has been very culture-driven. That is, the approach to advertising or promotion has been based on the mores and structures of the economy or society in which it was written. Thus, a text written in Australia really wasn't too relevant to someone in Hong Kong. Or a text developed in Germany had little interest in South Africa. This book is, to my knowledge, the first text that takes a "global" approach to IMC. That is, it is boundary spanning and culture crossing. It is a horizontal view of the marketplace, across countries, across cultures, across economies. It is what has often been described as a "transnational" approach. Yet, it is very practical for a student who never plans to get more than a couple of hundred miles from home. Global is a way of thinking and a way of doing advertising and communication which is as relevant in the local market as it is in a satellite-delivered Olympic venue which spans the globe. In short, *Principles of Advertising: A Global Perspective* practices what IMC is all about, the integration of marketing and marketing communication from the view of the customer, not just the view of the marketing organization.

Ethics. In most principles texts, ethics or ethical behavior in marketing and communication usually ends up somewhere near the end of the text. Thus, the student or instructor can often "just not have time to talk about or cover the ethical considerations of an advertising or communication program" during the course. More critical, ethics is often separated from how the communication is either developed or implemented. In too many cases, authors treat ethics and ethical behavior by communicators as something that is added at the last moment. Lee and Johnson integrate ethics and ethical behavior throughout the book. Ethical communication and behavior is at the beginning and throughout the text. And, that's important. Too many consumers believe marketing communication and advertising is hucksterism or even worse, misleading or manipulative or just plain dishonest. In my view, ethical behavior by advertisers and communicators is one of the most critical issues of the twenty-first century. The increasing availability of individual customer information raises all the questions of privacy and marketers' "need to know" that consumer groups so legitimately challenge. Ethics is, to me, the cornerstone of effective communication, and this text is permeated with an ethical view. That's important for the student to learn and more important for the practitioner to implement.

Voices from industry. "What's it really like out there in the 'real world'?" students often wonder. In this text, you will learn. Monle and Carla have asked their own students to tell, in their own words, their experiences. And, those experiences aren't the musings of a twenty-year veteran who foggily remembers what it was like to work in the 1970s and 1980s. These are "real-world," "day-to-day" experiences from new hires in the advertising and communication fields. They "tell it like it is, warts and all." Some of the experiences are good. Some are bad. But all are interesting and useful to a person who is considering a career in advertising, promotion, public relations, direct marketing, or IMC. So, those are the four things which I believe differentiate this principles text from all the others on the market. It's integrated. It's global. It's focused on ethics and ethical behaviors by communicators. And, it's "real world." It's how IMC is being done today and will be done tomorrow.

Most of all, this text passes the four-C test I use to evaluate any text. In my system, Cs are good, not bad. The Cs I use are Clarity, Conciseness, Completeness, and Currency. The text you are about to read passes all four of these tests with flying colors. So, rather than four stars, I give Carla and Monle four Cs. And that is about the best you can do in my classes.

Don E. Schultz
Northwestern University
Evanston, IL

Acknowledgments

The authors wish to thank their families for their love, support, and patience: Dariush and Jennifer Behzadi, Wuchi Lee, Helen Jackson, Roderick S. Johnson, James C. Kennedy, and Aaron H. Hoffman. We also wish to acknowledge with deepest gratitude the contributions of other special individuals: Stefan Horvath, graduate assistant at Indiana University South Bend, who helped in countless ways throughout the writing of this book; Joyce Perry, Celia Fallon, and Charles Peltier at Saint Mary's College; Paula Winicur for ad design and cover art created just for us; and Dana Hanefeld, Tara Krull, Catherine A. Narbone, Amy Codron Randolph, Eric Remington, and Kathy Evans Wisner for their invaluable assistance in securing illustrations and permissions. We are also indebted to a number of Saint Mary's College graduates who so generously agreed to write about their experiences in the "real world," and to Jon A. Shidler at Southern Illinois University at Carbondale for his contribution. Finally, the authors wish to acknowledge fellowships received from the Direct Marketing Educational Foundation, the Yellow Pages Publishers Association, and the International Radio and Television Society to attend their seminars and institutes, where much of the knowledge represented here was gained. In fact, the authors met at an IRTS seminar in New York City. Without that opportunity, this book would never have existed.

Chapter 1

Introduction to Advertising

In an unprecedented display of the power of deep pockets, Coca-Cola Company aired up to seventy different commercials just once each in prime time during the 1996 Summer Olympics on NBC. Coca-Cola paid a hefty $60 million to NBC to buy the nonalcoholic beverage category for the Olympics being staged in its hometown, Atlanta, Georgia. Coca-Cola used its Olympics commercial time to push a number of its beverages, including Diet Coke, Sprite, PowerAde sports drink, and Nestea. Coke also tied in a major retail promotion with the Olympics. Point-of-purchase displays declared the season a "Red-Hot Olympic Summer." Featured products were custom twelve-packs and two-liter bottles, and consumers were able to win bottles of Coke as well as Olympics-related merchandise.[1]

In 1998, an Indiana college professor sent an overnight Federal Express package to the American Council for International Studies (ACIS), headquartered in Boston. A call to the recipient revealed that the package had not yet been received by late morning. The professor phoned a toll-free FedEx number, provided the tracking number, waited a few seconds, and discovered that the FedEx van was on Bay State Road in Boston, en route to deliver the package. The reason for the later-than-usual delivery time was also discovered: the FedEx flight out of Chicago's O'Hare Airport had been delayed by early morning fog. As the professor again called the recipient, the ACIS representative spotted the FedEx van pulling into a parking space on the street. The same tracking information was also available to the professor on the Internet.

Welcome to the world of Integrated Marketing Communication.

In the first example, Coca-Cola's decision to integrate a mass media blitz with special packaging and retail displays reflects the growing trend to "include and involve the channels of distribution in the communications mix" when an advertising campaign is launched.[2] But what does the second illustration have to do with advertising? The availability of consumer information, including electronic ticketing and tracking, illustrates the wave of the future—the shift in marketplace power from the manufacturer or service provider to the consumer, or end user. That shift has impacted and will continue to impact the field of advertising. According to Northwestern

2   PRINCIPLES OF ADVERTISING: A GLOBAL PERSPECTIVE

ILLUSTRATION 1.1. One Sight, One Sound

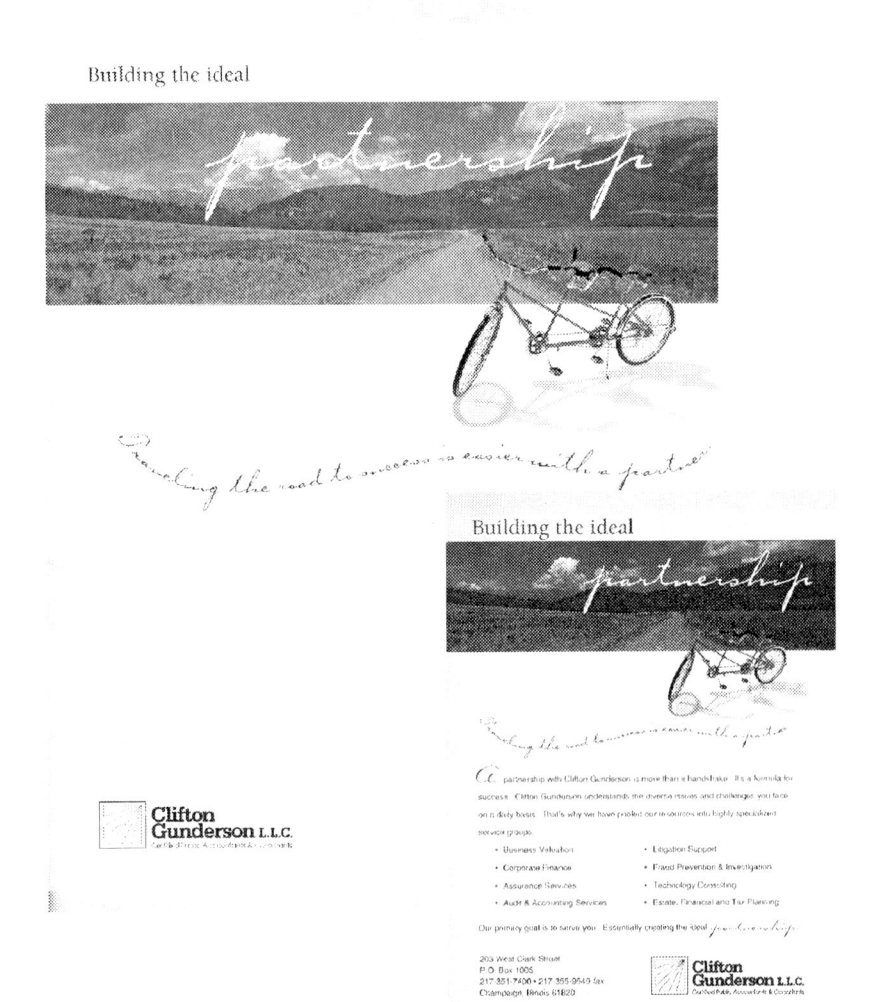

Clifton Gunderson L.L.C., one of the largest certified public accountants and consultants firms in the United States, employed a consistent image and message through integration of its public relations and advertising in Gunderson's "Building the ideal partnership" campaign. In the interest of consistency, the brochure (upper left) uses the same visual, as well as the same tag line and headline, as its print advertisement (lower right).

University advertising professor Don E. Schultz, the father of Integrated Marketing Communication (IMC), the concept of IMC starts with consumer needs and wants and works back to the brand.[3] Today, it is no longer enough for McDonald's to come out with a new product and spend $75 million on television commercials to promote it. Advertising plans must not only involve all the organization's communication systems but also the entire organization in total management of all brand contacts.[4]

Increasingly, those involved in the advertising profession recognize that future success depends on the ability to understand and use the tools of Integrated Marketing Communication. The evolution of IMC, or Integrated Communications (IC), will be discussed in this chapter. First, however, we must understand what advertising is and how it has evolved toward the twenty-first century.

ADVERTISING DEFINED

Advertising is a paid, nonpersonal communication about an organization and its products that is transmitted to a target audience through a mass medium such as television, radio, newspapers, magazines, direct mail, outdoor displays, or mass transit vehicles. In the new global community, advertising messages may be transmitted via new media, especially the Internet. Consultancy Jupiter Communications has predicted that online advertising will hit $500 billion by the year 2000.[5]

Advertising spending was expected to reach a record $200.3 billion in 1998, up 6.8 percent from the previous year. A 6 percent increase to $212.3 billion is forecast for the year 2000.[6] Individuals and organizations use advertising to promote goods, services, ideas, issues, and people. For instance, BMW of North America concentrated the bulk of its estimated $80 million media budget on television support for its 1996 Summer Olympic's sponsorship in Atlanta. The financial services industry, for example, American Express, Merrill Lynch, and the New York Cotton Exchange, spends an estimated $2 billion a year on advertising. In 1997, for the third year in a row, General Motors was the nation's biggest ad spender (see Table 1.1). For the top ad spenders by category, see Table 1.2.

Prescription drug advertisements targeting consumers have become a booming new ad genre; related ad spending doubled from $595.5 million in 1996 to nearly $1 billion in 1997 following the FDA's lifting of restrictions on TV ads for prescription drugs that year. According to a 1998 *Prevention* magazine consumer survey, 81 percent of U.S. adults are long-term users of prescription drugs. The first television commercials for the prescription drug Prozac aired on September 14, 1998.[7]

TABLE 1.1. Top U.S. Ad Spenders by Company

Company	1997 Spending Increase over 1996	1997 Dollars in Millions
General Motors	30%	$2,226.9
Procter & Gamble	12%	1,703.1
Philip Morris	8%	1,319.0
Chrysler	17%	1,311.8
Ford Motor	7%	973.1

Source: Adapted from Anne R. Carey and Quin Tian, "GM Top Ad Spender," *USA Today,* p. B1.

TABLE 1.2. Top Ad Spending by Category

Company	1997 Dollars in Millions	1997 Spending Increase	Number of Brands
Automotive	6.5	18.5%	26
Retail	3.4	24.5%	15
Restaurants	1.9	5.4%	8
Telephone	1.7	1.1%	7
Food	1.7	2.9%	10
Drugs and personal care	1.0	15.6%	8

Source: Adapted from "Top 100 Spend $20 Billion," *Advertising Age,* July 13, 1998, p. s2.

ADVERTISING CLASSIFICATIONS

No single, clear, all-embracing term describes advertising's complex character and multiple, interrelated functions. Advertising is frequently classified in several broad types.

Product Advertising

The major portion of advertising expenditure is spent on product advertising: the presentation and promotion of new products, existing products, and revised products. For example, in 1998, Apple signed with ad agency TBWA Chiat/Day and launched a $100 million marketing campaign to introduce its new iMac computer. Nationwide, the computer—first available in stores August 15—was almost or completely sold out by August 18. Many retailers reported taking hundreds of back orders. Apple shares rose to $42 $^{9}/_{16}$, a fifty-two-week high.[8]

Retail Advertising

In contrast to product advertising, retail advertising is local and focuses on the store where a variety of products can be purchased or where a service is offered. Retail advertising emphasizes price, availability, location, and hours of operation. Meijer, a Michigan-based superstore, which combines features of a discount store and supermarket, advertises frequently on local television and in local newspapers. Consumers are attracted to superstores by lower prices and one-stop shopping.

Corporate Advertising

The focus of these advertisements is on establishing a corporate identity or on winning the public over to the organization's point of view. Most corporate advertising is designed to create a favorable image for a company and its products; however, image advertising specifically denotes a corporate campaign that highlights the superiority or desirable characteristics of the sponsoring corporation. McDonald's Super Bowl XXX baby advertisement featured a baby in a swing, alternately crying and smiling when the baby sees the Golden Arches. This advertisement promoted a positive image of McDonald's restaurants, not a specific product.

Business-to-Business Advertising

This term relates to advertising that is directed to industrial users (tires advertised to automobile manufacturers), resellers (wholesalers and retailers), and professionals (such as lawyers and accountants). Advertising by professionals has gained momentum since U.S. Supreme Court decisions permitted such advertising.

Political Advertising

Political advertising is often used by politicians to persuade people to vote for them; therefore, it is an important part of the political process in the

United States and other democratic countries that permit candidate advertising. Critics are concerned that political advertising tends to focus more on image than on issues. In the 1996 presidential election, candidates ran many so-called comparison ads that were usually negative. Some defied the trend (see Illustration 1.2). Two-term state senator Dan Page (R-NC) ushered in one of the first negative television ads in the 1998 congressional campaign season—a spot showing newspaper headlines and magazine covers featuring President Clinton and Monica Lewinsky. A voice-over says, "Scandal after scandal. Day after day."[9] The advertising industry worries that it could face a regulatory backlash unless it can persuade media consultants to clean up political campaign advertising.

Governments as well as individual politicians may employ advertising. Facing financial crises in 1998, Thailand and Malaysia launched ad campaigns to improve their tarnished reputations and recover lost investors. Print ads appeared in global business publications, and television spots aired on the cable network CNN.

Directory Advertising

People refer to directory advertising to find out how to buy a product or service. The best known form of directory advertising is the Yellow Pages, although today there are many different kinds of directories that perform the same function. Yellow Pages directories were added to phone books after World War II. By the 1950s and 1960s, directory fees were invoiced on the advertising company's phone bill. The dual market structure of Yellow Pages advertising evolved into 80 percent local listings and 20 percent national. In 1975, the Yellow Pages Publishers Association (YPPA) merged from two previous Yellow Pages publishers' associations. A unique feature of Yellow Pages directory advertising has been the ability to measure response. The advertising company may carry two different phone numbers, one given in Yellow Pages advertising and the other used in alternative advertising channels, so that response to the Yellow Pages ad may be measured. Further, directory advertising is unique in that the user generally is ready to buy the product or service when the directory is consulted.

Direct Response Advertising

Direct response advertising involves two-way communication between the advertiser and the consumer. It can use any advertising medium (e.g., mail, television, newspapers, magazines), and the consumer can respond, often by mail, telephone, or fax. More and more companies now allow the consumer to respond online. The product is usually delivered to the consumer by mail.

Introduction to Advertising

ILLUSTRATION 1.2. No Negatives

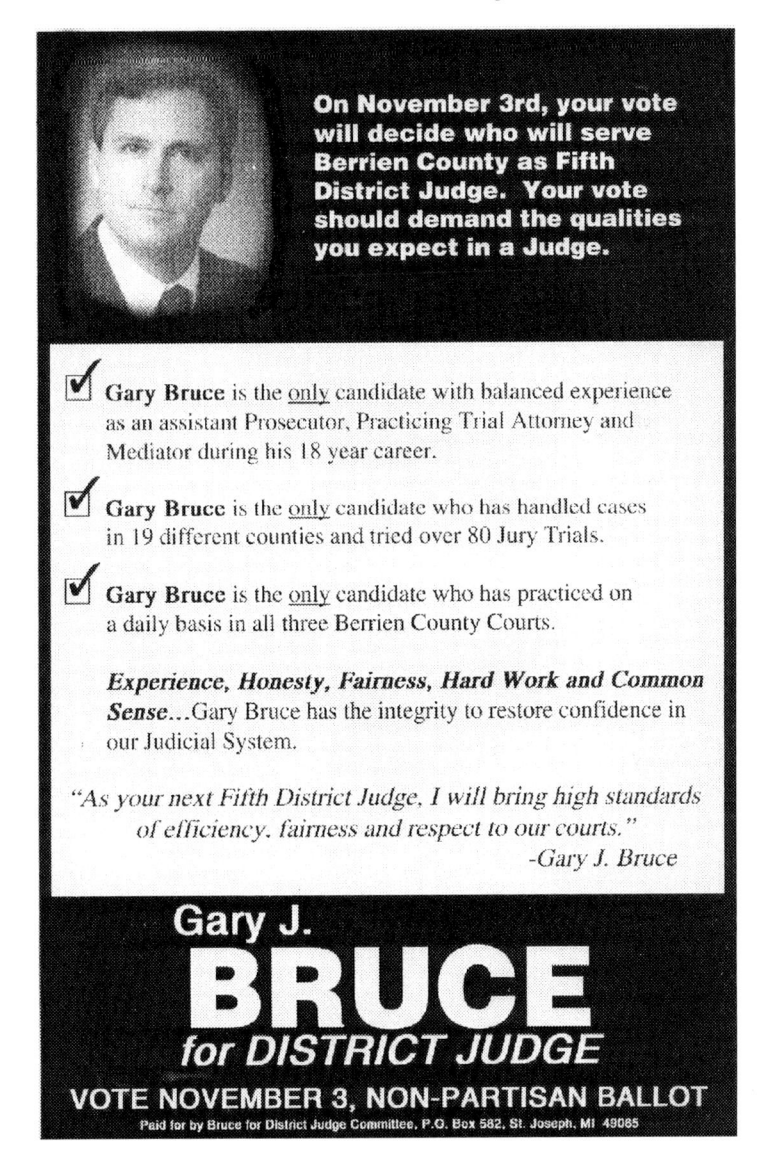

On November 3rd, your vote will decide who will serve Berrien County as Fifth District Judge. Your vote should demand the qualities you expect in a Judge.

☑ Gary Bruce is the only candidate with balanced experience as an assistant Prosecutor, Practicing Trial Attorney and Mediator during his 18 year career.

☑ Gary Bruce is the only candidate who has handled cases in 19 different counties and tried over 80 Jury Trials.

☑ Gary Bruce is the only candidate who has practiced on a daily basis in all three Berrien County Courts.

Experience, Honesty, Fairness, Hard Work and Common Sense...Gary Bruce has the integrity to restore confidence in our Judicial System.

"As your next Fifth District Judge, I will bring high standards of efficiency, fairness and respect to our courts."
—Gary J. Bruce

Gary J.
BRUCE
for DISTRICT JUDGE
VOTE NOVEMBER 3, NON-PARTISAN BALLOT
Paid for by Bruce for District Judge Committee, P.O. Box 582, St. Joseph, MI 49085

Gary J. Bruce, candidate for District Judge in Berrien County, Michigan, bucked the trend toward negative political advertising with this newspaper ad designed by Eric Remington. The only "negatives" are the sections of reverse type on black.

For instance, *Time* magazine uses a television commercial for direct response advertising; the commercial urges viewers to call an 800 number to order a subscription to the magazine or to receive more information. Similarly, the company uses cards inserted into newsstand magazines that are, themselves, response mechanisms. The consumer need only complete the card and mail it, postage free, to initiate home delivery. *Time* often also advertises an "offer," such as a free camera or video, that serves as a "gift" should the consumer decide to subscribe. The offer and the mailing list, if mail is the medium chosen, are said to be the most important criteria in direct response advertising success.

Public Service Advertising

Public service advertising is designed to operate in the public's interest and to promote public welfare. These advertisements are created free of charge by advertising professionals, and the space and time are donated by the media. Management and staff at Bozell and Jacobs, a U.S. advertising agency, donate time, talents, and money to community service organizations such as the American Cancer Society, American Red Cross, and United Way. Many local television stations have cooperated with Mothers Against Drunk Driving (MADD), creating and airing free public service spots that urge young people not to drink and drive at prom time. Over 200 ad agencies created ads at no charge for the government's largest ever ad campaign, a $2 billion antidrug effort, with networks airing 400 agency-created ads in 102 U.S. cities in July 1998.[10]

Advocacy Advertising

Advocacy advertising is concerned with the propagation of ideas and the clarification of controversial social issues of public importance. A growing number of firms have applied advertising strategies to such social causes as conserving wildlife.

ADVERTISING FUNCTIONS

Definitions and classifications only provide a common language in which to develop an understanding of advertising. The effects of advertising on an organization may be dramatic and also need to be explored.

- Advertising performs an "inform" function; it communicates information about the product, its features, and its location of sale; it tells the consumers about new products. Apple used an ad blitz to inform the public of its new iMac computer; another 1998 TBWA Chiat/Day

ad campaign ("Yo Quiero Taco Bell") introduced television viewers to Taco Bell's new Gorditas taco.
- Advertising performs a "persuasive" function; it tries to persuade consumers to purchase specific brands or to change their attitudes toward the product or company. The ABC television network employed Chiat in 1998 to create a network identity through ads designed to position it as "a smart, urban network."[11] Miller Beer spent between $60 million and $80 million on an ad campaign in 1996 for a new Miller brand, designed to favorably position the new brew to grab market share from Budweiser.[12] Sometimes advertising can be both informative and persuasive. As the Taco Bell ad campaign introduced the new Gorditas taco, it also encouraged viewers to choose Taco Bell for their fast food purchases through the emotional appeal of the now popular Taco Bell Chihuahua. (Sex, cute children, and small, furry animals are long-time staples of advertising.)
- Advertising performs a "reminder" function; it constantly reminds consumers about a product so that they will keep buying the advertised product instead of the competitor's brand. For years, McDonald's commercials have received top weekly exposure on television. Nielsen's listing is a good indicator of who's doing major advertising blitzes and how much support a marketer is putting behind a brand or advertising campaign. In 1998, McDonald's enjoyed a 42 percent share of the U.S. fast food burger market, though Burger King was putting up a good fight for number one fast food status. During the week of July 20 to 26, 1998, McDonald's aired sixty-one commercials, while Burger King aired sixty-nine. McDonald's ads reached 316.3 million households; Burger King's reached fewer, with 282.4 million exposures.[13] In 1997, McDonald's was the third largest overall ad spender among the megabrands and the largest spender on television advertising (see Table 1.3). The purpose of McDonald's advertisements was to remind consumers that when they get hungry, there is a McDonald's restaurant nearby.

TABLE 1.3. Top Ad Spenders by Brand in 1997

Megabrand	Total Spending	TV Advertising	Print Advertising
Sears stores	$664.6	$369.3	$251.2
Chevrolet	656.3	400.2	233.6
McDonald's	580.5	554.9	3.1

Source: Adapted from "Retail, Automotive Set Megabrand Direction," *Advertising Age,* July 13, 1998, p. s8.

Note: Figures are in millions of dollars.

ADVERTISING AND MARKETING

Four years of free-market reforms and strong agricultural output in India are cracking open that mammoth market for everything from toiletries to television sets. Colgate-Palmolive India Limited, a U.S. consumer goods company, is determined to draw more than half of its revenue from rural India by 2003, up from about 30 percent in 1996. It spent five times more on rural marketing in 1996 than in 1991. To get a foothold, however, consumer product makers cannot rely on conventional Madison Avenue marketing techniques: more than one-half of all Indian villagers are illiterate, and only one-third live in households with television sets. So Colgate's marketers turned to half-hour infomercials carried through the countryside in video vans. Many Indians in rural areas have never handled such products as a bottle of shampoo or a toothpaste tube. Fewer than 15 percent of rural Indians regularly use a dentifrice, according to Colgate-Palmolive. For generations, they have used charcoal powder and indigenous plants to cleanse their mouths. Farmers and field workers were drawn to the video van where the infomercial was shown to them. The subtext was clear: Colgate is good for your breath and teeth. The audience was offered free samples. A Colgate marketer demonstrated how to use the toothpaste and toothbrush. To encourage parents to buy a tube, the company offered free Colgate brushes to a few children, only to leave many little hands grabbing for more.[14]

The Marketing Concept

This story about consumer product giant Colgate-Palmolive Company suggests that advertising is just a part of the total marketing effort. It also suggests that marketing strategies, including advertising, are not easily transferred from one culture to another. Individuals, businesses, government, and nonprofit organizations all develop products to satisfy customers, the people or organizations that purchase a product, and advertising helps persuade customers to select one product rather than another. However, marketing is not just selling. The American Marketing Association defines marketing as "the process of planning and executing the conception, pricing, promotion, and distribution of ideas, goods, and services to create exchanges that satisfy individual (customer) and organizational objectives."[15]

According to the marketing concept, an organization should try to provide products that satisfy customers' needs through a coordinated set of activities that also allow the organization to achieve its goals. Today, manufacturers and service firms can produce more goods and services more efficiently than ever before, which means that supply is often greater than demand. Because people have so many product choices, an organization must give customers real reasons for choosing its products over competing products. Otherwise, the organization's profits will suffer as customers flock to rival companies. Therefore, the key to success is to apply the marketing concept.

Three main components make up the marketing concept:

- Meeting customer needs and wants—An organization must find out what will satisfy customers and use this information to create appropriate products. The organization must also continue to alter, adapt, and develop products to keep pace with customers' changing desires and preferences.
- Coordinating marketing efforts across the organization—Marketing is only one of the functions involved in meeting customer needs. Research and development, manufacturing, finance, and other functions are also important, so coordinating these functions with marketing efforts greatly increases an organization's chances of success.
- Achieving long-term goals—A firm that adopts the marketing concept must not only satisfy its customers' objectives, but also achieve its own goals, or it will not stay in business long.

The overall goals of a business might be directed toward increasing profits, market share, sales, or a combination of all three. When organizations truly implement the marketing concept, they find that customers will continue buying the products that best meet their needs, which fuels sales and profits over the long term.

The Marketing Mix

The marketing mix consists of four major components: product, place, price, and promotion. Marketing mix variables are often viewed as controllable variables because a marketing manager can decide what type of each component to use and in what amounts to achieve customer satisfaction. Thus, promotion (which includes advertising) must be balanced with product design, method of distribution, and price to create the overall marketing mix that customers consider when they choose a product.

Product

The product is a "bundle of value" that meets customer expectations. For example, an Acer laptop computer is more than just the computer itself; it also includes an instruction manual, access to a customer service hotline, a warranty certificate, and other components. An airline ticket promises more than transportation; other components, such as on-ground and in-flight services and timely and safe arrival to the destination, are expected by consumers. Advertising these features and benefits helps customers choose products or services that fit their needs. Branding and packaging are two important features of product. To translate the product's characteristics into something concrete that can be used to distinguish one product from another, many businesses advertise a distinctive brand, name, word, phrase, symbol, or a combination of these elements. For example, perfume companies invest a great deal of money in packaging their perfumes to distinguish them from competitors' perfumes.

Place

Place is also called channel of distribution or distribution channel. A channel of distribution refers to a group of individuals and organizations that directs the flow of products from producers to customers. Distribution activities include managing product transportation and storage, processing orders, and keeping track of inventory. The members of the distribution channel include wholesalers and retailers and industrial buyers in the industrial market. Channel decisions are critical because they determine a product's market presence and accessibility to buyers. U.S. automobile manufacturers believe that their cars have been difficult to sell in the Japanese market because Japanese dealerships are controlled by the major Japanese automobile manufacturers.

Price

Price is the value that is exchanged for products in a marketing transaction. A product's price has to cover all the costs involved in its production, distribution, and promotion, as well as any expected profits. In addition, price can support a product's image, take sales away from competitors, or induce people to change the timing of their purchases. For example, marketers give discounts to the customers who are willing to purchase air conditioners during the winter season. Setting a high price for Chanel perfume helps build an exclusive image for that product.

Promotion

Promotion—marketing communication—covers the variety of techniques used to communicate with customers and potential customers. Along with personal selling, sales promotion, and public relations (publicity), advertising is one of the four elements of the promotional mix. Personal selling is personal, paid communication that attempts to inform customers and to persuade them to purchase products in an exchange situation. Generally, personal selling is the most expensive element in the promotional mix. It is often used in the industrial market where personal contact is important to build relationships among industrial buyers. Sales promotion is increasingly important today for many organizations. Marketers often use free samples and coupons to reach consumers when they introduce new products. Public relations is a broad set of communication activities used to create and maintain favorable relations between the organization and its publics. These publics include customers, employees, stockholders, government officials, and society in general. Publicity is viewed as part of public relations. Organizations use media releases to gain free communication transmitted through a mass medium. Also, of course, advertising is paid, nonpersonal communication about an organization and/or its products, transmitted to a target audience through mass or alternative media.

THE EVOLUTION OF ADVERTISING

Advertising is hardly a new phenomenon. Even a hundred years ago, advertising was an integral, if sometimes unwelcome, part of daily life. The image of advertising has not improved over the years.

The very first U.S. newspaper, *Public Occurrences Both Foreign and Domestick,* appeared in 1690. In 1704, the *Boston Newsletter* was the first paper to carry an advertisement, which offered a reward for the capture of a thief. Two early colonial printers, James and Benjamin Franklin, started the *New England Courant* in 1721. By the time of the American Revolution, there were over thirty newspapers in the United States. Today, U.S. newspapers generally serve a specific geographic area, such as a local community. *USA Today* bucked that trend when it was launched in 1982 as a colorful national newspaper with jazzy graphics and brief, but punchy, articles. After *USA Today* led the way, many newspapers added color printing, allowing advertisers to show their products more realistically and to use snazzier art to snag reader attention.

The mid-1800s marked the beginning of the development of the advertising industry in the United States. A number of social and technological developments associated with the industrial revolution occurred during this period of time. The telegraph, telephone, and typewriter provided dramatic improvements in mass message delivery. Better printing technology and the ability to print photographs and detailed illustrations made magazine advertisements even more attractive to advertisers.[16] After the Civil War, *The Atlantic Monthly* and other U.S. magazines began carrying more advertisements. Advertising agency pioneer J. Walter Thompson prodded *Harper's Magazine* and other magazines to print advertisements for foods, soaps, and even patent medicines. By the dawn of the twentieth century, advertising had become a social and economic fixture in the United States. Magazines and newspapers were filled with advertisements for all kinds of products.

The first radio commercial in the United States was carried in 1922 by AT&T's station WEAF in New York. Within two years, radio expanded from a local medium to a national one, primarily because of the network, a group of stations that broadcast simultaneously in many markets. In 1926, AT&T sold its network of radio stations to the National Broadcasting Company (NBC).[17] Today, about 5,000 AM and 4,000 FM radio stations operate in the United States, all used by local, regional, and national advertisers.

The first commercial station was established in 1941. An early community antenna television system that started in Pennsylvania in 1948 was the forerunner of the cable systems that would pop up throughout the country during the 1970s and 1980s.[18] By 1954, NBC and CBS were the network leaders, trailed by ABC. In 1972, Home Box Office (HBO) began operation as a pay cable station. Today, cable networks, such as MTV and CNN, and local cable public access channels are widely available.

Advertising Phases

Advertising may be said to have evolved in phases. Until the early 1900s, advertising focused on product benefits with informational ads. These usually included the selling price and stressed product uniqueness and attributes. The 1920s saw the beginnings of status-conscious advertising. While the rich, upper classes enjoyed multitudes of luxuries, the so-called "Democracy of Goods" advertising formula promised that the lower classes could acquire at least some of these luxuries by purchasing certain products. For instance, a Chase and Sanborn's Coffee ad showed a butler serving coffee in an elegant home. The copy proclaimed that "no one—'king, prince, statesman, or capitalist'—could enjoy better coffee."[19] These ads frequently used such key words and phrases as "everyone," "anyone," and "any home."

By 1930, the focus of advertising messages had moved from the product to the user. Testimonials for various products, including tobacco, were common. Advertising themes included family, social status, and health.

Advertising shifted again following World War II. Wartime saw the cresting of America's producer economy, which necessarily shifted to a consumer economy after the war. As the unprecedented market created by the baby boom began to decline in the 1950s, manufacturers who had never geared down from wartime efficiency in mass production found themselves with product surpluses. To move these now stockpiled products, companies turned to the teams of psychologists who descended on Madison Avenue. Now advertising promised to transform the consumer. The 1960s saw a proliferation of guilt and fear appeals (some classic campaigns included "Ring around the collar" and "If she kisses you once, will she kiss you again? Be certain with Certs"). According to communication theorists Gary C. Woodward and Robert E. Denton, happiness, romance, and glamour would be possible for those who purchased the "prescribed product."[20] The image era of advertising has been attributed to David Ogilvy and his concerns with product image, long-term brand identification, and loyalty.

By the 1970s, products became emblems for group identification. Whereas the 1920s had been characterized by the elitist appeal of improved social status, advertising in the 1970s was characterized by populist appeals. According to Jack Solomon in "Masters of Desire: The Culture of American Advertising," the American dream "has two faces: the one communally egalitarian and the other competitively elitist."[21] The icons of populist commercials include "country music, small-town life, family picnics, and farmyards," as well as casual dress and an upbeat mood.[22] Thus, designer jeans defined particular groups of people, and a soft drink commercial proclaimed the populist message "I'd like to teach the world to sing/In perfect harmony . . ."

The 1980s carried through with the upbeat, populist mood until, late in the decade, a new kind of elitist appeal emerged. This "narrative played on the worries of young corporate managers struggling up the ladder of success," representing the "elitist desire to 'arrive'."[23] Meanwhile, McDonald's pioneered the strategically targeted commercial message. Resisting the one-size-fits-all campaign, McDonald's simultaneously targeted various age groups, classes, and races.[24] From the Ronald McDonald fantasy spots targeted to children, to appeals to the adolescent need to belong, to the more sophisticated "Mac Tonight," to "the new kid" commercials aimed at senior citizens, McDonald's defied overall trends and differentiated specific market segments.

In the 1990s, a skeptical consumer climate grew in response to public saturation with commercial messages and hyperbolic, manipulative appeals. The new consumer found the Energizer bunny's interruption of "a rather pretentious Gallo campaign . . . pitched to the yuppie market" to be refreshing.[25] The anticommercial has become a familiar response to consumer cynicism. Today, products are still advertised as solutions to personal problems and needs. Advertising may still suggest that a product can define status and group membership, but the groups targeted have become more diverse, reflecting the variable lifestyles in contemporary society.

Phases of Integrated Communications

In his article "The Evolving Nature of Integrated Communications," Don E. Schultz has redefined Integrated Marketing Communication. More commonly referred to today as simply Integrated Communications, Schultz says it is "not an activity or a field or an industry" but "a coordinated method or way of thinking about planning, development and implementation of communication programs for now and into the future."[26] He describes the following stages in the evolution of IMC, or IC.

Stage 1—"One Sight, One Sound" Approach to Integration

Prior to the mid-1980s, large, national brand marketing organizations, which had developed in the 1950s and 1960s, dominated the marketplace. Many communicators during this phase felt that they were practicing what has come to be called Integrated Communications by bringing advertising, sales, direct marketing, and public relations departments together to plan communications campaigns and programs. This first view of Integrated Marketing Communication was that it brought together previously segmented components of the promotional mix to produce a consistent image and message, in other words—one sight, one sound (see Illustration 1.1).

Stage 2—Process of Alignment and Integration

By the mid-1980s, scanner data and the creation of massive retailers shifted power from the manufacturer to the retailer. For instance, Wal-Mart's earnings for the second quarter of 1998 soared to $33.5 billion, and retail ad spending had increased 24.5 percent from 1996 to 1997 (see Table 1.2). The need and demand for integration shifted as well. Integration now needed to "include and involve the channels of distribution in the communications mix," according to Schultz. The integrated Coca-Cola campaign described at the beginning of this chapter illustrates how one company tied a traditional mass media advertising campaign to its retail promotions, and then tied the whole campaign to a major event (the Olympics) in the corporation's hometown. In this campaign, a spectrum of audiences and stakeholders was reached through what Schultz calls a "coherent, timely, customer-oriented" communication program involving all forms and types of distribution systems.

At the high end of this stage, developing and managing these communication programs involve the entire organization, Schultz contends. He believes that "IC has moved from a tactical activity which was practiced by Historical Marketers, to a more strategic, management-driven activity in the Current Marketplace."

Stage 3—IC in the Twenty-First-Century Marketplace

The evolution of IMC/IC has been driven primarily by the growth of information technology (computers, software, digital development, search engines, e-mail, Web sites, databases, etc.). The example of Federal Express tracking services detailed at the beginning of this chapter illustrates one way that new media enable organizations to more fully communicate with their customers. Interactive communication systems are controlled by the consumer. In recent years, information technology has been tipping the balance of marketplace power increasingly toward the consumer. In the next century, Schultz predicts that consumers will no longer be "targets" but "compatriots," not the recipients of advertising messages as much as those to whom advertisers listen and respond. Message flow is already shifting from outbound to inbound, with "customers and prospects making known their needs, wants and wishes, and marketers and communicators listening and developing responses." This, Schultz says, "will likely be the toughest integration task of all."

Changes in the business world and technology have also placed new pressure on advertisers to be accountable, to show how the organization has benefited from a particular communication program. While information technology makes "communication and IC more powerful and possible, the same sort of techniques are being offered as methods and manners in which to measure the *outcomes* of communication programs, not just the *output*," says Schultz.

In addition to these challenges, advertisers must now communicate in a global marketplace where what may be an appropriate, effective channel or message at home becomes impractical or culturally inappropriate in another part of the world. Colgate-Palmolive's attempt to market toiletries to villagers in rural India, mentioned earlier in this chapter, illustrates the challenges of advertising to people in another culture. The IMC/IC marketer must consider the different situations in which products may be used in other countries, as well as which of the traditional and the new, alternative channels of communication will work best. As Schultz says, IMC/IC advertisers will need to learn "where, in what form, at what time, under what conditions, and at what level" customers want to hear from them.

SUMMARY

Classifications of advertising include product, retail, corporate, business-to-business, political, directory, direct response, public service, and advocacy. Advertising may inform or persuade the consumer. In some cases, advertising serves to remind the consumer about a particular brand to maintain consumer loyalty. Advertising is just a part of the total effort carried out by the marketing mix (product, place, price, and promotion). The promotional mix includes advertising, public relations, sales promotion, and personal selling. Advertising in the United States has evolved in response to developments in the mass media and to other socioeconomic forces that have affected manufacturers, retailers, and consumers or industrial users. Integrated marketing communication, now known widely as integrated communications, has responded to the ways that information technology has changed both the consumer and the ways we communicate with the consumer.

* * *

THE GLOBAL PERSPECTIVE: GLOBAL BRAND CREATION

How do you create or reinforce a global brand? Magazine ads, television commercials—sure. But what about those "Heritage Tins" point-of-purchase displays? That Team Suzuki motorcycle race sponsorship? Those sexy retail posters sporting a barefoot, cat-suited blonde posing against the backdrop of an action-packed cityscape and tag-lined, "Get Lucky"?

Such iconography and images, now requisite for global branding, may be communicated via mass media channels, of course. A recent global campaign for Lucky Strike cigarettes integrated traditional advertising with place-based communications in bars, gas stations, and convenience stores. Bates North America, creator of the campaign, took a "sales promotion-style approach" rather than "beginning with the idea of an ad campaign." *Voila!* This IMC thinking brings Lucky's message (whether it be "An American Original" on the Tin Box Collection display or the entwinement of the Lucky Strike logo with Team Suzuki's logo, implying a close relationship between countries as well as between motorcyclists and cigarettes) to its targeted young adult audience through the group's own "underground and lifestyle" channels. Will such "media neutral" campaigns be crucial to global branding in the future?

Source: Kate Fitzgerald, "Beyond Advertising," *Advertising Age*, August 3, 1998, p. 14.

* * *

ETHICS TRACK:
DECEPTION IN ADVERTISING

Did Wal-Mart mislead its customers with its "Bring it home to the U.S.A." advertising campaign? The United Food and Commercial Union said that it did. In August 1998, the union asked the Federal Trade Commission (FTC) and the attorneys general in each of the United States to investigate Wal-Mart's "attempt to convince consumers that they're 'buying American'" when the products are really foreign made.[a]

Advertising is a dynamic public forum in which business interests, creativity, consumer needs, and government regulation meet. Deception is not the only ethics issue that advertisers face. A survey released in May 1998 showed that Budweiser's television commercials with talking frogs and lizards had become popular with youngsters from six to seventeen years old. Mothers Against Drunk Driving (MADD) and the American Association of Pediatricians have pressured Anheuser-Busch, the Federal Communications Commission (FCC), and the FTC to pull ads they feel encourage underage drinking.[b]

As traditional media—newspapers, magazines, TV, radio—become increasingly saturated with advertising, and as consumers become ever more resistant and skeptical, marketing managers search for new, creative ways to promote their products. Does this justify deception? Does the need to create new markets override the need to protect our children? Who should decide?

[a] "Union: Wal-Mart Uses Misleading Ads," *The South Bend Tribune,* August 11, 1998, p. B1.
[b] Ann Therese Palmer, "Why MADD Is Mad at Bud," *Business Week,* May 11, 1998, p. 6.

Lee & Johnson
:30 Spot
"Integrating an IMC Philosophy"

Despite the vogue that Integrated Marketing currently enjoys, it lacks many full-fledged homes. Few companies have embraced the kind of organizational and philosophical approach that is taught in graduate programs and espoused in books. Instead, many marketing professionals believe that integration is simply using all available marketing communication tools, such as public relations, advertising, direct marketing, and promotions.

As an alumnus of one of those graduate programs, I have come to find that the execution of the full arsenal of tools often touted as "integrated" is far less important than applying the overriding philosophies of Integrated Marketing in everyday business life.

In particular, I have long held the belief that customer focus—one of the primary tenets of IMC—should apply to a wide variety of groups: customers, consumers, employees, and shareholders, to name but a few. As an investor relations practitioner, it is paramount to expand this definition to meet the needs of the investment community, while maintaining a consistent, effective message. Imagine the dilemma of telling a sizable shareholder one message and then having a trade magazine or business publication publish another, only to tell employees yet a different story.

I suggest that treating every customer—broadly defined—as critically important and as a unique audience provides a powerful and necessary paradigm shift. Traditional business education says that businesses should be run to create shareholder value; thus, the shareholder's needs and satisfaction are at the forefront. Integrated Marketing generally teaches that the customer—narrowly defined—is the singular focus. Exploding these limiting definitions not only enhances the organization's potential for success, but it also gives the marketing or communications professional a philosophy of action that embraces all constituencies.

In my everyday world, I must recognize the importance of the needs of many audiences. Understanding what each requires represents a unique challenge. However, the payoff for successfully integrating the wants and needs of all customers is long-term prosperity for an organization, which is sure to make one's employer—yet another "customer"—quite happy.

Aaron H. Hoffman
Manager, Investor and Public Relations
GATX
Chicago, Illinois

Chapter 2

The Advertising Environment: Economy, Society, and Technology

Facing the profound changes in the U.S. population and the growing purchasing power among its diverse ethnic groups, Mobil has tried to do a better job of reaching certain ethnic segments. In the past, Mobil targeted minority segments using its general market agency, DDB Needham Worldwide, New York. To move its advertising from a general to a more ethnically targeted focus, Mobil hired African-American and Hispanic agencies to handle its marketing campaign in 1996. The campaign consisted of one 30-second television spot, two 30-second radio spots, outdoor advertising, event marketing, consumer promotions, and public relations. Mobil spends $35 million on measured media annually, but no budget was disclosed for the black consumers' effort.[1]

In 1997 YAR Communications and Kang and Lee Advertising, two of the nation's best-known ethnic ad agencies, combined to become One World Communications, the largest advertising agency targeting multicultural consumers.[2] One World's President and CEO Yuri Radzievsky estimates that 40 million Americans are multicultural by birth. It is generally acknowledged that cultural background affects the way a person perceives marketing messages.

The growing ethnic diversity of the United States is just one of a number of forces that create the advertising environment. This environment consists of external, or uncontrollable, forces that directly or indirectly influence advertisers, advertising agencies, media, and audiences. The advertising environment consists of economic, social, technological, and legal (and political) forces (see Illustration 2.1). The environment also involves ethical issues. Economic, social, and technological forces will be discussed in this chapter, and legal and political forces, in Chapter 3. The ethical considerations are so important that ethics issues appear in "Ethics Track" sections at the end of each chapter in this book.

ILLUSTRATION 2.1. "Wired"

In addition to other changes in the advertising environment caused by economic and social forces, the impact of the computer revolution on the field of communications has been phenomenal. © Dana Hanefeld.

THE ADVERTISING ENVIRONMENT

Environmental forces are always changing. Changes in the advertising environment create uncertainty, threats, and opportunities for advertisers. Although the future is not very predictable, advertisers try to forecast what may happen. We can say with certainty that advertisers continue to modify their advertising strategies in response to dynamic environmental forces. An advertiser can respond to the environment in two ways: reactively or proactively.

Reactive Response

When you believe you have no control over environmental elements, you will be reactive and simply try to adjust to them, many times after the fact. For example, a public relations consultant may be called upon to exercise damage control when an unanticipated crisis in a company occurs. The company must then react to what has already happened. Many crises could be averted if a company would proactively oversee all internal and external relations.

Proactive Response

When you think you have some control, you will be proactive and take steps to make changes that result in a more conducive environment for your activities. For instance, the number of immigrants into the United States has steadily risen during the last thirty years, resulting in a society that is becoming increasingly multicultural. The U.S. population has shifted from one dominated by whites to one consisting of three large racial and ethnic groups: whites, blacks, and Hispanics. Asians make up a fourth important group. Marketers recognize these profound changes in the U.S. population and the unique problems and opportunities they bring. A diverse population means a more diverse customer base, and advertising practices must be altered to fit it.

ECONOMIC FORCES AND ADVERTISING

Economic forces in the advertising environment influence both advertisers' and consumers' decisions and activities. Advertising expenditures today account for a significant part of the U.S. economy. When the economy is expanding, consumers and businesses have the money and the inclination to buy, and higher sales fire up advertisers to increase their advertising budgets, which in turn fuels retail and industrial as well as media sales. For instance, ad spending skyrocketed during the economic expansion of 1976 through 1988.[3] During most recessionary periods, profit pressures may cause some advertisers to cut back, despite studies suggesting that advertising during downturns can help firms increase sales and capture market shares from competitors who slow or stop advertising.[4] For example, in the recession of the early 1990s, retail bankruptcies, decreased real estate sales, and sluggish consumer spending dampened many advertising budgets. In turn, the reduced advertising spending set off a chain reaction that hurt the media, advertising agencies, and suppliers.[5] The impact of this situation was so serious that, in those years, many people working on New York's Madison Avenue, where many large advertising agencies are located, lost their jobs.

Multinational corporations, in particular, are affected by financial crises in other countries. Concern in mid-1998 about a devalued Mexican peso and Venezuelan bolivar, weak commodity prices of Latin American exports, and dependence by such U.S. giants as Coca-Cola and General Motors on emerging Latin American markets for profit growth reflected the extent to which economic conditions in one region or country impact others. "Latin America accounts for 21 percent of U.S. exports—compared with 14 percent for Asia, minus Japan."[6]

The link between advertising and the economy has traditionally been viewed in two ways. Some experts argue that advertising is the power in the hands of large firms with huge advertising budgets that create a barrier to entry. This condition makes it difficult for other firms to enter the market and results in less competition and higher product prices. Economists note that smaller firms already in the market find it difficult to compete against the large advertising budgets of the industry leaders and are often driven out of business. Defenders of advertising note it is unrealistic to attribute a firm's market dominance and barriers to entry solely to advertising. A number of other factors should be considered, such as product quality, price, and distribution effectiveness. Other experts view advertising as a source of information for consumers, enabling them to choose among available products. The debate over advertising's roles in the economy continues. Economists, scholars, and practitioners are divided over advertising's influence on several economic elements, including pricing and competition. Does advertising raise or lower the price that consumers pay for products? Does advertising serve as a source of information or a barrier to market entry?[7]

SOCIAL FORCES AND ADVERTISING

The role of advertising in society is controversial and has, at times, resulted in attempts at restricting or banning advertising of certain products or to certain groups. The controversy rages on over whether tobacco and alcohol advertising should be banned. These decisions involve very complex economic considerations, as well as social issues. Distillers such as Seagram's, in defending the decision to advertise on television after a decades-old, voluntary industry ban on television and radio advertising, promised not to advertise during prime time and other hours when children are most likely to watch television and not to use messages or symbols (including Santa Claus) especially attractive to children. The company also promised to push for "responsible consumption." However, antialcohol groups are foursquare against television ads for Absolut Vodka, Johnnie Walker Scotch, or any other liquor brands. They argue that, given the social harm already caused by alcohol—not only the thousands of deaths caused by drunk driving, but also aggressive behavior such as rapes, spousal and child abuse, fire and other property damage—the last thing the United States needs is an increase in television advertisements promoting more drinking.[8]

Criticism of Advertising

Advertising is claimed by its practitioners to be largely responsible for the good things in life and is criticized by its opponents as the cause of much of what is bad. Advertising copy is accused of playing fast and loose with the rules of language (e.g., twisting words or using incorrect spelling and grammar to make a point), which encourages the audience to do the same. A classic example of this is the 1954 tag line "Winston tastes good, like a cigarette should." The correct phrasing would be "as a cigarette should." More recently, Apple Computer used the slogan "Think different" instead of "Think differently," which would be grammatically correct.[9]

Another criticism is that advertising causes people to buy products or services that they do not need. The defenders acknowledge that the whole reason to advertise the product or service is to persuade consumers to purchase the right products. Another common criticism of advertising is that it perpetuates stereotyping, the process of categorizing individuals by predicting their behavior based on their membership in a particular class or group. The problem, critics say, is that advertisements often portray entire groups of people in stereotypical ways, for example, showing women only as homemakers and elderly people only as senile. These advertising stereotypes can reinforce negative or undesirable views of these groups, and this can contribute to discrimination against them.[10]

Advertisers have gradually realized stereotyping is not acceptable because it alienates potential customers. Moreover, by presenting minorities and women more realistically, advertisers can significantly expand their market segments for a wider variety of products. In looking for ways to make advertisements seem more realistic, some advertisers and advertising agencies are using real-life people in their ads rather than professional models or actors.[11]

The society in which we live and our own social standards influence advertising—the way it works and the ideas it uses. For example, before 1959, there were no women depicted in liquor advertisements in *Time* magazine, even though U.S. prohibition was repealed in 1933. This was because society did not approve of women drinking, and women were not allowed to drink in public places. Advertisements after 1959 showed the beginnings of a standard practice of including women in liquor advertisements. As society's attitudes changed, advertisers reacted and found that it was acceptable to put women in liquor advertising.[12] However, advertisers have generally been slow to reflect societal attitude changes toward women.

A 1996 Saatchi & Saatchi study made it clear that women did not feel advertisers were keeping up with the times in the 1990s. For the most part, women still found most advertising to be sexist, especially ads for beauty products, clothing, and food intended to keep women thin. Failure to "get the message right" carries consequences more serious than just not making a sale—it can "interrupt the consumer's connection with the brand."[13] When focus groups revealed that Kellogg's Special K ads offended the women targeted, the company's ad agency created a new ad campaign. Baby boomers could not relate to the models who "squeezed their drop-dead perfect bodies into clingy dresses and tight jeans" to preen in front of a mirror, so the new campaign, launched in February 1998, used women who projected a heavier, healthier look.[14] One ad in the campaign even pokes fun at men. A man gathered with friends at a bar worries about his too-large thighs, while another laments his big butt. The tag line says it all: "Men don't obsess about these things. Why do we?"

Advertising, in turn, affects society. Advertising pays many of the costs of the mass media and almost all the costs of the broadcast media. But if advertising pays the bills, doesn't it also control the media? A 1996 survey of 3,004 U.S. adults by the Center for Media and Public Affairs found that 58 percent think the media are too influential, and 63 percent say the media are often influenced by powerful people and organizations.[15] For instance, a local television station declined to cover an antifur demonstration staged by animal rights activists, caving in to pressure exerted by a furrier who regularly purchased a substantial amount of advertising time.

Ellen McCracken, a critic of mass culture, offers the case of *Ms.* magazine as an example of the effects of advertising. The magazine has claimed that it fights for the elimination of gender- and race-based subordination. However, $5.1 million of its $9.3 million annual revenues came from advertising in 1983. "Besides enabling the magazine to continue publication and providing money for women's causes," McCracken contends, "the advertisements in *Ms.* promote a consumption-based model of women's liberation and sometimes undercut the magazine's positive editorial messages."[16]

As with any controversy, the debate about the influence of advertising on society is not likely to come to a conclusion as we enter the next century.

TECHNOLOGICAL FORCES AND ADVERTISING

Technological developments provide important opportunities to advertisers who can use them to meet customer needs. For example, because of technological changes in communications, marketers now can reach large masses of people more efficiently through a variety of media. Quantum, a pay-per-view cable service developed by a division of Time Warner, Incorporated, uses fiber optics and coaxial cables to offer fifteen movies starting every half hour, twenty-four hours a day. For less than $5 a film, viewers can select a movie and the time it will air by pressing a remote control button to activate the on-screen guide. With fiber optics in place, Quantum is ready to offer HDTV (high-density television) and voice interactivity when these become available. As of May 1998, 64 percent of all U.S. households were cable subscribers; 43 percent also had home personal computers. Internet advertising revenues are expected to equal cable television advertising revenues in 1999.[17] The Internet has become an irrepressible force.

The Internet and Advertising

When HotWired was launched on the Web on Oct. 27, 1994, it pioneered the most explosive new advertising medium since the start of cable television. In the years since then, an entire infrastructure has sprung up to support the industry. There are companies to create advertisements, buy advertisements, sell advertisements, measure advertisements, and manage advertisements. There is even an industry group to promote Internet advertisements. Furthermore, marketer efforts on the Web have moved beyond the experimental. Many marketers make Web advertising a line item in their ad budget alongside magazines, television, and radio. The September 1996 Forrester Research survey of forty-four marketers found that 54 percent intended to spend less than $250,000 a year for Web advertisements,

38 percent planned to spend $250,000 to $1 million, and 8 percent, more than $1 million.[18]

The Internet is a reality that advertisers and marketers can no longer choose to ignore. The U.S. Commerce Department's first major study of the economic effect of the Internet revealed that "net traffic is doubling every hundred days and electronic commerce should reach $300 billion by 2002."[19] In 1997, Web ad spending hit $906.5 million.[20] With more than 100 million people "wired," growth of the digital economy is double the rate of the economy overall. According to the Commerce Department's report, Internet commerce represents over 8 percent of the gross domestic product. The report also found that, whereas "radio took 30 years to reach an audience of 50 million, and TV took 13, the Internet took just four years." By the end of 1997, 10 million people in the United States and Canada had purchased something online, up 4.7 million in just six months.

One clear-cut advantage the Internet holds over other advertising media is its accountability (see Table 2.1). The Internet makes it possible not only to record the number of "hits," or visitors, but also "to project the specific costs of bringing targeted visitors to sites."[21] Nevertheless, as late as 1996, many of the biggest advertising spenders still were not sure where, or if, Internet advertising fit into their plans. The head of promotion services at Campbell Soup Company did not see the Internet as an efficient delivery system for advertising soup, which largely sells for about a dollar a can. Internet ad spending only seemed more justifiable for big-ticket items.[22]

However, by 1998, the Campbell's Web site became a wonderland of advertising and promotions. On the homepage, a brick road winds through a colorful town, each building modeled from a Campbell's soup can, leading to a menu that includes the Creative Kitchen (recipes and menus), the Community Center (new products and other company news), the Financial Center (stock information), Labels for Education School (a program that

TABLE 2.1. Average Cost Per Visitor for Various Internet Marketing Vehicles

Business-to-Business Web Site Banner Ads	$2.10
Search Engine Key Word Advertising	1.70
Consumer Web Site Banner Ads	.93
Internet Sweepstakes Programs	.45

Source: Adapted from "Is the Price Right?" *Silicon Alley Reporter,* Iss. 12, March 1998, p. 6.

provides free educational and athletic equipment for schools), the Grocery Store (soup brand information), Fun and Games Park (arts and crafts ideas), and the Online Shop.

The Online Shop offers consumers a choice of two stores: the Campbell Shop and Pepperidge Farm. Although the Campbell Shop does not sell such small-ticket items as cans of soup, it does advertise and offer for sale a line of collectible dolls, die-cast vehicles, and artwork, as well as kitchen accessories, porcelain figures, an Art Deco watch, an Heirloom baby cup, and even a mouse pad. Consumers can purchase online by filling their shopping basket icon, then clicking on the "Check Out" button.

What may not have seemed possible or likely two years ago, may have become a reality today in the wild world of Internet advertising.

Results of a WebCensus poll conducted during a single week in January 1998 suggest that Internet advertising may be most effective as a complement to other media usage. Of those polled, 58 percent said that time spent on the Internet was in addition to, not instead of, time spent on traditional media.

Special Effects

Much video animation and most special effects, such as moving titles and whirling logos, can be done with a joystick. All major video production companies today use dedicated digital video effects units (DVEs) that can manipulate graphics on the screen in a variety of ways—fades, wipes, zooms, rotations, and so on. BBDO Agency has introduced computer-generated M&M/Mars candies. A recent trend has combined old clips of such classic film stars as Fred Astaire and John Wayne with new footage of such products as vacuum cleaners and soft drinks. For the 108th anniversary of the birth of Kentucky Colonel Harland Sanders, founder of the KFC fast food restaurant chain, the company decided to make its founder's image more visible. Instead of hiring an actor to portray the Colonel, as the company did in its unsuccessful 1994 campaign, or using clips of the real Harland Sanders—who made personal appearances until his death in 1980—KFC decided to create an animated likeness of the goateed gentleman in the white suit.[23] The company hoped the animated image would be less offensive to those who remembered the real Colonel than using an actor in commercial spots had been.

Special effects entertain viewers and win advertising awards. But if the sales message is complex or based on logic, another technique might be better. No technique should so enthrall viewers that they pay more attention to it than to the product being advertised. Although disputed by Energizer's (which used the mnemonic device—bunny) parent, Ralston Purina, some industry figures suggest that Duracell still outsells Energizer batteries.[24] The Energizer bunny may be lovable, but the public's affection does not necessarily lead to sales.

The available level of technology affects the way companies advertise their products and services in foreign markets. Seven of the world's ten fastest growing ad markets were in Asia in 1991. Hong Kong's satellite television, StarTV, launched the first pan-Asian network that year. With 2.8 billion people in thirty-eight countries under a "footprint" that runs from the Mediterranean through Southeast Asia and up to far eastern Russia, StarTV offers advertisers a new way to think regional (advertisements aimed at more than one country). Broadcasting across eight time zones allows StarTV to target its programming to a particular country's prime time.

Forget regional efficiencies—in Taiwan and India, penetration is deep enough to make advertising on StarTV as cost-effective as local television. When Lipton, a division of Unilever, launched its iced tea in Taiwan in 1992, its advertisement on StarTV was a hit. In addition, StarTV's ability to evade government broadcast regulations makes it an even better buy for some companies. Both United Distillers and Hennessy cognac used StarTV to target Taiwan, which limits advertisements for imported liquor.[25]

Advertisers, agencies, the media, and audiences are all part of a larger environment, influencing and being influenced by the economy, society, and technology. The impact of these complex environmental elements can be positive or negative, sometimes even both. Advertising is a source of information for consumers and a source of market power for advertisers. Advertising has been accused of harming society because it seems to go beyond merely selling products; it can also shape social trends and attitudes in powerful ways. With the Internet, a firm can present consumers with a combination of advertising, information, and entertainment related to its product. Consumers are able to control their exposure to a product and ultimately decide whether they want to learn more about it or even place an order. With advertising dollars tighter in the 1990s, accountability has become more important than ever. Internet advertisers are able to record the number of people who have actually viewed their ads and know in advance how much each Web site visit will cost them.

SUMMARY

Advertising is affected by economic, social, and technological forces. These forces are constantly changing. Advertising is inextricably linked to the economy, and the relationship between the two remains controversial. Just as controversial is the role that advertising plays in society. Advertising is also affected by technological change. With its advantages and disadvantages for advertisers, the Internet is a reality with which advertisers must grapple.

* * *

THE GLOBAL PERSPECTIVE: CONSIDERING CULTURE

You would expect to see shop signs in Hebrew in Tel Aviv's new shopping mall. Instead, expect to see mostly English-language advertisements for Benetton and other trendy franchises. Do not expect businesses and restaurants to be closed on the Sabbath. However, do expect Israel's ultra-Orthodox community to resent these artifacts of fast-spreading American consumerism. The young people who shop and work at the Tel Aviv mall may enjoy the freedom they believe these changes represent, but the older establishment wonders about the contradiction of having a Jewish homeland if it disregards "religious commandments to which other Jews were faithful, even on the point of death."[a]

The Israeli Embassy in Bangkok also reacted with indignation to a Thai television commercial that showed Adolf Hitler transformed into a "good person" after eating "X" brand potato chips. The ad's creator, Leo Burnett, immediately recalled the ad.[b]

Culture includes all traditions, habits, religion, art, and language. It consists of beliefs, morals, customs, and habits learned from others. As in domestic markets, the advertiser who wants to communicate with foreign consumers must consider the environments that influence people's tastes, attitudes, and the way they think.

The impact of religion on international advertising has become apparent. McDonald's had to introduce a vegetarian burger when it opened restaurants in India. Kodak avoided beach scenes in a commercial aired in Moslem countries in deference to local customs.

When to schedule international advertising is also an important decision for marketers. Religious holy days may affect the placement or timing of an ad. For instance, during the month-long Islamic observation of Ramadan, many Moslem countries do not allow the placement of any advertising.

[a] Judy Peres, "A Human Mosaic," *Chicago Tribune Magazine,* Special Edition: Israel at 50, May 10, 1998, Section 18, p. 57.
[b] Pichayaporn Utumpom, "Ad with Hitler Causes a Furor in Thailand," *The Wall Street Journal,* June 5, 1998, p. B8.

ETHICS TRACK:
MEDIA RESPONSIBILITY IN RUNNING ADS

In May 1998, the *Hartford Courant* refused to publish an ad promoting Janet Jackson's Velvet Rope Tour because the ad showed "ample cleavage." It was not just that the ad might perpetuate the stereotype of women as sex objects or love slaves. The paper's refusal reflected the publisher's sense of obligation to the newspaper's readership, especially to "the homes of readers with young children." The media have a role to play in advertising ethics. A television station or newspaper are not required to accommodate any and all advertisers who wish to purchase air time and print space. The *Hartford Courant* took a position in the controversy over the impact advertising has on society's tastes, values, and lifestyles.

Criticism of techniques used by advertisers includes arguments that advertising is deceptive or untruthful; advertising is offensive or in bad taste; advertising has the power to influence people to do things they would not do if they were not exposed to advertising; and advertising creates and perpetuates stereotypes (e.g., women are stereotyped as homemakers or sex objects).

Ethics refers to moral principles that define right and wrong behavior. The complexity of ethical issues in advertising requires the advertiser to make a conscious effort to deal with each situation. This presumes personal standards of what is right and what is wrong. However, what is or is not ethical is a judgment call made by imperfect individuals. When mistakes are made by advertisers, does the media have an obligation to serve as an ethics watchdog of the advertising it airs or prints?

Source: "Jackson No-Show," *USA Today*, May 5, 1998, p. A1.

Lee & Johnson
:60 Spot
"The Times They Are Changin'"

Market fragmentation, media segmentation, and diversity are key words in advertising today. Mass media is not what it used to be. Twenty-five years ago, an advertiser could purchase a "roadblock" (a thirty-second commercial on the three networks at the same time) with the potential to reach 93 percent of the viewing audience. The same technique today barely delivers 50 percent of the viewing audience. Advertisers seek to spend each dollar as efficiently as possible to reach the desired audience. This is the concept that has made Integrated Marketing Communication (IMC) a major topic. Consumers and their attitudes have changed also. Not only do they want more value, they want more convenience. They can shop twenty-four hours a day from retail stores, home-shopping channels, infomercials, the Internet, and catalogs. The old idea of considering each communications element separately no longer applies, from the consumer standpoint. A 1992 Consumer Survey by Leo Burnett U.S.A. revealed that consumers consider all messages—public relations, sales promotion, direct mail, billboards, event marketing, point-of-purchase signs and displays, Internet banners, product placements in movies and videos, etc.—advertising.

In an effort to reach and accommodate these consumers, advertisers, with advanced technology and capability, continue to define the target audience more and more precisely. Demographics and the traditional ethnic minorities are not enough. By 2010, there will be no "majority." African Americans, with substantial buying power, and Hispanics, soon to be the largest segment, are part of most major advertising campaigns. Asian Americans, the fastest growing segment, have already been targeted by some, such as Sears Roebuck, who launched a separate campaign in 1994. Additionally, key segments, such as women and the fifty-plus market (including baby boomers), are further defined by lifestyles and attitudes. Gays and lesbians and the disabled are already being targeted separately by advertisers. Computers allow for further analysis and segment identification than ever before, and media exist that allow advertisers to reach them directly.

Whereas mass marketing and mass media produced more product alternatives and lower prices, consumer loyalty to brands and products eroded. In one sense, the advertising challenge has come full circle. Key objectives for national advertisers now focus on building long-term relationships, offering real value, and creating brand loyalty. This was the initial purpose of most national television commercials and magazine ads in the 1960s.

Watching commercials on top-rated television events, such as the Superbowl, the Olympics, and the final episode of *Seinfeld*, reveals the importance of entertaining viewers as part of advertising strategy.

Both advertisers and consumers have more choices for products, services, and media than ever before. Indications are that these choices will increase rather than decrease in the future. As they say on the news, stay tuned, whether it be our television sets or our computers.

Jon A. Shidler
Associate Professor
School of Journalism
Southern Illinois University
Carbondale, Illinois

Chapter 3

Legal and Political Forces and Advertising

Since 1948, there has been a voluntary ban on hard liquor advertising on U.S. broadcast and cable television. However, legal decisions in the United Kingdom and Canada to permit television advertising for alcoholic spirits may have repercussions in the United States, possibly leading to revisions of a ban followed by most members of the U.S. Distilled Spirits Council. After bans were rescinded in the United Kingdom and Canada, Seagram's Beverage Company was the first hard liquor company to jump on this opportunity. TBWA Chiat/Day, New York, pitched a television campaign for Absolut Vodka with a number of cable networks, including CNN and Bravo. Bravo's lawyers, however, were very concerned that the ads might generate problems with cable subscribers in American cities and towns. Another reason cable networks were afraid to touch the ads was that Congress had only recently passed the new telecommunications bill and no one wanted the switchboard on Capitol Hill lit up by pressure groups because of the ads. Other liquor marketers are not looking to stir things up with changes. Spokespersons for the industry say that they would have to be certain that public officials, regulators, and the public itself would go along with broadcast advertising of hard liquor before they would seek any changes in the Distilled Spirits Council code regarding the voluntary ban on broadcast advertising.[1]

In 1997, the tobacco industry settled antitobacco litigation with a deal that would restrict tobacco advertising and sales in the United States (see Illustration 3.1). However, the agreement had to be ratified by Congress. Subsequently, Senator John McCain sponsored a bill that, among other things, would have further restricted tobacco advertising and marketing. In June 1998, the McCain bill met defeat in the U.S. Senate. Senate supporters of the bill failed to win the sixty votes needed to clear procedural hurdles, and the bill was dropped. President Clinton blamed the bill's defeat on an aggressive advertising campaign waged by tobacco companies.[2]

ILLUSTRATION 3.1. Outlawed?

This billboard for Doral cigarettes with its cartoon dog may soon be a historical artifact. The tobacco industry's settlement with forty-six states in November 1998 included the agreement to no longer advertise tobacco products on billboards or use cartoon characters in tobacco advertising. © Dana Hanefeld.

Welcome to the legal and political environments of advertising.

No one in the advertising business can afford to ignore government policies and the legal system. Many laws and regulations may not be designed specifically to address advertising issues, yet they can have a major impact on a firm's opportunities, both locally and abroad. For example, the U.S. Lanham Trademark Act (1946) provides protections and regulation of brand names, brand marks, trade names, and trademarks. Yet, copyright laws and violations are becoming an increasing concern for international executives. Many Asian countries have been problematic for international firms due to a lack of copyright protection. For instance, a Taiwanese manufacturer that had been producing running shoes for a U.S. shoe company decided to market itself to other shoe companies. The manufacturer advertised in an international magazine displaying the U.S. firm's brand name on the product. Although this was an honest mistake made by the Taiwanese manufacturer, it clearly violated the copyright law set by the United States. The manufacturer was subsequently sued by a major U.S. shoe company. U.S. trade representatives often watch over trading partners to ensure they are protecting intellectual property.

In another incident, a globally distributed Gap apparel ad featured unauthorized use of the "ultra-hip" eyewear of New York designer On Davis.[3] The designer filed a lawsuit seeking $10 million in punitive damages and additional compensation of more than $2 million, saying that the Gap just wasn't "hip enough" to qualify for free product placement of his high-priced spectacles in their advertising. Meanwhile, a federal court ordered *Polo Magazine* to print disclaimers on its cover, masthead, and contents page saying that it is not affiliated with Ralph Lauren or any Polo Ralph Lauren entities. The order resulted from a lawsuit initially filed by Westchester Media of Dallas, publisher of the quarter-century-old horseman's magazine, which asked the court "to protect the publisher's use of the Polo name."[4] Instead, the judge decided that the magazine had tried to capitalize on consumer familiarity with the Polo Ralph Lauren name by overhauling its contents and marketing.

Business does not function strictly by its own set of rules. It has to answer not only to its customers but also to the government, which sets the rules in the political-legal environment. This dimension of the marketing environment includes laws and regulations. The rapidly changing nature of the international political scene is evident to anyone who regularly reads, listens to, or watches the various news media. Political upheavals, revolutions, and changes in government policy occur daily and can have an enormous effect on international business, for example, international advertising strategies.

This chapter will deal with the political and legal environments in the United States, as well as in other selected countries of the world.

THE POLITICAL AND LEGAL ENVIRONMENTS IN THE UNITED STATES

In 1938, the U.S. Congress passed the Wheeler-Lea Act, which prohibits unfair and deceptive acts or unlawful practices, regardless of whether they injure competition. It specifically prohibits false and misleading advertising of foods, drugs, therapeutic devices, and cosmetics. The Wheeler-Lea Act also provides penalties for violations and procedures for enforcement. In 1946, Congress passed the Lanham Trademark Act. It, and a subsequent revision, the Trademark Law Revision Act of 1988, allows companies to challenge a competitor's false advertising claims about its own product and, in comparative ads, false claims by the competitor about the other company's product. Since the latter remedy was added relatively recently, most of the litigation has involved Company A suing Company B to halt B's advertising campaign on the basis that B was making false claims relative to B's own product.

For instance, Tropicana aired a television commercial using Bruce Jenner, a celebrated athlete, as its spokesperson. The athlete squeezed an orange while saying, "It's pure, pasteurized juice as it comes from the orange." He then poured the juice he squeezed into a Tropicana carton. In the advertisement, a voice-over claims that Tropicana's Premium Pack orange juice is "the only leading brand not made with concentrate and water." Coca-Cola, one of whose products is Minute Maid orange juice, sued to halt the advertisement on grounds that it was making false claims about Tropicana's orange juice. Coca-Cola requested an injunction to prevent the continuation of the advertising campaign.

Whether the plaintiff will suffer irreparable harm if the advertising campaign is not halted is an important factor in a court's determination as to whether an injunction will be issued. Marketing research studies can be critical in making such determinations. If consumers are misled into believing that Tropicana's product is more desirable, since it contains only fresh-squeezed juice, then it is likely that Coca-Cola will lose a portion of the chilled juice market and thus suffer irreparable injury. Advertisers need to turn to these marketing research studies to determine whether an advertisement is misleading or confusing consumers.

In viewing the thirty-second Tropicana commercial, the court decided that Tropicana's claim was false. Premium Pack juice is heated and sometimes frozen prior to packaging. Yet, in the advertisement, its celebrity spokesperson squeezes the orange and then pours the freshly squeezed juice directly into the carton.[5]

Government Regulation

At the national level, the primary instrument in the regulation of advertising is the independent regulatory agency, the Federal Trade Commission. The FTC was created in 1914 by the Federal Trade Commission Act and given regulatory authority in both the antitrust and advertising areas. It exercised the latter under directions to halt "unfair methods of competition." The Wheeler-Lea Act in 1938 significantly broadened its authority by authorizing it to prevent "unfair or deceptive acts and practices." As amended, the law now states, "unfair methods of competition . . . and unfair or deceptive acts or practices . . . are hereby declared unlawful."[6]

The major difference between the Lanham Act and the Federal Trade Commission Act is that the former only strikes at "false" advertising claims, whereas the latter is broader in scope by sweeping "deceptive" ads within the FTC's regulatory purview. It is considered deceptive for an advertisement to

1. offer two for the price of one, if both items were not sold at a normal price of one unit prior to the advertising campaign;
2. offer buy one, get one free, if the price of the former is marked up to compensate for the cost of the "free" item;
3. engage in "bait and switch" sales tactics;
4. utilize a celebrity endorser for a product if the celebrity does not actually use or prefer the item; or
5. use a mock-up in the advertisement while telling the viewer that the real item is being used.

The FTC regards an advertisement as deceptive if it contains a representation, practice, or omission likely to mislead consumers acting reasonably and the representation, practice, or omission is material to a consumer's choice. The FTC also regards as deceptive an advertising claim that is made without *prior* substantiation. Thus, if when challenged by the FTC, the advertiser conducts tests that prove the validity of the claim, those facts will not provide a safe harbor from the legal storm. The FTC requires that an advertiser have a reasonable basis, or substantiation, for the claim prior to their assertion in an advertisement. This substantiation requirement is applicable to both expressed and implied claims. Marketing research is once again vital in ascertaining what, if any, implied claims are made to consumers.

In 1995, the U.S. Supreme Court handed down an important ruling dealing with the power of the Bureau of Alcohol, Tobacco, and Firearms

(BATF) to regulate advertising on beer labels (*Rubin v. Coors*, 63 LW 4319 [1995]). The Agriculture Department possesses authority over certain aspects of food products. Under that authority, it issued a rule that, effective August 1996, poultry cannot be labeled and sold as fresh if it has been frozen. The Food and Drug Administration (FDA) has authority over certain other areas of food products. The agency made major news in August 1995 with its proposed widespread regulation of cigarette advertising. By declaring nicotine a drug, and tobacco a drug delivery device, the FDA proposed to ban brand-name advertising at sporting events and on products that are not tobacco related, such as T-shirts; forbid outdoor advertisements of tobacco within 1,000 feet of schools and playgrounds; limit advertising in publications that reach a significant audience of children; and require tobacco companies to fund a $150 million advertising campaign to stop young people from smoking (see this chapter's Ethics Track, pp. 49-50).

Other governmental agencies that have become involved in advertising regulation include the Department of Transportation, which regulates airline industry ads, and the Federal Bureau of Investigation (FBI) and U.S. Department of Justice, which launched an investigation in 1995 of a controversial Calvin Klein campaign. Klein had had previous problems with its emphasis on youthful models in what critics called pornographic poses. A 1980s Brooke Shields television commercial, which showed crotch shots of the fifteen-year-old model and featured the tag line "Nothing comes between me and my Calvins," met with some stations' refusals to air the spot—never mind that sales of the jeans almost doubled.[7] But, in 1995, a campaign that featured the nude body of Kate Moss in erotic poses caused the FBI and Justice Department to question whether the ads violated federal pornography laws. Although the investigation was dropped, Klein pulled the offending ads.

Such gutsy campaigns are said to have "attitude," a 1990s term that refers to a disposition or tone of hostility. Advertising with attitude generally reflects a view that conflicts with most people's perceptions of what is politically correct. For instance, Holiday Inn promoted its $1 billion renovation program during prized Super Bowl time in 1997 with a transsexual ad—the tag line declared, "It's amazing the changes you can make for a few thousand dollars." When clients were offended, Holiday Inn backed off by canceling a follow-up spot involving the Pope before it aired.[8]

Industry Self-Regulation

Self-regulation refers to actions taken by advertisers themselves rather than by governmental bodies. Several industry and trade associations and other organizations have voluntarily established guidelines for advertising within their industries. For instance, in 1936, makers of distilled spirits agreed collectively not to air ads on radio, and a decade later followed suit for television, which was just becoming popular in American homes. However, after a twenty-year drop in liquor consumption and a huge upswing in revenues to the beer and wine industries, Seagram's, the country's number two distiller, aired an advertisement for its Crown Royal whiskey on a local television station in Corpus Christi, Texas, in June 1996, breaking the industry ban honored over several decades.

Self-regulation by the Council of Better Business Bureaus' National Advertising Division (NAD) and National Advertising Review Board (NARB) has been the most publicized and perhaps most effective form of self-regulation. Complaints received from consumers, competitors, or local branches of the Better Business Bureau are forwarded to the NAD. After a full review of the complaint, the issue may be forwarded to the NARB and evaluated by a panel. Any unresolved cases may be forwarded to the appropriate government agency, such as the FTC, FDA, and FCC. For instance, The National Advertising Division of the Council of Better Business Bureaus ruled in favor of Papa John's Pizza in a substantiation claim initiated in 1998 by Tricon Global Restaurants, owners of the Pizza Hut chain. At issue was an ad that declared Papa John's pizza had bested Pizza Hut's pizza in a taste test. Papa John's struck back at Pizza Hut in full-page ads run in national newspapers on August 21, 1998. The ad featured a drawing of David holding a slingshot and wearing a Papa John's shirt as he faces the towering Goliath (with Pizza Hut emblazoned on his shield) and an army of lawyers. The headline said it all: "What's The World Coming To? Now Goliath Is Suing David For Pain and Suffering." The ad's text reiterated Papa John's claims that its advertising is truthful and accurate and that consumers prefer Papa John's over Pizza Hut. Although Papa John's substantiated the taste tests, the council did recommend that future ads be modified to only compare Papa John's pizzas to Pizza Hut's. Nevertheless, Pizza Hut's lawsuit against Papa John's remained unresolved early in 1999. The pizza advertising wars escalated in 1999 when a Pizza Hut commercial used Papa John's advertising footage without permission[9]

Campbell Soup Company modified its Soup in a Jar ads after losing its appeal of a 1997 decision made by the National Advertising Division of the Council of Better Business Bureaus. The National Advertising Review Board upheld the council's decision that Campbell's ads were deceptive in claiming that the glass jar soups contained fresh vegetables. More accurately, the soups had "been processed with" fresh vegetables.[10]

THE POLITICAL AND LEGAL ENVIRONMENTS IN OTHER SELECTED COUNTRIES

A country's political system, national laws, regulatory bodies, national pressure groups, and courts all have great impact on international marketing/advertising. A government's policies regarding public and private enterprise, consumers, and foreign firms influence marketing/advertising across national boundaries. In this section, we will discuss the political and legal environments in selected regions and countries.

Asia

China

International companies are concerned with the political uncertainty that influences the pace and direction of the economic transformation already under way in China. Since 1979, the year of the thirtieth anniversary of the People's Republic of China (PRC), authorities have permitted foreign advertising to influence how the vast country communicates, both internally and with the rest of an increasingly interdependent world. Although interest in China has begun to pay off for international advertisers and advertising agencies, questions about the effects of advertising are gradually being raised.

In May 1998, China announced "a ban on all forms of direct marketing, including Chinese versions of pyramid sales schemes and conventional direct-selling practices used by Amway and other U.S. companies," such as Mary Kay Cosmetics and Avon Products. Chinese authorities worry that the sales methods of these multinational companies—door-to-door selling "conducted by individuals who generally work with little supervision"—may be a potential "breeding ground for social unrest and economic havoc."[11] Representatives of the direct marketing companies hope to come up with a compromise. At stake is their $120 million investment in China.

Closer scrutiny is also being given to tobacco and pharmaceutical promotion and the link to poor public health. Spirits advertising—including corporate image campaigns for liquor products—has been banned from 7 to 8 p.m. (during prime time) on China's only national television station (CCTV). Spirits advertising had brought CCTV $36.8 million in revenues during 1997.[12]

China's domestic advertising agencies' concerns about competition from foreign joint venture advertising agencies have resulted in the Interim Regulations promulgated in 1993. The regulations clearly defined the roles of media and advertising agencies.[13] The Interim Advertising Censorship Standards were promulgated at the same time as the Interim Regulations of 1993. The Standards address emotional responses aroused by advertising. The second article of the Standards is devoted entirely to visuals and images displayed in ads. Use of sex appeals, fear appeals, and visuals that may lead to dangerous or negative behavior are forbidden.[14]

One of the more complex questions about the future of advertising in China has to do with the political future of Hong Kong. Besides Japan, Hong Kong has had the liveliest, most competitive advertising and commercial environment in Asia. As a British colony, Hong Kong had historically served as a center of foreign trade and communications. Many transnational advertisers, advertising agencies, and media have had offices in Hong Kong. Agencies such as Ogilvy & Mather and Leo Burnett used the colony as a base from which to try to expand into neighboring China. Hong Kong is such an important Asian business center that China itself has long had a state-owned advertising agency there to aggressively promote made-in-China goods. In 1998, Hong Kong reverted to China when Britain's ninety-nine-year lease expired. Only time will tell whether the Chinese will work out some means of continuing the status quo so that the mainland can continue to take advantage of Hong Kong's Western-oriented commercial and communications services, including advertising.

Reliable, quantifiable information about communications in China remains skimpy, and the government's policies continue in a state of flux. More specifically, China's advertising plans are not clearly articulated within the broad complex of the society's needs, aspirations, and resources.[15]

Japan

In April 1998, the tobacco industry ceased television, radio, movie theater, and Internet advertising. That limits tobacco advertising to print and outdoor media.[16] The restrictions on tobacco advertising will primarily affect foreign tobacco companies. Regulation of online communications that are viewed as pornographic or political is also under consideration.[17] New media and tobacco have been hot regulation issues throughout Asia as highly developed and regulated countries such as Japan and newer advertising markets such as Vietnam seek to protect their diverse cultures and religions.

Taiwan

To maintain fair competition among sellers and to protect consumers, the government of Taiwan ratified the Fair Trade Law on February 4,

1991. The law went into effect a year later, creating the Fair Trade Commission. Under this act, vertical price-fixing is prohibited. Also, it makes resale price maintenance, a common practice in Taiwan, illegal. Under the previous law, producers were not penalized if they attempted to control retail prices. It is now illegal for manufacturers and wholesalers to force retailers to accept a suggested retail price. The law specifies that sellers cannot engage in price discrimination unless there are provable differences between selling costs. Basically, this is an antitrust law that restrains unfair methods of competition.

While the Fair Trade Law protects competitors from one another, Article 21 of this law addresses the issue of false or misleading advertising. This article states that "an enterprise shall not make, on goods or in ads relating thereto, any false, untrue or misleading presentation which may likely cause confusion to or mistake by consumers such as their price, quantity, quality, content, manufacturing process, date of manufacturing, validity period, use method, purpose of use, place of origin, manufacturer, place of manufacturing, processor, and place of processing."[18] Furthermore, an enterprise shall not sell, transport, export, or import goods bearing false, untrue, or misleading presentations referred to in the preceding statement.

The Consumer Protection Law was promulgated on January 11, 1994, and became effective on January 13, 1994. This law was enacted for the purpose of protecting the interests of consumers, facilitating the safety of and improving the quality of the consumer life of the nationals. Because this second law is new, there may be some jurisdictional conflict between the Fair Trade Commission and the Consumer Protection Commission regarding deceptive advertising. Nevertheless, it is clear that a consumer who seeks damages from a company should go to the Consumer Protection Commission. A consumer may also complain to the Fair Trade Commission about deceptive advertising. If the Fair Trade Commission's investigation finds an advertisement deceptive, the commission has the power to fine the company.

It is useful to mention that it took more than ten years for these two laws, first envisioned in 1981, to be enacted. In the meantime, consumers endured misconduct from businesses, such as deceptive advertising and a low level of product quality.

Malaysia

Although there are numerous situations in which differing customer needs require tailor-made advertising campaigns, in many instances, the particular regulations of a country prevent multinational corporations from using standardized approaches. In countries such as Malaysia, regulations are a direct outgrowth of changing political circumstances.

The Malaysian government does not have an overall or comprehensive policy regarding advertising practices. In theory, the main set of regulations controlling advertising ethics is the Malaysian Code of Advertising Practice. This code is not a piece of legislation introduced by the government; it is a purely voluntary set of guidelines drawn up and administered by a private-sector organization, the Advertising Standards Authority (ASA). Although no comprehensive advertising legislation exists in Malaysia, the Trade Descriptions Act (1972) empowers the Ministry of Trade and Industry to act against companies that give misleading statements or suggestions in advertisements. The Radio Television Malaysia (RTM) Code of Advertising is not too different from the Code of Advertising Practice. Since it was first issued by the Ministry of Information on December 27, 1972, it has been updated several times. Several distinguishing features of the RTM code are bans on the following types of ads: alcoholic beverage ads; ads that use children to promote products not intended for them; ads for women's products, such as sanitary napkins, that are screened before 10 p.m.; and cigarette ads.[19]

Singapore

Advertisers, media, and advertising agencies find it in their own best interest to support self-regulatory bodies rather than wait until the government has to step in and take measures that might adversely affect the advertising industry. One of the best-organized self-regulatory bodies in Asia is in Singapore. The Advertising Standards Authority of Singapore (ASAS) has ties to consumer and trade union groups and includes representatives of agencies, advertisers, and the media. It sets standards, publishes a code of ethical advertising practice, and deals with complaints from the public and from within the industry. In a number of developing countries, however, codes either do not exist or are difficult to enforce.

First as a British colony, then as part of Malaysia, and now as an independent republic, Singapore has thrived as a regional commercial and communications center for foreign businesses. Transnational advertising agencies and their clients have flocked to Singapore because facilities for communications are excellent and there are no regulations against wholly owned subsidiaries.[20] Nevertheless, Singapore has become one of the "most policed" of the Asian countries, especially when it comes to new media. "The government has established the Proxy, a central master server and screening service for material on the Internet."[21]

Indonesia, Thailand, and Vietnam

Concern about growing advertising markets has led to tighter regulations—regarding tobacco and alcohol in particular—in these three countries. Although Indonesia allows cigarette advertising on television, spots cannot show the cigarette packs or scenes that involve actual smoking. A ban on all cigarette advertising has been under review. A change in Thai Censorship Board regulations now permits television advertising of alcohol, but only after 10 p.m. Whereas advertisers view Thailand as "modern" and receptive, Vietnam presents a hostile climate. Ad agencies, restricted to representative offices, must conduct financial transactions outside the country. Media buying may eventually be restricted to Vietnamese-owned agencies. Although currently there are no such regulations, and policies change often, the general atmosphere has been anti-Western.[22]

Europe and the United Kingdom

Issues facing the European Union's highest executive body, the European Commission, have included new media, protection of children, privacy, and a tobacco ban that has been resisted by Denmark, Germany, and the United Kingdom, among others.

The British advertising regulatory regime is a unique combination of case law, statutory law, and self-regulation. It differs from the regulatory systems of continental Europe and the United States in two major respects: (1) the absence of general statutory laws prohibiting misleading and unfair advertising and (2) the central role of voluntary self-regulation in the control of specific advertising abuses. The centerpiece of the British scheme is the self-regulatory system. Most complaints about advertising content are generally directed, in the first instance, to the nongovernmental Advertising Standards Authority or Independent Broadcasting Authority. The courts and the law provide legally enforceable alternatives when self-restraint does not succeed or when the abuse is beyond the scope of self-regulation. The scope of the law differs to some extent from the scope of the self-regulatory system. Self-regulation focuses principally on the content of ads, whereas the law has a much wider scope, including the behavior of the advertisers and agencies.

Although some countries are still dealing inadequately with public and industry complaints, the United Kingdom already has the Advertising Standards Authority (ASA) in place. The ASA tobacco advertising regulations of 1994 banned the use of humor in tobacco ads. The regulations also led to tobacco industry agreements to cut its poster advertising budget

40 percent, to stop putting posters within 200 meters of schools, and to increase the size of health warnings in advertising by 20 percent.[23]

The British Commonwealth of Nations

Many countries, members of the British Commonwealth of Nations, have adopted political and legal systems patterned on the English system. Industrialized Commonwealth countries, including Canada, Australia, and New Zealand, have also adapted many aspects of the British advertising regulatory scheme to their national situations. All these countries have central self-regulatory bodies somewhat comparable to the British Advertising Standards Authority, with the exception of New Zealand, which has established a less extensive system of voluntary restraints.

Although advertising in Canada is closely tied to U.S. industry, the regulatory system is independent. Canada pioneered a system of self-regulation in 1957. Today, the Advertising Standards Council (ASC) is the self-regulatory arm of the Canadian Advertising Foundation (CAF). The ASC cooperates with the government. The CAF was the first to outline educational guidelines for sex-role stereotyping and to establish a Broadcast Code for Advertising to Children, which it jointly administers with the Canadian federal government.[24]

Since outdoor advertising was banned in 1995, there has been no cigarette advertising in Australia. As the most regulated, Westernized country in its region, Australia has a number of regulatory agencies. The Australian Competition and Consumer Commission is a governmental regulatory body with codes governing, among other areas, the portrayal of women and children in advertising. These codes are administered by the Media Council. Other regulatory agencies include the Australian Association of National Advertisers and the Advertising Standards Council (which represents the public as well as the advertising industry).[25]

South America

Venezuela's congress has already banned tobacco advertising on radio and television. Advertising agencies in what has been described as a hardline country are represented by the Venezuelan Federation of Advertising Agencies. Chile and the Dominican Republic represent a less restrictive advertising environment in which marketers, advertising agencies, and the media practice self-regulation, pulling ads with "questionable content."[26] Silec, an ad trade group, resolves a high percentage of advertising conflicts in Mexico, Argentina, Nicaragua, and Venezuela. In Colombia, the lobbying group Asomedios represents advertisers.

Brazil has been self-regulatory since the early 1980s in the hope of avoiding governmental regulations. However, in the early 1990s, a strong proconsumer sentiment mandated visual and audio health warnings in tobacco advertising and banned the link of tobacco and alcohol products to such healthy situations as sports.[27]

Before a company enters a foreign market, it must thoroughly analyze the environment. If an advertising strategy is to be effective across national borders, the complexities of all the environments involved must be understood. In 1998, Asian economic problems adversely affected both the U.S. trade deficit and the stock market. The overthrow of the government in Indonesia in May 1998 also created a sense of caution among international marketers. Any change in the political and economic climate of a country will eventually impact the world of marketing and advertising.

Fortunately, these days, multinational corporations are paying more attention to the uncontrollable environments (e.g., political and legal issues) in foreign markets when they design their ads. For instance, few advertising and public policy issues have attracted more attention in recent years than the international controversy over the marketing of infant food. Infant formula manufacturer Nestlé has been boycotted and its activities in developing countries closely scrutinized. To improve its company image, Nestlé has gone out of its way to support social development efforts by emphasizing that teaching is satisfying work in ads created by Ogilvy & Mather in Kuala Lumpur. Gradually, in Malaysia and elsewhere, advertisers are becoming aware of the social value of reinforcing cultural traditions and the political value of supporting government policies.[28]

SUMMARY

No one in the advertising business can afford to ignore government policies and the legal system. Many laws and regulations may not be designed to address advertising issues, yet they can have a major impact on a firm's opportunities, both locally and abroad. The political and legal environments in the United States are influenced by federal government regulation, especially Congress and the Federal Trade Commission. In Taiwan, the Fair Trade Law and Consumer Protection Law have affected advertising. In other countries, the political system, national laws, regulatory bodies, national pressure groups, and courts all have great impact on international marketing and advertising. Before a company enters the international marketplace, it must thoroughly analyze each country's political and legal forces.

* * *

THE GLOBAL PERSPECTIVE: THE IMPACT OF ADVERTISING ENVIRONMENT ON INTERNATIONAL ADVERTISING

A 1994 Super Bowl commercial had no problem in other countries, but a Greek television network gave it the boot.

Pepsi had created the ad, which showed two chimps drinking cola—one guzzling Pepsi, the other Coca-Cola—specifically for the international market. Because many countries, including Greece, ban or restrict comparative ads that name a rival's product, Pepsi prepared different versions for different countries. In another version, which ran successfully in twenty countries, one of the chimps drinks Pepsi, the other Brand X.[a]

Following the growing influence of Moslem fundamentalists in many parts of the world, Malaysia, a country with a large Moslem population, outlawed ads showing women in sleeveless dresses and pictures showing underarms. These were considered offensive by strict Moslem standards. Obviously, this caused considerable problems to marketers of deodorant products.[b]

When India banned feminine hygiene product advertisements on terrestrial TV, Procter & Gamble used Hong Kong's StarTV, the first pan-Asian satellite television network, as a way to reach women in India.[c]

As these advertisers discovered, a country's political system, national laws, regulatory bodies, and interest groups all have a great impact on international advertising.

[a] Pat Guy, "Chimp Ad's Appeal Isn't Quite Global," *USA Today,* February 1, 1994, p. 2B.
[b] "Curbs on Ads Increase Abroad As Nations Apply Standards of Fairness and Decency," *The Wall Street Journal,* November 25, 1980, p. 56.
[c] Jonathan Karp, "Medium and Message," *Far Eastern Economic Review,* February 25, 1993, pp. 50-52.

* * *

ETHICS TRACK: TOBACCO'S WOES

According to *Newsweek* magazine, 3,000 children take up cigarettes each day, and "1,000 of them will die of smoking-related diseases." "More than one third of high-school students now smoke."[a] When the antitobacco bill sponsored by Republican Senator John McCain was defeated in the Senate in June 1998, many advocates of children—such as McCain—feared that tobacco advertising and other gimmicks tobacco manufacturers use to interest children in smoking would have far-reaching social effects.

A number of ethical issues are linked to advertising. Among the hottest topics being debated today are advertising to children and minority audiences and advertising controversial products (e.g., alcohol and tobacco).

Makers of alcohol and tobacco products have frequently employed billboards and other advertising media to target brands to African Americans and Hispanics. Billboards advertising alcohol and tobacco have been disproportionately more likely to appear in inner-city areas.[b]

Perhaps the most controversial advertisement has been R. J. Reynolds' character spokesperson, Joe Camel. Nine years after a campaign featuring the cool, sax-playing, cigarette-smoking camel first appeared, the company was forced to retire Joe to settle an onslaught of lawsuits. Research showed that Joe Camel had become as recognizable to children as Mickey Mouse, and critics believed that the cartoon character's appearance on such diverse public venues as billboards and racing cars encouraged children to smoke.[c]

An agreement between the tobacco industry and several state attorneys general in 1997 included a variety of "ad curbs" that had to be ratified by Congress. These ad curbs, defeated in McCain's bill, would have greatly limited tobacco advertising. However, on November 21, 1998, tobacco companies settled a lawsuit with forty-six states in a landmark deal that included the firms' agreement to no longer advertise tobacco products on billboards and to cease using cartoon characters in their ads. In April 1999, the Supreme Court agreed to hear the Clinton administration and the tobacco industry argue whether or not the Food and Drug Administration (FDA) has the authority to restrict cigarette advertising and sales. What did the Supreme Court decide? What other ways might cigarette advertising to children and minorities be curtailed? What should the advertising industry's responsibility be in resolving this controversy?

[a] "The Trouble with T Shirts," *Newsweek,* June 22, 1998, p. 28.
[b] "Fighting Ads in the Inner City," *Newsweek,* February 5, 1990, p. 46
[c] Christian Thompson, "Joe Camel Dies: Victim of His Own Success," *USA Today,* July 11-13, 1997, p. A1.

Chapter 4

The Advertising Business and Advertising Agencies

The global community in which we live has created complex challenges and made new demands on advertisers and their agencies. John Dooner, chairman of McCann-Erickson Worldwide, the largest international advertising agency, has set up a special team of the agency's top strategic and creative talent.[1] Its mandate is to develop clients' multinational businesses, taking globalism to a new level. The agency's growth will depend on growing the clients' global businesses by bringing marketing initiatives to its clients, as well as producing superior creative work. That McCann-Erickson is doing this now indicates how critical global advertising has become to the survival of the advertising agency. About 75 percent of its billings come from such global marketers as Coca-Cola, General Motors, Goodyear Company, Exxon, McDonald's, and L'Oréal. Global advertising is in fashion, and clients want to work more closely with fewer, worldwide agencies.[2] McCann-Erickson is owned by Interpublic Groups of Cos., the third-largest advertising organization in the world (see Table 4.1).

There is more to running a global business than global branding (developing a global market for either a domestic or multinational brand) and a multinational advertising campaign (although the advertisements might have different executions and emphasize different product features, the underlying message remains the same). Bozell International has helped clients find qualified local personnel, prescreened potential distributors, and even put clients in touch with plant acquisition opportunities. Bozell's philosophy is that by helping clients open up networks of distribution and marketing, the agency may create an unlimited partnership with them.

As McCann-Erickson, Bozell, and their clients know, creating an ad campaign, whether for a local market or a multinational market, involves a partnership between the advertiser and the agency. Two other key players are in the advertising business. The first is the media, which sell time in electronic media and space in print media to carry the advertiser's message

51

TABLE 4.1. The Global Perspective: Top Ten Advertising Organizations (Ranked by Worldwide Gross Income—1998)

1. Omnicom Group	New York	$4,812.0
2. Interpublic Groups of Cos.	New York	4,304.5
3. WPP Group	London	4,156.8
4. Dentsu	Tokyo	1,786.0
5. Young & Rubicam	New York	1,659.9
6. Havas Advertising	Paris	1,297.9
7. True North Communications	Chicago	1,242.3
8. Grey Advertising	New York	1,240.4
9. Leo Burnett	Chicago	949.8
10. Publicis	New York	930.0

Source: Derived from R. Craig Endicott, "Top 25 Global Advertising Organizations," *Advertising Age,* April 19, 1999, p. s18.

Note: Income figures are in millions.

to the target market. The second, the suppliers, includes the illustrators, photographers, printers, typesetters, video production houses, and other intermediaries who assist both advertisers and agencies in preparing advertising materials.

This chapter examines the advertisers and agencies—what they do, who they are, and how they work together.

THE ADVERTISING BUSINESS

The large and complex business of advertising involves many types of organizations and people. According to *Advertising Age,* international advertising agencies' billings rose to $117,490,000,000 in 1994, an increase of 9.1 percent over 1993 billings.[3] This information was derived from just the numbers reported by the top 500 major advertising agencies. Ad spending was predicted to increase to a record $186 billion in 1997, a 6.2 percent increase over the previous, banner year.

What Advertising People Do

Advertisers or the advertising agencies they hire must perform certain basic tasks. These include planning, budgeting, coordination, and ad crea-

ILLUSTRATION 4.1. Creative People

Agency employees develop and prepare advertising plans and produce advertisements and other promotional materials. Account executives must have writing and computer skills and be prepared to communicate via mass and new media. Catherine A. Narbone (pictured here), assistant account executive at Golin/Harris Communications, Incorporated, stresses the importance of writing skills in her :60 Spot "Writing the Road to Success" in this chapter. She also defines the function of public relations in Chapter 17's :60 Spot.

tion (see Illustration 4.1). In a large firm, the advertising manager is the person who is in charge of all the advertising tasks. In the advertising agency, the account manager generally pursues these tasks.

Planning

Planning is an ongoing process of defining and redefining goals and objectives, performing advertising research, developing and scheduling advertisements, and evaluating results.

Budgeting

The advertising manager, the person who is in charge of all the advertising tasks, or the account manager (or other personnel) formulates the annual budget and presents it to top management. This person then sees that the staff (either the advertiser's or the agency's) adhere to the budget.

Coordination

Business activities usually fall into three broad, functional areas: production, finance, and marketing. Advertising is a marketing activity. The person in charge of the advertising process must coordinate advertising activities with other marketing functions (e.g., sales), as well as with production and finance activities. Advertising agency personnel also need to coordinate the advertising activities with other marketing, production, and finance functions within their client's company.

Creating Advertisements

The creative tasks consist of three main elements: copywriting, art direction, and production. The advertising manager or other personnel need to ensure that the finished advertisements will fulfill the company's goals.

The Advertisers

Advertisers hire many people to create advertisements and buy ad time and space. Advertisers may be international, national, regional, or local; they may be global corporations, such as Coca-Cola, or small businesses. These advertisers range from one-person certified public accountant (CPA) offices that advertise only in the local Yellow Pages to national chain stores that advertise on television and in national newspapers. In fact, the *Standard Directory of Advertisers* (known as the advertiser's "Red Book") lists roughly 25,000 advertisers in the United States alone and includes their budgets and their advertising agencies. Virtually every company has an advertising department. Large companies may have a separate advertising department that employs many people and is headed by an advertising manager who reports to a marketing director or marketing services manager. Smaller companies may have just one person who performs all the advertising tasks and reports to the top management. In these smaller companies, this person may also be part of top management.

THE ADVERTISING AGENCY

The American Association of Advertising Agencies defines an advertising agency as an independent organization of creative people and businesspeople who specialize in developing and preparing advertising plans, advertisements, and other promotional tools. The agency purchases advertising space and time in various media on behalf of its clients—various advertisers or sellers—to find customers for the clients' goods and services.[4]

Advertising agencies range in size from small shops to giant businesses that hire thousands of employees. The smaller agencies usually have up to a dozen employees and handle accounts of up to $10,000. Medium-sized agencies bill an average of $10,000 to $100,000,000 annually. In 1997, J. Walter Thompson (JWT) pulled up from number three to number two in the *Advertising Age* U.S. brand rankings with a gross income of $387.8 million, replacing Leo Burnett, which had occupied the number two spot in 1996. JWT continued to hold the number two position in 1998 (see Table 4.2). Brand agencies do not handle their clients' specialty advertising and nonmedia components such as public relations. Worldwide agency brands are defined as international networks associated with the agency and the agency's U.S. brand. In 1998, Dentsu was the world's largest brand agency, with worldwide gross income of $1,786 million.[5]

TABLE 4.2. Top Ten U.S. Agencies (Ranked by U.S. Gross Income—1998)

1. Grey Advertising	New York	$422.3
2. J. Walter Thompson	New York	414.6
3. Leo Burnett	Chicago	380.2
4. McCann-Erickson Worldwide	New York	378.4
5. Y&R Advertising	New York	344.0
6. BBDO Worldwide	New York	336.6
7. DDB Needham Worldwide	New York	316.6
8. Foote, Cone & Belding	New York	298.0
9. Brann Worldwide	Deerfield, Illinois	287.6
10. Ogilvy & Mather Worldwide	New York	278.4

Source: Derived from R. Craig Endicott, "U.S. Shops Top $15 Billion in Revenue," *Advertising Age,* April 19, 1999, p. s4.

Note: Income figures are in millions.

Advertising agencies may be organized into departments based on functional specialties (account services, creative services, marketing services, and administration) or into groups that work as teams on various accounts. Advertising agencies can be classified by the range of services they offer and the types of business they handle. The two basic types are full-service agencies and specialized service agencies, such as creative boutiques and media-buying services.

Types of Advertising Agencies

Full-Service Agencies

A full-service agency performs at least four basic functions for the clients it represents: research services, creative services, media services, and account management. In addition to these functions, some advertising agencies are expanding their services by offering direct marketing, public relations, and even sales promotion services in the spirit of becoming Integrated Marketing Communication agencies. DDB Needham Worldwide's subsidiary, DDB Needham Marketing Communications, deals with sales promotion, direct response, and other marketing services.

McCann-Erickson Worldwide, which includes all its subsidiaries and specialty units except public relations, was ranked number one among U.S.-based agencies on a consolidated basis by *Advertising Age* in 1995.

Specialized Service Agencies

Creative boutiques. Creative boutiques are limited service advertising agencies. These relatively small agencies concentrate entirely on preparing the creative execution of client communications. The focus of the organization is the idea and the creative product. There are no staff for media, research, strategic planning, or other services that a full-service agency can offer. McDonald's Corporation surprised the industry when it hired Fallon McElligott, Minneapolis, basically a creative boutique, to handle its $75 million introduction of the Arch Deluxe in May 1996. It also went beyond its core advertising agencies (Leo Burnett USA and DDB Needham Worldwide) for creative resources for its other products.[6]

Health/medical agencies. This special type of agency concentrates on advertising for pharmaceutical companies such as Merck, Pfizer, and Upjohn. The health/medical agency carries out most of the functions a full-service agency performs but concentrates on the medical field. Health care is one of the fastest-growing segments in advertising in the United States today. Prescription and over-the-counter drugs account for much of this advertising. Many full-service agencies and holding companies have been buying health/medical agencies. In 1996, McCann-Erickson Worldwide bought Torre Renta Lazur Healthcare Group, one of the United States' leading health agencies. Large U.S. agencies have also made consumer health advertising a priority. For instance, Saatchi & Saatchi Advertising in New York has created a separate division called Healthcare Connection to keep up with its competitors.[7]

Direct marketing agencies. These agencies specialize in strategic planning, creative solutions, and execution, as well as database management for direct response advertising. However, some direct marketing agencies have expanded to full-service agencies. Such an agency is Rapp Collins Worldwide, a direct marketing pioneer almost thirty-five years ago, which is now the world's largest direct marketing agency, with global billings in excess of $1.8 billion, forty-five offices in twenty-five countries, and 2,400 employees. Relationship marketing and interactive communication have always been the special domain of direct marketers. Today, direct marketing agencies offer such services as Web site creation, e-commerce, Internet marketing, and data mining and modeling, along with traditional direct response services.

Ethnic agencies. Another example of a specialized agency is the ethnic agency. According to the latest estimate, the Hispanic population is growing at four times the rate of the general U.S. population. The Hispanic population in North America is expected to jump 14.8 percent to 31 million by the year 2000 and will soon represent the largest minority group in the United States. Many Hispanic magazines and television and radio stations have emerged specifically to serve this population. The group's buying power in 1995 surged to $240 billion. Many blue-chip marketers recognize the importance of this fast-growing consumer group, for example, IBM, General Motors, AT&T, and Revlon, which now place ads in Hispanic magazines.[8] American Honda Motor Company used its Hispanic agency, La Agencia de Orci & Associates in Los Angeles, to create advertising campaigns for fifteen Latin American countries. Although the advertising was designed for all markets, it allowed for alterations as needed in each country.[9]

Armed with statistics that show the African-American population will reach 39 million by the year 2010 and spending by this group has reached $300 billion, marketers are spending more than ever to reach black consumers. Seventeen advertising agencies are listed as specialists for this market in the *Standard Directory of Advertisers*. Most of them are small agencies of fewer than a dozen employees. Burrell Advertising in Chicago is one of the largest and most successful of the African-American agencies. In 1995, the agency gained target-marketing assignments from Mobil Oil Corporation and from Nabisco Foods for its A1 Sauce. Many general agencies realize the importance of the African-American market and vie for this market. Procter & Gamble urged national advertising agencies to aggressively diversify their ranks with full-time minority employees for their own benefit and for the good of the nation's top brands. George Fisher, the CEO of Eastman Kodak, has noted that customers do not all want the same things and cannot all be treated the same way. One of Kodak's four advertising agencies is Uniworld, a minority-owned agency whose advertising primarily targets African Americans.[10] Some companies even have an in-house agency to create advertisements aimed at African Americans.

Over 7 million Asians live in the United States, and by the year 2000, the number is expected to increase to slightly over 12 million. Asian Americans, on average, are better educated, have higher incomes, and occupy more prestigious job positions than any other segment in American society. Some firms have been successful in marketing to specific Asian groups by customizing marketing programs specifically to their values and lifestyles rather than merely translating Anglo programs. Often, an Asian agency is used by these advertisers. Muse Cordero Chen, a Los Angeles agency, specializes not only in marketing to Asian consumers but also to African-American and Hispanic markets.

AGENCY COMPENSATION

To survive, an agency must make a profit. Basically, agencies make money from three sources: media commissions, fees, and markups.

Media Commissions

The media channel may allow an agency to retain a 15 percent commission on the time or space purchased for clients. For example, a television station bills an agency $10,000 for airing a commercial. The agency bills the advertiser $10,000. The advertiser pays the agency in full, and the agency submits $8,500 to the station, keeping $1,500 (a 15 percent commission). An agency typically provides creative, media, research, and account management services to earn its 15 percent commission for its largest accounts. For outdoor advertising, the commission is usually more, at $16\ ^2/_3$ percent.

The 15 percent commission has been a matter of some controversy between the advertisers and agencies. Agencies argue that a 15 percent commission does not cover their costs; smaller advertisers must sometimes pay additional fees. On the other hand, many advertisers believe that a 15 percent compensation is too much. The disagreement has spurred the growth of other compensation systems. In fact, a 1995 study by the Association of National Advertisers revealed that only 14 percent of advertisers still pay a 15 percent commission. According to the study, the most common compensation method is a reduced commission system (less than 15 percent). Of the advertisers surveyed, 45 percent indicated that they use this form of compensation. An Andersen Consulting study revealed that most advertisers using agencies for full-service advertising pay commissions ranging from 8 to 15 percent, with larger advertisers paying an average of 13 percent. Other studies show an even lower range, from 8 to 10 percent.

Another controversy regards hidden costs extracted from advertisers by the media, especially television. Agencies say these fees further cut into their profits. For instance, the broadcast networks charge a $125 to $550 "integration fee" each time an ad runs. Networks say the fee covers the costs of ad screening and on-air placement. Agencies view the fees as unnecessary.[11]

Labor-Based Fees

A labor-based fee system has become popular in recent years. Of advertisers surveyed, 35 percent compensated agencies on time commitment. An hourly fee is negotiated between the advertiser and the agency. The agency then monitors the labor and bills the client on the time spent. This system is also used for special services the agency renders for its clients. For example, if an agency arranges a focus group study for its client, the client will receive a bill from the agency based on an agreed-upon hourly rate.

Markups

The agency may need to purchase photographs, illustrations, or other services from outside suppliers for its clients. The agency pays these suppliers a set fee and adds a markup, typically 17.65 percent, to the client's bill. For example, ABC Advertising Agency purchased illustrations from XYZ Services for $1,000. ABC would add $176.50 to its client's bill, which becomes $1,176.50. This additional $176.50 earned by the agency would become 15 percent of the final bill ($1,176.50) to the client. Therefore, the agency still earns the traditional 15 percent commission.

Finally, 7 percent of advertisers in the American Association of Advertiser's study stated that they compensate their agencies on the basis of a prearranged incentive-based system. In this system, agencies are compensated based on the extent to which a client's advertising objectives are accomplished. The agency earns more if the campaign attains specific, agreed-upon goals. The increased emphasis of top management in the 1990s on measurable results and accountability has placed added pressure on agencies to show *outcomes*, not just *output*. As mentioned in Chapter 1, the need for greater accountability is one of the driving forces in the evolution of Integrated Marketing Communication. Agencies now struggle with ways to bill for services and to quantify *outcomes* when the client's goal is long-term relationship marketing.

FUTURE TRENDS

Many advertisers employ a combination of the different advertising options (e.g., in-house agency, boutiques, and outside advertising agency) rather than using one of them exclusively. However, due to intense competition, the recent trend has been for advertisers to use the services of full-service agencies, moving away from in-house agencies. Some have also reviewed their relationships with advertising agencies they have used for years and welcomed other advertising agencies to compete for accounts. These agency reviews have created an area of both opportunity and contention between the advertiser and the agency. Advertisers have even begun asking agencies pitching an account to offer creative ideas that can later be used by the advertiser even if another agency gets the business.

- Grey's Advertising's MediaCom in New York lost its $100 million Canon USA account to Leo Burnett's Starcom Media Services in February 1999. Several weeks earlier, Kellogg Company had shifted its Honey Crunch Corn Flakes account to Leo Burnett USA, Chicago, in what was called "a wrist slap" to Kellogg's core shop, J. Walter Thompson.[12]
- Philip Morris's Miller Brewing Unit, the number two brewer, stripped its biggest brand, Miller Lite, from Leo Burnett. The new shop for the account, estimated at $80 million, is Minneapolis-based Fallon McElligott, known for its offbeat advertisements for Lee Jeans and McDonald's Arch Deluxe. Miller also reassigned its media-planning and -buying duties to Leo Burnett. In the first nine months of 1998, over thirty advertising accounts—worth more than $1.5 billion—changed agencies.[13]
- Lowe & Partners/SMS, creators of the "Pardon me, would you pass the Grey Poupon?" ads for Nabisco's high-class mustard, ended its

relationship with the manufacturer rather than participate in an agency review. Nabisco says it is looking for an advertising breakthrough with measurable results, not having met sales objectives with previous advertising.[14]
- Eastman Kodak dumped J. Walter Thompson after sixty-seven years, and United Airlines, Delta Airlines, and MasterCard all switched agencies in 1997.
- Ethnic marketing shop Chisholm-Mingo Group was considered a front-runner for the Seagram's Extra Dry gin account after an April 1998 agency shake-up at Seagram America. When Seagram's spent only $3.1 million on its gin product, out of a 1997 total spending of $68.3 million, sales dropped 6 percent. Seagram's hoped for a marketing overhaul that would, among other things, better target African Americans. Seagram's also dropped Ogilvy & Mather for its VO Canadian Whiskey account, picking up Grey Advertising instead.[15]

These shake-ups represent a change in the attitude of the advertiser. It is no longer enough for an agency to have a good, long-term relationship with its clients; to survive, the agency must also document not just *output* but *outcomes*.

Because advertising may have become too narrowly defined by its *output*, agency clients are "increasingly handing over their strategic-thinking chores to marketing consultants."[16] Consultants are perceived as providers of strategic advice, whereas advertising agencies have been perceived as producers of "clever commercials, amusing animated spokescharacters and punchy promotions."[17] Despite these perceptions, advertising industry leaders argue that the advertising profession and its agencies do understand the various consumer groups and know how and where to best connect with them—the industry just needs to work on reshaping these perceptions.

The "Total Communications" Agency

In the late 1980s, spending on public relations and other areas of promotion surged ahead of traditional ad spending. A philosophical shift among major ad agencies reflects the endurance of Integrated Communications thinking in the business world. Agencies now focus more on campaigns that are low in cost but high on measurable effects by auxiliary use of traditional media and strategic blending of special events, sponsorships, sales promotion, direct marketing, targeted radio, and new media.[18] That branding solutions *involve*, but are no longer necessarily *about*, advertising has led to the creation of special, integrated units within major agencies (e.g., J. Walter Thompson's Total Solutions Group and DDB Needham's Beyond DDB).

The Merger Boom

From the 1960s through the 1980s, Wells Rich Greene was known as one of Madison Avenue's "most glittering jewels."[19] The agency famous for its creation of ads for Alka-Seltzer ("Plop, plop, fizz, fizz") and Benson & Hedges ("Oh, the disadvantages") has now become famous for the speed of its dissolution. Wells Rich Greene became Wells BDDP when it was purchased for an exorbitant $130 million in 1990. After the sale, BDDP failed to keep ad legend Mary Wells Lawrence involved, to ensure a smooth transition. A series of leadership problems and bad decisions has plagued the agency throughout the decade, and now Wells' parent company GGT has been sold to the giant ad-holding company Omnicom.

In 1997, "agencies gobbled up one another to the tune of more than $1.25 billion," according to AdMedia.[20] Further, only 6 percent of respondents to an AdMedia survey predicted a merger and acquisition slowdown in the next few years. About 21 percent of those surveyed work for "goliath" agencies with revenues above $150 million. One force driving the merger boom is the demand of large advertisers for greater marketing efficiency, with their global ad dollars distributed to fewer agencies. Another force has been identified as "Wall Street's hunger for steady earnings growth," which has led such companies as Omnicom and Interpublic Groups to acquire smaller firms. Larger is not always better, however. Some goliaths have been less progressive than smaller agencies in developing such top-expansion interactive marketing areas as direct marketing, multimedia advertising, and database management. Also, mergers often lead clients to cut down their agency rosters.[21]

Another drawback of the goliath agency is that clients do not like to share their agency with a competitor. To remedy this problem, Britain's WPP Group created an entirely new company, Intuition Group, out of its J. Walter Thompson agency. The parent company will keep its Unilever and Warner-Lambert accounts, while the new company will handle the Bristol-Myers account in product categories that do not currently overlap. All three companies compete as drug and consumer product makers.[22]

In its own effort to minimize a disadvantage of the large-sized agency, Leo Burnett has decentralized its U.S. operations. Late in 1997, the Chicago agency created seven small agencies—miniagencies—within the large one. The miniagencies, which remain within Burnett's headquarters but are responsible for their own profits and losses, represent the agency's interest in communicating more closely with its clients.[23] And, although

Leo Burnett Chief Executive Rick Fizdale has dismissed rumors of an outright merger with MacManus Group, both companies "acknowledge talks" between their media-buying operations.[24]

SUMMARY

Advertisers range from small, local businesses to large, multinational corporations. Those hired by advertisers to create and place advertisements are involved in planning, budgeting, coordination, and creative tasks. Many advertisers are the clients of advertising agencies that provide the services of specialists in developing and preparing advertising plans, advertisements, and other promotional tools, as well as purchasing advertising time and space. In addition to full-service agencies that provide research, creative, media, and account management services for their clients, advertisers may choose from other types of agencies—creative boutiques (limited service agencies), health/medical agencies (which specialize in health care), and ethnic agencies (which specialize in communications with specific ethnic groups). Agency compensation, agency reviews, and mergers are areas of controversy as we enter the twenty-first century.

* * *

THE GLOBAL PERSPECTIVE: AGENCY SHOPPING

An increasingly competitive global marketplace has led some U.S. firms to go agency shopping. Financial services company Ernst & Young, with an advertising budget of around $13 million in its pocket, did some direct mail shopping in April 1998. Questionnaires sent to about ten New York agencies detailed what Ernst & Young hoped to find—an Internet-savvy agency with "extensive international business-to-business experience." Mergers were pending between Coopers & Lybrand and Price Waterhouse & Company, and Andersen Worldwide was involved in internal problems with its consulting and accounting units. The time seemed right for Ernst & Young to communicate a cohesive brand image against a fluctuating world marketplace. The company's "wish list" included differentiating itself from its competitors with an image that would paint the picture of *financial services*, not just an accounting firm.

However, at least one "store" closed its door to the shopping trip—BBDO was not interested in Ernst and Young's window shopping. What reasons would BBDO have had to decline? Should agencies expect more shopping trips from prospective clients in the future?

Source: Laura Petrecca and James B. Arndorfer, "Ernst & Young Opens Global Review," *Advertising Age*, April 27, 1998, p. 4.

* * *

ETHICS TRACK: AGENCY REVIEWS

The Budweiser lizards may be hearing more complaints and this time, not from the frogs. In summer 1998, Anheuser-Busch authorized "spec spots" (television commercials speculatively produced) for its Budweiser brand—a longtime practice that is no cause to raise eyebrows. However, in this case, Anheuser-Busch had its agency, DDB Needham Worldwide, shop storyboards around looking for producers "willing to produce them with no guarantee of payment."

Advertisers have already begun to use creative ideas pitched by agencies during agency reviews—even though they do not hire that particular agency. This practice, coupled with Anheuser-Busch's behavior in the storyboard shopping incident, especially troubles agency personnel. *Advertising Age* called this a "stunt," identifying the underlying issues as "the current state of agency/client relationships." After all, asking DDB to shop the storyboards under those circumstances could create problems between the agency and the production houses it uses.

Some agencies believe that these practices, at the very least, are disrespectful. At worst, they may be unethical. Aside from holding down production costs, is there any justification for what Anheuser-Busch did? Is cost reduction a sufficient justification?

Source: "No Respect," *Advertising Age*, May 11, 1998, p. 32.

Lee & Johnson
:60 Spot
"Writing the Road to Success"

How does one begin to climb the corporate ladder in public relations? Experience, experience, and more experience was the common answer in recent interviews I conducted with public relations practitioners. Internships, extracurricular activities, and classes are examples of ways to gain experience. Internships are a way to learn the craft from the very basics, from clipping client mentions out of the daily newspapers to the more advanced basics such as writing. Internships are a way to learn whether the public relations industry is for you.

As an intern at BSMG Worldwide in Chicago, I had the opportunity to interview public relations practitioners and ask what it takes to be successful in this industry. I have learned many important values in my internship; however, three of the most important values are time management, writing experience, and initiative.

Most public relations agencies require new employees to intern before taking an entry-level position. And not all agencies use the same titles for every position. For example, BSMG chose Assistant Account Executive as the title for an entry-level position, whereas Burson-Marstellar prefers Client Executive. From an AAE, one moves up to Account Executive, Senior Account Executive, Account Supervisor, Group Manager, Director, Managing Director, Chief Operating Officer/Partner, and President.

"With experience, one learns the basics such as writing, public speaking, English and grammar skills," said Rebekah White, a former BSMG Senior Account Executive. She acknowledged that college taught her how to think and to express thoughts in an articulate way to make a meaningful impact in day-to-day work. White also mentioned time management as a skill learned in college that prepared her for a life in public relations.

Time management is truly one key to success in public relations. Week by week, responsibilities increase. This is the point when managing your time is a priority. Organization factors into time management; thus, taking an assignment and finishing it in a timely manner shows dedication to the job. It also shows results on a daily basis, which gives an edge over other interns.

Next, when you are given a writing assignment as a public relations intern, it is a sign of your progress and the agency's trust in your ability. As writing is critical in public relations, all writing must be approved by your team. To show clips of your writing at a job interview is a great display of your accomplishments.

"Writing, writing, and more writing; be proactive about keeping up creative thinking skills during the first few years when most of the work will be tactical/executional," said Londonne Corder, a Senior Account Executive. Managing Director Amy Colton added, "Try to intern a lot of places, get writing assignments so you can show clips, because the real work counts more than anything."

Finally, taking the initiative shows ambition and sincerity. Practitioners at BSMG have repeatedly mentioned that thinking ahead and looking at the "big picture" sheds light on your creativity as well as your comprehensive training as an intern. The ability to take pieces of a puzzle and put them together to reach a solution is a valuable asset.

Although time management, writing experience, and initiative will lead you in the right direction as a successful intern, these practitioners agree that there are other qualities for success. Teamwork, out-of-the-box thinking, and resourcefulness are also essential qualities. Many factors can lead to success in a public relations internship, but only you can determine the combination of these factors and utilize them to the best of your ability.

Catherine A. Narbone
Assistant Account Executive
Golin/Harris Communications, Inc.
Chicago

Chapter 5

Market Segmentation, Target Marketing, and Product Positioning

To create one of the largest global food brands and secure the company's lead in the $17 billion global snack food market, PepsiCo, Incorporated's international snack food division made a series of marketing and operations changes in 1995 (see Illustration 5.1). These changes ranged from new packaging and advertising campaigns for Lay's potato chips, to overhauled manufacturing techniques, to higher quality standards for all PepsiCo products sold abroad. In 1994, the worldwide potato chip market was valued at $400 billion. Interviews with more than 100,000 consumers in more than thirty countries established the potato chip as, by far, the most popular snack.

In response to these facts, PepsiCo decided to market its dozens of company-owned potato chip brands abroad under the Lay's logo. To market the brand overseas, the company more than doubled its advertising spending—to $50 million. To satisfy the new consumers' culturally determined tastes, PepsiCo introduced a shrimp chip for the Korean market, a squid-peanut snack for Southeast Asia, and "cheeseless" Chee•tos for China. The company also built plants in targeted countries to ensure the quality of its international potato chip products.[1]

At the end of the first quarter of 1997, international business—mostly European—accounted for 34.6 percent of CFC International's total sales. The industrial specialty functional coating manufacturer, headquartered in Chicago Heights, decided to make a greater commitment to its Asia Pacific sales. The company appointed Shigemitsu Takashima as president and general manager of its Asia Pacific operations. CFC was responding to growing markets for a number of its products throughout Asia. Its simulated wood-grain laminates provide an alternative to expensive, imported lumber for the manufacture of furniture and other building products. The

68 PRINCIPLES OF ADVERTISING: A GLOBAL PERSPECTIVE

ILLUSTRATION 5.1. Culturally Determined Tastes

To tap into the $17 billion global snack food market, companies such as Pepsi-Co and Coca-Cola are adapting both their products and promotional images to meet the wants and needs of overseas consumers. © Dana Hanefeld.

company also found new markets for its pharmaceutical line—specialized, functional coatings for the heat transfer printing on IV solution bags, drainage bags, syringes, and so forth—in the Asia Pacific region. The company conducted a market study to see how it was perceived by customers and to determine which countries would be appropriate for various product lines. The company believed that Takashima's firsthand knowledge of the area and experience in business development, particularly in the chemical industry, would enhance CFC's business in the region.

The key to any company's success is its ability to attract and keep customers who are willing and able to pay for its goods and services. This means a company must be able to locate possible customers, wherever they are, and then be able to understand them and communicate with them. Marketing is the answer to this challenge. According to Pride & Ferrel, marketing is "the process of creating, distributing, promoting, and pricing goods, services, and ideas to facilitate satisfying exchange relationships in a dynamic environment."[2] The Lay's potato chip story exemplifies this definition. Improving the quality of potato chips by building the plants in foreign markets, increasing the advertising budget, conducting consumer research, and creating different flavors of potato chips for different foreign markets were all important to marketing the product. CFC conducted market research and identified a target market appropriate for each of its product lines. It also appointed as its Asia Pacific president someone with special knowledge of the area who can better understand and communicate with CFC's Asia Pacific customers. Advertising alone cannot do it all in enticing consumers to buy a product.

MARKET SEGMENTATION

Marketing and advertising people constantly scan the marketplace to see what needs and wants various consumer groups have and how they might be better satisfied. One of the techniques they use is market segmentation. PepsiCo realized the overseas snack business brings in more than $3.25 billion in annual sales and, in the long term, will be a very important business for the company. It also realized that not all consumers have the same tastes, especially in the global markets. It developed a paprika-flavored chip for Poland and Hungary, a squid-peanut snack for Southeast Asia, and "cheeseless" Chee•tos for China. The company treats each country as a different market and offers a different marketing mix to each different country, or market segment.

The purpose of using market segmentation is to enable a marketer to design a marketing mix that more precisely matches the needs of consumers in a selected market segment. A market segment consists of individuals, groups, or organizations with one or more similar characteristics that cause them to have relatively similar product needs. This market segment can be an ethnic group, a geographical region, or a specific country. In the United States, target marketing of different ethnic groups is now common practice. Philip Morris's Kraft foods unit launched a series of new commercials for its Velveeta cheese brand specifically aimed at Hispanic audiences, while Chrysler is known for aggressively marketing its vehicles to African Americans.[3]

A marketer using segmentation to reach a market can choose one or several methods. As Table 5.1 shows, the segmentation methods for a consumer market can be grouped into four categories: demographic, geographic, behavioristic, and psychographic. For the industrial market, segmentation methods can be grouped into three categories: geographic, type of organization, and product use.

TABLE 5.1. Methods for Segmenting Consumer and Industrial Markets

Methods	Variables
Consumer Markets	
Demographic	Age, sex, family size, stage of family life cycle, income, education, occupation, religion, race, nationality
Geographic	Region, population size, density, climate
Behavioristic	Benefits sought, volume usage, brand loyalty
Psychographic	Lifestyle, personality
Industrial Markets	
Geographic	Location
Types of organization	SIC codes*
Product use	Where used, how used

* The North American Industry Classification System (NAICS) replaced the Standard Industrial Classification system (SIC codes) beginning in 1997; it provides common industry definitions for Canada, Mexico, and the United States.

Methods for Segmenting the Consumer Market

Demographic Segmentation

Demographic segmentation involves dividing the market on the basis of demographic variables such as age, sex, family size, stage of family life cycle, income, occupation, religion, race, and nationality (see Illustration 5.2). Marketers rely on these demographic characteristics because they are often closely linked to customers' needs and purchasing behavior and can be readily measured. Time Incorporated is one of several publishers expanding its child-oriented titles. Among the new publications is the first advertising-supported regular edition of *Time for Kids* aimed at high school students and *Sports Illustrated for Kids*.[4] ABC Radio Networks launched its first Radio Disney outlets on AM stations in four U.S. city test markets in 1996. The new twenty-four-hour children's station format includes Top 40 music from the 1950s through the 1970s and programs such as *ESPN for Kids* and *ABC News for Kids*. Radio Disney attracted such national sponsors as Toys "R" Us and Kimberly-Clark Corporation's Huggies diapers.[5] Advertisers in banking, such as Visa, in communications, such as AT&T and MCI, and in automotive, such as BMW, have earmarked more dollars for Hispanic radio advertising in the United States in recent years, especially in major markets such as Los Angeles, New York, and Miami.[6]

Geographic Segmentation

Geographic variables, such as region, population size, density, and climate, also influence consumer product needs. People in one region of the country—or the world—have needs and purchasing behavior that differ from people in other regions. For instance, a large market for suntan lotion exists year-round in Florida, but only seasonally in northern states. Internationally, marketers compare the needs and preferences of various geographic segments to look for differences. Marketers have noted the markets of post-Soviet Central Asia as an attractive source of sales growth. Multinational corporations such as Coca-Cola Company and Procter & Gamble have built Central Asian plants and introduced their brands to 55 million people in this area—previously occupied by the Soviet Union—who had never heard of these brands or product categories before. Coca-Cola has created specific ads to fit the distinctions of each different country in the Central Asian area; for instance, one of largely Christian Armenia's biggest radio hits in December 1997 was a Coke advertisement that featured a church choir singing a Christmas carol-type theme.[7]

72 PRINCIPLES OF ADVERTISING: A GLOBAL PERSPECTIVE

ILLUSTRATION 5.2. Diversity

This Rapp Collins Worldwide/Chicago print ad for Lions Clubs International was part of a campaign that used images of people with different ethnic backgrounds and ages to show that the organization helps all kinds of people, all around the world.

Behavioristic Segmentation

Firms can divide a market into groups according to the benefits they seek, volume usage of the product, and brand loyalty. As an example, time is an important commodity for working mothers. Thus, this group seeks such product benefits as ease of use in appliances and quick preparation in microwavable meals. Because working mothers also seek quick, nutritious meals for their children, Boston Market introduced its first ever "kids' meals" in June 1997, with ads focusing on the meals' wholesomeness. *The Kids Market Report* estimated that parents would spend $117 billion on their children in 1998.[8]

Psychographic Segmentation

Dividing the market on the basis of lifestyle and/or personality is referred to as psychographic segmentation. The determination of lifestyles is usually based on an analysis of the activities, interests, and opinions (AIOs) of the consumers. One of the more popular studies of lifestyle is conducted by the Stanford Research Institutes's Value and Lifestyle Program (VALS). The VALS program places American consumers in three broad groups: outer-directed, inner-directed, and need-driven consumers. The VALS studies have been used to select advertising media and determine advertising content. A VALS 2 classification categorizes consumers into five basic lifestyle groups—strugglers, action oriented, status oriented, principle oriented, and actualizers.

Another important lifestyle study has been conducted for over twenty years by DDB Needham. The survey, mailed to 4,000 households each year, asks 1,000 questions on topics such as meal preparation, fashion choices, and social attitudes. *Advertising Age* is the exclusive reporter of the survey results, which depict a broad picture of the United States.

Methods for Segmenting the Industrial Market

Geographic Segmentation

In some cases, marketers find it beneficial to segment an industrial market geographically. Similar to those who segment geographically in consumer markets, industrial firms can concentrate their efforts on areas with high population growth rates. Or, due to differences in the climate and needs of markets in various countries, companies might target countries whose needs best fit the company's product lines.

Type of Organization

Another way to segment industrial markets is by type of organization. In the United States, the Department of Commerce classifies all businesses by Standard Industrial Classification (SIC) codes. These codes are based on broad industry categories. For example, major group thirty-six includes all firms that manufacture electronic and other electrical equipment and components, except computer equipment. Each major group is subdivided into subgroups and then detailed classes of firms in similar lines of business. SIC codes help marketers to segment different markets. SIC also helps investigate whether companies with the same codes satisfy similar target markets' needs.

Product Use

The way an organization will use a particular product is another basis for segmenting industrial markets. Basic raw materials, in particular, may be used in numerous ways. How an organization uses products affects the types and amounts of products purchased and business purchasing procedures. Computers, for example, can be used at an advertising agency for designing graphics or used in a university environment for word processing or accounting purposes. A computer producer may segment the computer market by types of use because companies' needs for computers depend on the purpose for which computer products are purchased.

TARGET MARKETING

Once marketers group consumers or possible product users by shared characteristics (demographic, geographic, or other variables), they can proceed to the next step: target marketing. The way this is accomplished determines the content, design, and implementation of the company's advertising.

Selecting the appropriate target market(s) is the key to implementing a successful marketing strategy and important to the company's survival. Failure to appropriately target can lead to low sales, high costs, and severe financial losses. A careful target market analysis places an organization in a better position to serve customers' needs and to achieve its own objectives. For instance, Meredith Corporation, publisher of *Ladies' Home Journal* and *Better Homes and Gardens*, spotted a market for a new fashion, beauty, and health magazine targeted to women ages forty to sixty-four. Meredith reasoncd that by 2012, this would be the largest, richest group of females. The publisher also determined that this group has felt "abandoned and unrepresented by glamorous publications such as *Vogue, Harper's Bazaar,* and *Elle*," yet is extremely interested in beauty and health topics.[9] In this case, the company created a product that would be highly appropriate for a specific target market when it launched *more* magazine in September 1998. The newspaper industry has witnessed a growth explosion of Hispanic newspapers over the past three decades (see Table 5.2).

Once a company defines its target market, it knows exactly where to focus its attention and resources. It can shape the product concept (e.g., special features for its product), establish proper pricing, determine the need for location of stores, and prepare the most convincing advertising messages. In other words, the marketing mix can be aimed at making the product attractive and accessible to the target market at the right time and in the right place. When Sears, Roebuck & Company noticed that almost one-fifth of its stores had a strong Hispanic customer base, the company began airing ads on *Sabado Gigante*, a four-hour Saturday night show that reaches 20 percent of the U.S. Hispanic population. Colgate-Palmolive Company has also advertised on the show, with a targeted commercial in which the audience sang an upbeat tune while a hip-swinging company spokeswoman extolled the virtues of Colgate Tartar Control toothpaste in Spanish (for a print example, see Illustration 5.3).[10] Other companies, such as Nike, have also joined the trend toward spending more on niche programming. Some advertisers contend that network television "just doesn't deliver the way it used to,"[11] but it might be more accurate to say that it is just more difficult to meet today's target marketing goals using the mass media.

A particularly hard group to successfully market to has been up-and-coming Generation Xers. Although this group now spends $125 billion a year, the generation that grew up in front of a television set is unusually

TABLE 5.2. Growth of Hispanic Newspapers in the United States (1970-1998)

Year	Number of Hispanic Newspapers	Circulation in Millions	Advertising Revenue in Millions
1998	515	12.7	$445
1990	355	4.2	111
1970	232	1.0	14

Source: Derived from Jeffery D. Zbar, "Hispanic One-Order, One-Bill Growing More Realistic," *Advertising Age,* April 26, 1999, p. s22.

76 PRINCIPLES OF ADVERTISING: A GLOBAL PERSPECTIVE

ILLUSTRATION 5.3. Target Market Ad

Colgate has been aggressive in targeting the growing U.S. Hispanic market by printing ads in Spanish. Credit: Colgate-Palmolive Company.

media savvy and especially cynical about advertising. Members of Generation X characteristically value honesty and are unmoved by slick, glitzy ad campaigns. A new genre of advertising has been created to embrace Generation X's skepticism—the "antiadvertisement advertisement."[12] For instance, in late 1997, Coca-Cola's Sprite campaign carried the tag line, "Image is nothing. Thirst is everything. Obey your thirst." One spot in the campaign used a voice-over that declared, "Trust your taste buds—not commercials."

Internationally, those who are sixty-five and older will become an increasingly larger target market for advertisers in the next century. Table 5.3 shows that, in some countries, senior citizens will constitute almost one-third of the population. One of the effects of the trend toward generational target marketing has been that fewer ad campaigns can reach all the income levels within these demographics. In 1998, *USA Today* reviewed more than sixty campaigns it had analyzed in its "Ad Track" feature to determine how these campaigns scored with various income groups. The newspaper's analysis suggests that "the link between income and ad tastes can often determine a campaign's success."[13] Two commercials spanned all age and income levels as the most popular ads since January 1997—the Budweiser Lizard campaign and the Taco Bell Chihuahua ads. Although other ads' popularity differed among age groups—for instance, whereas young consumers liked Levi's Wide Leg Jeans ads, which featured the 1970s nostalgia of Partridge Family tunes, older consumers preferred the sentimental, multigenerational family pitch of Hallmark Cards[14]—the Budweiser and Taco Bell spots were unusually successful, with "runaway hits" in all categories.

Once the target market has been selected, the company must find a way to fit the product to the selected market and to sell the product to that market. This is no small feat. Product positioning is one method marketers use to sell the product by setting it apart from competitors.

TABLE 5.3. Senior Population Growth in the Top Six World Economies

	1990	**2010**	**2030**
Italy	15%	21%	28%
Germany	15%	20%	28%
Japan	12%	21%	26%
United Kingdom	16%	17%	23%
France	14%	16%	23%
United States	13%	14%	22%

Source: Derived from Anne R. Carey and Elys A. McLean, "Aging Industrial Societies," *USA Today,* August 12, 1998, p. A1.

PRODUCT POSITIONING

Product positioning refers to the decisions and activities intended to create and maintain a certain concept of the firm's product in the customers' minds.[15] Clearly, product positioning refers to the decisions and activities intended to create and maintain a certain concept of the company's product, relative to competitors' brands, in consumers' minds. For instance, Volvo employed a positioning strategy founded on safety. The company used the strategy whenever it advertised in the media, whether in print or on television. Chief Auto Parts Stores, the number four U.S. retailer in aftermarket auto parts, has steered away from everyday low pricing and repositioned itself around quality with a $3 million campaign.[16] Marketers sometimes analyze product positions by developing perceptual maps. Perceptual maps are created by questioning a sample of consumers regarding their perceptions of products, brands, and organizations with respect to two or more dimensions.

Product differentiation is the competitive strategy of creating a product difference that appeals to the preferences of a distinct market segment. In advertising, nothing is more important than informing prospects how your product is different. The idea of consumer perception is critically important in differentiating products because the differences between products can be either real or perceived. Real differences might include features, price, or quality. Differences created by perceptions are typically based on a product's image. When an ad shows Michael Jordan eating Wheaties, the consumer may assume that eating Wheaties contributes to athletic performance, whereas consuming other cereals does not. Whether a teenager

TABLE 5.4. Perceptions of Clothing Brands (Consumers Ages 13 to 17)

Clothing brand	Percentage of target that perceived brand as "hot"*
Nike	73
Tommy Hilfiger	67
Calvin Klein	59
Oakley	50
Old Navy	48

Source: Adapted from Anne R. Carey and Julie Stacey, "Labels That Rule with Cool," *USA Today,* September 23, 1997, p. D1.

* Ranked brand as four to five on a scale of one to five.

believes a clothing label is "cool" or "uncool" depends not so much on the product as on the consumer's perception of that product (see Table 5.4).

Whether the differences between products are real or extrinsic to the product or service, all marketers/advertisers take steps to ensure that these differences do exist. Coca-Cola has long positioned itself as the all-American choice, whereas Pepsi has attempted to portray itself as "hip" and "cool" to make Coke seem "dull." However, Pepsi may have found itself targeting too narrowly with its "Generation Next" tag line, designed to appeal to the emotions of a very specific market segment—that tag line has been dropped. In summer 1998, the cola wars escalated when Pepsi filed a federal antitrust lawsuit against Coke. Pepsi accused its competitor of "trying to freeze it out of the business of selling soft drinks in restaurants serviced by independent food distributors."[17] A new, psychomachian Pepsi television commercial, created by Ominicom Group's BBDO New York, attempted to shift Pepsi's "cool" image to "good" in opposition to "evil" Coke. In the controversial ad, a little girl enters a diner and asks for a Pepsi. When she discovers that the diner serves only Coke, she makes an *Exorcist*-like transformation and, in Joe Pesci's voice, snarls at the stunned waiter, "What you really thought was that I don't know the difference between Pepsi and Coke." The girl returns to her former voice, saying, "I like this place," when the waiter serves her a Pepsi.

Product positioning is a customer's perception of a product's attributes relative to those of competitive brands. To position a new product or reposition an existing one, marketers need to know how consumers or industrial buyers in its target market perceive products in that category.

Advertisers often use comparative advertising to claim superiority to competitors in some aspect. Avis Rent-A-Car's positioning campaign is probably the most famous example. When Avis "was a small force in the market compared to category leader Hertz," Avis's tag line, "We're only number two. We try harder," made it a major contender in the field.[18] Such advertisements are legal so long as the comparison is truthful. In addition to being truthful, comparative advertisements must also make the comparison in terms of some objectively measurable characteristic of a product or service. In a 1998 ad campaign, American Express positioned its travel service with this print ad copy: "When the grind gets to be too much, American Express has the world's largest travel agency to get you out of here. Not to mention over 1,700 travel service locations worldwide to help you while you're there." In fact, American Express does operate the world's largest travel agency and does have 1,700 worldwide offices.

SUMMARY

A company must be able to locate possible customers, wherever they are, and then be able to understand and communicate with them. Marketing, the process of creating, distributing, promoting, and pricing goods, services, and ideas to facilitate satisfying exchange relationships, is the answer. Advertising alone cannot do it all. The consumer market segmentation process differs from the segmentation process for the industrial market, but each market must be segmented if the company's advertising is to be successful. Once a target market has been segmented, advertising must position and differentiate the product or service from its competitors.

* * *

THE GLOBAL PERSPECTIVE:
ONE PERSON'S HORROR, ANOTHER PERSON'S HUMOR

FBI agents arrive at the home of "Monica Lavinsky" to remove, wash, and return a dress that allegedly bears incriminating DNA evidence. Too bad they wash it in Biomat detergent. As they leave the house, they report by wrist radio that the dress is now "whiter than white"—only to be told by a voice in their earpieces, "White? But it's a blue dress."

During August 1998, people in the United States considered Ken Starr's investigation of President Clinton's relationship with Monica Lewinsky a serious matter. The Israeli television spot for Biomat soap powder was not intended for an American audience, of course. Suppose it had aired here. How would it have been received by American viewers?

The complexity of dealing with a large number of different customers in many countries offers a real challenge to international marketers. What is humorous in one country can be offensive in another. Many factors affect human perceptions of people, products, and situations. What geographic and psychographic factors might cause Israeli and American responses to the spot to be different?

Source: "Sex Sells," *USA Today,* August 18, 1998, p. C1.

* * *

ETHICS TRACK: TARGETING THE MIDDLEMAN

Is it better to target the consumer or the middleman? This was the question the veal industry pondered in the summer of 1997. Animal rights activists have peppered consumer publications with antiveal ads for years. With its product "under fire," veal producers decided to address a more sympathetic audience: chefs.

Veal ads in such publications as *Bon Appetit* and *Restaurant Business Magazine* bypassed the ultimate consumer in a narrowly focused campaign.

Was the veal industry's decision to target the more sympathetic "middleman" instead of the final consumer an ethical choice? Would it have been better to respond to animal rights criticism through informative advertising, addressing concerns about industry treatment of veal calves? Why or why not?

Source: Daniel Rosenberg, "Veal Industry Focuses on Chefs in Countering Animal Ads," *The Wall Street Journal*, March 18, 1998, p. B3.

Lee & Johnson
:30 Spot
"Paws-itively Hilarious"

May 28, 1998

Dear Dr. J.,

I started at Edelman Public Relations Worldwide last July and was promoted to Account Executive in April. I never knew life at age twenty-two could be so hectic!

So, you asked—what do I do? You better be sitting down for what I am about to tell you. I am currently going across the country looking for North America's Best Singing Pet! Yep, you read right—singing pets. If you have seen the commercials for Advantage® flea control for cats and dogs, then you might have an idea of what I am talking about. Cats and dogs are so happy to be flea free, they are literally singing the praises of Advantage!

I do the event planning and media relations for Advantage—which is made by Bayer's animal health group. Last year we generated over 300 million media impressions with our program, increased sales, and had superior placements on *The Tonight Show with Jay Leno*, *Regis and Kathie Lee*, and many other syndicated shows. People LOVE the cute animals and are already asking us when our 1998 winner will be announced! We even got a placement on the front page of *The Wall Street Journal*. If you are interested in checking out what these singing cats and dogs are all about, you can visit our Web site at www.nofleas.com, or call our help line at (800) NOFLEAS. It is "paws-itively" hilarious!

I also had the honor of representing Taco Bell® Home Originals™ and Kraft Foods, Incorporated, as a six-foot dancing Taco. I traveled the East Coast for a week to launch the new taco kits that are in grocery stores. We appeared on *The Today Show* window and several local market television stations, teaching the anchors the "Two-Step Taco"—two steps to the left, two steps to the right, and you do the taco! The fun never ends for me.

I never knew the "real" world would be so adventurous.

Take care,

Diane Grant
Account Executive
Edelman Public Relations Worldwide
Chicago, Illinois

Chapter 6

Consumer Behavior and Advertising

Japanese consumers were not supposed to want refrigerators such as the big General Electric model in Hiroshi and Yukie Tanaka's living room. The refrigerator's journey to the Tanaka's Yokohama apartment from a GE factory in Kentucky broke all the rules: that exporters must tailor their products to Japanese tastes, that foreigners must find Japanese partners to negotiate the distribution system, and that big American home appliances will not sell in Japan at any price. For years, many U.S. marketers have tried diligently to tap into the Japanese market, without too much success. However, in the mid-1990s, Japan's sick economy needed a revival, and this sparked demand for simpler, cheaper products. Also, more Japanese women are working after marriage and cannot shop daily for food as their mothers did. Big, inexpensive, two-door refrigerators (unlike Japanese-made three-door models that are more expensive) suddenly make sense.[1]

Consumers' needs and wants are constantly changing. To be successful, marketers need to make considerable effort to determine their customers' current needs. In this way, they may get a better grasp of their customers' buying behavior, as GE did in defying convention and offering American refrigerators to the Japanese market in the mid-1990s. Many foreign manufacturers, makers of everything from computers to cars, have done well by changing products to suit Japanese tastes. However, American marketers have come to realize that, in this decade, economic and social factors have changed Japanese consumers' needs.

Understanding individual consumer's product needs will become increasingly important in the twenty-first century. Already Levi Strauss has employed computer technology to custom fit women's jeans with its Personal Pair Program. Infrared scanners precisely measure the customer's foot in Custom Foot stores. A Japanese bicycle manufacturer uses the customer's instep measurement to construct a made-to-fit bicycle. Burger King has long been savvy to the consumer appeal of customized products and messages as illustrated by its commercial tag line "Have it your way."

Marketing involves developing and managing a product that will satisfy certain needs. It also focuses on making the product available in the right

84 PRINCIPLES OF ADVERTISING: A GLOBAL PERSPECTIVE

ILLUSTRATION 6.1. Customized Products and Messages

When your target market is a discerning, theatre-going segment of the public, advertising that is too "commercial" might offend. This print ad for Stratford Festival gift certificates uses the old-fashioned, nostalgic image of "Feste" the holiday bear to appeal to a consumer more interested in the artistic than in the mass-produced Christmas gift. The text stresses the customized features of this gift choice with the wording "something for everyone" and "Any way you package them . . ." Illustration and design by Karen Garratt, headline and copy by the Stratford Festival Marketing Department 1998, Stratford, Ontario, Canada.

place and at a price that is acceptable to customers. By knowing customers' buying behaviors, marketers can create marketing mixes that satisfy customers and lead to success in the marketplace. GE found that price was a deciding factor for Japanese consumers in the market for a refrigerator. The company then emphasized that its refrigerators cost half the price of a Japanese model. Constant research on consumer behavior and the factors influencing buying behavior is definitely important for marketers of any products. Chapter 7 will focus on the important topic of research methods.

The goal of advertising is to persuade the consumer to do something, usually to purchase a product. If advertising is to attract and communicate to audiences in a way that produces this desired result, advertisers must first understand their audiences. They must acquaint themselves with consumers' ways of thinking, with those factors which motivate them, and with the environment in which they live (see Illustration 6.1).

In this chapter, we will first examine the consumer decision-making process as it goes through the various stages of problem solving. In addition, we will discuss what occurs at each stage and how advertising and promotion can be used to influence buyer decision making. We will also examine the influences of various personal (such as demographic) and psychological (such as perception, motivation, attitudes, lifestyle, and personality) factors on the buyer decision process, as well as the effect of external influences (such as social factors). Finally, the chapter will examine the importance of understanding consumer behavior in the future.

THE BUYING DECISION PROCESS

All customers can be split into two general groups: consumers and organizations. The consumer market is made up of individuals and households who buy goods and services for personal use. The organizational market consists of businesses, governments, and nonprofit organizations. The ways in which the two groups respond to advertising and make purchase decisions are similar in many respects, but quite different in others.[2]

The buying decision process for both consumer and organizational markets is viewed as a series of stages through which the buyer passes in purchasing a product or service. The process includes five stages: need recognition, information search, alternative evaluation, purchase, and postpurchase evaluation.

Need Recognition

A buyer's first step toward a purchase decision is recognizing a need, which means that the buyer perceives a discrepancy between an actual state and a desired state. This discrepancy can be as simple as thirst for a drink or more involved, such as realizing that the company needs a faster computer to process its orders. At this stage of the decision-making process, the advertiser can try to influence buyers by helping them recognize needs that the advertiser's products can satisfy.

Information Search

When buyers have identified a need, they may look for information about how to satisfy that need. This information search is both internal and external, and the buyer's memory can be a key aspect of the process. If a buyer has satisfied a similar need in the past, he or she is likely to start the search for information by recalling how that need was satisfied. Often the buyer consults with other people in his or her reference group (e.g., relatives and friends). Buyers also acquire information from marketers through advertisements, packages, salespeople, and the like.

Alternative Evaluation

Based on the information gathered, the buyer identifies and evaluates ways to meet his, her, or a company's need, looking for the best choice in terms of quality, price, delivery time, and other factors deemed important. In this stage, the rational and emotional appeals of advertising play an important role.

Purchase

After considering the possible options, the buyer makes a purchase decision. This step includes deciding whether to buy and, if so, what to buy, where to buy, and when to buy. With large purchases in the organizational market, the buyer and seller must also work out delivery time, payment terms, installation, and so forth. At this stage, advertising continues to play an important role—preventing the buyer from changing his or her mind.

Postpurchase Evaluation

After buying a product, customers formally or informally evaluate the outcome of the purchase. Although consumers tend to be much less formal with their evaluations, in that they do not have set criteria to properly evaluate their purchases, organizational customers usually use standardized performance criteria to evaluate key suppliers.

In the case of large-ticket items, a common response is for the consumer to have doubts about the choice after the purchase. This feeling is called cognitive dissonance—a state of anxiety brought on by the difficulty of choosing from among several alternatives. Advertising can help buyers overcome dissonance if it continues to reinforce the reasons for making a particular choice.

FACTORS INFLUENCING THE ORGANIZATIONAL MARKET

Relatively few organizational purchase decisions are made by just one person; mostly, they are made through a buying center. These persons include the user, influencer, decision maker, gatekeeper (e.g., secretary), and purchaser. Identifying the roles in a buying center is a key step in planning effective advertising because people in the various buying center roles have different information needs and purchase criteria:

- *The user.* Users are the people in the organization who actually use the product.
- *The influencer.* Influencers are people who affect the buying decisions. For example, an engineer may help to develop product specifications.
- *Decision makers.* These are the people who actually choose the products.
- *Gatekeepers.* Those in the organization who control the flow of information into the buyer center are called the gatekeepers. Such people may include secretarial and technical personnel.
- *Purchasers.* The authority and responsibility to select suppliers and negotiate purchase terms resides in the person whose title is the purchaser or, in some cases, director of purchasing.

Derived Demand

Of all the differences between consumer and organizational buying behavior, perhaps the most important is the idea of derived demand, which means that the demand for industrial products derives from the demand for consumer products. When consumer demand for a product changes, a wave is set in motion that affects demand for all firms involved in the production of that consumer product. A tire manufacturing company may need to stimulate demand for cars in its advertisements so the company can sell tires to automobile manufacturers.

Supplier Selection

Supplier selection is often a formal process among organizational buyers, as customers try to find the best suppliers for each type of product they need. Many organizations have approved supplier lists, and employees are prohibited from purchasing goods or services from anyone not on these lists. This encourages advertisers to convince potential customers (e.g., members in the buying center) that they are capable and reliable sources of products. In turn, the buying organization may invite suppliers to submit formal proposals for buyers' purchasing evaluation purposes.[3]

Business-to-Business Advertisements

Businesses may advertise services or goods (products). Of the two, advertising for services lends itself more to the use of emotional appeals to develop a "service personality."[4] However, a research study conducted by Turley and Kelley found that only 4.4 percent of service ads studied employed emotional appeals. This reveals that "emotional appeals are rare in the business-to-business context," even where they might be expected—in service ads. Business-to-business advertising generally employs rational appeals, perhaps because organizational buyers "are believed to use a more rational decision-making process than final consumers."[5]

FACTORS INFLUENCING THE CONSUMER MARKET

Unlike the buying decision process in organizational markets, which is influenced by buying center personnel or other factors (e.g., derived demand and company policy), the buying decision process in the consumer market is mostly influenced by personal, psychological, and social factors.

Personal Factors

Personal factors are those unique to a particular person. Numerous personal factors influence purchasing decisions. Demographic factors are individual characteristics such as age, gender, educational level, occupation, and income. Given such differences, people tend to make different choices regarding, for example, cars, the media, and their patterns of spending. For instance, researchers have discovered that, although red violet is a popular fashion color with women, men are indifferent to the color. If an advertiser determines that a product is most likely to appeal to members of certain groups, a marketing mix can be developed that takes these differences into account.

Psychological Factors

Psychological factors operating within individuals partly determine people's general behavior and thus influence their purchasing behavior. Each individual consumer is influenced by his or her perceptions, motives, attitudes, and personality.

Perception

One reason that consumers respond differently to the same situations is that they perceive those situations differently. Perception refers to the way people gather and record information. Although marketers cannot control people's perceptions, they often try to influence them. In recent years, advertisers have found that men perceive athletes as "perfect," a quality to which most men aspire. In response to this perception, advertisers have been featuring more male athletes, rather than male entertainers, in their ads.[6]

The efficacy of subliminal messages—embedded material in advertising designed to "reach the consumer below the threshold of consciousness"—has been an area of controversy since the famous study in which messages to eat popcorn and drink Coca-Cola were projected on movie screens (sales of popcorn increased 57 percent and sales of Coke, 10 percent).[7] Opinion has been divided among skeptical academics and practitioners. Skeptics do not believe embedded material permeates the subconscious mind at all, and proponents may exaggerate the effects and frequency of the practice.

Motivation

The inner drive that propels consumers to fulfill a perceived need is called motivation. Basic human needs range from comfort and convenience to social acceptance to the need for love, sex, and power. Advertisers want to know what motivates consumers so that they can appeal to those motives. A DDB Needham lifestyle study sought to discover the motivation that drives today's consumers. The results were expressed in three words: "Gain without pain."[8] The study indicated that Americans in the mid-1990s were motivated by the need for comfort and traditional values—but only so long as those traditional values did not interfere with convenience, practicality, or individualism. The consumer desire for the continuity and consistency of traditional values also prompted the revival of old advertising themes and jingles.[9] For example, Johnson & Johnson revived its "I'm stuck on Band-Aids" tune, nearly a quarter of a century old, in commercials created by McCann-Erickson in 1997. Commercials for Ralston-Purina's Cat Chow once more feature a silver tabby doing the cha-cha, and the Meow Mix kitten is singing "Meow, meow, meow, meow" again.

Attitudes

When people are motivated to meet a need, the way they meet that need depends on their attitude toward the various alternatives. An attitude is an individual's enduring evaluation, feelings, and behavioral tendencies toward an object or idea. Consumer attitudes toward a company and its products greatly influence success or failure of the firm's marketing/advertising strategy. Therefore, marketers should carefully measure consumer attitudes toward advertisements, package designs, price, and other product features to ensure success in the marketplace.

One of the most impressive attitude-change advertising campaigns of the decade was launched by the National Fluid Milk Processor Promotion Board. When American attitudes toward milk became tepid, the "MILK: Where's *your* mustache?" campaign took to print with bold, full-page ads featuring celebrities with dramatically white milk mustaches. The celebrities—among them Super Bowl champion John Elway, country singer LeAnn Rimes, talk show host Conan O'Brien, and child star Jonathan Lipnicki—were chosen to gain the interest of an array of specific target groups and to change their indifference toward milk into positive attitudes.

Lifestyle

Consumers' attitudes can influence the lifestyle they adopt. A lifestyle can be defined as a person's activities, interests, opinions, and consumption patterns.[10] Marketers use lifestyle information to tailor the marketing mix to meet customers' needs. When American lifestyles left U.S. consumers uninterested in Unilever's "lifestyle" product, Persil laundry soap tablets, the company engaged WPP Group's J. Walter Thompson advertising agency in Great Britain to pitch the product to busy Europeans who live differently from their American counterparts. For one thing, European women "still do most of the washing even though more of them are working and have less time—and patience—for household chores."[11] The Unilever ads feature "rock music and irreverent interviews with denim-clad young people" who talk about lifestyle advantages of the tablets—they do not have to be "measured, scooped, or poured." The tag line stresses convenience—"A great wash, a great deal easier."

Personality

Another psychological element that has attracted the attention of advertising researchers is personality, a person's characteristic and consistent patterns of behavior.[12] A number of marketers are convinced that consumers' personalities do influence types and brands of products purchased.

Social Factors

External forces that affect individual buying behavior are called social factors. Most notable is the broad grouping of forces generated by culture, reference groups, and social status.

Culture

The beliefs, values, and symbols that a society shares and passes from generation to generation constitute its culture. Value differences in different cultures (e.g., the United States and Japan) can be especially notable in international marketing and advertising. For instance, the Domino's pizza chain offers squid and tuna toppings in Japan.

Reference Groups

In addition to culture, buyer behavior can be influenced by a reference group, including family, friends, and professional organizations. This group may consist of one or more persons who have a direct influence on the buyer's decision making. Reference groups influence people's decisions by providing information or by pressuring them to conform to group norms. Reference groups have the most impact when consumers are unfamiliar with a product. Advertisers need to find a way to gain the support of various reference groups in their efforts to sell their products to consumers.

Social Status

Social status is another important factor in buyer behavior. Consumers in every country are of different social classes. A social class is a group of individuals with similar social rank (e.g., similar income levels and skill). Social class determines to some extent the type, quantity, and quality of products that a consumer buys and uses. In some instances, marketers attempt to focus on certain social classes through advertisements, personal sales efforts, pricing, and other strategies.

CONSUMER BEHAVIOR: THE NEXT CENTURY

Automobile manufacturers such as Porsche, Mercedes-Benz, and BMW now cater not only to the wealthy as a group but also to individuals within that target market. Porsche upholstered a sports car for an American rancher with hides from his herd. Mercedes' Designo and BMW's Individual offer an array of options, including a pop-up television screen and a VCR for backseat passengers. Industry experts predict that 1950s-style custom ordering will return to popularity in the next century.[13] General Nutrition Centers (GNC) customizes vitamins, shampoo, and lotions. Customers also can e-mail personalized American Greeting cards on America Online.

In the mid-1990s, *American Demographics* reported that a typical American consumer no longer existed: "There is no average family, no ordinary worker, no everyday wage, and no middle class as we knew it."[14] Mass customization of both products and messages will be as important in the twenty-first century as mass production was in the twentieth. Marketers understand that consumers no longer want choices—they want what they want. Factors that have contributed to this consumer attitude include the growing diversity of the American public and the transition from the Industrial Revolution to the Information Age. Today, database technology allows marketers to store and retrieve precise details about individuals. The Internet allows for two-way communication and interactive relationships between the supplier and the consumer.

Computer technology, especially the database, has enabled marketers to gather more information than ever before about consumers' buying habits. Not surprisingly, information leads to insight. Consumers have become increasingly skeptical about the millions of new products and commercial messages that inundate them daily, and marketers hope that individualizing products and messages will better meet consumers' needs and wants.

Transforming the Agency:
The Role of the Account Planner

In response to the challenge to gain the deepest possible understanding of the consumer, advertising agencies have begun to employ account planners. The account planner's job is to convey insights about the consumer to other members of the traditional agency team and to be, in effect, the account executive's conscience.

The role of the account planner originated in J. Walter Thompson's London office in 1967. Jay Chiat of Chiat/Day, then a small West Coast agency, imported the practice to the United States because he believed that British advertising was superior to American. Although some traditional American agency researchers view account planners as simply qualitative researchers, in reality, the difference between the two is the role each plays, not the research tools each uses, according to Lisa Fortini-Campbell, a professor of Integrated Marketing Communication at Northwestern University. She predicts that agencies will become increasingly interested in people who can discover and express consumer insights.[15] This will be especially true as agencies find themselves competing with marketing consultants for clients. Understanding consumer behavior will continue to be crucial for advertisers in the competitive marketplace of the future.

SUMMARY

Consumers' wants and needs are constantly changing. If advertisers are to attract and communicate with audiences, they must acquaint themselves with consumers' ways of thinking, with those factors which motivate them, and with the environment in which they live. The consumer decision-making process involves various stages of problem solving. Consumer behavior is also influenced by various personal and psychological factors affecting the buyer decision process. External influences, such as social and economic factors, also affect this process. Computer technology, from the Internet to computerized production machinery, has also affected both consumer behavior and those who study it. With customized products and messages, marketers have begun to market the differences among people, not just the similarities. Some agencies now employ account planners who attempt to better understand consumer behavior in today's challenging marketplace.

* * *

THE GLOBAL PERSPECTIVE: GENEROUS EXPOSURE

To promote its new line of self-tanning lotion, The Body Shop put up display posters in its stores that showed a man with a bottle of the lotion tucked inside the front of his bathing suit. The words "Fake it!" spanned the poster.[a]

The man pictured in the poster was generously exposed, but the poster itself had a short exposure time in the United States. The London-based international cosmetics retailer had to remove the posters from 200 of its 300 U.S. shops after only a week's exposure time in May 1997. American men were offended, as they also had been the previous year when another Body Shop poster showed a rear view of three nude men jumping.

A survey published in the *American Journal of Public Health* in 1998 indicated that, although Americans surveyed were more critical of premarital and extramarital sex than their British counterparts, higher percentages of Americans reported having multiple sexual partners—13 percent of American men had twenty-one or more partners over a lifetime. Part of the American character seems to be moral contradictions. Americans may tolerate—and even enjoy—salacious confessions on television talk shows and deign to hear about politicians' sexual sins in the news, but when it comes to advertising, they are conservative and critical.

A number of U.S. agency creations, including a BBDO/Canada beer commercial that featured two women kissing, were up for honors at the 1997 Cannes International Advertising Festival.[b] However, many of these spots were too racy to be aired or printed at home. American agencies can dish up the sexy stuff that generates sales overseas, but they cannot show them at home.

Culture is an integrated pattern of behavior shared by people in a society. Some believe that the American attitude toward sexual explicitness in advertising derives from the social importance of traditional family values. A spokesperson for the American Family Association expressed the view that there is too much sexual explicitness in American advertising already. Although the number of single-parent and other nontraditional households has been increasing, Americans still consider a family with mother, father, and children to be the norm.

There is no doubt that American culture differs from other world cultures. Attitudes toward sex and what constitutes a traditional family unit are among the most prominent differences. The family unit outside North America tends to be much larger. In less developed nations, there is often an extended family that includes, but is not limited to, grandparents. The significance of the extended family to advertisers is that consumption decision making takes place in a larger unit. What factors must be considered—among other cultural differences—when designing an advertising message for a particular culture?

[a] Craig Wilson, "Tanning Lotion Ad Display Leaves Some People Burning," *USA Today,* May 30, 1997, p. D1.
[b] Melanie Wells and Dottie Enrico, "U.S. Admakers Cover It Up; Others Don't Give a Fig Leaf," *USA Today,* June 27, 1997, p. B1.

ETHICS TRACK: SUBLIMINAL MESSAGES

Outdoor billboards, magazine ads, and point-of-purchase displays appeared across the country like a rash when R. J. Reynolds Tobacco Company launched its $50 million campaign for Camel cigarettes. The 1998 blitz builds on a previous tag line, "What you're looking for," and appropriately so, since two ads featured embedded camel's heads. The advertiser did not try to conceal that the heads were embedded—they only concealed the camel's heads—using a mock warning label that read, "Viewer discretion advised: Subliminal imagery."

It may be that the tobacco company is fighting back against criticism of its industry. The subliminal ad spoofs critics' charges "that drawings of former spokesperson Joe Camel contained subliminal images . . ." However, critics now are concerned that smokers will take such humorous approaches as the "viewer discretion" warning to mean that warnings about the dangers of smoking can be taken lightly. Further, the company is positioning its brand as "offbeat and entertaining."

Advertising critics have long questioned the ethics of using embedded images to subliminally affect the attitudes and behaviors of target audiences. The controversy concerns the alleged manipulation of the subconscious mind of the person who views the subliminal aspects of the ad. The Camel ad in question is up-front about the fact that the picture includes embedded images, however. So can the subliminal ads—those which are marked with warnings—be considered unethical? Do you agree with critics who feel that the ads encourage smokers to disregard serious warnings about the dangers of smoking?

Source: Judann Pollack, "RJR Takes Brazen Tone in New Camel Campaign," *Advertising Age*, May 11, 1998, p. 2.

**Lee & Johnson
:60 Spot
"Marketing Professional Services"**

The job of marketing professional services for the twenty-first century holds tremendous challenges and opportunities. The Bureau of Labor Statistics forecasted marketing to be one of the four fastest-growing professions in terms of increased employment through the year 2006. Part of this growth can be attributed to a progressive embrace of professional services marketing that started in the late 1970s.

The late 1970s marked the period when certain processional organizations began to realize that marketing had become a critical factor in determining the success or failure of an organization. This movement led to the American Institute of Certified Public Accountants (AICPA) slowly lifting its ban on advertising and marketing of the profession. In addition, the landmark Supreme Court case *Bates v. State Bar of Arizona* (433 U.S. 350 [:1977]) gave attorneys the constitutional right to advertise under the First Amendment (*National Public Accountant*, 1996).

Marketing, as defined by Webster's dictionary, is the process or technique of promoting, selling, and distributing a product or service. However, as marketing as a function continues to grow and expand, so does the need to define the intricacies involved in the processes and techniques used in marketing professional services versus the marketing of consumer products.

Marketing professional services requires the targeted market to make an investment in the intangible. It involves creating superior value in something that lacks physical attributes, taste, or smell. Unlike product marketing, service marketing is a science that requires detail and precision in its technique. There is a large level of uncertainty associated with an intangible service. This leads to the current service marketing challenge of creating ways to erase uncertainty with value.

In my current position as marketing coordinator for a regional accounting and consulting firm, I struggle with this challenge every day. For example, one of our marketing strategies is built on the concept of "Clients First." Since characteristics of services (e.g., trust, competence) can only be assessed during or after the process, it is critical that clients feel that their goals and ideas are being valued and will never be compromised during or after the process. "Clients First" helps build stronger relationships with clients and will lead to additional revenue through additional services provided and referrals from these clients in the future.

Marketing is a concept that is here to stay. Your ability to add value to the service being marketed will determine your success. The challenge for professional service marketers in the twenty-first century will be defining, through focus and creativity, what marketing strategies can be used to unlock the key to additional profitability and continued success for your particular segment of the service industry.

The challenges are your opportunities. As General George S. Patton once said, "Accept the challenges, so you may feel the exhilaration of victory."

Source: Bates v. State Bar of Arizona, National Public Accountant, July 1996, Vol. 41, p. 22.

Amy Randolph
Marketing Coordinator
Clifton Gunderson L.L.C.
Champaign, Illinois

Chapter 7

Marketing and Advertising Research

The People Meter was first introduced to the United States by Audits Great Britain (AGB Advertising Research) in late 1984. Shortly thereafter, Nielsen Media Research followed with its own people-meter system. The meter has eight buttons for family members and two additional buttons for visitors. The family member (or visitor) pushes a designated button each time a particular program is selected. The meter automatically records the programs watched, the number of households watching, and which members of the household are watching. This viewing information is combined with each household's pertinent demographic profile to provide a single source of data. Nielsen conducts its survey "sweeps" four times a year in major market areas and publishes "sweeps books" that provide the basis for network and local station advertising rates. However, network ratings have been in a substantial decline. Following the 1993 season, the big three networks (NBC, CBS, and ABC) began to lose prime-time ratings to the new Fox network (see Table 7.1). Since then, the big three networks have lost millions of dollars in advertising revenue because their lower-rated programs are unable to command higher prices.

TABLE 7.1. 1993-1997 Network Television Prime-Time Ratings

	Rating Points			
	NBC	CBS	ABC	FOX
1993-1994	11.0	14.0	12.4	7.2
1994-1995	11.5	11.1	12.0	7.7
1995-1996	11.7	9.6	10.6	7.3
1996-1997	10.5	9.6	9.2	7.7

Source: Adapted from Jerry Mosemak, "TV Network Ratings," *USA Today,* January 14, 1998, p. A2.

ILLUSTRATION 7.1. Measures of Emotion

Research shows that ads which are better liked and which elicit positive emotions are more likely to be remembered and to persuade. This Children's Memorial Hospital ad, created by Rapp Collins Worldwide/Chicago to promote the hospital's corporate holiday cards in 1998, features the original work of a young artist, drawn during a stay at the Chicago pediatric hospital. The ad uses a combination appeal. The visual offers the emotional appeal of the child's drawing, and the copy offers the rational appeal of factual information.

Because critics have become convinced that people-meter numbers are flawed, six advertising agencies are investing $100 million and the four networks have allocated $10 million for the creation of a new rating service. Statistical Research of Westfield, Connecticut, plans to provide a new nationwide rating system, Smart, which resolves problems with channel identification—in some cities, cable companies may use different channels for the same station—by using a code instead of a channel number. Despite the agencies' investment in Smart and the networks' letters of intent issued to Statistical Research, Nielsen still plans to invest $300 million in new technologies.[1] This "passive" people meter would scan the room every two seconds to see which participants are actually watching specific channels.[2]

Employing another research method, TBWA Chiat/Day used focus groups to devise a clever ad campaign for the Weather Channel in 1997 to 1998. In an exercise with focus group members, it was discovered that without weather forecasts, people felt they could not exist, that their lives would collapse.[3] As a result of the focus group research, TBWA Chiat/Day came up with a tag line "WEATHER FANS YOU'RE NOT ALONE" and an innovative setting for the campaign's television commercial spots—The Front, a bar "where guys belly up to hear barometric pressure and every tornado junkie knows your name."[4] Marketing and advertising research employs a variety of techniques for a multitude of purposes. In this case, research facilitated the creative process rather than determining advertising rates, the purpose of Nielsen research.

Hundreds of billions of dollars are spent annually worldwide to market products and services. Sound business practice requires that efforts be made to determine whether these expenditures are justified. Accordingly, a significant amount of time and money are spent on testing marketing, including advertising effectiveness. Therefore, this chapter will describe many of the research techniques used in marketing, especially in the advertising research business.

MARKETING RESEARCH

Companies use research to identify and uncover problems with their market share, evaluate their competitive strengths and weaknesses, and measure consumer attitudes. Marketing research consists of all the activities that enable an organization to obtain the information it needs to make decisions about its environments (e.g., social, regulatory, and economic), its marketing mix (product, price, place, and promotion), and its present or potential customers. The marketing research process consists of five steps:

1. defining problems,
2. designing the research project,
3. collecting data,
4. interpreting research findings, and
5. reporting research findings.

Defining Problems

Problem definition is a statement of the topic to be examined via marketing research. A good problem definition directs the research process to collect and analyze appropriate data for the purpose of decision making.

Designing the Research Project

Once the problem is defined, there must be an overall plan to obtain the information needed to address it. The objective statement of a marketing research project should include hypotheses drawn from both previous research and expected research findings. A hypothesis is an informed guess or assumption about a certain problem or set of circumstances. When marketers need more information about a problem or want to make a tentative hypothesis more specific, they may conduct exploratory studies. The aim of exploratory research is to gain ideas and insights and to break broad, vague problem statements into smaller, more precise statements. Once an issue is clarified, conclusive research (survey, observation, and experiment) is used. Conclusive research is the structured collection and analysis of data pertaining to a specific issue or problem.

Collecting Data

If the project warrants continued investigation, the researcher must determine what additional information is needed and how to gather it. Secondary data, primary data, or both can be used in an investigation. Secondary data consist of information not collected for the issue or problem at hand, but for some other purpose. This information is available within a firm (e.g., sales reports) or externally (e.g., trade organizations, private research firms, and university libraries). Primary data consist of information gathered to address a specific issue or problem at hand. Such data are needed when a thorough analysis of secondary data is insufficient for a proper marketing decision to be made.

The three widely used methods of gathering primary data include survey (mail, telephone, and person-to-person interview), observation (human and mechanical), and experimentation (laboratory and field). Since the 1980s, focus groups have been widely used as a technique to gather primary data. The focus group is a special type of one-on-one interview conducted through survey panels. A moderator leads a group discussion of panelists' opinions to determine buying habits or perceptions of a specific product or idea. Panelists are drawn from the group targeted by the research. Sessions are usually videotaped and followed up with questionnaires.

Interpreting Research Findings

After collecting data to test their hypotheses, marketers require some type of data *analysis* to give the raw data meaning. SPSS or SAS statistical programs are often used to analyze quantitative data. However, before using any statistical program to analyze data, the researcher needs to check and verify whether the raw data are correct, whether they are complete, and whether all instructions were followed. This process is called *editing*.

After the statistical analysis has been completed, researchers interpret the research findings. Valid and reliable results depend upon a sufficient sample. Differences or distinctions determined by analysis must be large enough to offset the unavoidable margin of error. Incorrectly worded questions may also invalidate the data. Careful interpretation is required so that the findings will assist those making managerial decisions. If the results are determined to be valid, decision makers should take action.

Reporting Research Findings

The end product of the investigation is the researcher's conclusions and recommendations. Most projects require a written report, often accompanied by an oral presentation to management. At the end, researchers should follow up on their studies to determine whether their results and recommendations are being used.

Many standardized marketing information services are available for marketing researchers in the United States and other countries, although developing countries may lack these services. The top fifty research organizations had collective revenues of $5.5 billion in 1997. Business activities outside the United States accounted for $2.2 billion (39.5 percent) of these revenues. Research organizations are increasingly challenged to become more "worldly" in accommodating their multinational clients' interest in overseas markets.[5] A. C. Nielsen Marketing Research is by far the most widespread, with operations in eighty-eight countries.[6]

Marketing information services are available at some cost to the users and, in this respect, are a more expensive source of secondary data than published (e.g., government) information. However, such services are also typically much less expensive for a company than gathering its own primary data because, with the services, a number of companies share the costs incurred by the supplier in collecting and analyzing data. The main disadvantage of using secondary data from services is that they do not always ideally fit the needs of the user.

In today's increasingly competitive environment, firms must have an accurate assessment of how they are doing. A common yardstick for that assessment is sales and market shares. Historically, measurements have been handled in several ways, including the use of diary panels of households (e.g., the National Purchase Diary consumer panel, which is the largest in the United States) and the measurement of sales at the store level (e.g., A. C. Nielsen Company's Nielsen Retail Index). The NPD Group, Incorporated's Syndicated Tracking Service also provides database information on store movement and consumer purchasing.[7] Another area in which a great deal of commercial information is available for marketers relates to the assessment of exposure to, and effectiveness of, advertising.

ADVERTISING RESEARCH

Advertising is often the largest single cost in a company's marketing budget. No wonder its effectiveness is a major concern! Testing is the primary tool advertisers use to ensure their advertising dollars are being spent wisely. It can give the advertiser some measure (besides sales results) of a campaign's value.

Advertising research can be divided into two types: Media research concerns information about the circulation of newspapers and magazines, broadcast coverage of television and radio, and audience profiles. Message research addresses how effectively advertising messages are communicated to people and how well those messages influence people's behavior.

Media Research

A variety of resource materials are available to advertisers for determining the potential audience size for specific media vehicles (e.g., *Time* and *Life* magazines). The following techniques measure media audience.

Television Audience Measurement

A. C. Nielsen is one of the oldest, largest, and most influential research companies in the world. It is best known for its Nielsen National Television Index, which is responsible for determining the ratings that network television (e.g., ABC, CBS, NBC, and Fox) shows receive. Nielsen uses the people meter, an electronic device that records the daily network, cable, and home video viewing of members and guests in the 5,000 households that make up the U.S. market sample. It also measures television audiences through weekly mail diary surveys in 211 local markets, involving over 100,000 households.[8] With a high rating on the Nielsen National Television Index, a television program can command a high advertising rate. For instance, NBC's *ER*, the number one prime-time show in 1996 to 1997, received a rating of 22.6 in the week of December 26, 1996—with one rating point equaling 970,000 U.S. television households. As a result of this rating, a 30-second spot on *ER* cost advertisers $500,000.

Survey Research Group (China) Limited (SRG), an A. C. Nielsen unit, has been in China since 1984. It derives television ratings from fourteen cities, with 300 households in each city recording their viewing habits every quarter for a two-week period. After 1996, SRG had data from electronic people meters in Beijing, Shanghai, and Guangzhou.[9] In most countries, television stations pay for 70 to 90 percent of ratings research—a cost that can run into millions—because they use the ratings to price commercial air time.

Since the accuracy of Nielsen ratings has been questioned by the networks and a number of agencies, an alternative method of establishing the size of the viewing audience will continue to be explored.

Radio Audience Measurement

Arbitron Radio is the dominant radio audience research service, measuring audience sizes in more than 267 local markets in the United States. Arbitron researchers obtain data from more than 2 million randomly selected individuals a year. Respondents are compensated for maintaining diaries of their listening behavior for a seven-day period. From this information, Arbitron establishes radio station ratings. Arbitron Research is working to develop a new, portable device that can track radio listening both in and out of the home.[10]

Magazine Audience Measurement

Simmons Market Research Bureau's (SMRB) *Study of Media and Markets* is a major resource for consumer advertisers. It combines magazine and newspaper readership data, statistics on television viewing, product purchase data, demographic data, and other research results. The report helps advertisers with such tasks as profiling buyers in specific product categories and assessing the readership of a given magazine. Media Research, Incorporated (MRI) provides advertisers and agencies with an alternative magazine-readership source. MRI interviews 20,000 adults per year and, similar to SMRB, obtains readership statistics for over 100 magazines along with product/brand usage and demographic information.

Internet Audience Measurement

Media Metrix uses personal computer technology to provide new media audience measurement. In addition to determining audience reach and frequency, the company provides information on audience demographics.

Message Research

Advertising effectiveness is measured in terms of achieving awareness, conveying copy points, influencing attitudes, creating emotional responses, and affecting purchase choices. Based on these objectives, message research methods are generally divided into five different forms of response to ads: measures of recognition and recall, measures of emotions, measures of physiological arousal, measures of persuasion, and measures of sales response.[11]

Measures of Recognition and Recall

Recognition refers to whether a respondent can recognize an advertisement as one he or she has seen before. The most widely known service in measuring print advertising recognition is Starch INRA Hooper. In a typical Starch test, respondents look through a magazine and then they are shown the advertisements again to see whether they recognize them. The following four measures are generated for each advertisement: noted readers (the percentage of readers who remember having seen the advertisement); associated readers (the percentage who saw any part of the advertisement that clearly indicates the brand or advertiser); read-some readers (the percentage who read any part of the advertisement's copy); and read-most readers (the percentage who read half or more of the copy).

Recall refers to the proportion of a sample audience that could remember an advertisement. There are two kinds of recall—aided recall and unaided recall. In aided recall, the respondent is prompted by being shown a picture of the advertisement with the sponsor or brand name blanked out. In unaided recall, only the product or service name may be given. The best-known recall method in television advertising is called the Burke's day-after recall method (DAR). The DAR procedure tests commercials that have been aired as part of normal television programming. The day following the first airing of a new commercial, employees of Burke's Burke Marketing Research Division conduct interviews with a sample of 150 consumers. The sample includes individuals who watched the program in which the test commercial was placed and who were physically present at the time the commercial was aired. These individuals receive a product or brand cue, are asked whether they saw the commercial in question, then are asked to recall all they can about it.

IPSOS-ASI, known for its copy testing services, delivers advertising material (perhaps a videotape) directly to the consumer's home to test multiple measures of recall and persuasion in the natural viewing environment.[12]

Measures of Emotion

Research has shown that advertisements that are better liked—often because they elicit positive emotions—are more likely to be remembered and to persuade (see Illustration 7.1). A commonly used measure of consumers' feelings toward advertisements is a technique called TRACE that is used by the Market Facts, Incorporated, research firm. TRACE enables consumers to reveal their feelings toward what they are seeing in a television commercial by pressing a series of buttons on a handheld microcomputer.

Measures of Physiological Arousal

Several kinds of instruments are used to observe consumers' reactions to advertisements. In general, they attempt to capture changes in the nervous system or to record emotional arousal during the exposure sequence. The eye camera is a device that photographs eye movements, either by photographing a small spot of light reflected from the eye or by taking a motion picture of eye movement. Pupillometrics deals with eye dilation. The pupils dilate when something interesting or pleasant is seen and constrict when confronted with unpleasant, distasteful, or uninteresting sights.

Measures of Persuasion

Advertising Research Services (ARS) runs theater tests. Precommercial brand preferences are taken from a total sample of 400 to 600 persons in four cities in the United States. Viewers then watch a thirty-minute television program with three sets of two commercials embedded in the program. A second thirty-minute program is then shown, with six additional commercials included. Although only one of the twelve commercials is the test commercial, the measure of brand preference change is based on responses to all twelve commercials.

Measures of Sales Response

Information Resource, Incorporated's (IRI) BehaviorScan pioneered single-source data collection in 1979. Panel members provide IRI with information about the size of their families, their income, number of televisions owned, types of newspapers and magazines they read, and which household member does most of the shopping.[13] IRI then combines all of these data into a single source data bank to determine which households purchase what products/brands and how responsive they are to advertising and promotional techniques.

More recently, IRI offers InfoScan service that records the purchases of a national panel of 60,000 households with a checkout scanner. An additional 55,000 households record purchases with a handheld, in-home InfoScan device.[14] This is similar to A. C. Nielsen's SCANTRACK, which tracks mostly packaged goods through a panel of 119,000 households in fifteen countries (52,000 households in the United States). SCANTRACK's panel households use handheld scanners located in their homes to record every bar-coded product purchased. Panel members also use their handheld scanners to enter any coupons used and to record all store deals and in-store features that influenced their purchasing decision. Panel members transmit purchases and other data back to the Nielsen company every week by calling a toll-free number and holding up their scanner to the phone. The data are then recorded via a series of electronic beeps through the phone.

RESEARCH TRENDS IN THE 1990s AND BEYOND

Although traditional research methods still form the backbone of marketing and advertising research, marketers now look for ways to get beyond statistics and what consumers can articulate to get inside the consumers' minds. Focus groups became trendy in the 1980s, but the 1990s have seen widespread use of alternative research methods. Some of these unconventional research techniques include approaches as creative as asking people to color with crayons. In 1997, the Minneapolis agency Fallon McElligott employed this technique in its efforts to revamp a United

Airlines ad campaign. "Frequent fliers got eight colors and a map showing the different stages in a long-distance airplane trip and were told to let their emotions do the drawing—hot colors for stress and anger, cool ones for satisfaction and calm."[15] The research led the agency to create a tag line that would be responsive to passengers' desires for overall improved service: "UNITED RISING."

Because researchers suspect that focus group panelists may be influenced in what they say by peer pressure, including dominant and opinionated people who overwhelm other group members, marketers have begun to employ other methods similar to Fallon McElligott's coloring exercise. To better understand consumers' feelings, Chicago-based Leo Burnett has asked people to create collages using pictures from magazines.

Marketers have also borrowed techniques from anthropologists' practice of ethnography, the study of comparative cultures that employs observation to learn about various people and their distribution and characteristics. Research that includes observation of the consumer has extended from the focus group into the consumer's home. Home surveillance involves filming paid participants in their homes as they go about their daily rituals, including bathroom routines. In some cases, marketers even move in with the consumer. "Honda and Toyota have sent staff to live with families and observe how they use their vehicles—a tactic that Honda says confirmed its decision to add backseat room to the 1988 Accord."[16] Live-ins allow researchers to observe consumer behavior in a natural setting and even to learn the target market's lingo—information that is often quite useful in creating tag lines and copy for advertising campaigns. According to Joseph Plummer of DMB&B, New York, the consumer of the 1990s is not "some statistical model, or something to be manipulated like a marionette in the marketplace," but a living, breathing human being.[17]

SUMMARY

Advertisers and their agencies can take advantage of a wide range of commercial research services. The firms that offer these services deal with broadcast, print formats, and the media (who is watching, listening, or reading?) and messages (are the advertisements effective?). Some of these services are syndicated, whereas others are conducted on a custom basis for individual advertisers. Each research technique has advantages and disadvantages. The type of research employed must be determined by the client's purposes and needs. In the 1990s, advertisers still need to analyze facts and statistics, but they also need to discover insights into their consumers' minds.

* * *

THE GLOBAL PERSPECTIVE: INTERNATIONAL RESEARCH NEEDS

You have been assigned to work abroad. That is not unusual—about 300,000 Americans face that situation every year. Should you shake hands with native counterparts of the opposite sex? Is it polite or impolite to belch after dinner? Americans working abroad need to have information about local customs—and they need it fast.

Country Net (www.countrynet.com) provides "all the information employees need, whether they're on a three-week project or a three-year assignment."[a] Those who log on to Arthur Andersen's Web site access information, including tax and immigration laws, for eighty-four countries.

Marketing/advertising research involves more than just the information needed to assimilate gracefully. It plays the same important role in the development of international advertising and promotion strategies that it does in one's home country. However, many companies do not conduct advertising research in international markets. A main reason for this is the high cost of conducting that research (e.g., the likelihood that research methods will have to be adapted to local environments), coupled with the lack of basic data (e.g., demographic information).

Although the United Nations does offer some secondary demographic and economic data on more than 200 countries, many advertisers find it necessary to collect primary data on certain countries.

Do not be discouraged. Competent research personnel are available through local offices of major international research firms. A. C. Nielsen, the U.S. marketing research giant, acquired Asia's largest supplier of consumer market intelligence, Survey Research Group (SRG), in 1994. SRG has operations in Hong Kong (where it is based), Australia, Canada, China, Indonesia, Japan, Korea, Malaysia, New Zealand, the Philippines, Singapore, Taiwan, Thailand, Vietnam, and the United States.[b]

Information may also be gathered from research generated by companies and/or advertising agencies located in foreign cities.

[a] "Globetrotters' Friend," *Newsweek,* June 22, 1998, p. 8
[b] Ronald E. Yates, "A. C. Nielsen Grabs Asian Data Giant That IRI Had Sought," *Chicago Tribune,* July 6, 1994, pp. B1, B3.

* * *

ETHICS TRACKS: WATCHDOGS RESEARCH TOO

Manufacturers and their marketers are not the only ones who conduct research. Certain groups and institutions—consumer watchdog groups—do their research and report back to consumers on such issues as product quality and reliability. Among these watchdogs, the eighty-eight-year-old *Good House-*

keeping has the most recognized seal of approval among women ages twenty-five to fifty-nine. The percentages of this target group who recognize consumer watchdog groups' seals of approval are as follows:

Good Housekeeping	92%
USDA Choice (Department of Agriculture)	87%
ADA Accepted (American Dental Association)	82%
Consumer Reports	72%
Food and Drug Administration (FDA)	66%
Underwriters Laboratory	55%
J. D. Power and Associates	21%

Source: Adapted from Anne R. Carey and Marcy E. Mullins, "Consumer Emblems Women Know," *USA Today*, February 3, 1998, p. D1.

Lee & Johnson
:60 Spot
"Planning in Marketing: The Milk Mustache Story"

Campaign Background

Facing three decades of declining consumption, the U.S. milk processors joined forces to reposition milk as a contemporary beverage and get more people drinking milk. Market research was conducted to identify barriers to milk drinking. It revealed several, including health concerns, age appropriateness, and an uncool image. To reverse the situation, an integrated marketing campaign of advertising, public relations, and promotion was developed to give milk a more positive and compelling image to spur milk sales.

The cornerstone of the campaign is a series of ads featuring high-profile celebrities sporting their badge of milk enjoyment—a milk mustache. Instead of trying to break through the clutter of beverage advertising on television, the agency made a radical decision to focus the bulk of ad dollars on national magazines and utilize public relations to extend the campaign into other media.

Public Relations Campaign Strategy

Four audiences are targeted in the milk campaign: teens, college-age men and women, women ages twenty-five to forty-nine, and men ages twenty-five to thirty-four. Ad celebrities are selected based on their appeal to a specific target and their credibility in delivering relevant health messages about milk.

The role of public relations is twofold: (1) to educate and extend audience reach of the print ad campaign and (2) to partner with leading health professionals and organizations such as the National Osteoporosis Foundation (NOF).

Public Relations Campaign Tactics

In the beginning, the program was tailored to each target market's needs to educate about the benefits of milk.

Programs targeted to women were designed to communicate the target's need for constant bone replenishment through intake of calcium-rich milk—specifically, fat-free milk, since women tend to be more diet/weight conscious. For example, a "Drink 3" campaign led by milk mustache celebrity Florence Griffith-Joyner encouraged women to add an extra glass of fat-free milk to their daily diet to meet the recommended daily allowance (RDA) of 1,000 mg. The campaign kicked off with a press conference in Washington, DC, hosted by Secretary of Health and Human Services Donna Shalala.

For men, programs showcased recent research that proved calcium can reduce hypertension and positioned milk's high potassium and high protein content over that of the leading sports drink. The campaign also gained endorsement from winning sports teams such as the Denver Broncos and Chicago Bulls.

The hard-to-reach teen audience was literally taught the benefits of milk through a classroom program, "Crash Course on Calcium," featuring an MTV-style video with young actors telling teens—in kidspeak—why they should drink milk. Campaign celebrities and the nation's calcium and health experts endorsed the campaign to add an extra punch.

To capture the attention of the college community, milk mustache photo booths were set up on fifty campuses to draw attention and create a venue to teach students "Calcium 101" and bring the campaign to life. It also gave students an opportunity to see what they look like with a milk upper lip. Winning photos were placed in the school newspaper, and one finalist appears in an actual milk ad in *Rolling Stone* magazine.

Evolution Through Integration

In its fourth year, the campaign faces new challenges. Although awareness continues to grow, milk messages were mixed through the popularity of the "Got Milk?" campaign. Consumers often confuse the "Where's *Your* Milk Mustache?" campaign with the "Got Milk?" campaign, only remembering the visual of one and the tag line of the other. The two campaigns, running simultaneously, fragmented the efforts and did not affect milk sales as much as in the first year of the campaign. Also, it is a challenge to keep the media's interest in a four-year-old campaign and maintain the campaign's positive image of milk to consumers.

As a result, integration became a healthy solution for the two campaigns. Thus, the Milk Processor Education Program or MilkPEP ("Where's *Your* Milk Mustache?" campaign) and National Dairy Council/Dairy Management Incorporated ("Got Milk?") began the integration by replacing the "Where's *Your* Milk Mustache?" tag line with "Got Milk?" on print advertisements. By doing this, they maintain the powerful milk mustache as an icon with the equity of the "Got Milk?" line.

Campaign Results

Research was conducted at the beginning of the program to provide a baseline and at the end of each year's programming to evaluate the effort. The results of the first three years indicate a change in attitude toward milk and milk drinking, especially among women, the key target. Overall milk consumption increased 1 percent, the largest increase in a decade, and low-fat milk products showed increases of 4 to 6 percent.

Thus far, the integration has proved to be a success, as consumer awareness of the importance of drinking milk to strong, healthy bones continues to grow with the campaign.

Brandee Carlson and Angela Cataldo Tocci
Account Executives
BSMG Marketing Communications
Chicago

Chapter 8

The Marketing and Advertising Planning Process

Since the late 1980s, Nike has worked to transform its image from a brand of sneakers to a dynamic reflection of the booming sports entertainment industry itself—from pro sports arenas to inner-city basketball courts refurbished through Nike's P.L.A.Y. program, from Foot Lockers in shopping malls to the latest Niketown in New York City. Nike's advertising has depicted the vast scope of its business, as well as the unifying spirit of sports. The Nike name ranks, with Coca-Cola and McDonald's, among the world's top ten brands, according to Young & Rubicam, New York. The athletic footwear market is estimated at $7.4 billion at the American wholesale level. Nike's revenue for the fiscal year of 1996 was $6.47 billion. According to Sporting Goods Intelligence, Nike controls 37 percent of the American athletic footwear market, far ahead of Reebok International's 21 percent, and three times as much as number three Fila USA and number four Adidas America combined.[1] Nike's marketing formula has been to integrate its swoosh logo into the emotional and cultural tapestry of sports. The formula has proven successful, as Nike's growth has coincided with the growth in sports—at least until summer 1998 when Asian economic woes brought Nike its first loss in a decade, a fiscal fourth-quarter loss of $67.7 million.[2]

Nike was named the *Advertising Age* Marketer of the Year in 1996. Its strength across diverse sports segments has been clearly illustrated in its advertising campaigns. The "If you let me play" campaign underscored Nike's push into women's sports; "Nike vs. Evil," in which Nike's soccer endorsers do battle with Satan, reflects Nike's belief that it must dominate soccer to have global credibility. Nike's worldwide brand marketing and advertising strategy has been to take a global point of view, but with individual, country-by-country plans. For instance, responding to the Asian downturn of 1998, Nike dealt with Japan's inventory-reduction slowdown by shifting 540,000 sneakers from Japan to the faster-paced U.S. market.

Lee Jeans and Levi Strauss and Company, the two largest jeans manufacturers, engaged in a battle for the jeans market by launching new advertising

ILLUSTRATION 8.1. Riding the Light

This print ad is part of Qwest Communications' 1998 corporate identity and branding campaign. Tara J. Krull, Qwest's corporate marketing communications manager, discloses Qwest's marketing plan in this chapter's :60 spot. Photo © Tony Stone Images. "Gymnast" © Qwest Communications International, Inc., 1998.

116

campaigns in May 1998. Lee, with two-thirds of its customers women, decided to target seventeen- to twenty-two-year-olds with a new line of dungarees. To reach this target, Lee invested $13 million in a three-minute film reintroducing the company's seventy-six-year-old promotional doll, the dungaree-wearing Buddy Lee, on cable television's E! and Comedy Central channels. The research the company had done to determine how the target perceived its brand revealed that younger consumers think of Lee as the brand their mothers wear. Fallon McElligott, the agency Lee hired for the campaign, intends to alter that perception.[3]

Levi Strauss, on the other hand, sells two-thirds of its jeans to men. To remind its target market, mostly males fourteen and older, that Levi's is the original designer jean, the company launched a series of billboard ads featuring Tommy Hilfiger, Calvin Klein, and Ralph Lauren, all leading fashion designers. In addition to the billboard campaign, Levi Strauss sponsored round-the-world promotional events in celebration of the company's 125th anniversary on May 20, 1998.[4]

These vignettes illustrate how these companies and others, such as Qwest (see Illustration 8.1), have analyzed their current situations before developing a marketing plan and outlined objectives before undertaking advertising campaigns. Although the objectives of Lee and Levi's were the same—to recoup market share—their strategies differed, based on the different target audiences to which they hoped to appeal.

THE MARKETING PLAN

The Nike story demonstrates that marketing success depends on careful planning. It also suggests that a successful marketing plan needs advertising's help. Advertising is one part of the total marketing effort. Further, as Nike realized, marketing strategies, including advertising, are not easily transferred from one culture to another.

Although Integrated Marketing Communication theory suggests that a new, outside-in process may be more advantageous in the future, traditional marketing begins inside the organization and works out toward the consumer. The traditional, inside-out marketing planning process generally involves three steps, detailed as follows.

Conduct a Situation Analysis

The situation analysis presents all relevant facts about the company's history, growth, products and services, sales volume, market share, competitive status, strengths and weaknesses, and any other pertinent information. The situation analysis also includes information on key factors outside the company's control—for example, the social, technological, economic, political, or legal environments in which the company operates.

A situation analysis is sometimes referred to by the acronym SWOT, which stands for strengths, weaknesses, opportunities, and threats. The analysis of strengths and weaknesses focuses on internal factors; opportunities and threats analysis focuses on factors that are external to the organization.

Through analysis of external factors, Lee Jeans and Levi Strauss recognized that, although they were both competing for jeans market share, they appealed to different consumer groups. In analyzing its competition, Lee must have noticed that Levi's hold on the men's market had slipped from 48 percent in 1990 to 26 percent in 1997. Lee Jeans may have decided to take advantage of that slippage by specifically aiming its campaign at young men. Levi's slippage with the men's market did not escape its own situation analysis. External analysis also showed that, although Levi's share of the men's market was slipping, some of its competitors' annual sales were soaring. Levi's analyzed its internal situation, which revealed that it was the "original" blue jean creator and should position itself as such. Levi's hired Ominicom Group's TBWA Chiat/Day in February 1998. By May, nearly 20,000 billboards featuring comparative ads—declaring Levi's former market dominance through such messages as "Calvin [referring to Calvin Klein] wore them," dotted the nation in a month-long campaign.[5]

SWOT analysis also prompted PepsiCo Incorporated to spin off its three fast-food chains, Pizza Hut, Taco Bell, and KFC, in 1997. The breakup allowed PepsiCo to concentrate on its core soft drink and snacks businesses, free of the headaches that plague fast food restaurants. Fast food ventures have been especially vulnerable to mutable consumer preferences, slow growth, and managerial difficulties in the 1990s.[6]

Develop Marketing Objectives

The next step in marketing planning is to determine the marketing objectives of the organization's management. Marketing objectives must be designed so that their achievement will contribute to the corporate strategy and so that they can be accomplished through efficient use of the firm's resources. These objectives must consider the amount of money the company has to invest in marketing and production, its knowledge of the marketplace, and the competitive environment. They should also relate to the needs of target markets and to specific sales goals. Lee Jeans' objective was to change the consumer perception that theirs were jeans that only older women wore and to sell jeans to what was a new target market for them—men ages seventeen to twenty-two.

Develop Marketing Strategy

The third major step of marketing planning is to develop the marketing strategy, or set of strategies—the company's plan to accomplish its marketing objectives. In marketing terms, the objectives are what the company wants to accomplish, and the strategy is how the company will accomplish these goals. The organization's marketing program refers to a set of marketing strategies simultaneously implemented. Through the process of marketing planning, an organization can develop marketing strategies that, when properly implemented and controlled, will contribute to the achievement of its marketing objectives and its overall goals (see Illustration 8.2).

The first step in strategy development is to select the target market. Marketing managers use the processes of market segmentation and research to define their target market. Ohio-based regional bank KeyCorp newly defined its customer groups as small business, emerging affluent, mainstream, and upscale. One of its four magazine titles, *Business Vision*, targets small business owners. Rather than communicating generic information to customers, KeyCorp is using relevant communication channels more appropriately to tell stories and answer customer questions.[7]

The second step in developing the marketing strategy is to determine a marketing mix (product, price, place, and promotion) for each target market the company pursues. Database marketing and customer segmentation are playing a big role at KeyCorp, the nation's largest consumer lender of marine and recreational vehicle loans. The company has created an infomercial program to attract these marine and recreational vehicle buyers. In 1995, KeyCorp activated a database marketing system designed for cross-selling that triggers personalized letters each time a customer makes a bank transaction. Since the 1996 launch of a television and print campaign, the company claims its brand awareness has surged 50 percent.[8]

Companies have a wide variety of marketing strategy options. These include finding new uses for an old product, implementing discount pricing, increasing the number of stores that sell the company products, or expanding into new markets, local as well as foreign. The four marketing mix elements (product, price, place, and promotion) are interrelated; decisions in one area affect actions in another. Selection of each option depends on the product's position in the market and its stage in the product life cycle (introduction, growth, maturity, and decline).

Ultimately, management must select a combination of elements that will satisfy target markets and achieve organizational and marketing goals. For example, an industrial market company focuses more on personal contact than advertising. Distribution channels for the industrial market are also more direct. The company may need to decide whether to use one

ILLUSTRATION 8.2. Beneath the Covers

**TARGET MARKETING PLAN
FOR
LIFELINE PLANNING℠ SERVICES**

LIFELINE

LIFELINE PLANNING SERVICES
TARGET TOWN CSC

FY ENDING 5/31/98

Clifton Gunderson L.L.C.
Certified Public Accountants & Consultants

This title page opens to a marketing plan that includes among its goals concentrating the majority of its marketing efforts on existing clients. Such documents usually include strategies for accomplishing each goal, along with action plans, team members' responsibilities, and due dates. Courtesy of Clifton Gunderson L.L.C., Champaign, Illinois.

marketing mix to serve all its market segments or to change parts of the marketing mix for various segments of the total market.

A company's marketing strategy has a dramatic impact on its advertising. Even though the company may have the best product, lowest price, and appropriate distribution channel, success is unlikely without effective communication with target audiences. Today's most successful brand-name consumer goods were built by heavy advertising and marketing investments years ago. In 1996, the top twenty-five ad spenders put $17.8 billion into national advertising campaigns.[9]

The marketing strategy affects the amount of advertising used, its creative thrust, and the media employed. A new strategic trend has been the ad blitz, increasing the number of ads in a campaign from a few to over a dozen. For instance, Levi's billboard campaign, mentioned previously, was to be combined with at least ten television commercials. TBWA Chiat/Day has produced more than 700 Absolut vodka print ads since 1980. An image ad blitz for ABC included fifteen commercials, ten print slogans, and messages "on beach trash barrels, concert tickets, coffee cups, and on stickers on bananas in major urban markets."[10] Marketers who favor ad blitzes argue that money can be saved by airing more ads fewer times and that such expenditures make a company appear larger and more dominant. However, ad blitz critics say these campaigns are creating malaise among ad-weary consumers.

Marketing strategy also affects the creative thrust of an ad. For instance, in 1998, Iridium invested $140 million in a sophisticated print ad campaign to transform its high-priced, satellite-linked global phone into "an indispensable status symbol." To create that image, the romantic, sepia-toned ads portray as heroic the "mundane hassles of the harried business traveler" in foreign lands.[11] Marketing strategy also determined the media employed. The print ads ran in places "wealthy gadget-heads" were likely to see them—newspapers and magazines, such as *The Economist*, *National Geographic*, and *Forbes*. In addition to television commercials aired on seventeen different airlines, Iridium also chose direct mail as a medium—the direct mail materials could be easily translated into thirteen different languages. Booths in airport executive lounges and television program sponsorship in such countries as India extended the campaign's reach.

The Outside-In Planning Approach

Ideally, Integrated Marketing Communication's outside-in planning approach requires an exhaustive amount of consumer information. According to Don E. Schultz and Beth E. Barnes in *Strategic Advertising Campaigns*, the steps include the following:

- *The business review.* Similar to the situation analysis in internal and external examinations, the business review includes analysis of "what the organization might become," with an eye toward future development.
- *Consumer analysis.* This process uses databased information on individual customers.
- *Behavioral segmentation.* This is the area that most differs from the traditional process. It involves breaking down groups that appear to be homogeneous based on such demographic information as gender, age, and income. This is done using individual market behavior, such as purchase history, volume of use, place of purchase, and product use, available through in-store scanners, telephone records, airline flight data, and banking, financial, or credit card transactions.
- *Customer valuation.* Information on purchase loyalty, occasional buyers, price-reduced buyers, and so on, allows marketers to determine which customers are most profitable.
- *Behavioral objectives.* When marketers know what the customer does and what the customer is worth, then they can work to change current behavior to become more profitable.
- *Communications objectives.* This is the message, incentive, or activity needed to maintain or change consumer behavior.
- *Spending levels.* A budget is developed based on what needs to be done.
- *Tactics.* This compares to the step in the traditional model in which decisions are made about message, distribution, and so on.[12]

The emphasis on the consumer and the organization's long-term future are two features that distinguish this process from that of traditional marketing.

THE ADVERTISING PLAN

The advertising planning process is a distinct process within the marketing function. It consists of the six major steps that are detailed in the following material.

Reviewing the Marketing Plan

The advertising manager first reviews the marketing plan to understand where the company is going, how it intends to get there, and the role advertising will play in the marketing mix.

Analyzing the Company's Internal and External Situations

The internal and external situation analyses briefly restate the company's current situation, target market(s), short- and long-term marketing objectives, and decisions regarding the product's position in the market, its stage in the product life cycle, and its related marketing mix.

Setting Advertising Objectives

The advertiser's next step is determining what the firm hopes to accomplish with advertising. Advertising objectives should be stated clearly, precisely, and in measurable terms. Precision and measurability allow advertisers to evaluate advertising success at the end of the advertising campaign, assessing whether objectives have been met. The advertising objectives can be sales oriented or communication oriented. If an advertiser defines objectives on the basis of sales, the objectives focus on raising absolute dollar sales, increasing sales by a certain percentage, or increasing the firm's market share.

Even though an advertiser's long-term goal is to increase sales, not all campaigns are designed to produce immediate sales. Some campaigns are designed to increase product or brand awareness, make consumers' attitudes more favorable toward the product or brand, or increase consumers' knowledge of product features. For example, The National Fluid Milk Processor Promotion Board assigned Bozell Worldwide to its $36 million advertising campaign in 1996. The campaign's short-term goals were to change American consumer attitudes that caused the decline in per capita consumption of milk and to increase public awareness of nutritional facts. The long-term goals were to stem and ultimately reverse the decline and to maintain public awareness of milk nutrition.[13]

Developing and Executing Advertising (or Creative) Strategy

The advertising objectives declare where the advertiser wants to be with respect to market share or consumer awareness. The advertising (or creative) strategy describes how to get there. This strategy consists of the following elements:

- *Target audience.* The target audience is the group of people at which advertisements are aimed.
- *Product or service concept.* A product can be an idea, a service, a good, or any combination of these three. This definition also covers support-

ing services that go with goods, such as guarantees and maintenance. When writing the advertising plan, the advertising manager must develop a simple statement to describe the product concept—that is, how the advertising will present the product. To create this statement, the advertiser first considers how the consumer will perceive the product and then weighs this against the company's marketing strategy.
- *Advertising media.* Advertisers need a systematic method of determining which media to use, how to use them, when to use them, and where to use them to effectively and efficiently deliver their advertising messages.
- *Advertising message.* What the company plans to say in its advertisements and how it plans to say it—verbally and nonverbally—make up the advertising message. Each advertisement needs a headline or opening to create consumer interest and copy that presents the message. Content decisions also involve the use of color and illustration, advertisement size or length, the source, the use of symbolism, and the adaptations needed for foreign markets. The role of these factors depends on a firm's goals and resources.

Developing and Executing Media Strategy

Media planning helps answer such questions as the following: What audiences do we want to reach? When and where do we want to reach them? How many people should we reach? How often do we need to reach them? What will it cost to reach them? The media include traditional methods, such as newspapers, magazines, television, radio, or billboards, and supplementary media, such as Yellow Pages advertising, Internet advertising, and specialty advertising. In 1996, the top twenty-five advertisers spent $17.8 billion on national advertising. The breakdown of their expenditures by medium appears in Table 8.1.

TABLE 8.1. Ad Expenditures by Medium (Top Twenty-Five Ad Spenders in 1996)

Medium	Percentage of Total Expenditures
Broadcast Television	60
Magazines	16
Newspapers	13
Cable Television	8
Radio	2
Outdoor	1

Source: Derived from Anne R. Carey and Marcy E. Mullins, "Where Big Spenders Advertise," *USA Today,* July 10, 1997, p. B1.

Evaluating Advertising Effectiveness

In managing its advertising campaign, a company should carefully evaluate the effectiveness of previous advertisements and use the results to improve the quality of future advertisements. Top executives want proof that the advertising they purchase is worthwhile. They want to know whether the dollars spent on advertising are producing the sales volume that could be reaped from the same dollars spent on other marketing activities. An advertisement's effectiveness may be tested before it is presented to the target audience, while it is being presented, or after it has completed its run. The methods used to measure advertising effectiveness were discussed in Chapter 7.

MAKING BUDGET DECISIONS

After setting objectives and defining creative and media strategies, an advertiser faces the next advertising challenge: figuring out how to pay for it. The advertising budget is, in many respects, the most important decision made by advertisers. If too little money is spent on advertising, sales volume will not achieve its potential, and profits will be lost. If too much money is spent, unnecessary expenditures will reduce profits. Of course, the dilemma faced by advertising or marketing managers is determining what spending level is "too little" or how much is "too much."

Setting Advertising Budgets

Several methods and formulas for setting advertising budgets have been developed over the years, but none is adequate for all cases, and many advertisers try to employ several methods to help them arrive at the right figures. Here is a quick look a the most commonly used methods.

Percentage of Sales Method

The percentage of sales method defines the advertising budget as some predetermined percentage of past or expected sales. Assume, for example, that a company allocated 5 percent of anticipated sales to advertising and that the company projects next year's sales of a particular brand to be $50 million. Its advertising budget would be set at $2.5 million. Although this method's major advantage is that it is easy to apply (once an advertiser has arrived at the right percentage, that is), the major flaw in the percentage of sales method is that it does not rest on the premise that advertising can influence sales. An advertiser could spend too much (on products that may not need that much advertising) or too little (on products that could benefit from an advertising boost). In practice, most sophisticated marketers do not use percentage of sales as the sole budgeting method. Instead, they employ the method as an initial pass, or first cut, for determining the budget and then alter the budget forecast depending on the objectives and tasks that need to be accomplished.

Objective and Task Method

The objective and task method is used by two-thirds of the largest advertisers.[14] This method looks at the objectives set for each activity and determines the cost of accomplishing each objective: What will it cost to make 60 percent of the people in your target market aware of your product? How many people do you have to reach, and how many times?

Competitive Parity Method

Another budgeting method is to adjust the advertising budget so that it is comparable to competitors' budgets. The logic is that the collective minds of the firms in the industry will probably generate advertising budgets that are somewhat close to the optimal.

All You Can Afford Method

Firms with limited resources may decide to spend all that they reasonably can on advertising after other unavoidable expenditures have been allocated. Although some larger firms also use this method, the competitive parity method is most frequently used by smaller firms that tend to follow industry leaders. Smaller firms can also create community awareness by their owners' networking, for example, involvement in community events, talking to customers, and talking with others who have experience in the same type of business.

The budgeting decision is one of the most important advertising decisions and also one of the most difficult to manage. Perhaps the most important point to learn about budgeting is that no magic formula will deliver the right answer every time. Instead, experts recommend a logical process that can help identify minimum and maximum values. However, as with most business decisions, setting the budget requires judgment and experience.[15]

SUMMARY

Marketing success depends on careful planning. The marketing plan involves three steps: situation analysis, development of marketing objectives, and development of market strategy. The advertising plan involves analysis of the company's internal and external situations, setting advertising objectives, developing and executing creative strategy, developing and executing media strategy, and evaluating advertising effectiveness. Of course, budget decisions are, in many respects, the most important decisions made by advertisers.

* * *

THE GLOBAL PERSPECTIVE: SELECTING AN INTERNATIONAL AGENCY

When Starbucks Coffee Company decided to break into the market in Singapore, it abandoned its tradition of doing very little advertising, if any at all. Instead, Starbucks hired Saatchi & Saatchi Singapore to create outdoor and transit ads as well as newspaper ads that announced each new store. In other Asia/Pacific countries, Starbucks held to its customary use of special events, public relations, and promotional materials.

One of the most important decisions a company engaged in international marketing must make is the selection of an advertising agency. The company has three alternatives in agency selection. It can work with domestic agencies (in their own countries), local agencies (in foreign countries), or international affiliates in local markets (large advertising agencies with both domestic and overseas offices). The formation of mega-agencies and the trend toward mergers and acquisitions suggest an additional alternative: international affiliates in local markets may become the preferred arrangement for large companies. International affiliates are viewed as more efficient due, in part, to staffing adequate personnel, knowing the local market, and creating effective advertisements. Many advertisers have switched from using a variety of domestic agencies to global agency networks.

The largest of these networks is Omnicom Group. *Advertising Age* listed the following agencies as connected to Omnicom (those italicized are subsidiaries): BBDO Worldwide, *Baxter Gurian & Mazzei, Corbett HealthConnect, Doremus Company, Lyons Lavey Nickel Swift, Ross Roy Communications,* DDB Needham Worldwide, *Focus Group, Bernard Hodes Worldwide, Integer Group, KPR, PGC Advertising, TLP,* TBWA International (Chiat/Day), Alcone Marketing Group, Cline Davis & Mann, Della Femina/Jeary & Partners, Eagle River Interactive, Harrison Wilson & Associates, Harrison & Star Business Group, Ketchum Directory Advertising, Merkley Newman Harty, Rapp Collins Worldwide, Goodby/Silverstein & Partners, GGT Group, *GSD&M, Martin/Williams, BrightHouse, BDDP Group,* and *Batey Group.*

Of course, local shops thrive in key cities. In 1997, the following cities were at the top of the world as far as local shop billings were concerned:

City	Billings in Millions	Number of Agencies
1. New York	$37,697.2	152
2. Tokyo	31,449.3	51
3. London	15,316.8	57
4. Chicago	11,214.4	76
5. Paris	9,366.7	38

Source: Normandy Madden, "Starbucks Ships Its Coffee Craze to Pacific Rim," *Advertising Age*, April 27, 1998, p. 28.

Note: Table information is adapted from "Top 25 U.S. Cities by Volume" and "Top 10 Cities Outside the U.S. by Volume," *Advertising Age*, April 27, 1998, p. s13.

* * *

ETHICS TRACK: TOBACCO COMPANIES— THE DECISION TO CUT AD SPENDING

"Viewer discretion advised," says the ad's text. The visual shows a "disgruntled" maid flicking cigarette ashes onto food she has prepared for "a snooty rich couple."[16] The controversial R. J. Reynolds campaign for Camel cigarettes in summer 1998 startled people with its "irreverent scenarios" and messages. The ads clearly talked back to the overwhelming, long-running criticism of the tobacco industry and its advertising methods and messages.

When deciding where to put advertising dollars and how much to spend, a company must consider many factors. Some tobacco companies have pulled back from criticism—their response has been to cut back on ad spending (see the following list). But R. J. Reynolds (RJR Nabisco) has pushed aggressively ahead.

Ethics are never clear-cut. Countries such as Canada and Finland have banned all cigarette advertising. Critics of advertising regulation in the United States fear the power of "big government" and believe that consumers should have the right to receive information through advertising about legal products.

1996 Spending on Tobacco Ads

Company	1996 Change	Spending in Millions
Philip Morris	−10%	$232
B.A.T. Industries	unchanged	120
RJR Nabisco	11%	82
Loews	−1%	23
UST	59%	14

Source: Table information is adapted from "USA Snapshots," *USA Today*, July 3, 1997, p. B1.

Lee & Johnson
:60 Spot
"A Day in the Life of an Evolving Brand"

Most see only the physical and monetary growth of a company—I see the daily struggles of a brand that continues to grow and evolve in a state of constant fluctuation.

When I joined Qwest Communications in January 1998, the company had been public for several months, consisted of 1,500 employees, had acquired two small companies, and had just launched its first comprehensive corporate brand advertising campaign. As the proverbial end-of-the-year books close for 1998, Qwest will log a stock split, over 6,000 employees, a $4 billion acquisition of LCI International, and a joint venture with a European telecommunications company that consequently creates the world's largest interconnect network. To most Qwest employees, the general public, many of the company's stakeholders, and even some industry analysts, Qwest has had a successful and rather amazing year. It's hard for me to disagree with that, but my role as corporate marketing communications manager has enabled me to see the past ten months in an entirely different light.

Qwest's overall business position is the construction of a high-capacity fiber-optic network poised to reliably deliver high-speed broadband services and the framework necessary to empower businesses with the next generation of multimedia communications. Qwest's is the first network designed with enough capacity to send multimedia content—data, images, and video—as seamlessly as voice is carried on traditional networks. To communicate this, Qwest unveiled a new corporate identity as a public company along with its first corporate advertising campaign in October 1997.

The entire identity and branding campaign was intended to communicate, in a single phrase, the benefits of Qwest's unprecedented network technology—designed to erase the constraints of time and distance. Qwest's tag line, "Ride the light," was inspired by Albert Einstein's teachings about the Theory of Relativity (see Illustration 8.1). The tag line represented a clarion call to individuals and businesses to begin enjoying the benefits of twenty-first-century digital communications. The branding campaign and its respective advertising was designed to make Qwest synonymous with the simple, yet powerful, attributes of light, such as speed, clarity, simplicity, illumination, and enlightenment. To deliver these branding messages, Qwest rolled out a national print advertising campaign to communicate the power and possibilities of the Qwest vision and network. Later, we introduced additional print ads and corporate television spots to the media plan.

Qwest successfully emerged through a cluttered marketplace. Its brand evolved throughout 1998, reaching its target audiences with consistent messages about the network benefits. However, Qwest's merger with long distance provider LCI International in June 1998 posed the brand's greatest challenge. The Qwest brand, so carefully positioned as a high-tech, multimedia network, was suddenly forced to integrate with LCI, a brand that communicated "simple, fair, and inexpensive" long distance service—at odds with Qwest's benefits: speed, reliability, accuracy, and security. Fortunately, Qwest's overall business direction did not change as a result of the merger. Qwest continues to position itself as the company building a network for the next century. Because the Qwest network has been more fully deployed, enabling the company to offer more products and services than when the brand was first launched, and because we have acquired a massive customer base and additional product and service functionality from LCI, Qwest has much more to add to its story in 1999.

What's next? We don't have a firm response. This is a crucial time for the Qwest brand as it enters a new year with its new constituents. The magnitude of changes that the brand has incurred during the past year make it seem only natural that some confusion would exist about its future evolution. Although it is critical that corporate marketing's number one objective is to determine where we take the brand next, it is equally important to the brand's evolution that we acknowledge the company as a "player"—meaning that it can't be ignored. Neither can we in corporate marketing, as builders and protectors of the brand, ignore the fact that our brand is now visible and recognized around the world, not only because of a record-breaking year of successful business transactions but also because of the successful first year of a comprehensive, integrated campaign.

Tara J. Krull
Manager, Corporate Marketing Communications
Qwest Communications
Denver, Colorado

Chapter 9

The Creative Aspect of Advertising

The *Seinfeld* finale on May 14, 1998 rivaled the Super Bowl as an advertising extravaganza. Yet this occasion pushed ad creativity in a way the Super Bowl never could—the ads had to compete with the creativity of the innovative show itself. Some commercials used animals, a staple gimmick of advertisers. Foote, Cone & Belding had success by infusing the element of surprise into an old ploy in its Coors' commercial for Zima malt beverage. The spot featured a poodle in a bar. In another commercial, a basket of kitties charmingly sang the virtues of Advantage, a Bayer flea-control product. Another staple—the use of celebrities—bombed in an Herbal Essence commercial featuring Dr. Ruth. Others relied too heavily on special effects, with the exception of a Sony spot for its monster movie *Godzilla* (1998). The creative challenge was so daunting that long time Super Bowl contender Pepsi decided to warm the bench. Some nonparticipants, such as Pepsi, feared that the writing of the show—unusually artistic for a television situation comedy—could easily overshadow the writing of the commercials.[1]

Legendary ad creator George Lois, who worked for Doyle Dane Bernback in the 1960s, would not have been intimidated by the *Seinfeld* challenge. He firmly believed that advertising is an art, refusing to concede that it is at least part science and gagging at the value of precampaign message testing with focus groups. He believed his famous Braniff Airlines campaign ("If you've got it, flaunt it") would have bombed in ad tests. As it turned out, the ads tripled Braniff's business. What separated Lois from the rest was not that he strived so fervently for success—many do—but that he mastered the unexpected, the bold, the outrageous—in other words, he recognized the Big Idea when he stumbled on it. His definition of advertising flouts the scientific aspects of the business—advertising is an art, and the process is intuitive. It is hard to argue with success like that.[2]

What is the Big Idea? Don E. Schultz and Beth E. Barnes describe it in their book *Strategic Advertising Campaigns* as "usually very simple, but it brings a realism, an understanding of the marketplace, and an empathy with the target market that literally makes the advertisement jump off the page or television screen and into the life of the reader or viewer."[3] As examples, they offer Life Cereal's "Mikey" commercials and a Cheer detergent ad that

ILLUSTRATION 9.1. The Big Idea

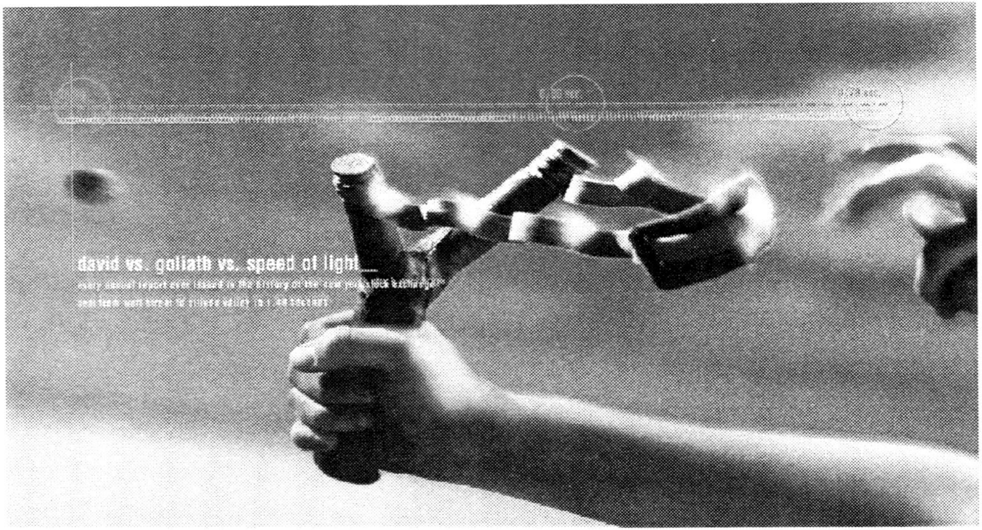

To make concrete its abstract "product," one of the world's most advanced fiber networks, Qwest, employs visual representations of the speed of light in its 1998 advertising campaign. For instance, one of its television commercials shows the dramatic image of a lightning strike and ends with the tag line "ride the light." The print ad above recalls one of the most memorable displays of unexpected, unseen power in history—David striking down Goliath—in its visual of a youthful hand and a slingshot and its headline: "david vs. goliath vs. speed of light." "Slingshot" © Qwest Communications International, Inc., 1998.

132

showed a man washing his clothes in ice water. The Cheer ad got across the detergent's longtime "all-temperature" message in a fresh, memorable way. For one thing, to see a man—instead of a woman—washing clothes in a detergent ad is unusual in itself. Beyond that, what is the probability that *anyone* would wash the laundry in ice water?

CREATIVE CONCEPTS OR CREATIVITY IN ADVERTISING

Behind every good advertisement is a creative concept, a Big Idea that makes the message distinctive, attention getting, memorable (see Illustration 9.1). Some advertising experts argue that for an advertising campaign to be effective, it must contain a Big Idea that attracts the consumer's attention, gets a reaction, and sets the advertiser's product or service apart from the competition's. Although really great ideas in advertising are difficult to come by, some examples of Big Ideas have resulted in memorable, effective advertising. The Energizer bunny's "It keeps going and going" has had endless applications (the cultural icon of the bunny has popped up in cartoons, conversations, and political campaigns, and even been reproduced as a mechanical toy). Another icon, the Morton salt girl, first said, "When it rains, it pours," back in 1912.[4]

It is often difficult to pinpoint the exact source or inspiration for Big Ideas or to teach advertising people how to find them. However, several methods can guide the creative team's search for a major selling idea and offer alternative solutions or options for developing effective advertising. These methods include the "incubation" technique of James Webb Young, the process of lateral thinking, and the storytelling process.

A Technique for Producing Ideas

In *A Technique for Producing Ideas*, James Webb Young proposes a five-step process for idea generation. A creative executive with J. Walter Thompson, Young developed this process in 1940. To begin, gather specific information (elements and information directly related to the product or service) and general information (observed information about life and events). Then, digest this material and give it a mental work over. Next, in the "incubation" period, forget about it and let the subconscious mind go to work. Young predicts that the idea will appear "out of nowhere." Finally, shape, develop, and adapt the idea to advertising.[5] The idea of consciously forgetting about the project and letting the subconscious *mull* ideas over time is typical of the creative writing process. Insights may come from the subconscious mind as mental pictures. For instance, the American playwright Arthur Miller said that his play *Death of a Salesman* initially came to him as images, many derived from his observations of people and their lives—the image of "a little frame house on a street of little frame houses, which had once been loud with the noise of growing boys, and then was empty and silent"; images of futility—"the cavernous Sunday afternoon polishing the car"; images of aging—"so many of your friends already gone"; and the image of a private man "in a world of strangers."[6] From these mental pictures, Miller understood his main character, Willy Loman, and wrote his masterpiece play.

Lateral Thinking

Another process for idea generation widely used today is lateral thinking. This process explores new relationships, breaking established thought patterns to generate new ideas and escape old ways of thinking. Since ideas are turned upside down and looked at in new ways, this concept is also called out-of-the-box thinking. In his book *Lateral Thinking for Management*, Edward deBono contrasts vertical ("traditional logical thinking") with lateral thinking.[7] Some of these contrasts are depicted in Table 9.1.

The Cheer ad showing a man washing his clothes in ice water broke "out of the box" in which detergent ads generally operate to present a surprising, improbable picture—most likely born from lateral thinking. A 1998 Leo Burnett campaign for Kellogg's illustrates out-of-the-box thinking that led to a surprising approach to the campaign's execution. Burnett chose to use a generic approach—usually employed to increase sales in an entire product category, not for just one brand. For instance, the National Pork Producers Council ran generic ads to jump-start sales in a declining product category. Since cereal sales figures had been flat in the United States, Burnett decided to hype the general health benefits of eating any brand of cereal with the tag line, "Cereal. Eat it for life."[8]

Storytelling

Advertising at its best is a form of storytelling. The most compelling advertisements have all the components of a short story. They introduce characters, identify tensions and problems, develop toward a conflict, and then offer a resolution—usually provided by the product or service being promoted. Some of the best television commercials could be called lyrical: they have the poetic quality of condensing legendary and mythic stories familiar to the target's culture into spots as brief as fifteen seconds.

For instance, an award-winning Australian commercial for Levi's 501 jeans alludes to both the myth of the American cowboy and the legendary

TABLE 9.1. Differences Between Vertical and Lateral Thinking

Vertical	Lateral
selective	generative
analytical	provocative
sequential	makes jumps
has to be correct	does not have to be correct
uses negatives to block pathways	recognizes no negatives
excludes the irrelevant	welcomes chance intrusions
follows most likely path	explores least likely path
finite	probabilistic

Source: Adapted from Edward deBono, *Lateral Thinking for Management,* New York: American Management Association, 1971, cited in Don E. Schultz and Beth E. Barnes, *Strategic Advertising Campaigns,* Fourth Edition, Lincolnwood, IL: NTC Business Books, 1995, pp. 18-181.

rebelliousness of the 1950s. With no dialogue, the spot uses the classic rock single "Be My Baby" as the musical backdrop for a sixty-second fantasy. Employing the familiar journey motif of American film, the commercial begins with an establishing shot of an isolated stretch of desert highway. A dark car travels the highway, down a sun-drenched hill, into a valley, where it breaks down. The driver, a bespectacled young man in a conservative suit, disappoints his wholesome-pretty, girl-next-door companion when he is unable to fix the car. Rescue comes as another young man arrives in a pickup truck. The first image of him shows his dusty cowboy boots hitting the sand as he jumps from his vehicle. The car is overheated, so the handsome rescuer, bare-chested except for an open denim jacket, takes off his Levi's jeans, an action observed with admiration by the young lady. In the closing sequence, using the legs of the jeans as a towing rope, the hero and the girl drive off into the sunset. As they drive away, the jeans split in two, leaving the "square" behind. The splitting of the jeans' legs is reflected in the commercial's clever tag line: "Separates the men from the boys." For a product targeted largely to young men, this story taps into that group's interest in the Old West, in the rebel characters of the 1950s, such as Marlon Brando and James Dean, and in winning the heart of a pretty girl.

To create effective advertisements, ad creators must be familiar with the target's cultural interests—the music target group members enjoy, the books and magazines they read, the movies they have seen, the problems that typically occupy their minds, and so forth. For instance, in summer 1998, the American Film Institute selected the top 100 American movies, then released the list in its "100 Years . . . 100 Movies" publicity campaign. Several magazine publishers followed with reader surveys and their own lists based on these surveys. Those who aspire to create great ads by tapping into the American psyche should familiarize themselves with film classics that appeared on all the lists, such as *Gone with the Wind* (1939), *Casablanca* (1942), and *The Godfather* (1972/1974/1990) series.

Another award-winning Australian television commercial alludes to the famous 1953 film *From Here to Eternity*. A scene in the movie that shows its stars, Deborah Kerr and Burt Lancaster, making love on a beach became a turning point in the intensity of passion and sexual explicitness that might be acceptable in American film. In the Australian commercial, two lovers—clad in black bathing suits, similarly to the film's stars—appear in the same prone position on the sand, washed by a raging surf, as they commence lovemaking. The only dialogue is the young woman's question: "Do you have any protection?" In response, the man puts the bolle (the advertised brand) sunglasses on his face. Although the black-and-white film used a day-for-night filter to suggest its lovers met at night, the commercial is shot in full color, in blazing sunlight. This difference is key to the man's response to the woman's question—he needs the sunglasses to protect his eyes. By tapping into viewers' existing perceptions of the classic film, the spot resonates with associations and meanings far beyond what it could otherwise present in thirty seconds.

Ford's Mercury division broke out of the conservative approach usually taken by U.S. automakers when it became obvious that obscure references to design and safety features were not resonating with consumers and increasing sales. Mercury decided to take a risk and spoof the film classic *Casablanca* and such classic television shows as *Perry Mason* and *Gunsmoke* in ads introducing its 1998 models.[9]

Creative giants in the United States today include partners Rich Silverstein and Jeff Goodby (the "Got Milk?" campaign), Dan Wieden of Wieden & Kennedy (Nike's "Just Do It"), and TBWA Chiat/Day's Lee Clow, who sees advertising as "an uplifting social force, as a way not only to persuade but to inspire and entertain."[10] In May 1998, Clow launched his agency's first campaign for Levi Strauss & Company by opening a box conspicuously placed outside Levi's San Francisco headquarters. "Inside the container was . . . nothing," illustrating that Levi's "now thinks outside the box."[11]

Of course, however creatively the Big Idea may be conceived, the ad must do more than resonate with the consumer. It must also be grounded in sound strategy. The consumer who views the ad must be able to understand, among other things, the product benefit and selling message.[12]

DEVELOPMENT IN CREATIVE STRATEGY

Similar to any other area of the marketing and promotional process, the creative aspect of advertising is guided by specific goals and objectives that require development of a creative strategy. A creative strategy focuses on what the advertising message will say or communicate and guides the development of all messages used in the advertising campaign. Some of the best-known and most discussed approaches include the following:

- *Unique selling proposition approach (USP).* With this approach, developed by Rosser Reeves of the Ted Bates agency, an advertiser makes a superiority claim based on a unique product attribute that represents a meaningful, distinctive consumer benefit. Many of the successful USPs, such as "M&M candies melt in your mouth, not in your hand," result from identifying real, inherent product advantages.[13]
- *Brand image approach.* Whereas the USP approach is based on promoting physical and functional differences between the advertiser's product and competitive offerings, the brand image approach, popularized by David Ogilvy, founder of the Ogilvy & Mather agency, involves psychological rather than physical differentiation. Advertising attempts to develop an image identity for a brand by associating the product with symbols. Perhaps the most successful image advertising of all time is the Marlboro campaign. The campaign has focused on western imagery, such as cowboys, horses, and ranching. Since the United States is said to have two major myth systems, the Old West and the Old South, the cowboy is a strong and compelling image.
- *Positioning approach.* The concept of positioning as a basis for advertising strategy was introduced by Jack Trout and Al Ries in the early 1970s. According to this approach, successful advertising must implant in the customer's mind a clear meaning of what the product is and how it compares to competitive offerings. One of the most famous advertisements using the positioning approach was that of the Avis rental car company—"We're No. 2, and No. 2 tries harder."
- *Generic brand approach.* When you are the number one brand, you have no need to acknowledge the competition or claim superiority. Such an approach can be used only as long as a product or service truly does dominate the brand category. A 1998 television commercial for the Gap shows numerous couples, all wearing khaki pants, executing the popular 1940s dance, the swing. The tag line makes no mention of any brands. It simply says, "Khakis swing," followed by "The Gap." There is no claim of superiority; for instance, a less dominant brand might claim, "Khakis swing better." As already mentioned, Leo Burnett chose to use a generic approach for Kellogg's "Eat it for life" campaign—a surprising but innovative choice.
- *The resonance approach.* This approach requires that the creative team have a deep understanding of the target audience's world, including

their experiences and emotions. Advertising created with this approach "does not focus on product claims or brand images, but rather is designed to present situations or emotions that evoke positive associations from the memories of the respondents."[14] For example, Hallmark uses this approach in appealing to the emotions of those who buy greeting cards with their familiar tag line, "When you care enough to send the very best."

The copy platform, or creative brief, is the written document that specifies the basic elements of the creative strategy. The format of the copy platform varies from agency to agency, but it generally contains some variations of the following: a profile of the target audience; the problem, issue, or opportunity that advertising is expected to address; the advertising objective; the key customer benefit; supportive benefits; and a creative strategy statement (a campaign theme or Big Idea, an advertising appeal, and the creative execution style to be used). Kathy Evans Wisner of Rapp Collins Worldwide elaborates on the importance of the creative brief in the :30 spot in this chapter.

The basic content and form of an advertising message are a function of several factors. Characteristics of the people in the target audience (income, age, race, gender, occupation, etc.) influence both content and form. An advertising campaign's objective(s) also affects the content and form of an advertising message. If an advertiser faces the problem of low brand awareness and its advertising objective is to increase brand awareness, the message may need to repeat its brand name many times. To persuade consumers to buy its product, the key and supportive customer benefits should also be included in the advertising message.

Advertising Appeals

Advertising appeal refers to the basis or approach used in the advertisement to attract the attention or interest of consumers and/or to influence their feelings toward the product, service, or cause. Advertising appeals can be broken down into two categories—informational/rational appeals (hard sell) and emotional appeals (soft sell).

Informational/Rational Appeals (Hard Sell)

These appeals focus on the consumer's practical or functional need for the product or service and emphasize features of a product or service and/or the benefits or reasons for using or owning a particular brand. Many rational motives can be used as the basis for advertising appeals, including comfort, convenience, and economy.

Emotional Appeals (Soft Sell)

These appeals use an emotional message and are designed around an image intended to touch the heart and create a response based on feelings and attitudes (see Illustration 9.2). Advertisers can use emotional appeals in many ways in their creative strategy. Humor and sex appeals, or other types of appeals that are very entertaining, upbeat, and/or exciting, affect the emotions of consumers and put them in a favorable frame of mind. Fear appeals can be equally dramatic in arousing emotions but have an opposite effect on the viewer's frame of mind.

Humor appeals. Consumers have historically given high ratings to humorous advertising (e.g., see Illustrations 9.3 and 9.4). The Energizer bunny that "just keeps going and going" and the hip, singing-and-dancing California raisins are among consumers' all-time favorite ads. Recently, the Taco Bell Chihuahua with its meaningfully raised eyebrows and suave style made consumers chuckle and catapulted the ad to the top rating spot.

Sex appeals. The old adage "sex sells" may not always be true. For instance, men gave high ratings to Special K ads featuring nearly nude, extremely thin women copping sexy poses in front of a mirror, but the ads did not appeal to the targeted group—women. Although the Australian ad for bolle sunglasses, mentioned previously, successfully evoked viewer passion, an I Can't Believe It's Not Butter commercial featuring heart-throb Fabio was effective with only 15 percent of its audience, according to ratings released by *USA Today*'s Ad Track in September 1996.

Fear appeals. Long a staple of advertising, these appeals have heightened consumer fears about social acceptance and isolation (expressed in ads for anti-itch creams and diarrhea remedies), personal hygiene (advertisers originated the term athlete's foot and made halitosis a household word), and motherhood (ads for cheese and peanut butter products commonly consumed by children have used such guilt-producing slogans as "Choosy mothers choose Jif"). A new ad category—high-tech phone service—now employs fear appeals. A 1998 Iridium ad for its worldwide, mobile phone service plays to today's fear of being out of touch, and a Nextel commercial appeals to financial worries. In the Nextel spot, a cellular phone user driving out of his local calling area is stopped at a "border" on a bleak landscape where a crazed guard vacuums all the money from the cell phone user's pockets and even sucks up the coins in his penny loafers. The ad creates a terrifying image of being fleeced by cell phone roaming charges.

Fear appeals have also been heavily used in campaigns designed to combat drug addictions and other health-related problems. In 1998, the Hepatitis Foundation International ran a print ad showing a young woman wearing a bright bathing suit and eating a salad. The advertisement resembled a travel

ILLUSTRATION 9.2. Soft Sell

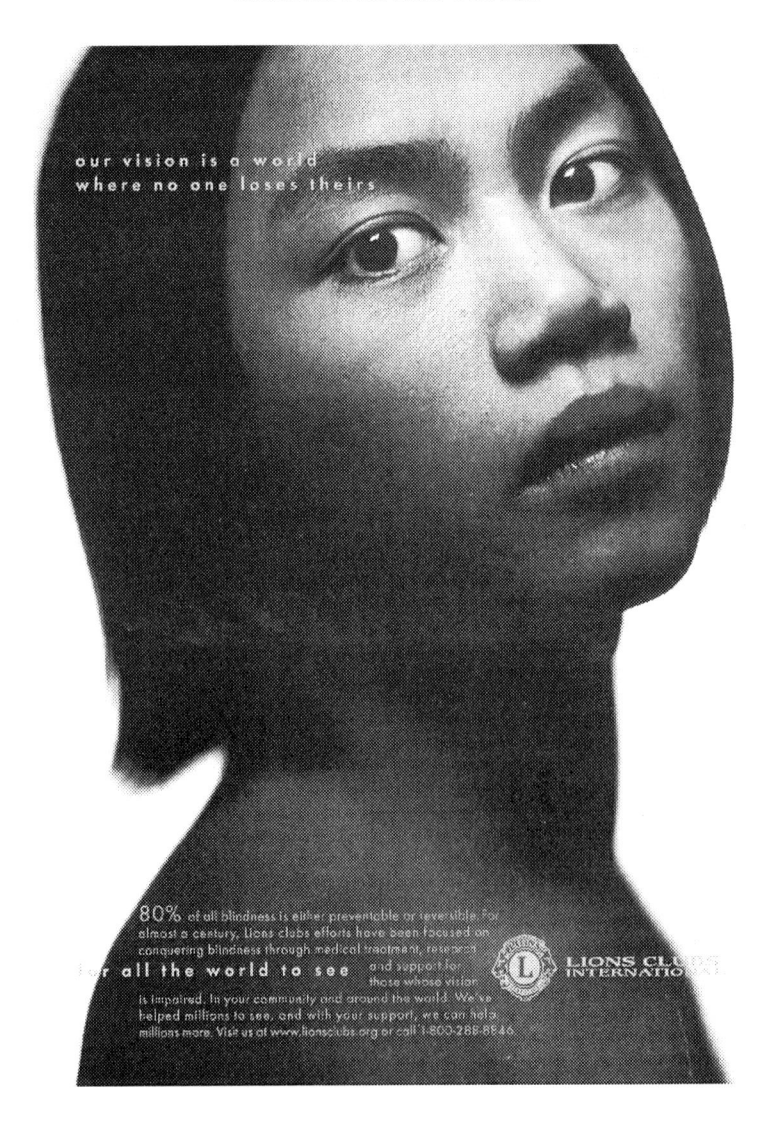

Rapp Collins Worldwide/Chicago designed its message around a dominant, emotional image of a child for this Lions Clubs International print advertisement. Even the headline appeals to the heart in a clever play on the duality of the word vision: *our vision is a world where no one loses theirs.*

The Creative Aspect of Advertising 141

ILLUSTRATION 9.3. High Ratings

We interrupt your Year 2000 project to offer you a little piece of advice.

Run!

from all the half-baked Year 2000 solutions out there. The "quick fixes" that don't really fix anything. The products that lock you into long-term consulting. Take cover with PLATINUM TransCentury solutions, instead. Our easy-to-learn tools work well, get any job done fast, and come with consulting services only if you want them. Whether you need a single tool or a complete "find-it, fix-it, test-it" solution, call us at 1-800-890-7828, ext. 40160. Or log onto www.platinum.com/y2k

PLATINUM
TECHNOLOGY

You're Not Alone.™   ©1997 PLATINUM technology, inc. All rights reserved.

Humor appeals score high with consumers. In this Rapp Collins Worldwide print advertisement for PLATINUM technology, the childlike drawing sets a lighthearted tone for the two-part headline: *We interrupt your Year 2000 project to offer you a little piece of advice.—Run!*

ILLUSTRATION 9.4. Integration for Even Higher Ratings

Rapp Collins Worldwide/Chicago created a direct mail piece for PLATINUM technology that coordinates in image and tone with the print ad shown in Illustration 9.3. The same picture and the first half of the ad's headline appear on the mailing's cover. Inside, a figure drawn in the same style, by the same artist, dives through a tube into the water while minimal text proclaims, "Find it *fast.*"

142

ad for a tropical resort. The travel industry claimed that the headline, "She just picked up a virus to bring home to her family and friends," and a color-coded map that showed most parts of the world as danger zones for hepatitis inflamed travelers' fears about diseases. Although the ad raised the ire of tourist offices and travel agencies, it also successfully raised the demand for hepatitis vaccinations, which was the purpose of the campaign.

Combination Appeals

These appeals combine informational/rational and emotional appeals. In many advertising situations, the creative specialist does not choose an emotional over a rational appeal, but instead decides how to combine the two. Consumer purchase decisions are often made on the basis of both emotional and rational motives, and copywriters must give attention to both elements in developing effective advertising. For instance, the success of Pepsi's advertising for Super Bowl 1998 was credited not only to its customary product focus but also to the use of humor, minimal dialogue, and an underlying universal truth. The commercial spots were directed by Joe Pytka, who has used the appeals of animal magnetism (e.g., the goldfish and chimps) and big stars (e.g., Cindy Crawford) in thirteen of Pepsi's sixteen highest-scoring ads.[15]

Rational and emotional appeals have been further differentiated by Foote, Cone & Belding. In 1978, the advertising agency developed a model based on the assumption that consumers' buying decisions are affected by their degree of involvement in the decision. The model, shown in Table 9.2,

TABLE 9.2. Foote, Cone & Belding Model

High Involvement	
Thinking	**Feeling**

Products:
   cars, house, furnishings
	Products:
	   jewelry, cosmetics, clothes

Message Variables:
   long copy, informational
   demonstration, comparative
	Message Variables:
	   emotional, visual

Low Involvement	

Products:
   food, household items
	Products:
	   liquor, candy, cigarettes

Message Variables:
   coupons, samples
	Message Variables:
	   creativity, lifestyle

Source: Adapted from Richard Vaughn, "How Advertising Works: A Planning Model," *Journal of Advertising Research,* October 1980, pp. 27-33.

provides a matrix, with each quadrant detailing how the purchasing decision relates to consumer involvement. In this matrix, "thinking" refers to rational appeals, and "feeling" refers to emotional appeals. The following are examples of different levels within this matrix.

- *High involvement/thinking.* This type of appeal can be successful when advertising a product of high importance to the consumer, such as a car or computer. Long, informational copy would be appropriate.
- *Low involvement/thinking.* For products or services that are routinely purchased, rational appeals that encourage trial purchases (such as cents-off coupons) will be more effective than long copy.
- *High involvement/feeling.* Emotional appeals work best for products or services related to the consumer's self-esteem, such as makeup, fashion accessories, and clothing (e.g., see Illustration 9.5). The emotional value of some types of clothing has been illustrated by the lengths to which some teenagers have gone—including theft and violence—to acquire name-brand athletic shoes. Teenagers are especially vulnerable to esteem appeals.
- *Low involvement/feeling.* Emotional appeals also work well for products and services that satisfy desires for personal gratification, such as soft drinks, beer, liquor, and tobacco products. Since such purchases are often enjoyed socially, appeals to the desire to be accepted by a certain group can also be a factor. For instance, the circular argument "Coke Is It" has no valid logic but implies social acceptance.

It is clear that most advertising works. It is also clear that not all advertising works equally well. What is unclear is what makes one campaign more effective than another. For years, experts have tried scientifically to pinpoint the ingredients that make up an exceptionally effective campaign. However, these efforts have seldom been conclusive. Opinions about what works and what does not generally fall into two schools: the straightforward and the creative.

Members of the straightforward, no-nonsense, factual school like advertisements that deliver relevant facts in support of the product. They want presentations to be professional, but they do not believe it is important for the advertisements to be artistic. Those in the second school favor a creative, emotionally based approach. They believe that advertisements focusing heavily on information are likely to be ignored and that focusing on emotion is more likely to create the desired response.

Evidence suggests that one of the approaches is quantifiably more likely to bring success. The evidence comes from the Effie Awards, sponsored by the American Marketing Association's New York Chapter, which are given based on measurable results, not on creativity alone. Analysis of

ILLUSTRATION 9.5. High Involvement/Feeling

BE AN ANGEL. Buy Our Cards.

LIFT THE SPIRITS OF OUR YOUNG PATIENTS, JUST BY BUYING OUR CORPORATE HOLIDAY CARDS.

Ah, a breath of fresh air in a world of computer-generated holiday cards. It's the Children's Memorial Hospital Collection, and it features only original works of art created by children during their stay with us. There's a watchful angel...a festive city scene...even a holly-adorned "Chicago Bull." Each design is reproduced on a high-grade paper and printed large to capture every precious detail. But beyond the charm and quality of these cards lies the best reason of all to buy them——a full 100% of the net proceeds will go toward our Child Life program, which sponsors creative and therapeutic activities for our young patients and their families. So this holiday, be a messenger of hope to our children. And get some wonderful, one-of-a-kind cards in return.

Another Rapp Collins Worldwide/Chicago print ad, this one for Children's Memorial Hospital's corporate holiday cards, responds both to the motivation of desired self-esteem associated with greeting card buyers and to the high importance to the corporate consumer of purchasing the right holiday cards to send to clients and customers. While the angel drawn by a hospitalized child appeals to emotion, the long copy satisfies the need for information in making an important decision.

the 1995 Effie Gold Award winners revealed that a wide majority were based on emotional appeal. Indeed, humor seems to improve a campaign's chances for success—the 1998 "Grand Effie" went to the M&M/Mars Snickers commercial, "Hungry? Why Wait?" Next to humor, the most successful element seems to be an empathetic understanding of the customer. In the end, the advertisements that achieve exceptional results more often communicate a deep understanding of how consumers feel rather than relying on rational advertising.[16]

Creative Execution Styles

Once the specific advertising appeal that will be used as the basis for the advertising message has been determined, the creative specialist or team must then turn its attention to execution. Creative execution refers to the way in which an advertising appeal is carried out or presented. In addition to using humor, an advertising message or appeal can be presented in numerous ways, such as the following:

- *Testimonial.* Also called "word of mouth" advertising, this approach uses well-known figures or an unknown, "typical" person to provide product testimonials.
- *Problem-solution.* This tactic presents the viewer with a problem to be solved and the solution is provided by the advertiser's product.
- *Demonstration.* This is designed to illustrate key advantages or benefits of the product or service by showing it in actual use or in some contrived situation.
- *Slice-of-life.* A variation of the problem-solution approach, this technique attempts to portray a real-life situation involving a problem or conflict that consumers might face in their daily lives. The ad then focuses on showing how the advertiser's product or service can resolve that problem.
- *Fantasy.* This approach uses special effects to create an imaginative place, events, or characters.

Advertising Format and Copy Elements

Once creative strategy, appeals, and execution styles have been decided, it is time to create the actual advertisement. The three basic components of a print ad are the headline, body copy, and visual or illustration. The headline and body copy portions of the advertisement are the responsibility of the copywriters, and artists—often working under the direction of an art director—are responsible for the visual presentation of the ad. Artists also work with copywriters to develop a layout. The layout involves the arrangement of the various components of the ad, such as headlines, subheads, body copy, and tag lines. The tag line is a memorable saying or slogan that conveys a selling message, such as the tag line used by a 1998 Tylenol advertising campaign: "Take comfort in our strength."

Television copy consists of two elements—the audio and the video. The video (visual elements) is what the viewer sees on the television screen. The video generally dominates the commercial, so it must attract the viewer's attention and communicate a key idea, message, and/or image. The audio includes such elements as voices, music, and sound effects. Broadcast commercials are demanding to make, and they must be credible and relevant. Research shows that the following techniques work best: the opening should be a short, compelling attention getter; demonstrations should be interesting and believable; the content should be ethical, in good taste, and entertaining; and the general structure of the commercial and copy should be simple and easy to follow.[17]

Radio copy presents a particular challenge to advertisers and their agencies because it lacks the visual aspects of both print and television. Successful radio spots usually enable listeners to visualize the product or something related to it. For this reason, radio advertising is often referred to as "theater of the mind." A radio spot for Kruse Farm Supply in Bristol, Indiana, (the script is given in Table 9.3), illustrates how a radio advertising spot can evoke images and associations in the listener's mind. This particular spot alludes to Alfred Hitchcock's famous film *The Birds* (1963) to gain attention and to generate mental pictures. Also, the writer covers all the copy points (specific details about the product, price, and place—the retailer's location) that the retailer requested.

One of the most challenging aspects of writing for radio is making the script fit the time slot.[18] The copywriter should read the script out loud for

TABLE 9.3. Radio Ad Script

Kruse Farm Supply
:60 Radio
"The Birds"

SFX: MUSIC SIMILAR TO THE SOUNDTRACK OF ALFRED HITCHCOCK'S *THE BIRDS*

MAN: Aahh . . . this is so relaxing . . . watching the birds eat at the bird feeder . . . I hope it's enough . . . it's the last of the bag. Why are they looking at me like that? I don't have any more seed. Hey, guys, the show's over . . . the buffet's closed . . . don't hurt me. I'm the hand that feeds you . . . what about my fine feathered friends . . . this is not an Alfred Hitchcock movie . . . AHHHH!

SFX: MUSIC FADES UNDER

ANNCR: Don't let another senseless bird attack happen. Be prepared for fall feedings—stop by Kruse Farm Supply during their sale going on Monday through the fourth. Save 20 percent on bird feeders and accessories. Thistle seeds are only 79 cents a pound. Fifty-pound bags of black oil sunflower seeds, just $10.50, and premium ear corn is a low $5.50 for a 50-pound bag. Sign up to win 100 pounds of free birdseed at Kruse Farm Supply—no purchase is necessary! And see Kruse's bird room . . . a section dedicated to bird enthusiasts. Keep your flock of birds a happy one—with birdseed and feeders from Kruse Farm Supply . . . stop by during their sale starting Monday. Kruse Farm Supply. On County Road Six in Bristol!

Source: Michelle Egan, South Bend, Indiana. Printed with author's permission.

timing. With electronic compression, recorded radio advertisements can now include 10 to 30 percent more copy than text read live.[19]

To appear professional and to be easy to produce, copy must adhere to the appropriate industry format. Table 9.3 shows the correct format for radio copy. All copy begins with the name of the advertiser in the upper left-hand corner. The size of the print ad or length of the broadcast script, followed by identification of the medium to be used appears on the second line—for example, "Full page, magazine" or ":60 radio." The name given to the advertisement appears on the third line. Often a series of advertisements are created for a specific advertising campaign. In this case, all the ads created for the campaign may have one name that unifies the series.

SUMMARY

Advertising is both an art and a science. The art comes from writing, designing, and producing exciting messages. The science comes from strategic thinking and planning, including research. The creative specialist or team must first deal with the problem of developing a concept. Then the specialist or team must devise a creative strategy, determine appropriate appeals, and select a style of execution. The ad must then be cast into a print, television, radio, or other format. At this stage, copywriters generally collaborate with artistic or production teams to create the actual advertisement. From start to finish, the process of ad creation involves a multitude of decisions that require understanding of both the product and the consumer, as well as knowledge of the various formats and media.

* * *

THE GLOBAL PERSPECTIVE: HARD SELL IS A HARD SELL OVERSEAS

"Akiko is late, isn't she?" a young woman says to her friend as they wait in a theater lobby for the missing Akiko. In the boredom of waiting, conversation turns to hair. It seems that one of the women attributes her beautiful, "supple" hair to Rejoy hair rinse: "It's much better than before." The spot concludes with an announcer's voice-over, "A much better rinse. Single-step Rejoy. You'll feel the difference when you touch (your hair). From P & G."

This commercial may not seem very remarkable unless the stereotypes of Japanese commercials—as frequently humorous, emotional, and less than informative—are considered. Japanese creatives are said to employ indirect, emotional advertising appeals (soft sell) as opposed to the direct, hyperbolic hard sell that characterizes Western advertising. A study of 464 American and 863 Japanese commercials in 1993 confirmed suspicions that Japanese commercials were less informative with their soft sell approaches than American commercials.

However, Michael L. Maynard's qualitative, interpretive analysis of the Rejoy commercial suggests that "the persuasive strategy in Japanese television advertising is indeed more complex." The commercial does present product information (the rinse has been improved, it makes hair feel supple, yet it is light), and its dialogue employs repetition of the product name and its attributes—the selling points. In fact, the Rejoy commercial's slice-of-life format presents the minidrama of two ordinary people in an ordinary situation. What makes the commercial interesting to the viewer, in this case, cannot be attributed to humorous or emotional appeals. The viewer becomes drawn in as an "eavesdropper" to a private conversation—a casual, friendly "story." Maynard attributes the spot's complexity—its blend of hard and soft sell characteristics—to Japan's cultural norms. Does the American hard sell approach work best abroad when it *blends* with the native culture rather than assaults it? In this case, the approach may have been chosen to evoke the best response from a Japanese viewer presented with an "overtly labeled" American product from Procter & Gamble.

Source: Michael L. Maynard, "'Slice-of-Life': A Persuasive Mini Drama in Japanese Television Advertising," *Journal of Popular Culture*, Vol. 31, No. 2, Fall 1997, pp. 131-142.

* * *

ETHICS TRACK:
ETHNIC GROUPS IN THE MAINSTREAM

By 2050, people of color are expected to represent 55 percent of the U.S. population. The "Ethics Track" in Chapter 3 addressed the debate over advertising controversial products to minority audiences. Advertising and other forms of marketing communications are often criticized because they are directed at specific target markets, such as children and minorities, and these groups, for various psychosocial and economic reasons, are vulnerable to marketing messages.

But, does advertising *have an obligation* to address the diverse groups that make up the "multihued mosaic" of the United States? The answer is *yes*, according to Alfred L. Schreiber, VP and general manager of Stedman Graham & Partners, a unit of True North Communications' True North Diversified Cos., a specialist in Integrated Marketing Communication programs targeted to ethnic communities.

Schreiber believes that advertising has a vital role in placing the growing ethnic groups in the media mainstream. In an *Advertising Age* guest column, he asserts that the advertising industry "must make a conscientious effort to create advertising that reflects the way America looks today," thereby "narrowing the mainstream-versus-ethnic marketing gap" and making "great strides in narrowing the nation's cultural gap." He concedes that some "protest that such lofty aims shouldn't be part of advertising's job description." He also argues that such narrowcasting would not only be ethically responsible but also be otherwise advantageous to agencies and their clients.

Schreiber believes that the tremendous power of advertising to persuade Americans "not only what to buy but also what to think" is the power clients seek when they invest their million-dollar budgets in agencies. Look up Schreiber's column at the library. What arguments does he give for the advantages of ethnic narrowcasting? How do the tenets of Integrated Marketing Communication complement the sort of advertising climate, rich with consumer dialogue, that Schreiber believes agencies can create for their clients?

Source: Alfred L. Schreiber, "Defining the 'New America,'" *Advertising Age*, August 3, 1998, p. 21.

Lee & Johnson
:30 Spot
"The Key to Great Creative"

In advertising, there are "Suits" (account people) and "Creatives" (copywriters and art directors). The creative brief is the document that the Suits provide the Creatives so that the Creatives can do their job (i.e., create advertising). The better the creative brief, the better the advertising—plain and simple.

So, what exactly is a creative brief? It's a document that describes an assignment that is given to an advertising agency by one of its clients. Usually, account people from the agency work with the client to put together an initial draft of the brief, and then they pass it on to the Creatives for their input. All parties must agree to the brief before any creative is done.

Each agency has its own version of the creative brief, but the contents are generally the same. A typical brief starts with some *background* information about the company, marketplace, and competition and goes on to describe the *benefits* of the particular product or service (not just the features), including the *key benefit* that the advertising should focus on.

Next, the *target audience* is defined, along with relevant information about their attitudes and past behaviors. A *key insight* about the audience is given to help further focus the creative. Finally, the *purpose* and *scope* of the specific assignment is spelled out, including the tone, media, offer (if any), deadlines, budget, legal copy, and desired end result.

What makes a good creative brief? Simple language (not a lot of marketing jargon). A lot of details about the target audience. A good key insight. And a leverageable point of difference for the product or service. Deliver these, and you're bound to get some really great advertising!

Kathy Evans Wisner
Associate Creative Director
Rapp Collins Worldwide
Chicago, Illinois

Chapter 10

Advertising Production

The newest medium experiencing advertising clutter is the Internet. Banner ads allow Internet users to surf without paying site subscription fees—advertisers provide the financial support. Nevertheless, these ads are often viewed by site visitors as a "necessary evil."[1] Multimedia companies such as Narrative Communications have been developing software to "jazz up" banner ads with animation and audio. Eddie Bauer, Godiva Chocolate, and 1-800-FLOWERS recently installed Narrative Communications' Enliven/Impulse software that allows users to conduct secure sales transactions within the banner ad. For instance, buyers merely click on an "Order" icon on an Eddie Bauer banner ad to begin a sales transaction. One of a series of screens even depicts swatches of stonewashed fabric in various colors. Banner technology companies have expanded the production possibilities for banner advertising, allowing sites such as Bauer's to stand out from the clutter.

Art directors are also using typography to break through the clutter of competing print and Internet advertisements. Long one of advertising's humblest tools, typography has taken on new importance in the Information Age. The most eye-catching new face on Madison Avenue in 1996 appeared in a Nike advertisement showing a little girl in a swing and the slogan "If you let me play." That face was Bell Gothic—a clean, streamlined typeface with elegantly curved edges and the suggestion of cyberspace. A similar typeface adorned a UPS campaign, as well as recent advertisements for Epson, Discover Card, Chrysler, Budweiser, Citibank, Samsung, and Compaq. Bell Gothic and its lean, simple look-alikes also counterbalance the visual chaos of many of the collagelike advertisements intended to simulate computer screens. Further, designers say that such typefaces suit the contradictory corporate image that Madison Avenue seems to be selling these days: strong yet sensitive, technologically sophisticated yet back to basics.

The search for banner ad technology and distinctive, unique typefaces reflects a larger concern for advertisers: how to grab attention when more

151

152 PRINCIPLES OF ADVERTISING: A GLOBAL PERSPECTIVE

ILLUSTRATION 10.1. Visual Interest Enhancement Using Varied Typefaces

Karey Welde and Paige Inglis designed this ad for *The Elkhart Truth* using interesting typefaces and reverses. Because color is expensive and not always reliable in newspaper advertising, ad designers occasionally use reverses to add visual interest. The black banners with the reversed type create a top and bottom frame that helps lead the eye to the dog's poignant face.

advertisements than ever are appearing on billboards, at sports arenas, on television, in magazines, and on the Internet. Although the spread of computer graphics has enlarged the art director's bag of visual tricks, the trend cannot last forever. Some designers already worry about simple-type burnout. Even the greatest message can be perceived as too trendy or overused if, as some graphic designers fear, type styles become as typecast as actors identified with just one part. Then, the purpose of creating a distinct, fresh identity could be defeated as typefaces such as Bell Gothic are used over and over again.[2]

Production is what happens between the time an ad idea is okayed and the time it finally appears in its proper medium. Production of print advertisements embraces the separate technical skills of typography, reproduction, and printing. Broadcast production is a different world from print production. You will need to deal with audiotapes, sound effects, recordings, film or videotape, camera operators, directors, performers, and editors. Producing advertisements for the Internet involves all the skills of Web site creation, as well as knowledge of typography, graphic design, and the latest multimedia software.

PRINT ADVERTISING PRODUCTION

Every print advertisement (both newspaper and magazine) represents the outcome of a highly complex process: reproduction of visuals, precise specification and placement of type, and the checking, approving, duplicating, and shipping of printing materials to newspapers and magazines in time to meet their deadlines. This production process requires good planning, and those involved must understand layout and design, typography, and desktop publishing.

Layout and Design

Once headlines and body copy have been written, copywriters prepare rough sketches to convey their concept to the art directors. These sketches rough out the desired placement of headlines, subheads, body copy, the company logo, and visuals. Basic advertising layouts include these types: Copy Heavy (ad space dominated by text), Frame (graphics or other images frame the copy), Grid (space divided by squares of equal size), Mondrian (space divided into boxes or sections, not necessarily of equal size), Picture Window (space largely occupied by art—a photo, drawing, or other image), and Type Specimen (space dominated by the headline, which substitutes for art). Subheads are often used to break up long copy. Italicized copy and reverses (white print on black) should be used sparingly.

Typography

Typography is the art of selecting and setting type. Because almost every advertisement has some reading matter, type has tremendous importance. Typefaces affect an advertisement's appearance, design, and readability (e.g., see Illustration 10.1). As illustrated by the opening vignette, art directors rely on stark, eye-catching typefaces to help break through the clutter of competing advertisements.

Type Families

All typefaces (or type fonts) come in families, just as human faces do. Many of them have proud family names, usually inherited from the original designer of the typeface, such as Bodoni, Gothic, Goudy. Certain families offer all kinds of variations. To present his client's product well, Steve Ohler, creative executive of McCann-Erickson, tapped graphic designer David Carson's talents to invent a new typeface for AT&T Lucent Technologies. The type font he used is a member of the Bell Gothic family, with angular wings on the edges of its ns and diagonal tops on its ts.[3] Most traditional types have small cross-strokes, called serifs, that appear on the arms of certain letters. Some of the more modern type designs do not have these tiny extensions on the ends of letters. Such typefaces are called sans serif. Each family offers capital letters and small letters, referred to by typographers as uppercase and lowercase, and may usually be italicized.

Typefaces

Families of type fall into one of several "faces." These include roman (Bookman, New Century Schoolbook, and Times), sans serif (Franklin Gothic, Futura 2, and Helvetica), square serif or egyptian (Aachen Bold), script (Calligrapher and Nuptial), and Pi faces (Woodtype Ornaments and Zapf Dingbats). Typographic noise is said to occur when type families of the same face are mixed in an advertisement. Sans serif types are best used for headlines and serifs for body copy, as the serif enhances readability. According to Tom Lichty in *Design Principles for Desktop Publishers*, the serif makes reading easier because "it cuts down the reflection of light from around the letter into the reader's eye (halation); it links the letters in a word and provides a horizontal guideline; and it helps distinguish one letter from another."[4] The word Illinois provides a classic example. Table 10.1 demonstrates this. Because of their superior readability, serif types are also preferred for copy that will be faxed, as individual letters lose clarity in faxing. Most of the type you see in textbooks, novels, newspaper stories, and magazine articles is roman type.

Points

Type is measured in points. There are 72 points to 1 inch vertically. Most families of type offer sizes from tiny 6 point to giant 72 point and

TABLE 10.1. Sample Typefaces

Illinois   Illinois   *Illinois*

On the left is the familiar roman typeface, New Century Schoolbook. In the center is the sans serif typeface Helvetica. On the right is a script typeface, Amazone. All are 18-point size. Notice the improved legibility and character recognition of the roman type.

Source: Adapted from Tom Lichty, *Design Principles for Desktop Publishers*, Second Edition, Belmont, CA: Wadsworth, 1994, p. 34.

larger. When fairly long text is being set in type, 10-point, 12-point, or 14-point size makes for good reading. Beyond 14 point are the display or headline sizes. The ad layout includes the amount of space between the headline, any subheads, and the text, as well as the actual length and width of the advertisement itself.

Pica Measurements

In typography, the unit of area measurement is called a pica. There are 12 points in a pica, 6 picas to an inch. A copy block might be termed 16 picas wide by 36 picas deep.

Desktop Publishing

Enormous technological progress has taken place in graphic arts due to the revolutionary application of computers and electronics. Today's graphic artist or designer can do much of the work previously performed by hand retouchers and pasteup artists on the computer. In fact, small IBM PC and Macintosh-based systems are ideal for desktop publishing—the process that enables individuals with desktop computers to "publish" print materials. In fact, most large circulation newspaper editors now scan photographs directly into computers, eliminating the time-consuming process of halftoning photos. Also, writers type their stories directly onto computer layouts, eliminating the need to typeset and paste up newspaper pages.

Desktop publishing software enables the user to word process text, to create or import and manipulate graphics and other art, and to bring these elements together in sophisticated layouts with a variety of page dimensions (for example, legal, tabloid, and magazine size), formats (including Compact Disc), and orientations (using the page Wide or Tall). A brochure that previously took days or even weeks to be typeset, halftoned, pasted-up, and printed via an outside vendor can now be produced in just a few hours with a desktop publishing program.

The two leading desktop publishing programs are Aldus PageMaker and Quark Xpress. PageMaker enjoys popularity with book and magazine publishers, as well as public relations professionals, because the program is geared toward the desktop publication of brochures, newsletters, and the double-page spreads often required for books and magazines. Quark Xpress is used by many newspaper publishers and advertising agencies because its text boxes allow for a wide range of layout possibilities and for easy layering of text and graphics. Adobe Photoshop and Adobe Illustrator are also used in advertising production. Whereas Photoshop is commonly used to manipulate photographs and other art, Adobe Illustrator allows artists to draw their own pictures and graphics. Adobe Illustrator's tools enable artists to draw, paint, and "mix" exactly the desired color from a full-spectrum color wheel.

BROADCAST ADVERTISING PRODUCTION

Broadcast media production (both television and radio commercials) is, indeed, a different world from print media production. Both print and broadcast production require skilled talent, of course. However, the production process is very different. The television or radio production team requires specialized training and technical skills. The advertising team, from the account executive to the copywriter, must understand the broadcast production process and how television and radio communicate advertising messages. They also must have command of basic broadcasting terminology.

Television Advertising Production

The purpose of television production is to translate the narrative of the written script into an audiovisual medium. Concepts for commercial television spots must employ the medium's predominantly visual storytelling vocabulary. It is important to think in terms of how the Big Idea can be communicated with an emphasis on visual image, with as few spoken words as possible. Television's distinctive feature is that it provides moving pictures. It is not a good choice for relaying instructions or for informational listings. For instance, retailers who wish to detail sale items and prices most often choose print advertising as the appropriate medium. Since the advent of MTV and the music video in the early 1980s, many television commercials have been conceived in this fast-paced style, which combines lightning-fast, rhythmic editing with a strong musical integration. The visual image and the sound and words of the music work together to tell a story or to create a mood or feeling that viewers come to associate with a certain brand or product. For instance, the Levi's 501 commercial described in Chapter 9 used a series of meaningful images to tell a story, but the lyrics of the background music contributed to the story as well, with the singer's plaintive plea, "Be my baby."

Advertisers also use computer-generated graphics to animate TV commercials for many products. Arm & Hammer baking soda's Boxman helped introduce PBS's new *Baking with Julia* in a fifteen-second segment that opened the show. In this animated TV commercial, Boxman beckons baking utensils to come on camera.[5] In a TV spot from Kellogg Company, produced by Leo Burnett USA, Chicago, the animated Malcolm the Toaster character is distressed that the extra two Pop-Tarts in the new Pop-Tarts package may make him blow a coil.[6] Computers can also digitally manipulate music and sound. Special effects entertain viewers and win advertising awards. However, no technique should so enthrall viewers that they pay more attention to it than to the product or the message.

The most talented production team cannot salvage an unworkable concept or a muddled script. Commercial television scripts must be written so that the production team recognizes the format and understands the creative team's vision of how the concept or story will unfold. To do this, copywriters must be familiar with broadcast format and the terminology. To keep the scripts as brief as possible, many terms are abbreviated.

Camera Shots

What do you want the viewer to see on the screen? It depends on the product and concept, or Big Idea. The shot that will best fulfill the need of the product and story should be specified. The following are some basic camera shots.

Extreme close-up (ECU). In an extreme close-up, the camera gets as close as possible to show part of a person's face or body or a close-up detail of a product. The ECU may be used for dramatic effect (for instance, an ECU of someone's wide-open eyes and raised eyebrows may convey the person's surprise), for persuasive appeal (an ECU of a model's lips may show the dewy, moist quality of a lipstick), or for demonstration purposes (an ECU might show a close-up of a blemish before and after the application of a concealing medication).

Close-up (CU). In a close-up, a face or product dominates the screen. The CU is often used to draw viewer attention to food products. For instance, the only image on the screen may be the advertiser's new fast food sandwich. Cosmetic and hair products also use close-up shots—for instance, a head shot of a model showing what the advertiser's shampoo has done for her hair. A close-up communicates the importance of an image or creates a sense of intimacy.

Medium shot (MS). In a medium shot, the camera shows a person from the waist up. In a two-shot, two people appear. Often the MS is used to feature spokespersons so that their facial expressions are visible yet the viewer can discern their appropriate roles by their attire. For example, Karl Malden appeared in American Express commercials for over twenty years wearing a businesslike suit and hat, which suggested his credibility to discuss financial matters. Michael Jordan might appear in his team jersey to bolster his credibility to advise on sports equipment. The basketball court may appear behind him in the shot.

Long shot (LS). Because a long shot may give the viewer a frame of reference as to location, it is often called an establishing shot. Although a person or persons may appear in an LS, it is the setting that fills the screen. Although long shots are used in commercials to establish place, such a shot is less effective on the small television screen than on theater screens where panoramic shots have great impact. Therefore, establishing shots in commercials are used sparingly. However, a long shot may also be used to show crowds of people, as in the 1998 Taco Bell spot that showed a dog on a balcony addressing the huge crowd below him in a takeoff on a famous scene from the 1997 movie *Evita*. A 1998 commercial for The Gap's line of khaki pants uses a long shot to show a chorus of couples dancing in their khakis. The long shot suggests an impersonal physical or emotional distance.

Pan. In a pan, the camera moves from a fixed point to follow a moving object or to give a panoramic effect. Sometimes a pan can be used to invoke a "searching" camera that takes in meaningful objects that shorthand the story. For instance, in the 1990 film *Dances with Wolves*, a pan of an uninhabited landscape contrasts the gruesome beginning footage that depicts the carnage of war. The natural beauty of the scenery panned provides what the film's hero, Lt. John Dunbar (Kevin Costner), has been seeking—a respite from the brutality of the "civilized" world.

Zoom. In a zoom-in, the camera moves in so that the image gets larger and appears to be closer; a zoom-out has the opposite effect.

In most cases, a television commercial will employ a variety of camera shots. For example, the storyboard for the "Stop Hate" public service announcement in Illustration 10.2 shows the variety of camera shots envisioned by the creative team and also shows how these visuals will correspond to specific parts of the script. "Stop Hate" begins with a medium shot (MS) of Jason Alexander, followed by a cutaway to a medium shot of a crowd of people. After the initial medium shots, the camera is to show a close-up of Alexander's face, followed by a long shot of a burning cross, an image dramatized by its contrast with the black night sky. Medium shots, such as those of Alexander, are typical of testimonial spots. However, the close-ups of his face allow viewers to get "inside" his thoughts and feelings. Every camera shot is chosen for meaningful communication of the television spot's message.

The Storyboard

Just as a print ad concept is conveyed to the art department by a rough sketch, the concept of a television commercial is conveyed to the production team through the storyboard. The storyboard displays inside a frame, shaped like a TV screen, a picture of each individual camera shot. The appropriate portions of the script appear beside or below these "screens" so that the producers of the spot can see how the visuals correspond to the script. Advertising agencies may also use the storyboard to sell the commercial to a client. It is difficult for people to visualize the concept from just a script, without the storyboard. Agencies identify the storyboard in the upper left corner with the name of the company or product, the running time, and the commercial's title. The storyboard for the ADL public service announcement (see Illustration 10.2) might have been identified with the following three lines:

> Client: ADL
> Time: :30 TV (film)
> Title: "Stop Hate"

Notice that, after the time designation, the storyboard identifies the medium on which the spot will air (TV, radio, or film). For instance, film is the medium for a movie trailer, an advertisement shown in the movie theater that previews an upcoming film. In parentheses, the medium in which the commercial will be produced is identified. The three basic types of production in television are live, film, and videotape, detailed as follows:

160 PRINCIPLES OF ADVERTISING: A GLOBAL PERSPECTIVE

ILLUSTRATION 10.2. Screening the Television Spot

ANTI-DEFAMATION LEAGUE
"STOP HATE" :30 PSA

JASON ALEXANDER: My wife and I have a son. Perfect little boy.

And suddenly I looked at the world in which he'd live,

and was terrified.

Hate crimes

don't just devastate their victims.

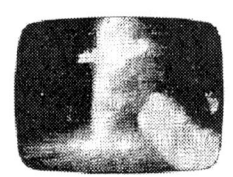

They reach past individuals

to strike at the very heart of communities.

The best response is to fight.

Unite under the banner of decency, equality, respect.

I want to give my son a better, wiser, more loving world than this one.

STOP HATE

ADL

(Localized for your area)

The storyboard allows the client and/or the production team to preview a television commercial. This storyboard shows the shots that will make up "Stop Hate," a public service announcement for the Anti-Defamation League (ADL). The spot's final screen may be used by a television station to localize for its viewing area. The station might add its own call letters or record a voice-over that identifies the station as the commercial's sponsor.

1. *Live production.* Live TV production is action as it takes place. Such a proposition is risky because anything can go wrong, and you only have one take. Most advertisers—local as well as national—prefer the assurance of videotape.
2. *Film production.* Since the first television commercial was made, film has been the most popular form for TV production. The majority of America's commercial film production for national advertisers is done in Hollywood and New York. Film has long enjoyed superiority over videotape in several areas, including resolution (clarity and distinction of the components of a picture) and depth of field. Especially in long shots, depth of field adds dimension to filmed images. Whereas the movie camera can capture distinctions between backgrounds, midgrounds, and foregrounds, the video camera produces a flat image. Also, prior to the introduction of the computer as an editing option, film could be more precisely edited. Film strips can be spliced on the exact frame intended, whereas video editing, which involves the copying of one tape onto another, is less precise. Picture quality is lost each time a tape is copied.
3. *Videotape production.* The most wondrous development in television production has been videotape because the tape does not have to be processed, as film does, and—after editing—is immediately ready to air. The majority of local television commercials are recorded on videotape because it is less expensive than film. However, increasing numbers of television commercials for national advertisers are also being videotaped. The reason for this is the computer. As already noted, the computer has made animation in commercials much easier and more sophisticated. Further, computer editing of videotape is faster and more precise than with previous editing equipment.

The Final Process

The client generally has to approve the commercial before production begins. The visuals and camera shots depicted on the storyboard submitted at this point in the production process are either drawn by hand or created with computer programs such as Adobe Illustrator. For the big national advertiser with a big agency and a big budget, the television production process begins the moment the storyboard is okayed by its management. At the same time that the idea is okayed, a tentative budget is approved. Once the advertiser approves a storyboard and budget, the production process begins. At the advertising agency, a producer is assigned. The producer (either in-house or freelance) is responsible for completing the job on schedule and within budget. The commercial is not produced in the agency. Instead, copies of the storyboard are first sent to several independent production companies selected by the agency producer.

Video production is always a team effort. Once an independent production company is hired, the next major step is the preproduction meeting. Here, the producer, director, set designer, talent director, and various other key people meet with the agency producer and copywriter to iron out many details that must be settled before going into the studio to shoot the film. The cast is selected, the set is built, and all other details are arranged. Only then can a television commercial be produced. Because the television producer is especially skilled in that medium, the producer may make changes in the script based on experience of what will and will not work in communicating messages on television. A "rough cut," the first edited version of the spot, is usually shown to the advertiser and/or the agency. Further changes can then be made so that the produced commercial meets everyone's satisfaction.

Editors are responsible for much of the art in film and television production. Basic editing terms include the following:

- *Cut.* This is a film-editing term referring to the actual cutting of a strip of film between frames to change quickly and cleanly from one shot to another. Since video actually involves the dubbing of a master tape onto another tape, video-editing equipment allows the editor to select a precise image on a videotape to make a "cut"—or to copy that image—within a frame or two of another shot.
- *Dissolve.* Instead of abruptly cutting from one shot to another, a dissolve allows one image to fade out before being replaced with another, which fades in. The two images may also be superimposed—appear simultaneously on the screen.
- *Super.* Instead of superimposing one picture on top of another, this term refers to placing graphics or text over a shot. For instance, the advertiser's name and logo may be "supered" (appear) over the final footage of a commercial shot.
- *Voice-over.* Off-screen narration creates a situation in which the viewer cannot see the person speaking but can hear a voice. The voice-over was made famous when Sir Laurence Olivier used the technique in his 1948 production of Shakespeare's *Hamlet* to suggest that Hamlet's "To be or not to be" soliloquy reflected his innermost, unspoken thoughts, eliminating the modern conception that a soliloquy is just talking out loud. In many commercials, an authoritative "announcer's" voice reads the tag line as the advertiser's name and/or logo appear at the end of the

spot. Sometimes the text of the tag line may also be supered on the screen so that the viewer both hears and reads the words.

The Role of the Computer in Production

The personal computer (PC) created a revolution in video production. Desktop video production employs a variety of computer-driven equipment. In addition to animation, which has already been discussed, the benefits of this type of equipment include image manipulation—accomplished by Digital Video Effects (DVE) systems. DVEs can rotate, flip, shrink, or expand an image. A flipped picture can give the impression that someone has just turned a page. Picture shrinkage allows for a smaller picture to be layered over another image that fills the screen; for instance, a graphic of a gun may appear in the corner of the screen, above the anchor's shoulder, while the anchor talks about a local shooting. The digital image is actually a series of stored numbers, so the computer changes the image through numerical recalculation.

Perhaps the most often used equipment in television commercial production is the character generator. Today's sophisticated character generator (CG) is used primarily to put text on the screen. Text is often placed on the lower third of the screen if it is to be juxtaposed with a picture. Many commercials conclude with the tag line and/or company or product name and logo generated in the center of the screen. The background on which the text appears may be just color or it may be a continuation of the commercial's final shot. It is not unusual for the last frames—with the tag line and identification of the company or product—to be voiced-over. For instance, an announcer might read the tag line aloud as it appears on the screen. Sometimes, for dramatic effect, the last frames appear with text only and no sound.

Radio Advertising Production

Once the concept (Big Idea) for a radio commercial has been decided and the spot has been scripted, the creative team must be certain that the commercial's producers will understand what they want. The more specific the script is regarding SFX (sound effects), music, and distinctions between voices as well as tones of voice, the more likely the commercial will be produced as it was conceived. However, as with television production, flexibility can be a virtue—sometimes changes made in production work better than the original script would have and create a more effective or aesthetic commercial. Also, as is customary with television production, the production team works with the company's or agency's creative team. Script changes usually must be approved and the final product reviewed by the advertiser and/or its agency.

Radio commercials are produced in one of two ways. They are either taped and duplicated for distribution, or they are recorded live. The more common form is the taped radio commercial. National radio commercials are produced by an advertising agency, and duplicate copies of the tape are distributed to local stations around the country. Commercials for local advertisers might be produced by local stations, with the station's staff providing the creative and production expertise. The recording is done in-house using the radio station's studio. Those involved in radio production should be familiar with the following basic terminology:

- *Music In, Music Out, and Fade Under.* Some radio spots begin with music (in) that ends (out) when an actor begins to speak. The volume of the music may also be gradually decreased (fade) so that the music can be heard faintly under the speaker's voice.
- *Up, Down.* Volume may be increased (up) or decreased (down).
- *SFX.* The use of sound effects (abbreviated SFX) is common in radio commercial spots; for instance, a spot that begins with children coming home from school may be enhanced by the sound of hurried feet hitting the pavement and a door slam.
- *Segue.* This term refers to a musical or verbal transition to bridge sections of a commercial.

With live radio advertising, a typewritten script is read by whichever regular station announcer is on duty. The inclusion of sound effects, music, or additional speaking parts would require studio production. The live script is advantageous to the local retailer who must get a message on the air in a matter of hours. However, as with live television, the live radio spot is risky due to the possibility of human error. Occasionally, the copywriter leaves five seconds open at the end of the script so that the announcer can add a live tag line to the taped commercial. Such copy points as sale prices and dates can be easily updated without having to produce a completely new audiotape.

Radio production depends upon the talent of the performers, as well as on effective sound effects and music that grabs attention, enhances the mood or story, or otherwise contributes to conveying the Big Idea. Since generally only national advertisers have sufficient budget to pay royalty fees for the use of popular music and artists, local radio stations buy rights to generic music tracks to provide inexpensive alternatives. Also, local radio announcers often perform in commercial spots, which eliminates the need to pay for outside professional talent and helps local advertisers cut costs. Some radio station personnel are adept at doing voice impersonations of celebrities and politicians. Such spots can gain attention and appeal to the listener's sense of humor.

Some local advertisers like to perform in their own spots. Because the voice of a "real" person at the company or organization can personalize the spot for a local audience, this technique can work—but only when the person has a background in acting or some natural talent. The difficulty for the production team arises when the company's representative lacks this talent and still insists on doing the spot: sometimes a way must be found to tell a client that he or she cannot act, and that is a treacherous situation.

INTERNET ADVERTISING PRODUCTION

Internet advertising differs from print and broadcast in its ability to reach a narrowly defined niche audience, to enable immediate interaction between the consumer and the advertiser, and to link the consumer to other product or company information. Internet advertising resembles print and broadcast advertising in its purpose—to market goods, services, and images with persuasive messages. Copywriters work with graphic designers to develop the concept for the Internet advertisement. Ads may be of any length, from banner ads to deep, multiple-page advertisements. Banner ads are the primary advertising method used on the Internet. They generally span the width of a page and are an inch or so deep. Typically, they feature bold or decorative headlines, a graphic image, and a link to further information with a "Click Here" button.

The nature of the Internet (which makes frequent updates possible) and the demands of the Internet (browsers expect current information) make it an advertising medium in a class of its own. Products, prices, and promotional messages can be changed as often as circumstances dictate. A growing number of Web design services have formed to meet the needs of this new advertising medium. Such companies provide monthly activity reports to give the advertiser an accurate account of traffic on the site and will make regular changes after the site has "gone live." For example, Shamrock Net Design is a full-service interactive communications consulting firm that specializes in interactive marketing and Web site design. Omnicom, U S Web, and iXL in Atlanta are among the "aggressive acquirers" of an expanding number of interactive agencies.[7]

In cyberspace, a Web site must compete with hundreds of thousands of other sites, many of which link visitors to still more channels (see Illustrations 10.3 and 10.4 for one company's interrelated Web site pages). Therefore, the Internet designer and producer face immense challenges. Those creating Internet Web sites and advertisements should keep in mind the guidelines detailed in Table 10.2.

TABLE 10.2. Guidelines for Web Site Creation

1. A Web site should serve as a forum for the exchange of ideas rather than as a corporate brochure.
2. Content should be organized in a thoughtful, accessible manner with creative visual design and navigational clarity.
3. Encourage interaction, offering the customer an outlet for comment, question, or complaint, as well as a way to immediately receive additional information.
4. The Web site should function in the same role as a trade show exhibit, enhancing corporate image, generating leads, and enabling direct sales through online ordering.
5. Register the Web site on all major search engines (such as Yahoo and Alta Vista). Work to have your site recognized with a "What's Cool" or "What's Hot" rating by one of the major search engines. These ratings will guarantee that the engines pull your site up first and increase traffic to your site dramatically.
6. Draw attention to your site by holding contests and giveaways.
7. Encourage the advertiser to promote the URL (Web address) of the site as part of the company's existing corporate communications strategy, placing the URL on letterheads, business cards, press releases, print and broadcast advertising, envelopes, and mailing labels. This increases public awareness of the site and its advertising messages.
8. Engage in cooperative advertising with another company. The Internet is built on cooperation, and it rewards companies that leverage off one another's efforts.

Source: Adapted from Shamrock Net Design's Web site, http://www.ShamrockNetDesign.com

Advertising production on the Internet follows the same process as print and broadcast advertising—the advertising concept results from research, planning, and creative collaboration. It has been said that interactive advertising is one part creativity, one part technology, and one part business.[8] The graphic designer, programmer, and copywriter often work together to produce the Internet advertisement. Web producers and the creative teams must have technical skills and a knowledge of Internet applications. Most production is done in HTML (Hyper Text Markup Language), which enables the hypertext links to be embedded in the docu-

ILLUSTRATION 10.3. Creative Concepts and Tag Lines

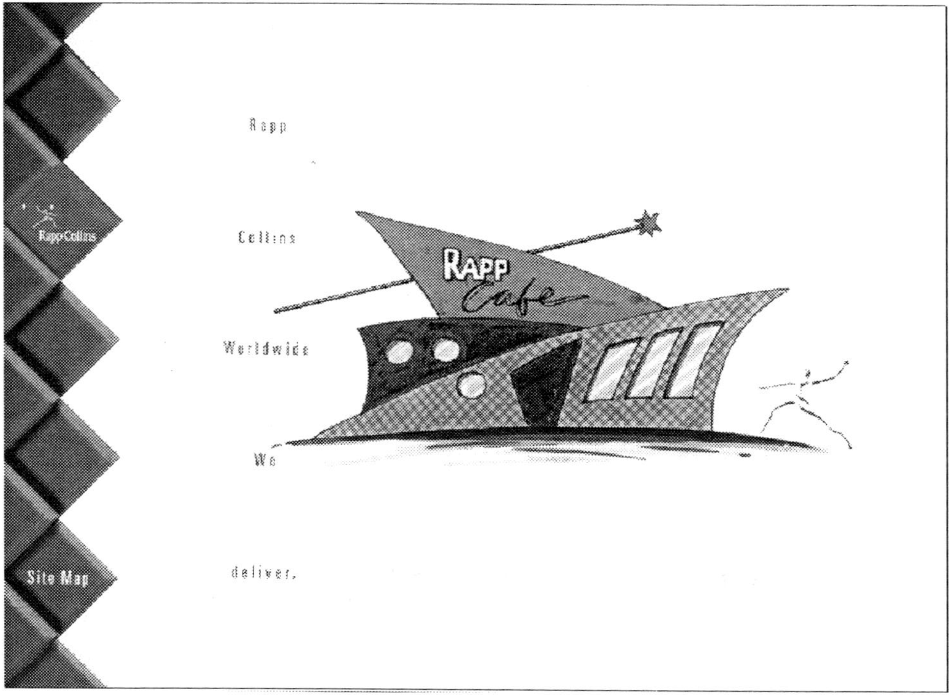

The Rapp Collins Worldwide Site Map sets up the creative concept of the diner with the Rapp Cafe image and the tag line, "We deliver."

ILLUSTRATION 10.4. Visually Exciting Advertising

Following up on the Cafe idea, this Rapp Collins Worldwide Web site page offers visually exciting, colorful click options.

168

ment. FTP (File Transfer Protocol) uploads files from a computer to the Internet—Fetch is a common FTP application. Web servers host or maintain the site once it is "live."

SUMMARY

Production is what happens between the time an idea is okayed and the time it finally appears in its proper medium. Print, broadcast, and Internet production all have some common characteristics: they rely on the creative team's prior research, planning, and scripting of the advertising concept. It is important for the creative team to convey the concept envisioned to the production team in the expected format and as descriptively as possible. In all cases, the production team generally works with members of the creative team to ensure that the advertisement, as it was conceived, has actually been produced. This is where similarities end. Print, broadcast, and Internet production—because they involve very different channels of communication—employ distinctly different processes. Each has its own specific terminology and format. Because advertisers today often employ multiple media channels to communicate their advertising messages, those who are responsible for the strategic or creative side of advertising need to have a basic understanding of the terminology and processes used in the new arena of print, broadcast, and Internet production.

* * *

THE GLOBAL PERSPECTIVE: DEVELOPING THE BIG IDEA ABROAD

The *Seinfeld* television show began with a whimper in 1989, but it went out with a ratings bang in 1998 (and, even then, the final episode was bemoaned by fans and critics alike as less than laughable). Except for urbanites, American television viewers initially did not find the "show about nothing" very funny. But as the show persisted and the 1990s progressed, a cross-section of the American public began to identify with the show's depiction of the everyday frustrations of living in a culture fraught with indifference.

Stand-up comics such as Jerry Seinfeld are well aware that comedy is difficult to pull off. If the punchline does not resonate with the audience, the whole business falls flat. Nevertheless, as the *Seinfeld* show demonstrates, if humor does work, the payoff can be big. When it showed fifty national print and television advertising campaigns to 11,000 U.S. adults, *USA Today* discovered that the top choices for likability and effectiveness had one common characteristic: they were funny.[a]

Although humorous appeals may be effective in the United States, many consumers in other countries do not respond as favorably to them.[b] The creative team must have a clear idea of the characteristics of the audience that will receive the message. In this sense, the principles of creating effective advertising are the same as in the domestic marketplace, for example, consider that *Seinfeld* was most popular with U.S. *urban* audiences.

The advertiser must determine what foreign consumers are actually buying—that is, determine the customers' needs, motivations, and attitudes. Then the Big Idea can be developed, and specific appeals and execution styles chosen. Market research conducted by Grey International in London established that Procter & Gamble's Pantene shampoo's perceived benefit of shiny, healthy hair had universal appeal. It was then able to develop a global advertising campaign that had as much impact on women in Japan and China as it had on women in Scandinavia.[c]

Let's face it. Americans laughed at the idea of an "atomic wedgie" (defined in *The Entertainment Weekly Seinfeld Companion* as "Underwear torture in which the waistband is stretched up over the victim's head—George suffered it in high-school gym class").[d] But, would such a joke resonate with those who live in countries where there may be no gym class, and perhaps not even a public school? Could the idea of a "wedgie" be offensive in certain cultures?

[a] Dottie Enrico, "Humorous Touch Resonates with Consumers," *USA Today*, May 13, 1996, p. B3.
[b] Dana L. Alden, Wayne D. Hoyer, and Chol Lee, "Identifying Global and Culture-Specific Dimensions of Humor in Advertising: A Multinational Analysis." *Journal of Marketing,* Vol. 57, April 1993, pp. 64-75.
[c] Rachel Kaplan, "Ad Agencies Take on the World," *International Management,* April 1994, pp. 50-52.
[d] Bruce Fretts, *The Entertainment Weekly Seinfeld Companion,* New York: Time Warner Books, 1993, p. 21.

* * *

ETHICS TRACK: CULTURE JAM

A rearranged Benetton ad shows a man with a mouthful of green paper money. It resembles a Benetton ad, but Benetton had nothing to do with it. Although Benetton has tried to portray a "green" (environmentally friendly) image, this ad suggests that the company consumes resources for money just like everyone else. The tag line reads, "THE TRUE COLORS OF BENETTON."

Sometimes the Big Idea can come back to haunt you. At least, the international consumer movement known as Culture Jam hopes it will.

These rearranged, irreverent ads are created by a sophisticated group determined to undermine the power of advertising messages and icons. Concerns about planetary resources and rising global consumerism have led these grassroots critics to produce "culture jam"—ads with visuals and messages rearranged to parody a widely recognized ad. Many of these ads have appeared in the nine-year-old Canadian quarterly *Adbusters*, which now reaches 30,000 subscribers, most of them in the United States.

Source: Mary Kuntz, "Is Nothing Sacred?" *Business Week*, May 18, 1998, p. 130.

Lee & Johnson
:60 Spot
"Vicki's Choice: Healthy Challenges"

7:55 a.m. Monday—I arrive at LeSEA Broadcasting and check my e-mail. I find a message from the production manager saying that I have a :30 spot that needs to be shot and edited by 5 p.m. today for Making Healthy Choices Angle Pack. Quite an unrealistic goal, but that's the way it mostly happens around here.

8:10 a.m.—I walk down the hallway to see if Terri or Krista is available to talk about what the most important copy points are so that I can write the script. After that, I sit at my desk and quickly try to write so that I can have the copy approved before the production coordinator leaves for the day.

8:57 a.m.—The copy for the spot is approved. I have decided on a spot featuring children eating unhealthy food given to them by their mom. It's a great script. There is only one problem: I have to come up with a location, children, and a mom so I can start shooting by 11 a.m.

9:32 a.m.—I am on the phone with the engineer's wife asking if she can pick up some lunch and meet me at her mother-in-law's with her kids so we can shoot the spot. She agrees.

9:35-11:00 a.m.—I build the graphic in Adobe Photoshop that will be used to tag the spot at the end. It has the name of the pack, the contents, and price. I have developed a graphic for Making Healthy Choice already, so I stay with the same format, knock out the graphic, and save it to disc to be transferred into the Avid. I also drop the script off to radio so that I can have the voice-over done when I get back.

10:45 a.m.—I pack up a camera, tripod, lights, microphones (just in case), batteries for the camera, a beta tape, and a card for the white balance.

11:10 a.m.—After laying bars and tone and doing a white balance, I begin shooting. I start with product shots. I always want to have more footage than I actually need, so I shoot a minimum of thirty minutes for a :30 spot.

12:45 p.m.—I head back to the station to start editing.

1:00 p.m.—I take my lunch into the Avid suite and begin to digitize the material. If the shot is :15 long, it takes :15 to enter into the computer. The nonlinear editing system allows me to go back and make corrections in the middle of a shot without having to re-create the beginning or end again. While all this is going on, I pick up the script from audio, dub the voice-over from the reel to a beta tape, and pick out background music.

2:08 p.m.—I have digitized enough footage, the music, and the script. I am now ready to put the sequence together. Most people think that a :30 spot takes :30 to edit. That's a misconception! From my experience, a :30

spot takes about two hours to put together, providing there are no major changes.

3:54 p.m.—I have completed the spot with enough time to get it to Master Control so they can log it and get it on air. I call Terri down to see if she can give me the final approval so I can dub it to tape.

4:29 p.m.—Terri finally comes down and says that the graphic is wrong. I run to the computer, rebuild the piece, retransfer the graphic, and have the spot reapproved.

4:59 p.m.—Terri is satisfied with the spot. I dump it to a recycled beta tape and drop it off at Master Control.

5:02 p.m.—I head upstairs to my desk to check my voice mail, and then start to fill out the paperwork on the spot that I've just completed.

5:24 p.m.—It's too late for me to start working on another spot that needs to be done Wednesday, so I decide to call it a day and begin the whole process tomorrow. However, I remind myself why I went into television in the first place: the excitement and the challenge of being creative on the fly.

Learn the Term

Avid System—A nonlinear, computer-based editing system

Bars and tone—Set machine recording and playback levels. Bars set video levels at the proper hue, brightness, and black levels. Tone helps the machine calibrate audio levels at zero.

Beta tape—Beta cameras and beta tapes are used in television production in preference to VHS, which is the prevailing type used by home video producers. Beta utilizes half-inch oxide tapes to record audio and video.

Digitize—The term refers to the transformation of analog video into digital. Tape is shot in analog in order to edit the video, then converted to digital.

Master Control—This department at a television station plays videotaped programs and commercials for on-air viewing.

White Balance—The act of telling the camera what is white by placing a white card in front of the lens. This allows all the other colors to be true since all colors make white.

Vicki Palk
Associate Producer/Editor
LeSEA Broadcasting
South Bend, Indiana

Chapter 11

Advertising Media Planning and Selection

Hoping to beat back rivals and change its image, Motorola launched a $100 million-plus corporate image campaign in April 1998. Splashy television and print ads carried the new corporate slogan: "Wings." Motorola's traditional bat wing symbol grows wings and flies around like a bat at the end of a television commercial that aired in a "roadblock" of ad time (a new ad-buying tactic) on Sunday, April 18, at 9 p.m. The :60 spot appeared simultaneously on over a dozen channels, including Fox (during the highly rated *X-Files*), ABC, NBC, and MTV. In the same week, print ads appeared in *Fortune, Time, People, Entertainment Weekly,* and *Sports Illustrated* magazines.[1] As corporations posture to create new images for the next century, advertising spending is expected to continue its current upward trend. McCann Erickson's Robert Coen, a fifty-year forecast veteran, predicted that U.S. advertising spending would reach a record $200.3 billion in 1998, up 6.8 percent from 1997.[2]

However, the money might be better earmarked for free product samples and cents-off coupons. A study by Yankelovich Partners and Gannett's *USA Weekend* magazine of 1,000 consumers nationwide shows that only 25 percent of those questioned said that a television advertisement would induce them to try a new product or brand. Only 15 percent said a newspaper advertisement would entice them to buy, and 13 percent said a magazine advertisement would influence them. Advertisements in supermarkets would entice only 15 percent of those questioned. Also, advertisers who shell out a small fortune to hire celebrity endorsers will be dismayed to learn that only 3 percent of those questioned said a star would sway them to try a new product. More consumers are buying in new ways: 80 percent have ordered from a catalog, 59 percent have used an advertisement to purchase by mail or telephone, 44 percent have mailed in a coupon from an advertisement, and 27 percent have ordered a product seen in an infomercial.[3]

Advertisers spend tremendous amounts of money on advertising media. These amounts have grown rapidly during the past two decades (see Table 11.1). To derive maximum results from media expenditures, marketers must

ILLUSTRATION 11.1. Global Image

If this is your idea of geographic exploration...

It's time to call **TravelZone.**

We travel to cities across the world for less than you thought possible.

Call us at 1-800-TRAVELZ or visit our website at www.travelzone.org

Paula Winicur's design uses a picture window format, one of the basic print ad layouts, for a travel advertisement. Her generous use of white space frames the globe, which dominates the page. The ad also refers the consumer to an 800 number and Web site address, increasing the number of media choices.

TABLE 11.1. Advertising Spending Increases

Largest 1998 U.S. Advertising Spending Increase by Product Category (based on first-quarter 1998 figures)	
Automobile expenditures	+17%
Toiletries and cosmetics	+14%
Largest 1998 U.S. Advertising Spending Increases by Medium (based on forecaster predictions)	
Cable TV expenditures	+13.0%
Newspaper and radio	+7.5%
Magazine and network TV	+ 5.5%

Source: Information adapted from "Ad Spending Increases," *USA Today,* June 24, 1998, p. 6B.

develop effective media plans. Some marketers believe that traditional media, such as television, newspapers, magazines, and radio, are not as effective in producing sales as they were in the past because markets rapidly change and advertisers must be much more selective in reaching the product's best prospects. To use media effectively, it is important to understand not only the media but also how best to plan for and buy media space or time. Media planners are challenged now, more than ever, to choose the best media to reach increasingly segmented consumers. As Integrated Marketing Communication theory gains dominance in the corporate world, marketers have come to realize how crucial it is to use all available channels of communication, both traditional and nontraditional, to reach both mass markets and individual consumers (e.g., see Illustration 11.1).

MEDIA PLANNING

Media planning is the process of directing the advertising message to the target audience at the appropriate time and place, using the appropriate channel. Media planners must consider the following:

- What audiences do we want to reach?
- When and where do we want to reach them?
- How many people should we reach?
- How often do we need to reach them?
- What will it cost to reach them?

When all questions have been asked, answered, and decisions made, the recommendations and rationales are organized into a written document called a media plan. When approved by the advertiser, the plan becomes a blueprint for the selection and use of media. Once the advertiser has approved the plan, it also serves as a guide for actually purchasing the media.

Media planning involves the coordination of three levels of strategy formulations: marketing strategy, advertising strategy, and media strategy. The overall marketing strategy provides the impetus and direction for the choice of both advertising and media strategies. The media strategy consists of four sets of interrelated activities: (1) selecting the target audience, (2) specifying media objectives, (3) selecting media and vehicles, and (4) buying media.

Selecting the Target Audience

Successful media strategy requires that the target audience be clearly pinpointed. Because people who have common characteristics tend to act in similar ways, advertisers like to break down the population into consumer segments, groups of potential buyers with key similarities. This process of segmentation allows advertisers to design messages specifically for the people who are most likely to buy their product. The consumer segments considered the best prospects for a product or service are called target groups. Advertising messages are directed to these potential buyers.

Specifying Media Objectives

A firm usually has certain organizational objectives that shape the marketing objectives. The advertising objectives must then work with the higher-level marketing objectives, and media objectives must contribute to the advertising objectives. Five objectives are fundamental to media planning: reach, frequency, weight, continuity, and cost.

Reach. What proportion of the target audience must see, read, or hear the advertising message during a specific period (e.g., one month)? Reach is a measure of how many different members (or what percentage) of the target audience is exposed at least once in a given period (usually four weeks) to the advertiser's message.

Frequency. How often should the target audience be exposed to the advertisement during this period (e.g., at least two times a week)? Frequency measures the average number of times people in the target audience are exposed to—see, read, or hear—the advertiser's message during a given period.

Weight. How much total advertising is necessary during a particular period to accomplish the reach and frequency objectives? Message weight is the size of combined target audiences reached by the advertiser's message in a single media plan.

Message weight is calculated by adding all the reach numbers for each ad in the plan, ignoring any overlap or duplication. Message weight can be expressed in terms of gross impressions or gross rating points (GRPs). Impression represents one person's opportunity to be exposed to a program, newspaper, magazine, or outdoor location. Impressions measure the size of the audience either for one media vehicle (one insertion in *Time* magazine) or for a combination of vehicles (*Time* and *Business Week*, for example) as estimated by media research. In practice, media planners discuss gross impressions—the sum of the audiences of all the media vehicles used in a certain time spot when dealing with multiple vehicles in a schedule. The summary figure is called "gross" because the media planner has made no attempt to calculate how many different people have viewed each show. Gross values simply refer to the number of people viewing, regardless of whether each viewer saw one, two, or all of the TV shows.

The numbers for gross impressions for mass media such as network television can become very large. For convenience, media planners sometimes express message weight in terms of GRPs, which are the sum of the ratings of all programs in the television schedule; in the context of one media plan (TV, for example), GRPs measure the total target audience exposed to all the vehicles in that plan. One percent of the target audience is equivalent to one rating point. To calculate GRPs for the entire media plan, multiply the proportion of the target audience reached by the frequency (GRP = R × F).

Continuity. How should the advertising budget be allocated over time? Continuity involves the matter of how advertising is allocated during the course of an advertising campaign. Advertisers have three general alternatives related to allocating the budget over the course of the campaign: continuous, pulsing, and flighting schedules. In a continuous advertising schedule, a relatively equal amount of advertisement dollars is invested throughout the campaign. In a pulsing advertising schedule, some advertising is used during every period of the campaign, but the amount of advertising varies considerably from period to period. In a flighting advertising schedule, the advertiser varies expenditures throughout the campaign and allocates zero expenditures in some months.

Cost. What is the least expensive way to accomplish the other objectives? Media planners must resolve cost issues as they attempt to allocate the advertising budget in a cost-efficient manner, while still satisfying other objectives. One of the most important and universally used indicators of media efficiency is the cost-per-thousand criterion (abbreviated CPM, with the M representing the Roman number for 1,000). The basic formula for CPM is

$$\text{Cost per thousand} = \frac{\text{cost of media unit} \times 1000}{\text{number of total contacts}}$$

The term contacts is used here in a general sense to include any type of advertising audience (television viewers, radio listeners, magazine or newspaper readers, etc.). To illustrate how CPM is calculated, consider the following situation: According to A. C. Nielsen TV ratings on a given week, NBC's top-rated *ER* commanded a rating of 22.6. (Note that a rating point is equal to 970,000 U.S. TV households; the total U.S. TV households were 97 million then.) The broadcast prime-time thirty-second spot TV ad rate for *ER* is $500,000. Therefore,

$$\text{CPM} = \frac{\$500{,}000 \times 1000}{97{,}000{,}000 \times 22.6\%} = \$22.81$$

The CPM statistics are useful for comparing the cost efficiency of reaching your target audience through various media. They must be used cautiously, however. These cost comparisons do not take into account variations in media audience, comparability across different media, and creative execution. CPM can be a handy yardstick to support media selection and a good way to measure cost, but it does not measure the effectiveness of an advertisement in certain media.[4]

Selecting Media and Vehicles

As an element of media strategy, the media are the channels of communication that carry messages from the advertiser to the audience. Media organizations sell space (in print media) and time (in broadcast media). The most frequently used advertising media are television, newspapers, magazines, radio, outdoor and transit, and direct response, although the Internet is becoming a contender.

Vehicles are the specific broadcast programs (e.g., the television program *ER*) or print choices (e.g., *Time* magazine) in which advertisements are placed. Each medium and each vehicle has a set of unique characteristics and virtues. Advertisers attempt to select those media and vehicles whose characteristics are most compatible with the advertised brand in reaching the target audience and conveying the intended message.

The study mentioned in the opening vignette divides U.S. consumers into five different groups: networkers, interfacers, retroactives, neo-bytes, and disconnecteds. People communicate back or react to advertisements in different ways. For example, networkers, about 23 percent of the population, are the heaviest users of print media. They do their own research rather than buying products simply out of brand loyalty. Diet colas and 100 percent fruit juices are the beverages of choice of networkers. Interfacers, 15 percent of consumers, prefer face-to-face contact when it comes to shopping. They are the most ethnically diverse segment, with four in ten being non-Caucasian. Interfacers are heavy users of television, and they like to be first with the latest trend. Their preferred beverage is regular cola.[5]

An advertiser might use only one medium (e.g., television) to reach the target audience when it is believed that this concentration will provide special impact. On the other hand, an advertiser might reach the target audience by building a media mix of two or more media (e.g., television and magazine). A media mix makes sense when a single medium will not reach the target audience in sufficient numbers or with sufficient impact to achieve media objectives (e.g., product awareness).

For instance, the Colgate-Palmolive Company introduced its Colgate Baking Soda & Peroxide toothpaste with a $32 million multimedia marketing budget. The campaign included television spots, ads in free-standing inserts (FSIs) in newspapers, direct mailings, samples distributed through dentists' offices, and trial-size displays in retail store aisles.[6]

Commercial time on network television has become amazingly expensive. Fox network sold :30 spots during the 1998 Super Bowl for a record $1.2 million.[7] Approximate costs for other prime-time shows in January 1998 are shown in Table 11.2.

TABLE 11.2. Costs for :30 Spots on Prime-Time Shows—January 1998

Show	Network	Approximate Cost
ER	NBC	$490,000
Spin City	ABC	350,000
Dateline	NBC	100,000
High Incident	ABC	60,000
Diagnosis Murder	CBS	45,000

Source: "USA Today Snapshots," *USA Today,* January 22, 1998, p. B1.

MEDIA BUYING

The eventual selection of a medium and specific media vehicles depends on the availability of media research and information supplied to media planners and buyers on the size and profile of the audience and the media costs for space or time. Buying and selling media is not the straightforward process it once was. There are many more media and vehicles to choose from these days. Moreover, to get a bigger share of the advertiser's budget, larger print and broadcast media companies now bundle the various stations, publications, or properties they own and offer them together as a packaged incentive.

Media buying can be a lucrative part of an advertising agency's business. For instance, Leo Burnett's media-buying division, StarCom, took in over $800 million in 1997, including important new media assignments from Procter & Gamble, Miller Brewing, the Gap, and Walgreens. StarCom was given responsibility for all consumer print planning and buying for P&G's more than 100 brands.[7] This much-needed business came to the agency at the time when it had laid off seventy-four people, including 4 percent of its creative staff.

Today, many media planners and buyers are hired right out of college and given entry-level salaries for work that requires a great deal of responsibility and long hours. Media departments at agencies constitute starting points for advertising careers. Because these twenty-somethings control millions of ad dollars in placements, their power is often disproportionate to their salaries. Some media executives complain that young planners and buyers have no understanding of older targets and no interest in media channels that specifically target affluent baby boomers—they are uninterested in publications they see as targeting their parents. Agencies do make an effort to educate young planners and buyers about the "different targets and demographics so that they'll be aware of media for older audiences."[8] Nevertheless, clients who hope to target an aging population may prefer to work with media department personnel who have industry experience and an understanding of that market's needs—and it is the client who pays the bill.

If media buying ever was predictable, it certainly is not anymore. NBC decided to charge all advertisers the same amount for the coveted ad spots on the *Seinfeld* series finale in May 1998. Advertising agency executives theorized that since NBC's asking price was $2 million per spot and there was no rating guarantee for the final episode, NBC would then be free to drop the asking price if all twenty of the available 30-second spots were not purchased.[9] Marketers have traditionally purchased network advertising during the so-called "up-front" period in May when fall schedules are announced. However, in May 1998, networks sought to dramatically increase rates (for instance, NBC asked at least $650,000, a 16 percent increase over 1997, for a 30-second spot on its top-rated *ER*, even though its star, George Clooney, would be departing from the show). With *Seinfeld* and Clooney out of NBC's golden Thursday night lineup, viewership is down (household viewing shares for ABC, CBS, NBC, and Fox fell from 68 percent in 1992 to 1993 to 59 percent in 1996 to 1997), program costs soaring, and cable channels (whose viewing shares increased from 24 percent to 34 percent over one season) offering serious competition with their own hit shows, media buyers went into a state of malaise.[10]

Internet ad buys have added to the confusion. Disagreement exists over whether the Internet has audience units consistent with those associated with television, radio, and magazines. The argument has been made that the cost per 1,000 banner ad impressions on a high-tech Web site compares favorably with the cost of 1,000 impressions for a magazine ad.[11] In that case, traditional concepts of reach and frequency may be appropriate in selecting Web site media schedules. However, without an "average" audience, Internet ad buyers cannot measure in terms of a day, week, or month; instead, they tend to purchase "hits" (clicks or page exposures). Whether reach and frequency can be discussed in traditional ways is not likely to be quickly resolved. Two different techniques are currently used to measure Internet reach and frequency: a consumer-centric approach and a site-centric measurement:

- *Consumer-centric approach.* This measurement uses a PC meter to determine the length of time a user has spent on various activities. The measure of interactivity is referred to as the "click-through."[12]
- *Site-centric measurement.* This approach involves analysis of server activity log files. Since the vehicle is the unit of measurement in traditional media, with the advertising cost based on potential audience delivery capabilities of the vehicle, John D. Leckenby and Jongpil Hong believe that "the site would seem to be a compatible object of measurement."[13] A disadvantage of this method is that measurements taken at the Web site track "hits," but do not record movement back to pages previously viewed.

Current data suggest that reach/frequency models developed for traditional media can be applied to the Internet. The biggest issue that remains to be resolved is how accurate the "old methods" will be in the "new media environment."[14] In her study of both consumer-centric and site-centric methods, Leslie Wood of Leslie Wood Research, Incorporated, did not expect to discover that, although total sites "deliver a lot of frequency, segments of sites, particularly smaller segments, deliver mostly reach."[15] But that is exactly what she found. Another key finding she reports is the "continued steep growth of reach. Television reach curves tend to flatten out and have diminishing returns at the upper levels of GRPs."[15] Wood believes this lack of flattening may be explained by continued Internet growth and the continuous introduction of new visitors.

The use of computers has made the media planner's job easier. However, even with computer technology, it is still up to the media planner to know the product, the market, and the media and to make the call. Computers help in the planning process, but—with subjective judgment now such a crucial part of the process—they cannot take the place of people.

SUMMARY

The tenets of Integrated Marketing Communication have affected media planning: the marketer must now, more than ever, choose the right media to reach increasingly segmented consumers. That challenge is compounded by the proliferation of media from which to choose today. To develop an effective media strategy, media planners must select and understand the target audience, establish media objectives, choose the right medium (or media) and vehicle(s), and buy media and construct media schedules. The final step is to prepare and implement the media plan.

* * *

THE GLOBAL PERSPECTIVE:
THE OPTIMIZER AND THE BRITISH INVASION

Producers of original American plays have complained for over two decades about the British invasion of Broadway. Andrew Lloyd Webber's *Cats* slinked onto the scene in the early 1980s, and the parade of British imports has not stopped since. However, one of the latest British imports in the business world, the "optimizer," received red-carpet treatment from U.S. media buyers and planners in 1997.

European users had found the optimizer helpful, and representatives of Super Midas and X*pert were "quite modest" about their software's advantages and disadvantages.[a] However, that did not repress America's "optimizermania." Optimizer has become an industry buzzword. Procter & Gamble has gone so far as to require "agencies competing for its billion-dollar media buying assignment to include optimizing systems in their proposals."[b]

Europeans have used optimizers, "computer programs that use algorithms to evaluate schedules" and compare alternatives, for a number of years.[b] The programs assist media buyers and planners in identifying the best media and the schedule that "maximizes efficient reach" to better meet clients' objectives at the best price.

In his *Advertising Age* article, Neil Braun cautions that an optimizer program can help implement strategies, "but it cannot design a strategy for you." Still needed is a media planner with "a Midas touch."

[a] Neil Braun, "There's No Magic in TV's Optimizers," *Advertising Age,* May 11, 1998, p. 36.
[b] "Optimizers and Syndication," *Advertising Age,* April 27, 1998, p. A22.

* * *

ETHICS TRACK: GREEN MARKETING

"Save the whales" and "Save the trees" have become familiar promotional slogans. Environmental groups, including members of Europe's Green Party and international members of such organizations as World Wildlife Federation and Greenpeace, are making their voices heard through sophisticated global advertising and public relations campaigns.

Earth Day, celebrated in the United States in April, has become an increasingly well-observed event over the past couple decades. Activities include in-school education programs and projects; community awareness campaigns, demonstrations, and clean-up efforts; and media coverage of these events. Reversing the effects of years of damage to natural resources—the cutting down of forests, the endangerment of the species that live there, dumping of waste products into rivers and streams, industrial pollution of the air, and so forth—is now a higher priority with the American public than ever before. Americans are concerned not only about environmental problems in the United States but also about the devastation of the Brazilian rainforests, the poisoning of lands in countries previously occupied by the Soviet Union, and the loss of plant and animal life in the oceans and seas.

With the "greening" of America, many businesses today are trying to promote their positive environmental qualities. Green marketing is another major social responsibility in marketing and advertising. Green marketing is any marketing activity of a firm that is intended to (1) create a positive impact on the environment or (2) lessen the negative impact of a product on the environment. In this way, the marketer hopes to respond to consumers' concerns about environmental issues. Green marketing efforts range from simply altering advertising claims to the development of entirely new products.[a]

Since the first Earth Day, Americans have increasingly placed greater emphasis on quality of life than on the quantity of goods they buy. The proportion of consumers who buy environmentally friendly products, at least occasionally, is rapidly growing. The New York consulting and research firm FIND/SVP lists four criteria as key success factors for any environment-conscious business: product, packaging, price, and promotion.[b] FIND/SVP considers a product to be green if it runs cleaner, works better, or saves money and energy through efficiency. Businesses are considered to practice being green when they voluntarily recycle and attempt to reduce waste in their daily operations. Green promotion requires businesses to be honest in their promises to consumers.

What green product or packaging changes do you know about that have occurred in the 1990s? How does price factor into the green marketing effort?

[a] Michael J. Etzel, Bruce J. Walker, and William J. Stanton, *Marketing*, New York: McGraw-Hill, 1997, p. 612.
[b] J. Stephen Shi and Jane M. Kane, "Green Issues," *Business Horizons*, January/February 1996, pp. 65-70.

Chapter 12

Print Media

Every year, when Thanksgiving approaches, many food marketers that advertise minimally the rest of the year make their annual pilgrimage to the pages of women's service magazines. The reason is that, for example, about 30 percent of all whipped cream sales occur during November and December. Also, Thanksgiving records the biggest sales gain of the year. Reddi Wip (a whipped cream product), which spent $1.1 million in 1995 to 1996 on media advertising, concentrated on print ads that included recipes, themes for the fall holidays, and themes for berry season in the summer. Cranberry Jell-O sold 15 percent of its volume for the year during the Thanksgiving season. The company ran a campaign featuring its ubiquitous holiday molded gelatin in 1996. ConAgra's Swift Butterball turkey, the centerpiece of many Thanksgiving tables, appeared in print, radio, and Internet advertising using the tag line, "Always Juicy. Always Tender. Always Butterball."[1]

Although over half the U.S. population is female, news magazines have long geared their content toward men. Therefore, their advertisers have traditionally targeted men, and few food product ads have appeared on news magazine pages. That may be changing. In its June 1, 1998 issue, *Newsweek* magazine featured prominent ads for Tostitos and DiGiorno pizza. The Tostitos ad shows a man wearing a lounging robe and slippers, relaxing on a chaise lounge. He holds a giant plate of Tostitos tortilla chips with nacho toppings; the copy reads, "You don't have to be lazy to make 'em, but it helps." This ad appears on page two, closely followed by a DiGiorno ad on page seven, which also pitches convenient food preparation to men. A picture window ad design showcases a color photograph of three wide-eyed Boy Scouts serving a DiGiorno pizza. Copy printed across the picture implies that the boys have honestly provided fresh-baked pizza—not delivery pizza—for their meeting. One boy raises his hand in a pledge to honesty and truthfulness, and long copy reprints the official Woodchuck pledge. The group's leader responds, "Good Jimmy. Now, for the last time, who delivered the pizza?" The ad uses the ability of

ILLUSTRATION 12.1. The Wave of the Future

Graphic artist Paula Winicur chose a font for this dramatic ad that would appeal to a youthful target. The wave crashes diagonally in a dynamic visual to match the excitement and energy associated with the jeans-wearing generation.

print to present long copy and the facial expressions and actions that can be captured in a large color photograph to convey a fairly complex story line. In this case, the story reveals that even the youngest males can prepare snacks and meals if the proper food product is purchased.

These messages to men, telling them that they can easily prepare food, encourage them to join the majority of grocery shoppers—women—in buying the advertisers' products. Because magazine subscriber demographics can be pinpointed relatively easily, ads can be confidently targeted to niche markets. Certainly, pitching retail food ads to men requires creating and placing ads in venues other than the traditional women's magazines, and magazine publishing has such audience diversity.

Each advertising medium and vehicle has a set of unique characteristics and virtues. Advertisers attempt to select those media and vehicles whose characteristics are most compatible with the advertised product and which will enhance the product's image (e.g., see Illustration 12.1). Many magazines are able to reproduce ads with excellent color fidelity. The necessity for fine color reproduction is obvious for certain kinds of product advertising such as food and makeup. This chapter explains how print advertising (magazines and newspapers) enhances the advertiser's media mix.

MAGAZINE ADVERTISING

Over the past several decades, magazines have been a rapidly growing medium that serves the educational, informational, and entertainment needs and interests of a wide range of readers in both the consumer and business markets. The wide variety of magazines makes this an appealing medium to a vast number of advertisers. The magazine industry recorded a 2.1 percent increase in advertising revenues for the first quarter of 1999 compared to the first quarter of the previous year.[2] A new trend, custom publishing (a roughly $3 billion category of publications tailored to their sponsoring marketer) has grown quickly in the last five years. For instance, USAir's in-flight magazine handled by New York Times Custom Publishing is distributed in all USAir flights to its passengers.[3]

Classifications of Magazines

Thousands of different magazines are published in the United States. They are so diverse that it is helpful to classify the main types. Magazines are commonly categorized by the broad audiences they service: (1) consumer magazines, (2) business magazines, (3) farm magazines, and (4) computer/Internet magazines. An emerging new category is the online magazine.

Consumer Magazines

Advertisers do not choose magazines as a medium as often as they once did for general mass-appeal products. Yet, magazines are very good at reaching certain kinds of consumer segments—target groups (see, e.g., Illustration 12.2). *Better Homes and Gardens* is oriented toward homemakers and family service. *Sports Illustrated* is oriented toward sports enthusiasts. Even for the same general target market, for example, women, there are magazines that appeal to nearly every specific consumer interest and lifestyle. For instance, there are publications for women who decorate, garden, cook, and sew. There are also magazines about weddings, travel, fitness (see Table 12.1), fashion, careers, and health. Still others (general interest magazines) try to cover a little bit of it all. Although the general interest magazine has survived for over a century, magazines targeted to niche markets have become increasingly popular and successful in the last decade. For instance, *Fitness* magazine's circulation more than doubled, increasing from 300,000 in 1992 to 700,000 in 1996, according to the ABC audit.

Magazines are also becoming better at reaching target markets within geographic areas. Many magazines sold throughout the United States publish regional editions that are distributed only in certain parts of the country (e.g., North, South, East, and West). Advertisers can use these regional editions to advertise only in certain areas or to change their advertising messages from one region to another. Some magazines, such as *Midwest Living*, target only a specific geographic area (see Table 12.2).

TABLE 12.1. Demographics of *Fitness* Magazine Readers

Age:	The median age is 30.4 years, with 94.7% in the 18 to 49 age bracket.
Marital Status:	45.1% are married; 38.8% are single.
Children:	49.8% have children in the household.
Education:	71.9% attended college.
Employed:	77.7% are employed, 59.5% of them full-time.
Household Income:	Median HHI is $47,148, with 73.7% at $30,000+.

Source: Adapted from the Fall 1995 MRI.

Print Media   189

ILLUSTRATION 12.2. Pain Management

New Sports Massage Video!

The Latest Proven Sports Massage Technique is the Huston Method c.

The 10 top reasons massage therapists want to learn what this man has to teach....

1. President of his own chapter of Massage therapy
2. Counts top Olympic athletes as his clients
3. Stays booked 60 hours a week
4. Makes more money than 96% of the therapists
5. Works the NCAA circuit
6. Has been Endorsed by the top Sports Massage Educators in the country
7. Has one of the best sports massage *videos on the market*
8. Volunteers countless hours to service for the good of massage
9. Professional and amateur sports teams have used him *(Notre Dame & Detroit Red Wings Professional Hockey team)*
10. Because these people just like you endorse his video course

"The The Huston Method is great. Thank you Dale for teaching to us...We're eager to learn more.." Ellen Rithison Massage Practitioner, French Lick Springs Resort

" Dale Huston is a great instructor! I really Enjoyed his class. He makes learning enjoyable and fun." Stella Deutsch massage practitioner, Kentucky

" Dale Huston's Seminar opened a new door for me... I feel that if I have a client now for sports massage I can give them a great sports massage." Shannon Nolan Indiana

" I liked it! I 'm very visual and to actually see it done the way he does it helps me to understand it much quicker." John Settle Heltonville, Ind

Now You Can Learn The Huston Method

Order your own Video for 59.95 +P&H.
Credit Cards Accepted or send Check or Money Order
to : Tresgano Group
8141 N. Cuzco Rd.
French Lick, Ind 47432
Or Call 1-888-778-2072
Money Back Guarantee!

National marketing expert Ken D. Lochner specializes in massage business marketing. His ad for the Huston technique sports massage video ran in niche magazines that reach a specific target group—massage therapists.

TABLE 12.2. Geographic Information—Midwest (*Midwest Living* Magazine's Target Market)

	Percent Comp Index (U.S. Average = 100)			
	Midwest	Northeast	West	South
Entertain Friends/Relatives at Home	114	104	112	81
Prepare Food from Scratch	119	105	97	86
Own a Microwave	120	99	99	88
Use a Microwave	120	104	99	85
Heavy Microwave Use*	126	105	91	85
Percent of Total U.S. Households	24	20	21	35

Source: Based on 1995 Spring MRI.

Note: Midwest Living's Media Kit provides demographic information about a specific geographic region—the Midwest—which may be of special interest to advertisers of food products and kitchen appliances. The second largest region in the United States, the Midwest is number one in entertaining with food and friends, in cooking from scratch, and in microwave use.

* Twelve-plus times in the last seven days.

Business Magazines

Whereas consumer magazines are directed at those who buy products for their own consumption, business magazines are directed at business readers. There are several types of business magazines: industrial magazines directed toward manufacturers (e.g., *Chemical Week*), trade magazines directed toward middlemen (e.g., *Progressive Grocer*), and professional magazines directed toward a specific profession (e.g., *National Law Review*). By paid circulation in 1997, the top three business magazines were *Journal of Accounting* (351,602), *Nursing* (344,434), and *ABA Journal* (309,541).[4]

Farm Magazines

The third category of magazines is farm publications, directed toward farmers and their families or to companies that manufacture or sell agricultural equipment, supplies, and services. *Successful Farming* had the highest paid circulation in the category in 1997 (476,357), followed by *Progressive Farmer* (286,383) and *Farm Journal* (197,370). Some advertisers overlook the farm publication marketplace. And, even if they do use farm publications as an advertising medium, they may not use them well.

Computer/Internet Magazines

A new category of magazine, targeted to computer and Internet users, has seen its growth spurt in the mid- to late 1990s. For instance, one Barnes & Noble Booksellers store may carry as many as twenty titles in just the Internet niche. These titles include everything from the general (*Internet Basics* and *Webguide Monthly*, which covers more than 1,000 Web sites) to the very specialized (*Online Investor*). The most popular computer magazine titles are *PC World* (1997 paid circulation 1,176,351) and *PC Magazine* (1997 circulation 1,124,589), which feature general information on computer/Internet topics, including the latest in software.

Online Magazines

Print publishers were initially hesitant to launch online versions of their magazines, afraid that they would "cannibalize their print properties."[5] Nevertheless, the field of online magazines has been pioneered by such publishers as Time Warner, which expanded from a Web site supported by only five advertisers in 1994 to the current Time Warner's Pathfinder Network that houses the online editions of *Time, People, Money, Fortune,* and *Entertainment Weekly*, among other titles. The main advantage of online magazines is said to be reader loyalty. Niche targeting is also possible. Time Warner has found that reader demographics differ somewhat from print to online versions of the same magazine (see Table 12.3). Monthly page views also have rivaled or overtaken the print monthly circulation numbers, with *Time* online garnering 12.2 million page views in Spring 1998 compared to a monthly circulation of 4.2 million for the print publication.

TABLE 12.3. Comparison of Online and Print Statistics for *People* Magazine

People online		*People* offline	
Monthly page views	10.9 million	Monthly circulation	3.6 million
Median household income	$45,000	Median household income	$47,851
Median age	32 years	Median age	40 years
Male/female ratio	30%/70%	Male/female ratio	34%/66%
Graduated college	44%	Graduate college	26%

Source: Adapted from "Inside Time Warner/Audience Demographics," *Silicon Alley Reporter,* Iss. 19, Vol. 2, No. 11, November 1998, p. 60.

Controlled or Paid Circulation

Magazines may be distributed on either a controlled-circulation or paid-circulation basis. The top three non-paid-circulation (controlled-circulation) magazines for the second half of 1995, based on Audit Bureau of Circulations and BPA International figures, were (1) *The Disney Channel Magazine*, which is distributed free, with a circulation of 5,502,575; (2) *CompuServe Magazine* (2,118,529); and (3) *U—The National College Magazine* (1,568,363).[6] A paid-circulation magazine requires the recipient to pay a subscription price to receive it. The top paid-circulation magazines in 1997 included *Modern Maturity*, published by the American Association of Retired Persons (AARP) (20,390,755); *Reader's Digest* (15,038,708); and *TV Guide* (13,103,187).

Advertisers pay for the controlled-circulation magazine, and the publisher mails the magazine free to a select list of individuals the publisher thinks can influence the purchase of advertised products. *PROMO* magazine is written for brand, product, promotion, and marketing managers, promotion specialists at advertising and promotion agencies, and other people in marketing/advertising-related fields. Besides its paid-circulation basis, people such as college professors who teach in these fields can receive it free. To receive a free copy, college professors or other interested individuals must indicate in writing a desire to receive it and give their professional designation or occupation.

Advantages and Disadvantages of Magazine Advertising

Magazines have a number of characteristics and qualities that make them particularly attractive as an advertising medium.

- The ability to pinpoint specific audiences is the feature that most distinguishes magazine advertising from other media.
- Magazines are noted for their long lives and high reader involvement. Most readers spend a couple days with new magazines, then keep them in their home for a long time. Magazine subscribers (primary readers) often pass along their copies to other readers (secondary readers or pass-along readers), further extending a magazine's life.
- Magazine ads have very good printing and color quality. For example, food items advertised in magazines such as *Bon Appetit* always look real and tasty.
- Magazines offer flexible formats that permit different ad sizes, as well as inserts and scent strips. Perfume companies often add scent strips to their ads so that recipients can actually smell the product. A bleed page is one in which the dark or colored background of the ad

extends to the edge of the page. Magazine publishers usually charge a 10 to 15 percent premium on them. The advantages of bleeds include greater flexibility in expressing the advertising idea, a slightly larger printing area, and a more dramatic impact. A junior unit is a large ad (60 percent of the page) in the middle of a page surrounded by editorial matter. Similar to junior units are island halves, except that more editorial matter surrounds them.
- Sometimes, rather than buying a standard advertising page, an advertiser uses a magazine insert. The advertiser prints the ad on special, high-quality paper stock and then ships the finished ads to the publisher for insertion into the magazine at a special price.

Although the advantages offered by magazines are considerable, this medium is limited by certain factors. The most salient disadvantages are high cost, long lead time, clutter, and competition:

- Advertising in mass circulation magazines such as *Time* can be very expensive. However, the costs of ad space in more specialized publications (e.g., *Home Gym* and *Fitness*) with smaller circulations is less.
- Magazine ads must be submitted well in advance of the publication date, usually thirty to ninety days.
- Magazines generally gauge their success in terms of the number of advertising pages they attract. Thus, clutter becomes a very big problem for advertisers.

Buying Magazine Advertising Space

Magazines provide rate cards offered by Standard Rate and Data Service that show how much they charge for their advertising. Standard Rate and Data Service (SRDS) contains more than just advertising rates. It also contains an estimate of the circulation, closing dates, mechanical requirements, readership profiles, and additional information. Advertising space is generally sold on the basis of space units, such as full page, half page, and quarter page, although some publications quote rates on the basis of column inches. Ads can be produced or run using black and white, black and white plus one color, or four colors. The more colors used in the ad, the greater the expense because of the increased printing costs. The rates for magazine advertising space can also vary according to the number of insertions during a specific period. Cumulative quantity discounts offered by magazines are based on the total space purchased within a contract year and provide clear incentives for advertisers to maintain continuity with a particular magazine. Advertisers can also save money by advertising in magazine combinations (e.g., two different magazines).

The CPM measure is used by advertisers to compare different magazine buys. The magazine with the lower cost per thousand will be the more economical.

$$\text{Cost per thousand} = \frac{\text{Page rate}}{\text{Circulation}} \times 1{,}000$$

Cost-per-thousand information for each magazine is available from two syndicated magazine services: Mediamark Research, Incorporated (MRI), and Simmons Market Research Bureau (SMRB). Cost-per-thousand data are useful in making magazine-vehicle selection decisions, but many other factors (e.g., readership profile) must also be taken into account.

New Media Magazines

Magazine Publishers of America (MPA) and Ernst & Young conducted a survey of forty-seven companies, publishing 304 magazine brands, in 1996. Of these forty-seven companies, 82 percent had already developed an online magazine. Most online magazines promote the company's printed publications, providing general and subscription information about the associated print publication(s). A 1997 Ernst & Young study revealed that advertising had produced only 53 percent of magazine publishers' total revenues for their new media magazines, but projected that total revenues would rise dramatically in 1999.[7] At an MPA conference in November 1996, Bill Bass of Forrester Research predicted that Web site magazines would not generate enough revenue from advertisers to be profitable until the year 2000.[8] Nevertheless, online magazine advertising should become an increasingly viable advertising option in the next century.

NEWSPAPER ADVERTISING

Newspapers have historically been the leading advertising medium in the United States, but recently, television surpassed newspapers as the medium that receives the greatest amount of advertising expenditures. However, people continue to turn to the daily newspaper for the in-depth news coverage and other current information that is not available on television. According to surveys conducted in 1997 by Scarborough Research for the Newspaper Association of America, about 59 percent of all adults in the fifty largest markets read a newspaper on a typical day. That is a bigger audience than those tuned in to broadcast or cable TV during prime time or to morning drive-time radio. Readership is especially high in cities with colleges and more than one daily newspaper.[9] See Table 12.4 for a listing of the country's top ten newspapers by circulation.

TABLE 12.4. The Top Ten U.S. Newspapers As of March 31, 1998

Newspaper	Average Weekday Circulation
1. *The Wall Street Journal*	1,820,186
2. *USA Today*	1,715,245
3. *The New York Times*	1,110,143
4. *Los Angeles Times*	1,095,007
5. *The Washington Post*	808,884
6. *New York Daily News*	730,761
7. *Chicago Tribune*	655,522
8. *Newsday*	571,283
9. *Houston Chronicle*[a]	553,387
10. *The Dallas Morning News*[b]	509,775

Source: Adapted from Ira Teinowitz, "Dailies See Small Gains for 2nd 6-Month Period," *Advertising Age,* May 11, 1998, p. 56.

[a] Rank based on Monday through Saturday circulation.
[b] Figure adjusted by *Advertising Age* to indicate average weekday circulations.

Newspapers are still an especially important advertising medium to local advertisers and, particularly, to retailers, who account for a large amount of newspaper advertising. Because newspapers allow for immediate communication, retailers use this medium to announce sales and offer discount coupons. Many people buy the newspaper specifically for the coupons and sale information.

Classifications of Newspapers

As with magazines, there are different classifications or types of newspapers: daily, weekly, national (e.g., *The Wall Street Journal* and *USA Today*), special audience (e.g., *Advertising Age* for those in the advertising and marketing fields), and *Pennysavers* (local publications with newspaper format and minimal nonadvertising content, primarily funded by advertising and delivered free of charge to all addresses in a geographic area).

Newspaper magazines are a hybrid of the two print media. The newspaper has a separate magazine editor and staff, and the format resembles that of a magazine, with longer feature stories illustrated by large color photos. Since newspapers easily target geographic areas through special editions, *The Chicago Tribune Magazine* targets prosperous Chicago-based areas through a special VIP edition. This allows advertisers more precise targeting, as it reaches households in selected areas where median income exceeds $55,000 and 60 percent of its readers will be professional women and/or college-educated adults. Similar to other magazines, the newspaper magazine may offer special themed issues such as "Weddings" and "Summer Activities."

Newspapers are typically available in two sizes. The first, referred to as the tabloid (e.g., the *National Enquirer*), is about fourteen inches deep and eleven inches wide. The standard size, or broadsheet, is about twenty-two inches deep and thirteen inches wide and is divided into six columns. The newspaper industry in the United States uses a standard advertising unit (SAU) system that uses column inches as the main unit of measure for advertisers to place ads. There are fifty-six standard ad sizes for broadsheet papers and thirty-two for tabloids.

Advantages and Disadvantages of Newspaper Advertising

Advantages of Newspapers

- Newspapers provide complete coverage and are not restricted to specific socioeconomic or demographic groups—almost everybody reads newspapers.
- Newspaper advertising is timely (see Illustration 12.3). Short lead times (the time between placing an ad and running it) permit advertisers to tie in advertising copy with local market developments or newsworthy events. The results of newspaper advertising are also quick.
- Ads can be quickly and easily changed.
- Newspapers appeal to those already interested in reading, so newspapers provide both the audience and space for long, detailed copy, including lists and prices.
- Special editions allow for precise targeting, for example, those who read Food sections are looking for ads with recipes and coupons, and so forth.
- Most newspapers are geographically targeted—even big city newspapers have special editions for the various neighborhoods and suburbs.

Disadvantages of Newspapers

- Newspapers do not have the long life of a magazine—most are recycled or thrown away.

- The national advertiser must deal separately with each newspaper publisher. Another problem for national advertisers is that the rates charged to them may be higher than those charged to local advertisers.
- There are also great variations in printing and color quality in newspapers. Newspapers have traditionally been printed by the rotogravure process. If color work is desired, the advertiser provides halftoned color separations for the separate color plates used in the rotogravure four-color printing process. Most newspaper presses are geared toward speed, not quality. Generally, do not expect the printing and color quality of magazine publishing. Paper quality is also inferior—you usually will not get the slick magazine paper surface.
- Similar to magazine advertising, many newspaper ads appear amidst the clutter of other ads.

ILLUSTRATION 12.3. Timely and Targeted

SIGNAL TRAVEL & TOURS, INC.

Your Honeymoon Specialists
Making Honeymoons Memorable Since 1968
Ask About Our Bridal Registry

FOUR CONVENIENT LOCATIONS

Niles	South Bend	Dowagiac	St. Joseph
219 E. Main St.	North Village Mall	146 S. Front St.	223 State St.
(616) 684-2880	(219) 271-8700	(616) 782-9825	(616) 983-7323
1-800-535-1070	1-800-327-1032	1-800-535-1025	1-800-535-1035

Being The Best Doesn't Mean Being More Expensive!
Voted Best Travel Agency In Michiana

AMERICAN EXPRESS
Travel Services
Representative

Retail and service ads often have a "creative handle." This Signal Travel & Tours, Incorporated, ad ran in newspapers in June 1998, tying into the proliferation of June weddings and the subsequent proliferation of honeymoon bookings.

Types of Newspaper Advertising

Classified Advertising

Classified ads usually appear under subheads (e.g., Help Wanted, Cars for Sale) that describe the class of goods or the need the ads seek to satisfy. Classified rates are typically based on the number of lines the ad occupies and the number of times the ad runs.

Display Advertising

Display advertising is found throughout the newspaper and generally uses illustrations, headlines, white space, and other visual devices in addition to the copy text. Display advertising is further divided into two subcategories—local (e.g., local retail stores) and national (e.g., national advertisers).

Preprinted Inserts

Preprinted inserts are ads that do not appear in the paper itself but are printed by the advertiser and then taken to the newspaper to be inserted before delivery. A retail advertiser who wants to reach only those shoppers in its immediate trading area can place an insert in the local editions.

Public Notices

Public notices include a variety of governmental and financial reports and notices and public notices of changes in business and personal relationships (such as marriage announcements provided by a government agency).

Buying Newspaper Space

Buying newspaper space follows the same basic procedure as buying magazine space. The advertising rate is the amount the newspaper charges for advertising space. As noted previously, newspapers may charge local and national advertisers different rates, with the national rate generally higher. Newspapers attribute the higher national rates to the added costs they incur serving national advertisers (e.g., they may have to pay an ad agency a 15 percent commission).

There are two ways to measure newspaper advertising space—by the column inch and by the agate line. However, in recent years, national advertising rates in newspapers have been based solely on the column inch measurement. The column inch is a space one inch high and one newspaper column wide. Usually, there are about 126 or 129 column inches for a one-page newspaper ad. Some newspapers charge the same advertising rate (flat rate) no matter how much space a single advertiser buys. Most newspapers, however, offer a lower rate (discount or volume rate) for advertisers who buy space regularly or in large amounts. An open rate is the highest advertising rate. It is used for advertisers who do not earn a discount. An advertiser who contracts to buy a specific amount of space during a one-year period at a discount rate and then fails to do so is charged a short rate.

Combination rates are often available for placing a given ad in (1) two or more newspapers owned by the same publisher, (2) in morning and evening editions of the same newspaper, and (3) in some cases, in two or more newspapers affiliated in a syndicate or newspaper group. Run of paper (ROP) advertising rates entitle a newspaper to place a given ad on any newspaper page or in any position it desires. An advertiser can ensure a choice position for an ad by paying a higher preferred position rate. When advertisers want to experiment with two different creative approaches, some large newspapers will print an ad using one approach in half its papers, then stop the printing presses to substitute an ad using the other approach for the second half. This is called a split run. This way, the advertiser tests the pulling power of each ad.

As with other media, advertisers are interested in comparing different newspaper buys. Since most newspapers have switched from the agate line to the column inch-based rate method, the cost-per-thousand method is now used to make cost comparisons among newspapers:

$$\text{CPM} = \frac{\text{Cost of one-page ad}}{\text{Newspaper circulation}} \times 1{,}000$$

Circulation figures provide the media planner with the basic data for assessing the value of newspapers and their ability to cover various market areas. Data on newspaper audience size and characteristics are available from commercial research services and from studies conducted by the papers. Statements regarding newspaper circulation are verified by the Audit Bureau of Circulation (ABC), an independent auditing group that represents advertisers, agencies, and publishers. Members of the ABC include only paid-circulation newspapers and magazines. Commercial studies providing readership information for the top 100 or so major markets are supplied by the Simmons-Scarbough Syndicated Research Associates. The audience information available from these studies is valuable to the media planner for comparing newspapers with other media vehicles that generally have similar data available. Many newspapers commission and publish their own audience studies so as to provide current and potential advertisers with information on readership and characteristics (e.g., demographics and shopping habits) of readers.

Magazines and newspapers play an important role in the media plans and strategies of many advertisers. Television Bureau of Advertising researcher Harold Simpson discovered that, on average, in 1995, 88 percent of adults nationwide watched some television, 71 percent listened to the radio, and 56 percent read a newspaper.[10] A number of magazine publishers have expanded child-oriented titles. Although broadcast is still the most important medium to reach children, print is increasingly important due to its extended reach.[11]

Rising costs and declining readerships continue to present problems for print publications. For instance, due to skyrocketing paper costs, many magazine publishers (e.g, *Redbook, Good Housekeeping,* and *Country Living*—all Hearst magazines) have increased magazine ad rates, angering advertisers. Kraft, a unit of Philip Morris, withdrew a huge chunk of advertising it had planned to run in Hearst magazines in 1996.[12]

Print publications also face increasing competition from other media, such as TV, direct mail, and the Web. Newspaper publishers themselves are flocking to the World Wide Web like gold miners to the hills, chasing the promise of a vast, but so far elusive, vein of $150 million in advertising revenue. The number of U.S. newspapers on the Web doubled from 1995 to April 1996.[13] By 1998, creative Web sites and interactive advertisements were included in the print category at the Forty-fifth International Advertising Awards in Cannes, France. IBM and Carnation were among the ten U.S. Internet winners. With a total of fifteen awards given, the United States dominated interactive advertising awards in the print category. Online publication is viewed by U.S. journalists and advertisers alike as the wave of the future.

SUMMARY

Each advertising medium has its own set of unique characteristics and virtues. Advertisers attempt to select those media and vehicles whose characteristics are compatible with the advertised product and which will enhance the product's image. Many magazines are able to reproduce ads with excellent color fidelity and to specifically target niche markets. Online magazines promise to be a future venue for the same color fidelity and specific targeting. Newspapers have abdicated their previous position as the leading U.S. advertising medium, but they remain a force in the marketplace nonetheless. The print advertisement of the future will most likely appear online, simultaneously with paper publications or exclusively online.

* * *

THE GLOBAL PERSPECTIVE:
AVON CALLING—WITH INTERNATIONAL ADS

When that doorbell rings in the Philippines, it may be Avon calling.

In fact, over $450 million of Avon's 1997 pretax income came from international sales, compared to slightly more than $200 million in U.S. sales.[a] Already marketed in 135 countries, Avon expects 70 percent of its total sales to come from global brands by the year 2000.[b] To enhance its international expansion, the cosmetic retailer consolidated its $66 million worldwide advertising account at MacManus Group. Avon plans to increase global ad spending to about 3 percent of its total sales by the millennium.

International advertising—advertising designed to promote the same product in a number of countries—is a relatively recent development in international commerce. During the Middle Ages, Holland traded tulip bulbs internationally in exchange for various products and services, but international commerce did not appear in any organized manner until the late nineteenth century. Current patterns of international expansion emerged largely in the twentieth century.[c]

North America, Europe, and the Asia-Pacific region are the world's three largest marketplaces. Total advertising spending worldwide increased 7.8 percent in 1996, then slowed a bit in 1997 to 6.9 percent.[d] If Avon and other countries interested in increasing global marketshare are any indication, numbers could rise again as we approach the twenty-first century.

[a] Leslie Kaufman, "Avon's New Face," *Newsweek,* November 16, 1998, p. 60.
[b] Laura Petrecca, "Avon Awards MacManus Units $66 Mil in Ads," *Advertising Age,* August 3, 1998, p. 3.
[c] William Wells, John Burnett, and Sandra Moriarty, *Advertising: Principles and Practice,* Englewood Cliffs, NJ: Prentice Hall, 1995, pp. 735-736.
[d] "Forecast for '97: Advertisement Spending Expected to Remain Strong," *Marketing News,* January 6, 1997, p. 21.

* * *

ETHICS TRACK: COVERT ADVERTISEMENTS,
ADVERTORIALS, AND OTHER PUFFING

A "Summer Beauty Tips" column in a women's magazine may recommend a suntan lotion that is advertised on a facing page. A feature on new trends in makeup may begin on a page facing an ad for a cosmetic company's new line of eye shadow. These placements are not accidental.

Covert advertising refers to "promotions disguised as editorial material so that they appear to be non-advertising."[a] Under the guise of presenting advice or information, covert advertising favorably positions consumers toward the company's overt ads. Advertisers convey covert messages in women's magazines, for instance, by obtaining cover credits for makeup or clothing, by receiving mention of an advertised product in an advice column, and through ad placement next to complementary articles.

Advertorials, a type of covert advertising, present an ad that appears to be a feature story, blurring the traditional distinction between magazine content and purchased advertising.[b] Because editorial material in a print publication carries a high credibility with its readers, and because readers rarely see advertising text as an interruption in their reading (unlike television commercials, which are clearly viewed as interruptions), critics view covert advertising as a particularly clever way of duping the public.

Advertisers also have been accused of exaggerated claims. Puffery is defined as "advertising or other sales representations which praise the item to be sold with subjective opinions, superlatives, or exaggerations, vaguely and generally, stating no specific facts."[c] Because the federal government does not pursue cases involving obviously exaggerated claims, the question of puffery has become an ethical issue rather than a legal one.

A statement such as "We have the best hamburger in town" is a good example of puffery in advertising because it is obviously a subjective opinion. Critics say puffery is misleading, but defenders say people can tell when an advertiser is exaggerating.

Bring a women's magazine to class. Can you find examples of covert advertising? Do some ads inflate claims (use puffery)? Would the use of these techniques have been obvious if you were not looking for them?

[a] Ellen McCracken, *Decoding Women's Magazines,* New York: St. Martin's Press, 1993, p. 38.
[b] Ibid., pp. 50-51.
[c] "The Image of Advertising," *Editor and Publisher,* February 9, 1985, p. 15.

Lee & Johnson
:60 Spot
"First Day"

Starting a new job is always a little unnerving—sometimes even a little scary. No one really knows what to expect the first day. It is usually the endless paperwork for the personnel files, the tax information, and all those other little documents you must fill out before officially becoming an employee. So, just imagine my surprise when my first job after graduating from college turned out to be not quite what I expected.

I was very nervous and more than a little scared of this new career I was embarking upon. I remember thinking, "I survived college, so I can handle anything." I just reminded myself over and over how prepared I was to do this job. However, my first day in my new career proved to be very interesting, to say the least.

I drove to work, excited, nervous, and praying that I was ready to handle all the marketing duties for Signal Travel & Tours, Incorporated, a travel agency nationally affiliated with American Express. I knew I would have a lot of responsibility since I would be the only marketing person in the department. The president/owner decided that she could no longer handle all the marketing responsibilities for all four offices branched in different cities—so the new marketing director would do it all. That was me.

As I was praying I would be successful, I was speeding through the small town where the Signal headquarters is located. I was pulled over by the local police. Not only was I embarrassed—I was going to be late. What a great first impression! I walked into the office to find that everyone already knew I was pulled over. To this day, I don't know how the news spread so fast, but when I walked in the door, everyone—including the president—knew about it. That was only the beginning.

I was sent to the personnel department for the paperwork. That was easy. Then I came downstairs, preparing myself for some on-the-job training. Instead, I was informed that we had a half-page advertisement due for a Bridal Extra in the local newspaper that was due yesterday, and I had a one-day extension—the end of the day. I had completed ads in college, but even then, I had direction and time. I had to complete an ad that would be viewed by at least 35,000 people, and it had to be done in two hours. Talk about pressure. I also had to utilize suppliers that had cooperative funds to defray the cost of the advertisement. I quickly learned that day what cooperative funding was and how to obtain it.

Needless to say, since I am still the marketing director at Signal, I completed the ad and the president liked it. I will have to admit I learned a lot that day. I realized I had what it took to succeed in the marketing field. Plus, my first day reaffirmed that all those late-night study sessions, all those exams, and all those papers actually did pay off.

I guess the one thing I learned from my whole experience was that you should never assume what your days will be like in marketing and advertising. Something different, surprising, and scary always pops up day to day. Some people may call these things "problems," but I call them "opportunities." Yes, really great opportunities.

Judeanne Wilson
Director of Marketing
Signal Travel & Tours, Inc.
Niles, Michigan

Chapter 13

Broadcast Media

The Super Bowl provides Madison Avenue with a showcase for creativity: frogs croak for beer, a goldfish plays dead for a soft drink, and a city slicker leads a cattle drive in a snazzy four-wheeler. Usually the most-watched event of the year, the game typically attracts 100 million or more viewers. With that much attention, the networks have been able to boost advertisement rates higher each year. The average :30 spot sold for $1.3 million in 1998. Advertisers and their consultants say the Super Bowl offers an unmatched one-time opportunity to introduce a product, deliver a sales theme, or show off an arresting, creative idea.[1] Online auto marketer Auto-by-Tel was basically an unknown prior to its ad appearance during the 1998 Super Bowl. Thirty days later, the company boasted more than 110,000 purchase-information requests, compared to only 80,000 in the previous thirty-day period. Primestar reported similar Super Bowl megasuccess, with call volume up 50 percent following its 1998 ad appearance.[2]

On May 14, 1998, the final episode of the top-rated, long-running *Seinfeld* show on NBC rivaled the draw of a Super Bowl. The show—with :30 spots going for $1.5 to $1.7 million—drew a whopping 76.3 million viewers, according to the Nielsen ratings. One advertiser, Gardenburger, reported a phenomenal response to its :30 finale spot. Within a week of the show, Gardenburger sold more veggie patties than the entire category had during the same period in 1997. The ads also created national awareness, garnering piles of press clippings with mention of the Gardenburger brand. The "power of the *Seinfeld* finale buy," advertisers discovered, was more than anecdotal.[3]

Broadcast media include both television and radio. Advertisers have been spending more and more on them in recent years, mainly because of the growth of broadcast media. Most of this growth comes from television. In this chapter, we will explore broadcast media and their place in advertising.

TELEVISION ADVERTISING

A major reason the Super Bowl is advertising's biggest showcase is that it appears on America's primary form of entertainment—the television set.

ILLUSTRATION 13.1. Helping

Who will feed your starving neighbors?

Every year around the holidays, hundreds of your Southwest Michigan neighbors go hungry. 70,000 pounds of food goes a long way to feed our community's needy. Thanks to Z-County Radio, hundreds of your neighbors in Southwest Michigan won't go hungry. Every year, prior to Thanksgiving, Z-County teams up with Value Save-More Markets and the S.G. Scooner's Food Bank to collect food for the needy. Last Year, Z-County collected 70,000 pounds of food in just 5 days.

Z-County and the rest of *The Local Radio Stations of Southwest Michigan* care about your community. In 1960, our flagship, WSGW was born. Since then, our company has grown to include eight radio stations right here in Southwest Michigan. While other companies may come and go, we promise to stay here where we belong, in our home . . . and yours, Southwest Michigan.

THE LOCAL RADIO STATIONS of Southwest Michigan

Community service helps radio stations establish visibility as a positive part of the community. When The Local Radio Stations of Southwest Michigan sponsored a Thanksgiving food drive, Glenna Revis created this emotionally appealing print ad encouraging community participation and emphasizing the stations' down-home ("where we belong, in our home. . . and yours. . ."), local ties ("other companies may come and go").

TV has virtually saturated households throughout the United States, and many other countries as well, and has become a mainstay in the lives of most people. For over forty years, television has been the world's most powerful medium, although network television's audience size has decreased in the last decade. A 1997 poll demonstrated TV's gradually diminishing hold on America's free time. Television watching as a free-time choice was down 6 percent from 1995, compared to no change in the number polled who favored reading, walking, and family time as free-time options.[4] Television watching is expected to continue its decline due also to the proliferation of alternative media. A 1998 Nielsen Media Research study showed that those who have Internet and online services in their homes watch 15 percent less television than those in nonwired homes.[5] Nevertheless, television remains the advertising medium with the broadest reach.

Two major categories of television broadcasting are important in advertising: network and cable. In network television, an independent business, called a network (e.g., ABC, CBS, NBC, and Fox), joins individual television stations that broadcast its programs and advertising. Usually, only one station per market carries each network's programs. Rather than go through the networks, advertisers may also deal directly with the local television station, an individual station broadcasting within a small geographic area. In fact, few advertisers are large enough to afford expensive network advertising time, so most of them deal with local stations.

Perhaps the most significant development in the broadcast media has been the growth and expansion of cable television. In May 1998, 65 percent of U.S. households subscribed to cable TV.[6] Although bolstered by such events as the Super Bowl, the Olympics, and presidential elections, spending on network television has been fairly flat—as low as a 2 percent 1997 increase. On the other hand, cable ad spending has vaulted as much as 18 percent, to over $5 billion in 1997.[7] Based on the May 1998 up-front buying season, Bill McGowan, the senior vice president at Discovery Communications, predicted a $500 million shift from network broadcasting to cable in 1998. This adds up to a 20 percent increase for cable and another flat year for broadcasting.[8] In fact, two cable networks overtook traditional networks in actual 1998 rating point revenue (see Table 13.1).

Cable subscribers pay a monthly fee for which they receive on average thirty or more channels, including the local network affiliates and independent stations, various cable networks (e.g., CNN, MTV, and ESPN), superstations (e.g., WTBS-Atlanta and WGN-Chicago), and local cable system channels. As with network television, cable television advertising can be purchased on a national, regional, and local level.

TABLE 13.1. Cable Revenue Leaders—1998

Rank	Network	Advertising Revenue Per Rating Point
1	ESPN	$1,083.3
2	MTV	1,037.5
3	NBC	993.3
4	ABC	962.5
5	CBS	883.3

Source: Derived from Joe Mandese, "Matching Ratings to Ad $$, ESPN Comes Out Tops," *Advertising Age,* April 12, 1999, p. s2.

Advantages and Disadvantages of Television

Advertisers would not invest large sums of money in television commercials unless these advertisements were effective. The major strengths of television that make it appealing as an advertising medium include the following:

- The cost-per-thousand method can be efficient: for an advertiser attempting to reach an undifferentiated market, a :30 spot on a top-rated show may cost a penny or less for each person reached.
- Television allows for the demonstration of products or services.
- Television is versatile, allowing for the combination of sounds, color, and motion. As a primarily visual medium, TV employs pictorial storytelling, a strong point in a world where the amount of time spent reading has declined. Research also shows that visual images bypass the logical brain processes and are directly conveyed to the brain's emotional center, creating the strong emotional impact characteristic of television and film.
- It is hard for viewers to tune out a commercial: television advertisements engage the senses and attract attention even when one would prefer not to be exposed to an advertisement.

As an advertising medium, television suffers from several distinct problems, including the following:

- The absolute cost of producing and running commercials has become extremely high. In 1975, a :30 spot during the Super Bowl cost $110,000. In 1998, a :30 spot sold for an average $1.3 million.
- With the invention of the remote control and the VCR, much of a viewer's time is spent switching from station to station, zipping com-

mercials (skipping through commercials in programming that was recorded on a VCR) or zapping commercials (changing channels at the beginning of a commercial break using a remote control).
- Clutter has been created by the network's increased use of promotional announcements to stimulate audience viewing of heavily promoted programs and by the increase in shorter, ten- and fifteen-second commercials. Jean Pool of J. Walter Thompson, New York, views this clutter as industry desperation to pay for its high-budget shows—the cost for one episode of *ER* rose to $13 million in 1998—and to offset its declining audiences.[9] In May 1998, the average number of commercial minutes in an hour of prime-time television rose to twelve minutes, up 14 percent since 1991.[10] Commercial time now represents nearly a quarter of total broadcast time.

Buying Television Advertising

The purchase of television advertising time is a highly specialized phase of the advertising business, particularly for large companies spending huge sums of money. The large advertiser that makes extensive use of television advertising generally utilizes agency media specialists or specialized media-buying services to arrange the media schedule and purchase television time. Agencies buy television time on both the networks and cable television (see Tables 13.2 and 13.3). In 1997, Leo Burnett's media-buying division, Star-Com, took in more than $800 million in media-buying assignments. A $60 million TV-buying account from Paramount Pictures catapulted TeleVest, New York, into the top spot as "the country's largest national TV buyer" in mid-1998.[11]

TABLE 13.2. Top Agencies by Network Television Billings

Company	1997 Billings (in billions of dollars)	Increase over 1996
Young & Rubicam	$1.3	36.1%
Televest	1.3	14.6
BBDO Worldwide	1.1	18.0
McCann-Erickson	1.1	5.4
J. Walter Thompson	1.1	13.8
Leo Burnett	1.1	30.4

Source: Adapted from Paula Hendrickson, "Net's Pace Slow, but Buyers Don't Expect Price Drop," *Advertising Age*, May 11, 1998, p. s12.

TABLE 13.3. Top Agencies by Cable Television Billings

Company	1997 Billings (in millions of dollars)	Increase over 1996
Grey Advertising	$290.3	15.6%
BBDO Worldwide	259.8	26.9
Young & Rubicam	255.5	37.4
Leo Burnett	243.3	23.8
TeleVest (D'Arcy)	230.0	20.4

Source: Adapted from Charles Waltner, "Cable Nets Covet $500 Mil Shift of the Upfront Pie," Advertising Age, May 11, 1998, p. s10.

Methods of Buying Advertising Time

A number of options are available to advertisers that choose television as part of their media mix. Some of these options include sponsoring an entire program, participating in a program, purchasing spot announcements between programs, and purchasing spots from syndicators. An advertiser can also sponsor an entire program. For example, Hallmark Cards has sponsored the critically acclaimed *Hallmark Hall of Fame* since the 1950s. Under a sponsorship arrangement, an advertiser assumes responsibility for the production of the program and, usually, the content of the program, as well as the advertising that appears. However, the costs of producing and sponsoring a thirty- or sixty-minute program make this option too expensive for most advertisers today.

Under a participation option, advertisers pay for ten, fifteen, thirty, or sixty seconds of commercial time during a particular program. Although this is less expensive, participations do not create the same high impact as full sponsorship, and the advertiser has no control over program content. Although Olympic sponsorship has been popular with major advertisers throughout the 1990s, IBM has already declined to renew its sponsorship for the Sydney Games in 2000 because of skyrocketing costs. In addition to worldwide sponsorship fees of $40 million, the price tag can triple—to over $100 million—with other expenses, including network ad costs. John Hancock, Xerox, and Visa brand managers expect accountability questions from corporate executives about the value of Olympic 2000 sponsorships. Beyond that, sponsors will be faced with renewal decisions regarding the Salt Lake City Games in 2002.[12]

Spot announcements refer to the breaks between programs that local affiliates sell to advertisers who want to show their advertisements locally.

Note that the word spot is also used in conjunction with a time frame, such as a 15-second spot, and that this usage should not be confused with spot announcements.

Syndicated programs are an increasingly popular alternative to network advertising. In the early days of television, stations purchased shows on a cash basis and sold all the commercial time on these shows to local advertisers. Today, syndication comes in three forms: off network, first run, and barter. Off-network syndication refers to reruns of network shows that are bought by individual stations. First-run syndication includes original shows produced specifically for the syndication market, such as HBO's original shows. Under barter syndication, both off-network and first-run syndicated programs, such as the popular TV shows *Wheel of Fortune* and *Oprah*, are offered free or for a reduced rate to local stations, but with some advertising time presold to national advertisers.

Local businesses and retailers, often in cooperation with nationally known manufacturers, may buy time from local network affiliates or independent stations. Most local stations sell spot announcements. However, some local advertisers do develop and sponsor local programs or buy the rights to a syndicated series.

Categories of Television Time

Television time is divided into dayparts (see Table 13.4). There are different levels of viewing during each day part, the highest being prime time (8 to 11 p.m. Eastern Standard Time or 7 to 10 p.m. Pacific Time). The network advertising time just before and just after prime time is called fringe time because it is on the fringes of the highest audience-viewing times. Daytime and late nighttime tend to have smaller audiences and lower advertising rates than prime and fringe times.

Costs of Buying Television Advertising

Network television advertising rates are negotiable. Larger advertisers may be able to get more economical, discounted rates than smaller, occasional advertisers. An advertiser must contact the networks to begin buying advertising time and negotiating the prices. As much as 98 percent of TV time is purchased by advertising agencies that have the experience and expertise to negotiate the best rates and programs. For example, J. Walter Thompson was expected to spend $1 billion during the summer 1998 up-front buying period for the networks' fall season.[13]

The Standard Rate and Data Service (SRDS) can help advertisers find local advertising rates for individual television stations. Each station bases

TABLE 13.4. Television and Radio Day Parts

Television Day Parts	
Morning:	7:00 a.m.- 9:00 a.m.
Daytime:	9:00 a.m.- 4:30 p.m.
Early fringe:	4:30 p.m.- 7:30 p.m.
Prime-time access:	7:30 p.m.- 8:00 p.m.
Prime time:	8:00 p.m.-11:00 p.m.
Late news:	11:00 p.m.-11:30 p.m.
Late fringe:	11:30 p.m.- 1:00 a.m.

Radio Day Parts	
Morning drive:	6:00 a.m.-10:00 a.m.
Daytime:	10:00 a.m.- 3:00 p.m.
Afternoon/evening drive:	3:00 p.m.- 7:00 p.m.
Nighttime:	7:00 p.m.-12:00 a.m.
All night:	12:00 a.m.- 6:00 a.m.

Source: Adapted from William F. Arens and Courtland L. Bovee, *Contemporary Advertising*, Fifth Edition. Burr Ridge, IL: Irwin, 1994, pp. 440, 450; George E. Belch and Michael A. Belch, *Advertising and Promotion: An Integrated Marketing Communications Perspective*, Fourth Edition. 1998, Boston: McGraw-Hill, pp. 354, 371.

Note: All times are Eastern Standard Time (EST).

its rates on the demand for its advertising time and the size of its audience. Media planners analyze the cost efficiency of television advertising by using the CPM formula. For example, assume that *60 Minutes*, a CBS news magazine, has a rating of 11.4 and reaches 11,172,000 U.S. households (there were 98 million total U.S. TV households during the week of August 10, 1998, according to A. C. Nielsen TV ratings, × 14.4 percent) and commercial time costs $165,000 per 30-second spot. Then,

$$CPM = \frac{\$165,000 \times 1,000}{11,172,000} = \$14.77$$

The CPM formula for assessing cost efficiency of television advertising is as follows:

$$CPM \text{ (broadcast)} = \frac{\text{Cost of a commercial}}{\text{Audience size}} \times 1,000$$

Although the media buyer uses CPM to compare the efficiency of different television programs, CPM-TM is a more appropriate cost-per-thousand statistic due to its use of target market (TM) instead of total market in the calculation as shown here:

$$\text{CPM-TM} = \frac{\text{Cost of a commercial} \times 1{,}000}{\text{Number of TM contacts}}$$

Cooperative Advertising

Because of the high cost of television advertising, two companies—often a manufacturer and a distributor—may arrange to share the cost. Not all cooperative advertising involves buying television time, of course. Manufacturers of brand-name products encourage retailers to carry and promote their products through cooperative print advertising, such as free-standing inserts placed inside newspapers. Cooperative advertising gives both partners more exposure at a reasonable price, effectively doubling both advertising budgets. For example, a travel agent that serves a local market area might share the cost of a television spot with an international cruise line. The final screen will typically show the name of the travel agent and its logo next to the name and logo of the cruise line. In addition to cost benefits, cooperative advertising may also result in a higher commercial quality. The cruise line may be able to provide professionally filmed footage so that the local spot will look like a national commercial.

The Advent of WebTV

Some media experts predict that such alternatives as WebTV will eventually rival the importance of broadcast television. WebTV, a trademark of WebTV Networks, Incorporated, refers to a Sony and Philips Magnavox Internet terminal. The system requires a television set, a phone line, and an Internet terminal and operates via remote control. A monthly subscription fee is paid to WebTV. A home page guides the viewer to a menu that includes Arts & Books, Education, Entertainment, Lifestyle, Marketplace, News, Sports, and Travel.

WebTV's user advantage is convenience: instead of waiting for the sports report on the nightly news, the user can access WebTV's sports news twenty-four hours of the day, every day of the year. WebTV provides the advantages of both the personal computer and the television. A main difference between using WebTV and the standard PC is that WebTV's remote control allows the user to sit on the couch and "zap." WebTV differs from traditional television in the features it offers, including EXPLORE (an Internet browser) and AROUND TOWN (information on local restaurants, movies, and weather).

One of WebTV's advantages for advertisers is that they may include a "www" address in a commercial. Users can then go directly to that site to learn more about the product. However, a disadvantage is that users can also "zap" commercial breaks during WebTV programming. Advertisers may find WebTV one of the most challenging media of the future.

RADIO ADVERTISING

Radio advertising is available on national networks (e.g., ABC, CBS, NBC) and in local markets (spot ratio). Many local or regional stations belong to more than one network, with each network providing specialized programming to complete a station's schedule. Advertisers may use one of the national radio networks to carry their messages to the entire national market simultaneously via stations that subscribe to the networks' programs. In spot radio advertising, an advertiser places an advertisement with an individual station rather than with a network.

Advantages and Disadvantages of Radio

Radio is popular in local retail advertising because of its relatively low cost and its localized coverage. However, it is not for every advertiser. If retailers use radio properly to promote their products, the store will benefit from advertising. Radio ad revenue grew to $13.6 billion in 1997, up 10 percent from the previous year.[14] Retailers are the largest radio ad spenders. The biggest spending increases for retail advertisers in 1996 were expected to occur in toiletries and cosmetics, followed by travel, hotels, and resorts (see Table 13.5).

TABLE 13.5. Growth Areas for Radio Advertising (Based on Spending Through July 1996—in Millions of Dollars)

Category	Amount Spent As of 7/96	Percentage of Increase over 1995
Toiletries/cosmetics	$77	98
Travel, hotels, resorts	137	56
Candy, snacks, soft drinks	85	50
Publishing, media	163	14
Business/consumer services	418	11

Source: Adapted from Anne R. Carey and Marcia Staimer, "Growth Areas for Radio Ads" USA SNAPSHOTS, *USA Today,* July 1996, p. B1.

It is important to understand the relative strengths and weaknesses of this medium to make smart decisions. The advantages include the following:

- Radio is flexible. Advertisements can run almost anytime and on short advance notice.
- Radio commercials are also inexpensive to produce. Live commercials read by an announcer are least expensive because they eliminate production costs. The cost of radio time is also relatively low. The low cost of radio also means that, given a fixed budget, advertisers can build more reach and frequency into their media schedules.
- Radio can reach specific (niche) audiences, such as men, women, the elderly, and ethnic markets. Ethnic groups such as Hispanics enjoy programs specifically dedicated to their interests. It has been possible to reach almost every niche audience in an area by advertising on multiple stations. However, this advantage has been offset somewhat by the effects of the Telecommunications Act of 1996. The radio provisions of this act "enlarged the number of stations a firm can own."[15] The impact will be discussed as a disadvantage of radio advertising in the following section.

As with any medium, radio has its disadvantages:

- Although "goliath" consolidations have created wider audiences and record advertising revenues, they have adversely affected minority ownership of FM stations (black-owned stations fell 26 percent, and Hispanic-owned, 9 percent from 1995 to 1997) and AM stations (no gains from 1995 to 1997).[16] For instance, Inner City Broadcasting's KSJL-FM in San Antonio, Texas, owned by former Malcolm X lawyer Perry Sutton, has served the needs of the city's African-American population since the late 1980s.[17] The station was purchased in May 1998 by Clear Channel Communications, the fifth largest U.S. radio station owner with 196 stations (see Table 13.6). At the same time, the Commerce Department listed only three Native American-owned FM stations and just two owned by Asian Americans.
- Radio is strictly a listening medium, and listeners cannot see the product. Therefore, radio would not be appropriate for advertising that requires demonstration. It is also necessary for listeners to hear the commercial more than once for it to be effective. A good radio script will repeat the company and/or product name at least three times to be certain that the listener has heard it. Such repetition may not be aesthetic, but it is necessary.
- Another problem with radio is the high level of audience fragmentation that occurs because of the large number of stations. Radio listen-

ers can choose from a large number of stations, and the percentage of the market tuned into any particular station is usually very small. Thus, advertisers may have to buy time on a number of stations to have broad reach, even in a local market. The advertisers must deal with each individual station, and the rate policies may differ. This problem has diminished somewhat in recent years, as the number of radio networks has increased and the number of syndicated programs has grown, offering a package of several hundred station expands.

TABLE 13.6. Top Radio Station Owners As of June 1998

Owner	Number of Stations Owned	1997 Revenue (in millions of dollars)
1. CBS	160	$1,529.4
2. Chancellor Media	108	996.0
3. Jacor Communications	204	602.2
4. Capstar Broadcasting Partners	299	537.7
5. Clear Channel Communications	196	452.3

Source: Derived from "Top 10 Station Owners," *USA Today,* July 7, 1998, p. A2.

Buying Radio Time

The following are major considerations that influence where and how to buy radio time:

- Radio advertisers are interested in reaching target customers at a reasonable cost, while ensuring that the station format (classical, country, etc.) is compatible with the advertised brand's image.
- Radio advertising is offered both on a national network (with complete market coverage) and on an individual local market spot basis (with air time purchased from individual stations in various markets). Many station groups have developed and made available computerized reach and frequency programs that help planners measure the effects of different combinations of stations in delivering both gross impressions and frequency estimates against selected audience segments.
- An advertiser has to decide on a schedule of radio advertisements. Most stations offer anywhere from two to five day parts (see Table 13.3)—

morning drive time, daytime, afternoon/evening drive time, nighttime, and all night. Rate structures vary, depending on the attractiveness of the day part. Information about rates and station formats is available in Spot Radio Rates and Data, published by the Standard Rate and Data Services.
- Radio commercial time is usually sold in ten-, thirty-, or sixty-second time slots.

Advertisers are continuing to discover ways to make effective use of radio in their media plans, often using radio as a supplement to other media such as print (newspaper, magazine, etc.). However, as with all other advertising media, radio was hurt by the cutback in advertising spending in the 1990s. Agency media executives have recently complained about skyrocketing prices for national radio spots. Two broadcast groups reportedly "spiked rates 30 percent and higher in top markets"; stations controlled by Chicago's Chancellor Media Corporation increased prices a colossal 50 percent in 1997, and Westinghouse's CBS Radio hiked prices 30 percent.[18] Some suspect consolidation is the culprit. Meanwhile, the Radio Advertising Bureau reported a 13 percent increase in revenue. In a competitive media market, radio must deal with its problems carefully to sustain its growth (see Illustration 13.1).

SUMMARY

Broadcast media include both television and radio. Advertisers have spent more and more on broadcast media in recent years, mainly because of the growth of the broadcast industry. Most of this growth has come from television, especially cable. Experts expect WebTV to become an important advertising medium in the future. Both radio and television offer advantages and disadvantages to advertisers that must be understood when making advertising decisions.

* * *

THE GLOBAL PERSPECTIVE:
KIA SHUMA'S CULTURE CLASH IN SOUTH KOREA

The woman in the ad looks too much like Princess Diana. The paparazzi chase of her Kia Shuma is just too reminiscent of the tragedy in Paris the night Diana died. Okay, this time she gets out of the car, unscathed and winking at the camera. Still, Kia Motors Corporation was slapped with worldwide criticism for a spot intended to air only in South Korea—one that had not yet aired.

During the commercial shoot in Boston, English Diana look-alike Nicky Lilley had "walked off the set is disgust—and apparently started giving interviews—when the commercial's message became clear to her." The British press subsequently condemned the unaired spot. Bewildered, the account director at Seoul-based MBC Adcom quickly replaced her with someone who did not look like Diana. Kia sent apologies to the British ambassador in Seoul as well as to the British media, but had to deal with people in its own country who were upset about the flack. South Koreans felt that the British had infringed on their own freedom of expression.[a]

The ad was clearly intended to be localized for South Korean television. Although Kia did not avoid global offense in this case, some advertisers believe all international advertising should be localized, that is, vary significantly from country to country. They believe that consumer habits, customs, and attitudes differ too much among countries for the same campaign to work everywhere. Certainly, the British and South Korean views regarding the propriety of the Kia car chase ad were diametrically opposed.

Several studies support the contention that the standardization of marketing programs is virtually impossible in markets that represent distinctive differences between home and host environments.[b] Multinational corporations should consider the cultural factors, competition, marketing institutions, and legal restrictions of the various foreign markets. Although people around the world may react similarly to certain products, such as soft drinks, responses to the same advertising image, approach, or message may be quite dissimilar.

[a] Normandy Madden, "Kia Backpedals Amid Int'l Furor over Diana Spot," *Advertising Age,* May 11, 1998, p. 30.
[b] S. Douglas and Yoram Wind, "The Myth of Globalization," *Columbia Journal of World Business,* Iss. 22, pp. 19-29.

* * *

ETHICS TRACK: CELEBRITY ENDORSEMENTS AND OTHER DECEPTIONS

Schering-Plough Corporation recently went to the Food & Drug Administration (FDA) to get clearance for television personality Joan Lunden to endorse the prescription drug Claritin in a direct-to-consumer (DTC) spot. The advertising industry has been hesitant about using celebrity endorsers in DTC ads since mid-1980 when the FDA halted Mickey Mantle's promotional endorsement of Voltaren, an arthritis drug.[a]

It might be okay that a movie actor picks up a soft drink and viewers see that it is a Pepsi or a Coke as opposed to a generic brand, if no harm is done. On the other hand, a pharmaceutical manufacturer must not dress an actor in a doctor's gown to appear in its advertising about prescription or over-the-counter drugs because viewers could be deceived into believing that they are receiving medical advice rather than a promotional message. In the case of the Claritin spot, Lunden did not pretend to be a doctor, but to be herself—in real life, an asthma sufferer—hosting a fictional television show. Lunden was expected to act as host of a new Warner Bros. Television morning show planned for fall 1999.

As discussed in the Ethics Track in Chapter 12, it would be unethical for an advertiser to use a column format for newspaper advertising without clearly identifying the material as an advertising message because the reader might believe that the message was the opinion of the newspaper rather than a profit-seeking promotion. Either the marketer or the newspaper staff must label the space clearly as advertising.

To blur the distinctions between advertising and nonadvertising, to camouflage an advertiser's promotional message, may be an effective way of reaching more potential customers more frequently. However, this involves significant risks. The first is that advertisers invite some sort of government regulation. The second risk is that advertisers may lose the goodwill of their customers. People do not like to feel foolish, not to mention deceived. How might marketers decide at what point creativity crosses the line and becomes deception?[b]

[a] Michael Wilke, "FDA Gives OK for Claritin to Use Celebrity Endorser," *Advertising Age,* July 13, 1998, p. 8.
[b] Kirk Davidson, "When Does Creativity Become Deception?" *Advertising Age,* September 23, 1996, p. 12.

Chapter 14
Alternative Advertising Media

By May of 1998, Taco Bell's televised advertising campaign featuring its facially expressive Chihuahua and his tag line, "Yo Quiero Taco Bell," extended to specialty advertising. Retail stores and mail-order catalogs began to sell T-shirts and embroidered caps bearing the image of the popular dog, the tag line, and the Taco Bell logo. Each person who purchased and wore one of these T-shirts or caps became a walking billboard for the Taco Bell "Revolution" campaign. In fact, research conducted for Jerzees Activewear suggests that about one-quarter of T-shirts owned by adults promote a charity event, and a third promote a company, product, sports event, or concert.[1]

In addition to the traditional media (television, radio, magazines, newspapers, and out-of-home advertising), marketers find themselves looking at unique, new, and, sometimes, odd media: school buses, police cars, garbage trucks, and even the moon. New York City has studied the possibility of selling advertising space on city trash cans, school buses, and playgrounds. In a test, marketers paid up to $3,300 to buy advertisement space on school lunch menus. Under an Adopt-a-Car program in Crown Point, Indiana, police cars carry signs with two-inch letters saying, "This vehicle equipped by . . ." Local businesses paid $1,500 each to fill in the blank. Space Marketing of Roswell, Georgia, said it plans to offer corporate sponsorship of a U.S./Russian research mission to put unmanned lunar rovers on the moon. The rovers will be interactive, allowing earthbound consumers to drive the vehicles on the moon by remote control.[2]

In 1997, out-of-home media spending hit $3.8 billion, an increase of $2.6 billion since the decade began. Alternative advertising is now said to fill "the nooks and crannies of everyday life" with gimmicks ranging from protective pole covers emblazoned with Pepsi-Cola, Coca-Cola, and McDonald's logos (in 5,000 airports, sports arenas, and other indoor/outdoor sites by 1999), to perfume ads printed on the back of subway passes, to Coca-Cola and Perrier logos on traditional Egyptian sailboats, the *feluccas* of the Nile.[3]

The five traditional advertising media are television, radio, newspaper, magazines, and out-of-home advertising. Newspaper and magazine adver-

ILLUSTRATION 14.1. Alternative Seating

Outdoor advertising includes such alternative media as park benches. © Dana Hanefeld.

tising were discussed in Chapter 12. Television and radio advertising were discussed in Chapter 13. This chapter will cover out-of-home advertising, including outdoor (billboards and signs) and transit (both inside and outside the vehicle). A variety of alternatives, such as specialty advertising, yellow pages advertising, infomercials, and cross-promotions, will also be discussed in this chapter.

OUT-OF-HOME ADVERTISING

Media that reach prospects outside their homes are called out-of-home media. This includes outdoor advertising (e.g., billboards and signs) and transit advertising (e.g., bus and taxicab advertising, subway posters, and terminal advertising). Out-of-home advertising, or outdoor advertising, is regarded as a supplementary advertising medium (for an alternative example, see Illustration 14.1). According to the Outdoor Advertising Association of America, the industry enjoyed the largest jump in revenue in more than a decade in 1995, hitting $1.83 billion, an 8.2 percent gain over the previous year. In 1997, Greyhound buses, for the first time, accepted exterior and interior advertising, with income projected to be $16 million a year.[4]

A major reason for the continued success of outdoor advertising is the ability of this medium to remain innovative through technology. Universal Pictures, to tease its release of *The Frighteners*, used new special effects posters with three-dimensional images. The studio was the first marketer to use Extreme Vision in the United States. In the poster for the Universal movie, a skull seemed to move closer to the viewer as the words "Dead yet?" appeared. The advertisement appeared on bus shelters, vending machines, and the sides of delivery trucks.[5]

Outdoor Advertising

Billboard advertising is the major outdoor medium due to cost efficiency—the ability to reach more people at less cost than other media. Although billboard advertising has high visibility, viewing time is brief—about ten seconds. The major forms are poster panels and painted bulletins.

Posters are lithographed or silk-screened by a printer and shipped to an outdoor advertising company. They are then prepasted and applied in sections to the poster panels that face oncoming traffic. The standard sizes of poster boards are the thirty-sheet poster, with a printed area of 9 feet 7 inches by 21 feet 7 inches, surrounded by margins of blank paper, and the bleed poster, with a printed area of 10 feet 5 inches by 22 feet 8 inches that extends all the way to the frame. Smaller eight-sheet posters are 5 feet high and 11 feet wide. These "junior posters" are used by grocers and local advertisers and are generally placed for exposure to pedestrian traffic as well as vehicular traffic. The design for an outdoor board is supplied by the advertiser or agency. Copy should be limited and emphasis given to art (pictures), headlines, and the product or company name.

For poster panels, art is printed on a set of large paper sheets. Thousands of copies can be printed and distributed around the country. The sheets are then pasted like wallpaper onto existing boards by local outdoor advertising companies that own the boards. Painted bulletins are hand painted directly onto the billboard by artists hired by the billboard owner. The standard size of painted bulletins is 14 feet by 48 feet. Some follow a rotary plan and are moved to different places every thirty, sixty, or ninety days for greater exposure. The time commitment the advertiser makes can be a disadvantage of the medium. Some billboards remain permanently at one location.

Outdoor advertising is purchased through companies that own billboards, called plants. Plants are located in all major markets throughout the nation. Companies such as Gannett Outdoor (which was acquired by Outdoor Systems in August 1996) have the larger plants with operations in multiple metropolitan areas. To simplify the national advertiser's task of buying outdoor space in multiple markets, buying organizations—or agents—facilitate the purchase of outdoor space at locations throughout the country.

When an advertiser needs to saturate a market with a new product introduction or to announce a change in package design, outdoor advertising makes possible broad coverage overnight. The basic unit of sale for billboards, or posters, is 100 gross rating points daily or a 100 showing. One rating point is equal to 1 percent of a particular market's population. Buying 100 gross rating points does not mean that the message will appear on 100 posters; rather, it means that the message will appear on as many panels as needed to provide a daily exposure theoretically equal to the total size of the market's population. Actually, a showing of 100 gross rating points achieves a daily reach of about 88.1 percent of the adults in a market over a thirty-day period.[6]

Until recently, the tobacco industry has been one of the largest outdoor advertisers. Although as much as 50 percent of poster panel and painted bulletin space used to be filled with cigarette and liquor advertising, social pressures, lifestyle changes, and governmental regulations have decreased these categories to less than 20 percent. Since 1990, advertisers of cigarettes and alcohol have voluntarily restricted placement of advertising for their products on billboards within 500 feet of schools and churches. In

November 1998, to settle a forty-six-state lawsuit, tobacco companies agreed to cease billboard advertising altogether. As a result, antitobacco message ads have replaced tobacco ads on outdoor boards. In this new, "nicotine-free world," outdoor advertising is thriving with such categories as local services and amusements, hotels and resorts, retail, and restaurants.[7] These categories topped 1998 outdoor advertising expenditures.

The outdoor advertising business has picked up new clients these days. The boom comes as advertisers hunt for cheaper alternatives to other media, such as TV, where it is becoming tougher and tougher to stand out. Also, even though the outdoor industry faces a movement toward stiffer regulation of tobacco billboards, it is picking up new business, ranging from fashion and apparel to local governments. Universal, based in Chicago, primarily serves Midwest markets. Its big advertisers include upscale retailers such as Nieman Marcus and Nordstrom, as well as automakers and car dealerships.[8]

Transit Advertising

A second form of out-of-home advertising is transit advertising. Transit advertising includes the posters seen in bus shelters and train, airport, and subway stations. Occasionally, we also see trucks that carry billboards on the highway.

The three basic types of transit advertising are inside cards, outside posters, and terminal posters. Inside cards are placed above the seats and luggage area, usually 11 inches high by either 28, 42, or 56 inches wide. Outside posters may appear on the sides, back, and/or roofs of trains and taxis. External panels or posters are designed similar to small billboards—simple, bold, catchy, and legible. Terminal posters are located at railroad, subway, bus, and air terminals. In cities with major mass transit systems, advertisers can also buy space on bus shelters and on the backs of bus-stop seats.

As with outdoor advertising, the cost basis for transit is the number of showings. A full showing (called a number 100 showing) means that one card will appear in each vehicle in the system (e.g., bus system in one city). A showing of fifty would mean that half the vehicles would carry the advertisement.

OTHER ALTERNATIVE ADVERTISING MEDIA

Speciality Advertising

Specialty advertising has been defined as "an advertising, sales promotion, and motivational communications medium which employs useful articles of merchandise imprinted with an advertiser's name, message, or logo."[9] Specialty advertising is often considered both an advertising medium and a sales promotion medium. More than 15,000 different advertising specialty items with the advertiser's name printed on them are used by businesses. Specialty items can be sent to consumers and business customers. These specialty items can serve as continuous, friendly reminders of the advertiser's business. Examples of specialty advertising include the Rolling Stones concert calling cards and the Taco Bell Chihuahua caps and shirts described at the beginning of this chapter.

Yellow Page Advertising

More than 6,000 Yellow Pages directories are distributed annually to hundreds of millions of consumers.[10] With national long distance carriers (e.g., AT&T and MCI) gearing up to compete in the local phone market, Yellow Pages advertisement agency executives anticipate parallel competition in directory publishing. Local businesses place the majority of Yellow Pages advertisements, but national advertisers are also frequent users of the Yellow Pages. The next century will see widespread availability of online yellow pages, with the Yellow Pages directory predicted to become completely paperless within the next two decades.

A new category of yellow page-type advertising is emerging on the Internet in the form of "shopbots," Web sites that offer software "agents" to assist consumers in sorting through the proliferation of online stores. Jupiter Communications has determined that 77 percent of online shoppers are looking for a specific product, so Web sites such as Excite and Compaq provide a virtual database of available products. Some "shopbots" allow the consumer to select by price, brand, or company. Featured stores pay to be listed.[11]

Infomercials and Home-Shopping Networks

Infomercials were introduced to television in the early 1980s. Most are thirty minutes long—a substantial time increase from the usual :30 to :60 television spot. Infomercials are produced by advertisers, yet are designed to be perceived as regular television programming. They typically offer consumers an 800 number so that a free call may be made to place an order or to obtain further information. Many advertisers have found the infomercial to be an extremely effective promotional tool for moving merchandise.

Although often associated with products that sell for such small-ticket prices as $19.95, the infomercial can also hawk big-ticket items. For instance, in July 1998, Chrysler Corporation aired a thirty-minute infomercial on national cable TV and United Airlines Sky TV. The infomercial pitched the new Chrysler 300M and redesigned LHS and Concorde sedans—all of which sell for considerably more than $19.95.[12]

Much of the criticism of infomercials regards the medium's resemblance to regular programming, which some view as deceptive. Many infomercials use a talk show-type format with celebrity hosts. Further, the 800 number makes ordering so easy that some viewers lose perspective and "max" their credit cards with gadgets they do not need. In response to this problem, *Good Housekeeping* tested ten popular infomercial "gizmos." Ratings—based on overall performance, truthfulness of claims, and cost—appeared in the magazine's June 1998 issue. Citrus Express received the highest rating, with nine out of ten possible points, followed by George Foreman's Lean Mean Fat Reducing Machine and Space Bag Home Storage System, each awarded eight points. The Brown & Crisp Microwave Cooking Bags offer was rated zero, that is, it was viewed by the testers as "a total dud."[13]

Despite criticism, a growing number of consumers order from infomercials, and in 1994, 22 million said they watched home-shopping programs.[14] These programs appear on cable TV channels such as QVC. To encourage ordering, an 800 number appears on the screen throughout talk show-type programming in which hosts of such exotic programs as *Brazilian Amethyst* chat with phone-in callers. QVC uses on-screen information boxes to give the item number, brief description, and price (often "special introductory" or "one time only") of the product being sold. Similar to infomercials, home-shopping programs frequently employ product demonstrations and hyperbolic rhetoric, such as, "Isn't this just absolutely gorgeous!"

New Media

Conventional advertising media have served advertisers' needs for many years, but advertisers and their agencies have been increasingly interested in new media that might be less costly, potentially more effective, and less cluttered than the established media:

- Recognizing that U.S. teens spend $100 billion a year on everything from cosmetics to sports gear to hamburgers and other fast food, cities in the United States now sell advertising space in public schools. The largest sponsors for the 33,000-student Colorado Springs, Colorado, school district each pay $12,000 a year for advertising that includes 2- by 5-foot posters in school halls and buses and recognition by sports announcers at high school games. At Colorado Springs' Audi-

bon Elementary, a Cub Foods grocery chain poster in the library urges kids to read. In the gym, a cartoon figure reaches for a Mountain Dew, a Pepsi product. Waterfield Mortgage Company has an advertisement in the hallway where parents drop off their children for preschool.[15]
- Now floor tiles bearing ads are being tested by Market Media for possible use in schools. Such imprinted tiles are already in place in Massachusetts and California grocery stores.[16]
- Teller machine talking ads are being tested by Electronic Data Systems Corporation.
- Avis rental cars will soon come equipped with cassette tape ads that pitch local restaurants, hotels, and other vendors. Advertisers may pay as much as $1,500 a month for single-city ad spots.[17]

Product Packaging

Although advertising using famous athletes is hardly a new idea, the advent of relationship marketing may change the face—or faces—displayed on cereal boxes. Some cereal boxes now feature the faces of local heroes instead of national ones. Carlisle Cereal in Bismarck, North Dakota, prepackages cereal for a major manufacturer; the packages feature hometown heroes for limited, specific geographic markets. General Mills has started to feature amateur athletic teams on its cereal boxes.

If amateur athletes on cereal boxes sounds like an innovative idea, consider Miller Brewing Company's scratch 'n' sniff package labels for novelty. A summer 1998 promotion featured scented labels on Miller Lite multipacks. Those who sniffed a coconut-scented label won a trip to Barbados, one of the promotion's 3.5 million prizes.[18]

Product Placements

For more than a decade, Hollywood has provided moving billboards for advertisers' products. The deals are a matter of mutual back-scratching. Advertisers supply edibles and drinkables for the movie crew, cars, computer equipment, helicopters, clothing, hotel scenery and lodgings, phones, electronics, and even cash or promotions for the film. In return, the movie provides exposure for the products. *Tomorrow Never Dies*, the James Bond film released in December 1997, provided alternative advertising for Visa, Heineken, Smirnoff, BMW, and Ericsson in what has been called "an unprecedented cross-promotional partnership."[19] In addition to featuring products in the film (James Bond rides a BMW motorcycle, Agent Q carries a Visa CheckCard), eight promotional partners also spent $98 million on a worldwide advertising blitz tied to the film.

Product placement in Hollywood movies gained momentum in 1982 when E. T. ate Reese's Pieces and increased candy sales for Reese's. With the cost of producing a movie now as high as $100 million, product placements supplement studio production and promotions budgets, while also helping to generate product sales for manufacturers through what is called the "halo effect." BMW reported 10,000 preorders for the Cruiser motorcycle that Bond rode in *Tomorrow Never Dies* and in the numerous televisioned trailers (film commercial spots) for the 1997 film.[20]

CROSS-PROMOTIONS

Various media, both traditional and alternative, may be employed in an advertising or marketing campaign. Cross-promotions involve the use of one product to promote another product and may be reciprocal. Although cross-promotion is nothing new (Bob Hope used his radio show during World War II to promote his movies), with the advent of new media, the possibilities for cross-promotion now seem endless.

- In addition to promoting via electronic press kit (trailers and features intended to air on television or in movie theaters), print advertising, and outdoor advertising (posters and billboards), MGM promoted *Tomorrow Never Dies* on its own Web site. The home page features a dramatic picture of Pierce Brosnan as James Bond, wearing a tuxedo and brandishing his handgun. The site provides a menu with subject categories similar to those of the electronic press kit—Cast, Characters, Story, Production, Media, and Soundtrack. However, the Web site provided options that no other media could—a TND Shockwave Game, access to sweepstakes entry information, and interactive contacts.

- For the release of its videotape of the film *Liar, Liar* in late 1997, Fox chose to place advertisements on 12 million apples in supermarkets at a cost of only $6.50 per thousand apples, compared to $450,000 or more for a thirty-second commercial. Placements of advertising on consumer products could be a future trend, perhaps leading to a vodka ad on a lemon or a miniature canned tomato soup label on a tomato.[21]

- In spring 1998, McDonald's McRib sandwich cross-promoted Disney's Animal Kingdom with the commercial tag line "Get Wild with McRib" and product packaging that featured jungle prints and the words "Animal Kingdom." *Time* magazine questioned this alliance: "Isn't it odd to connect frolicking animals and a rib sandwich?" Nevertheless, McDonald's stood by its marketing venture.[22]

- Vending machines in thirty-four East Coast theater lobbies dispensed movie-themed T-shirts for a multimillion-dollar movie, *Lost in Space*, in

1998. A long-familiar marketing device, the vending machine is now viewed as an alternative channel for promotions and merchandising. Live bait vending machines have appeared at gas stations, state parks, and boat launches, and Hewlett-Packard set up 200 HP Supply Stores, vending office supply merchandise, in summer 1998. Canned cold drinks still account for the majority of the $31 billion-a-year automatic merchandise business.[23]

- MSNBC may be the mother of future cross-promotions, pioneering ways that promotions may cross media in the next century. Launched July 15, 1996, MSNBC is a twenty-four-hour news, information, and talk network available in 30 million U.S. cable households and on the Internet. The number one television network, NBC, joined with Microsoft in anticipation of an Internet-driven future, projecting that cross-promotions would increase MSNBC cable subscriptions from 30 million at the time of the launch to 55 million by the year 2000.[24]

The MSNBC concept is to target network and cable television viewers and personal computer users with promotional messages designed to send NBC's viewers to its cable station CNBC and to the MSNBC Web site. PC users receive frequent updates on network news stories, and the cable station sends viewers to both the network and the Web site. Programs for MSNBC are developed simultaneously for cable and the Internet using crossover staff, including such network personalities as Tom Brokaw, Katie Couric, and Maria Shriver. The concept seems to have worked for CNBC, which topped the Nielsen charts with its 50.9 percent prime-time ratings growth from the first quarter of 1997 to the first quarter of 1998. Its main competitor, CNN, came in with 44.8 percent growth for the period. For business news, CNBC boasted an ever more dramatic 68.3 percent increase, perhaps because computers are so widely used in the business world—and CNBC was getting a constant plug from Microsoft.

- In 1998, NBC strengthened its Internet promotional clout with the purchase of 19 percent of Snap, a CNET Web directory service, and an option to buy up to 60 percent of the Internet service provider. Web users searching for news, weather, and entertainment are expected to make Snap a popular "jumping-off point," and advertisers may pay top rates to appear on Snap pages.[25] NBC did not expect conflicts to arise regarding its partnerships with CNET and Microsoft, owners of the Web directory service Start and NBC's partner in MSNBC.

SUMMARY

This chapter offered just a sample of the increasingly extensive and diverse use of alternative advertising and new media. Today, any space (or time) is a potential medium for a marketer's advertisement. From the T-shirts and caps bearing the image of the Taco Bell dog to the sophisticated cross-promotional expertise of NBC, alternative advertising provides a way to make products and services stand out from traditional media clutter.

* * *

THE GLOBAL PERSPECTIVE: CROSS-TRAINING ACROSS BORDERS

When a brand marks $4 million in Internet sales a day, would television commercials be a logical choice for the bulk of the brand's ad spending? J. Walter Thompson's Total Solutions Group—the overseer of Dell Computer Corporation's 1998 global campaign and Dell's $70 million account—did not think so.

Major agencies with Integrated Marketing units are now cross-training their staffs so that, for example, direct marketing experts are learning about point-of-purchase strategies. Such training helped DDB's Beyond DDB unit launch an innovative campaign for U.S. Gypsum's wallboard brand. The campaign included a construction site contest, "radio spots aired at 4 a.m., or 'construction drive time,'" and print ads in construction trade publications. A DDB campaign for Comedy Central's animated children's TV series included a "mobile marketing effort" that crisscrossed the country.

Alternative advertising channels may be considered for global accounts where countries lack up-to-date broadcast and postal services, making television commercials and direct mailings impractical. Furthermore, mailing lists may not be available around the world in the same degree to which they are in the United States. Pan-regional radio stations have become a popular alternative as a result of satellite technology. Some advertisements can virtually run worldwide, but others must be tailored locally to mesh with both the culture and the available communication channels.

Agency staffers who have been cross-trained will be better equipped to deal with the challenges of global advertising. Also, taking the time to train people has to be worthwhile. After all, international business transactions generate trillions of dollars a year in global sales. Moreover, virtually every nation in the world engages in significant international business.

Source: Kate Fitzgerald, "Beyond Advertising," *Advertising Age*, August 3, 1998, p. 14.

* * *

ETHICS TRACK: THE SQUAWK OVER L'EGGS' EGGS

Plastic eggs are artificial, sure. But why would a plastic egg offend consumers? L'eggs got pecked by the public in the early 1990s for using environmentally unfriendly plastic egg-shaped cartons to package its pantyhose. For more than twenty years, the company had sold its hosiery in cleverly egg-shaped containers, but it quickly changed to recycled paperboard packing in response to public pressure.

The squawk over L'eggs' containers arose about the same time McDonald's and other companies were publicly pressured to show social responsibility by packaging products in biodegradable containers. Plastic was choking America's landfills, and consumers were concerned about such landfill offenders as McDonald's Styrofoam carryout containers. Packaging is perhaps the most noticeable step a company can take in going green (see our discussion of green marketing in Chapter 11's Ethics Track).

Most advertisers today strive to maintain high ethical standards and socially responsible advertising practices regarding the environment. Once an unchecked business activity, advertising is now closely scrutinized and heavily regulated. For example, the U.S. Federal Trade Commission (FTC) has published *Guidelines for the Use of Environmental Marketing Claims,* a publication that attempts to interpret the laws regarding labeling and packaging using real-world examples. The regulations apply to labeling, advertising, promotional materials, and other forms of marketing. In addition, consumer groups, special interest groups, and even other advertisers review, check, control, and change advertising.

Although governmental regulations and self-regulation may make an advertiser's job more difficult, do the benefits of such programs and efforts outweigh the cost and effort they entail? Does the company itself benefit from greater environmental awareness?

Chapter 15

Direct Marketing/ Direct Response Advertising

Each fall, close to 3 million U.S. shoppers await the arrival of the Neiman Marcus Christmas catalog with almost as much excitement as the holiday season itself. This retailer/direct marketer decided to find out whether brand-conscious Japanese consumers could get into the same spirit. After all, Japan's total mail-order business hit U.S. $19.1 billion in the early 1990s.[1] Financial giant JCB had already experienced great success with its introduction of The Cashmere Store of Edinburgh, Scotland, to the Japanese direct market, which requested 20,000 Cashmere Store catalogs. On September 18, 1996, Neiman Marcus Company launched its first ever overseas marketing effort, mailing the 1996 Christmas catalog to as many as 100,000 Japanese buyers.

Many Japanese, especially young people, celebrate Christmas by exchanging gifts, even though Buddhism remains the predominant religion. Neiman Marcus did not veer from its U.S. roots; the Japanese version of the catalog was almost identical to the original, with a few exceptions, such as food items that might spoil during overseas shipment. Instead of buying mailing lists for direct marketing of the catalog, Neiman Marcus placed Japanese-language advertisements in upscale magazines, large circulation newspapers, and mail-order publications. The campaign also included promotional inserts in credit card mailings. Handled by the Tokyo office of J. Walter Thompson, advertisements offered subscriptions to the Japanese catalog for $13.50, more than double the $6.50 U.S. price tag for the Christmas catalog. The response was encouraging, with 100,000 catalog subscriptions—and the direct marketing venture had just begun (see Illustraiton 15.1 for another example of a direct marketing mailing).[2]

Whereas mail-order catalogs represent "classic" direct marketing, the Information Age has ushered in the era of multichannel direct marketing. Neiman Marcus combined traditional advertising with invoice inserts to market its Christmas catalog in Japan. Other companies employ electronic chan-

ILLUSTRATION 15.1. A Dimensional Mailer

To cut through mailbox clutter, Rapp Collins Worldwide created this "Year 2000" direct mail package for PLATINUM Technology, Incorporated. The mailing included a pound of coffee, two glass mugs, and a letter on stationery with a bagel on top. Such innovation ensures that the direct mailing will be effective. The recipient will not only open the mailing but will also, most likely, keep the mailing's contents, which serve as a reminder of the company or product.

234

nels to provide immediate, convenient, personalized service. Electronic commerce may also be supported by print and television advertising. For example, IBM has responded to changes in the buyer behavior of technology-product customers. Its Web site offers seven-day-a-week, twenty-four-hour availability. Traffic patterns indicate that IBM Web site activity continues some days as late as 2 a.m. IBM's customers expect the company to be "customer driven."[3]

As early as 1995, 68.7 percent of the U.S. adult population had ordered merchandise or services by phone or mail, according to the Direct Marketing Educational Foundation, Incorporated. We include examples of direct response advertising in other chapters of this book, for example, infomercials, home-shopping channels, magazine subscription advertising that features toll-free numbers and operators standing by to take orders, and Internet advertising, much of which employs a mechanism for two-way communication. This chapter explores direct marketing/direct response advertising in greater depth.

DIRECT MARKETING

What Is Direct Marketing?

The Direct Marketing Association, a trade group whose members practice various forms of direct marketing, defines direct marketing as an interactive system of marketing that uses one or more advertising media to effect a measurable response and/or transaction at any location.[4] Embedded in this definition are four components:

1. Direct marketing is an interactive system in that it entails personalized communications between marketer and customer. With the advent of computers and the development of extensive databases, it has become possible for an advertiser to develop one-on-one, two-way communication with those most likely to be in the market for a certain product when those customers are ready to buy. Some industry leaders believe that all Internet advertising should be categorized as direct marketing.
2. Direct marketing involves one or more media (e.g., mail and telephone).
3. Direct marketing is measurable. That is, direct marketing allows the marketer to calculate precisely the costs of producing the communication effort and the resulting outcome.

4. Location is not an issue in direct marketing. Direct marketing takes place at a variety of locations—by phone, mail, or Internet—and the order can be made at any time of the day or night. Product delivery can also be made to the consumer's home or to the business client's workplace.

According to a study by the Direct Marketing Association, overall media spending for direct marketing advertising expenditures rose to $153 billion in 1997, up from $104 billion in 1992, an increase of 8 percent annually. Direct marketing advertising expenditures have grown to represent 58.3 percent of total U.S. advertising expenditures. Business-to-business direct marketing expenditures accounted for 54 percent of total direct market expenditures in 1996. From 1996 to 2001, business-to-business growth is forecast at 8.3 percent on an annual basis. On the consumer side, the expected growth is 5.9 percent per year.[5] The DMA predicts that total direct marketing sales should reach $1.86 trillion by 2002, $880 billion of which is expected to be business-to-business, and $979 billion for consumer direct marketing. As will be discussed more fully in the final section of this chapter, global direct marketing has a bright future. According to the Direct Marketing Educational Foundation, the top five most profitable non-U.S. direct markets for U.S. marketers currently are Canada, the United Kingdom, Germany, Japan, and Mexico, in that order.

DIRECT RESPONSE ADVERTISING

Direct response advertising is a term used synonymously with direct marketing. Direct response channels include direct mail, catalogs, telephone, print, television and electronic shopping, and interactive media. Lists and databases assist direct response advertisers in identifying customers and demographic trends. Direct response advertising is not limited to consumer marketing, but includes business-to-business and financial services customers as well. Nonprofit organizations use direct response advertising extensively for fund-raising and membership retention. Direct response advertising differs from other forms of advertising in a number of ways, but most distinctly in its concern with the sales transaction process, which includes back-end activities such as order fulfillment and customer service.

Direct response advertising has become a fast-growing segment of the advertising industry. The industry's growth has been attributed to both social and technological factors. The rise in the number of single-parent homes and the influx of women into the workforce in recent decades are two societal factors. Furthermore, with both men and women spending long hours working in or out of the home, out-of-home shopping can sometimes be a nuisance or a waste of time. The credit card has also made direct marketing more attractive to the consumer. The previous payment system—cash on delivery (COD)—was less convenient (the shopper having to be at home when the delivery was made) and less reliable (customers not having the cash on hand, etc.). Now people can just sit at home, make purchases with their credit cards via telephone or computer, and find the prepaid packages on their doorsteps when they come home from work.

Technological advances have made direct marketing more efficient for marketers and more beneficial for shoppers. Advances in computer technology in the 1960s accelerated the industry's growth. Initially, the database allowed marketers to identify customers and prospects by name and to determine the best possible purchasers and prospects for a given offer at a given time through the availability of quantifiable information. The advent of cyber shopping was made possible by the Internet. Such household names as Wal-Mart, JC Penney, and the Gap already maintain online storefronts. A 1997 Georgia Tech survey of online shoppers gave the industry good and bad news. Forty percent of shoppers found what they were looking for within five to fifteen minutes; however, many shoppers found sites hard to use, too slow, or confusing.[6] Some potential online shoppers fear credit card fraud or loss of privacy, such as being placed on unsolicited mailing lists. Nevertheless, the number of online shopping revenues is expected to reach $2.77 billion by the year 2000.

DIRECT MARKETING HISTORY

Direct marketing is an industry that spans seven centuries, developing from the rural distribution of seed catalogs to database marketing. According to Susan Jones in *Creative Strategy in Direct Marketing*, the history of direct marketing begins around 1450 with Johann Gutenberg's invention of the printing press.[7] The new invention allowed European merchants to publish product catalogs, such as those in which English nurserymen advertised seeds and plants to farmers. In the United States, Benjamin Franklin began the first "continuity-style book club," with members selecting from almost 600 book titles by 1744.

Early direct marketers learned their trade from an abundance of door-to-door peddlers who traveled with such wares as soaps and medicines. Aaron Montgomery Ward was one such peddler who decided to advertise and sell by catalog. This catalog grew to 240 pages by 1884. Richard Warren Sears was a peddler of watches before he teamed with Alvah Curtis Roebuck and started Sears, Roebuck & Company. The two created a catalog that reached 75,000,000 customers through the mail by 1927. The catalog business was catalyzed by Rural Free Delivery in the 1890s and Parcel Post in 1913, allowing direct marketers to ship to the most remote areas of the United States.

The Direct Marketing Association (DMA) was established as the Direct Mail Advertising Association in 1917. After World War II, the baby boom created a demand for goods that were in short supply in neighborhood stores, and consumers turned to catalog shopping in greater numbers than ever. Advances in computer technology and the widespread availability of credit cards in the 1960s and 1970s further accelerated direct marketing growth.

Computer technology allowed for the storage and retrieval of information about customers, paving the way for more effective marketing and the creation and management of relationships between the buyer and seller. For this reason, some industry leaders argue that direct marketing is synonymous with "relationship marketing." Others use the term "database marketing." Database marketing has led to more efficient new customer acquisition, value maximization (i.e., development of product bundles or cross-sell opportunities), customer status change identification, identification of customer problems, participation of customers in contact management, and win-back opportunities to target good customers who have defected.[8]

What information about customers do direct marketers most often add to a database? According to the DMA's *1996 Statistical Fact Book*, customer loyalty is most valued, with 68 percent of marketers maintaining information about the length of time an individual or company has been a customer. Table 15.1 lists other information frequently included in a database. Marketers build models to cast diverse information into predictive patterns. These are called predictive models.

TABLE 15.1. Types of Customer Data Most Marketers Maintain

Type of Data	Percentage Who Maintain It*
Length of time individual/company has been a customer	68.0
Dollar value of purchases	67.1
Number of annual purchases	63.2
Source of original lead or contact	56.8

Source: Adapted from Direct Marketing Association, *1996 Statistical Fact Book*, New York-Direct Marketing Association, 1996, p. 24.

* According to surveys conducted by *Direct Magazine* in 1994.

DIRECT MAIL

Direct mail advertising refers to any advertising matter sent directly to the person the marketer wishes to influence. These advertisements take the form of letters, catalogs, and so on. This direct marketing medium constitutes what has been commonly referred to as "junk mail"—the unsolicited mail you find your mailbox. Direct mail can be anything and look like anything, but most pieces follow a fairly conventional format (e.g., see Illustration 15.2). A direct mail package usually includes a letter, a brochure, supplemental flyers, and a reply card with a return envelope inside an outer envelope. Mailing lists drawn from consumer and/or customer information databases are key to the success of a direct mail campaign. Database information allows for market segmentation. Lists have become increasingly more current and more selective, eliminating waste coverage. The most commonly employed lists are of those individuals who have been past purchasers of direct mail products.

List brokers have thousands of lists tied to demographic, psychographic, and geographic breakdowns. Most major firms can put together a list for a buyer by combining (merging) lists and deleting (purging) repeat names.

Although direct mailings are less constrained by the time and space considerations of print, broadcast, and other media, they do need to adhere to postal rules and regulations. The creative possibilities of direct mail materials are almost endless. Mailings may involve any combination of pieces, including outer envelopes, letters, brochures, response cards, reply envelopes, inserts, postcards (see Illustration 15.3), and product samples, informational computer disks, and/or videotapes. Of these, the letter has been the single most important piece because it can stand alone, personalize the mailing, and enhance the mailing's credibility through its length—a factor that, as research has shown, adds to the receiver's perception of the marketer's credibility. Typically, direct mail letters

- employ attention-getting openings;
- communicate product benefits;
- establish a personal relationship by using the receiver's name in the salutation, a real person's signature, a friendly tone, and you-oriented language; and
- close with a final pitch.

A postscript (PS) is recommended since it is one of the parts of the letter that receivers tend to read first. The PS may "restate the prime

ILLUSTRATION 15.2. Outer Envelopes

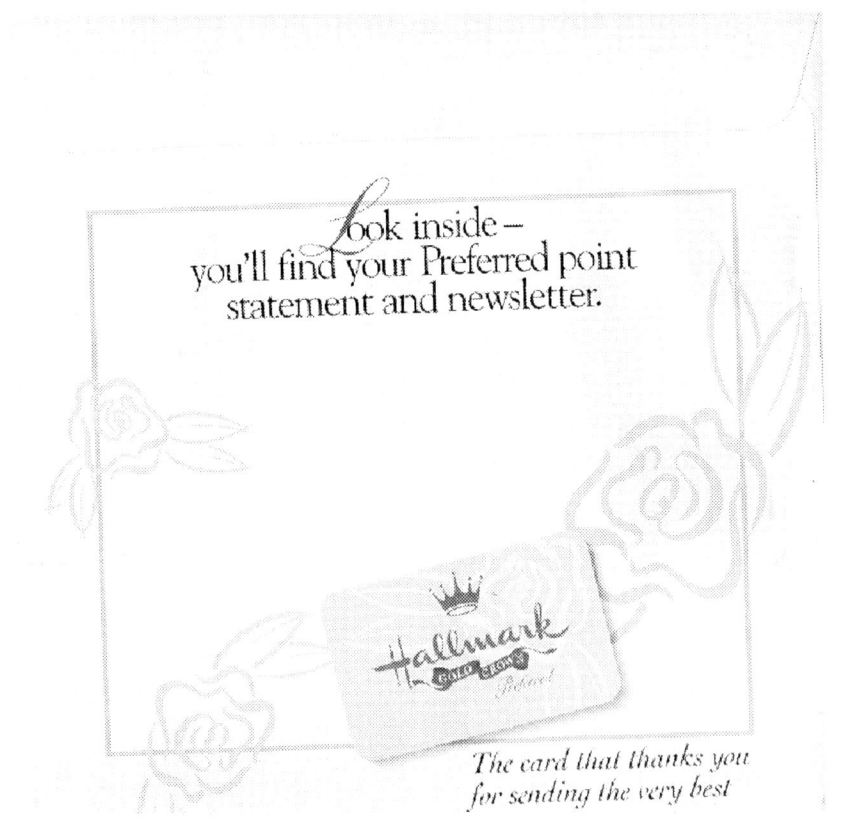

look inside — you'll find your Preferred point statement and newsletter.

The card that thanks you for sending the very best

Direct mailings can look like anything and be enclosed in envelopes of any shape or size as long as they adhere to postal regulations. The message on the back of the 9- by 9-inch outer envelope in this Hallmark Gold Crown Card Program mailing to preferred members directs the recipient to look inside for a bonus point statement and newsletter. The unusual shape and size of the envelope attracts attention, and revealing the contents encourages the recipient to open it. A window on the envelope's front makes the mailing look more official and important.

product benefit; highlight the urgency of the offer; refer the reader to the brochure, order form, testimonials, or other component of the package; remind the prospect about the premium; offer a toll-free number for ease in ordering; or emphasize the risk-free nature of the offer."[9]

Direct Marketing/Direct Response Advertising 241

ILLUSTRATION 15.3. Postcards

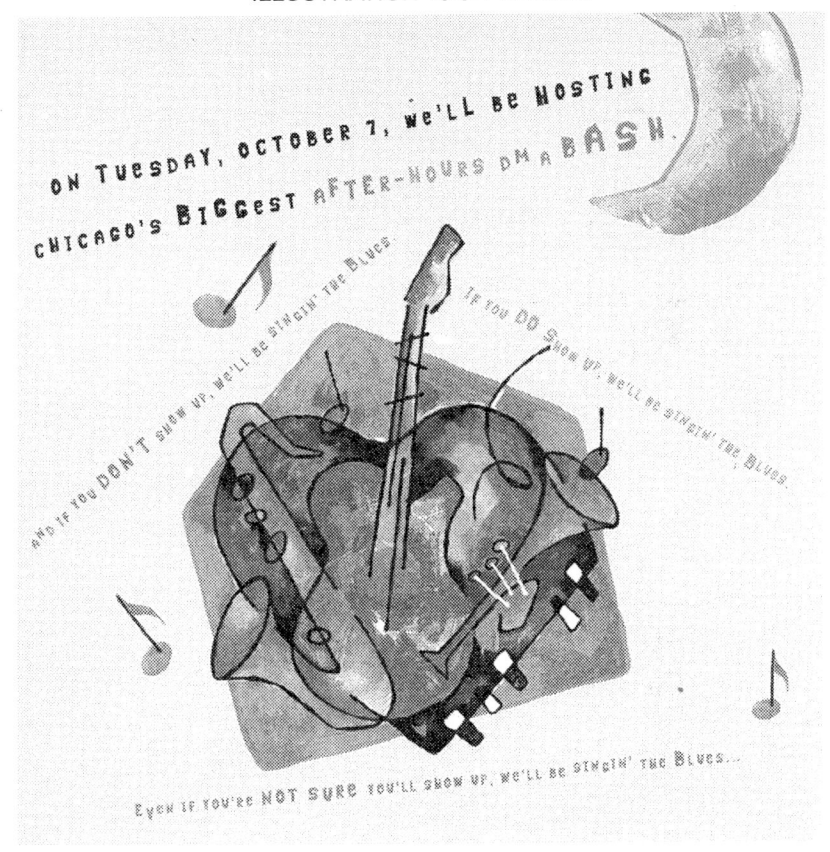

The postcard provides a cost-effective mailer. Rapp Collins Worldwide/Chicago mailed this card as an invitation to Direct Marketing Association conferees to "make a little room on your calendar" to attend a party at Chicago's House of Blues for "the biggest baddest blues club in the world's best blues town."

CATALOG MARKETING

Now an industry over 500 years old, catalog marketing is one form of direct mail. With more high-income families shopping at home, specialized niche catalogs are becoming big business. Name a product, and at least one company is probably marketing that item via catalog—clothing, health and beauty products, sporting goods, gardening supplies, office supplies, and other types of products (e.g., see Illustration 15.4). For example, L.L. Bean markets its sporting goods via catalog. Some big retailers, such as JCPenney, have their own full-line merchandise catalogs. Business-to-business marketers send catalogs to their customers to supplement their sales force's time and effort.

Although catalog marketing is pervasive, this industry has reached the mature life-cycle stage. As a result, some companies, notably historic catalog pioneers Sears and Montgomery Ward, have pulled out of the mail-order business. Some previously mail-order-only firms have opened retail stores, such as Banana Republic. L.L. Bean cut twelve pages from its Christmas 1996 holiday catalog because it expected flat sales. Spiegel's

ILLUSTRATION 15.4. Unlimited Creativity

The cover reveals the catalog's theme. The child's drawing of a personified star, the splash of stars, and the words "Brighten the life of a child" suggest that buying cards from the Children's Memorial Hospital's 1998 Holiday Card Collection catalog will do more than the purchase of other cards might. The theme is reinforced with the words "You have a hand in the future when you're taking care of children," written in star-colored gold across the sky blue inside cover paper. Courtesy of Rapp Collins Worldwide/Chicago.

holiday catalog is down to twelve pages. Some catalog makers have been so distraught with the slow-growing domestic market that they are searching overseas for new business.[10]

According to the Direct Marketing Association, the U.S. catalog business in Japan has grown rapidly, to $750 million in sales.[11] Before its Christmas catalog was sent to 100,000 Japanese customers, Neiman Marcus had conducted year-long Japanese tests of two other Neiman Marcus-owned catalogs, Horchow and Trifles. Lands' End, a U.S. catalog retailer comparable to L.L. Bean, has begun a fresh thrust into Hong Kong and Singapore. The main reasons for the company to enter these two countries are as follows: (1) both countries are small enough to be manageable; (2) they have efficient postal and express delivery systems; (3) they boast highly educated consumers and a sizable number of Americans, providing an existing Lands' End customer base; and (4) they have large and growing professional classes proficient in English.[12] These are some of the areas that must concern catalog marketers as they seek to expand globally.

The catalog offers room for almost unlimited creativity. The catalog cover is a major consideration in catalog design. The cover often reveals the catalog's theme; for instance, a department store's Christmas catalog might feature a snowy, winter scene with an old-fashioned, decorated pine tree in a city square. Cover art also defines the company's image, for example, the tree might reflect the store's long tradition, while the city square would suggest its sophistication. The back cover customarily features the products most likely to generate customer interest. Inside, key pages on which top-selling or new products are often pictured include the inside pages of the front and back covers and the center spread.

Other creative decisions include the catalog size (both dimensional and number of pages), paper quality, art and graphics (products may be photographed or illustrated), and layout style. Some catalogs are now quite distinctive in style—for instance, the SelfCare catalog features customer testimonials in shaded boxes next to pictures and descriptions of the products being praised; Victoria's Secret often features full-page photographs of glamorous models posed against deep-hued Victorian backdrops; The Tog Shop shows its clothing lines in stylized illustrations.

The catalog message has become crucial in an industry that, in the 1990s, must come to terms with saturated markets. The most important part of the catalog message is the graphics. Products are displayed in attractive settings showing as many details and features as possible. People scan through a catalog, looking at the pictures. When a visual appeals to the customer, the person stops scanning and decides to read the copy blocks. Magazine-style pages may have headlines and subheads. Both copy style and the size and style of the type in which the copy is set should complement the layout and, overall, reflect the personality or image of the issuing store or company. Copy may be long and detailed or very short. Typically, copy describes the product, notes distinctive features, and provides such additional information as fabric and color choices, sizes, and price.

Catalogs may encourage purchases by offering sale merchandise, free gifts with purchase of certain products or an order in a set dollar amount, discounts for volume orders, gift wrapping and cards, and gift certificates. Blank space on the reverse side of the order form may be used to prominently display these encouragements. Many order forms also include a section for referrals so that customers can have catalogs sent to others who might be interested in the products.

DIRECT MARKETING AND THE ENVIRONMENT

One of the biggest concerns consumers express about catalogs and other direct mail regards paper waste. Electronic catalogs provide an option, of course. However, direct marketing industry spokespersons have been quick to point out that there is a great deal of misinformation about and exaggerations of, the problem of junk mail—a derogatory term used by direct mail opponents—in the waste stream.[13] To offset a negative environmental image, the Direct Marketing Association provides *The DMA Environmental Action Kit* to its members. The association urges its members to act as environmental activists by recycling paper and working with their trade associations to incorporate environmentalism into their business strategies. Others ship merchandise in biodegradable packing material. Furthermore, environmental groups themselves routinely utilize direct mail for recruitment of members, informing members, and fundraising.

TELEMARKETING

With the escalation of the cost of the personal sales call over the past decade (see Table 15.2), many companies now use the telephone to support or even replace their conventional sales forces. Business-to-business marketers spent 12.3 percent of their 1995 direct marketing expenditures on telemarketing, according to an *Advertising Age* study.[14] Although $292 was the national average for the cost of a business-to-business sales call in 1997, in some industries, personal sales calls were more expensive, e.g., $322 per

TABLE 15.2. Average Cost of a Personal Sales Call

Year	Average Cost Per Call*
1980	$128
1984	$196
1988	$240
1993	$295

Source: Adapted from Direct Marketing Association, *1997 Statistical Fact Book,* New York: Direct Marketing Association, 1997, p. 219.

*Cost includes salary, benefits, commissions, travel and other expenses, promotional materials, and samples.

call for electronics and computer manufacturing companies. Compounding the cost is that it may take as many as four to six personal calls to close a sale.

Personal sales calls are very expensive, but very persuasive. Telemarketing is almost as persuasive, but a lot less expensive. However, telemarketing is not appropriate for all organizations. Telemarketing has to be efficient to be justifiable. The revenue has to justify the bottom-line costs. Forty percent of business-to-business marketers reported that they used telemarketing as a communication tactic, according to the DMA's *1997 Statistical Fact Book.*

Most companies that use telemarketing hire a specialized company to handle the solicitations and order taking. Companies usually do not have the facilities to handle a mass response, and that response, known as back-end marketing, is crucial to the process. For example, a company may advertise a product on television and be flooded by calls into the company's switchboard. Respondents have come to expect immediate information and/or order taking, as well as prompt product delivery. In today's competitive direct marketplace, if that company cannot quickly gratify the respondent, another company will.

Two forms of telephone marketing are practiced. One involves inbound calls for orders, inquiries, and complaints. The other involves outbound calls from telephone salespersons. The company may handle its telemarketing in-house, employing and overseeing its own telemarketers, or it may contract a telemarketing company to provide the service. In-house telemarketing is generally preferable, as company employees may know the product line better and may have a greater sense of company loyalty.

In addition to the use of telemarketing calls in business-to-business activities, such calls are also made to consumers. According to a national survey reported in the DMA's *1997 Statistical Fact Book*, 63 percent of consumers surveyed said they had received telemarketing calls from long distance telephone companies. Other types of calls consumers frequently received included local charities (62 percent), household product companies (49 percent), magazine subscription services (46 percent), and credit card offers (45 percent). Consumer responses to the calls ranged from highly favorable ratings for calls from charities to the greatest dissatisfaction with calls offering free vacations, household services, and sweepstakes.

Many consumers are disgusted with all forms of telephone marketing. They are besieged by calls from telemarketers at undesirable times, particularly during dinner hours. Telemarketing scams are everywhere. In response to consumer complaints, government regulators have taken action to try to prevent further abuses. Telemarketers need to be aware of the negative image of their industry and abandon practices that annoy and anger consumers. A better-designed message can reduce complaints and sell products more effectively. The outbound message needs to be simple, compelling, and short. Most people will not stay on the telephone longer than two to three minutes for a sales call.

NONPROFIT DIRECT MARKETING

Total donations, mail-order sales, and traffic generation brought in $59.94 billion to nonprofit organizations in 1997.[15] Religious organizations typically raise almost half of these monies, followed by human service organizations, educational institutions, health-related groups, and arts, culture, and the humanities, in that order.[16] The bulk of charitable giving comes from individuals—as much as 92 to 94 percent, with the remainder derived from corporate giving and foundations.

Direct mail and person-to-person communication have been the most common fund-raising techniques for decades. Direct mail has provided a cost-effective, measurable way to target prospective donors, providing the organization's "story" in such written formats as letters and brochures.[17] Database marketing has increased the efficiency of direct mail solicitations, and computers have allowed for personalization of appeals through individualized salutations. Some organizations follow up direct mail appeals with phone calls.

Direct mail pieces for fund-raisers generally utilize the same methods as profit marketers, e.g., human interest, personalization, and celebrity endorsements.[18] Many organizations now send membership cards, merchandise and insurance offers, organization newsletters, and notices of conventions or social events to fulfill the donor's need for a sense of affiliation. Nonprofit organizations such as AARP offer special insurance rates, a motor club program, and discounts at participating hotels, among other member benefits. Animal rights organizations such as the World Wildlife Federation, People for the Ethical Treatment of Animals (PETA), and the United States Humane Society all send attractive, sophisticated newsletters to contributors. Some send unsolicited gifts, especially greeting and note cards, along with appeals for additional contributions once an initial contribution has been made.

Nonprofits have reached beyond direct mail solicitations to utilize other direct response strategies in their fund-raising campaigns. A recent trend in fund-raising, troubling to some, has been the use of merchandising to raise dollars for charities. For instance, the Paralyzed Veterans of America, a fifty-year-old nonprofit charitable organization, anticipated an $800,000 surplus when it ran newspaper advertising in October 1996 to announce its new line of collectibles. Such organizations use merchandising "to obtain some discretionary dollars that were not earmarked for philanthropy."[19]

WGBH, a public television station in Boston, raises additional dollars by selling merchandise through its *Signals* mail-order catalog. PBS, a private nonprofit corporation owned by the nation's public service television stations, raises money through the sale of merchandise advertised in its slick, four-color catalog, *PBS Home Video*. Public television stations routinely offer merchandise premiums during their pledge drives. When the nation's number one PBS station, Chicago's WTTW, offered those who pledged $250 a videotape of *Les Miserables* as an exclusive on-air promotion in a 1996 pledge drive, the station had 2,500 takers. However, the station discovered a problem with merchandise-for-pledge offers. Since the technique focuses as much on merchandising as philanthropy, it has proven difficult to get first-time pledgers to renew during the next drive unless the station can come up with comparable merchandise.

As federal dollars for nonprofit organizations have declined and the number of nonprofit organizations has continued to grow (from 200,000 nonprofits in 1970 to 600,000 in 1996), competition for fund-raising dollars has become intense. Individual and corporate donors expect more for their money than purely philanthropic givers of the past. WTTW hired an outside fulfillment house to ensure that its pledgers would receive their premium merchandise as quickly as they would receive goods ordered from a mail-order company. Tax deductions; mentions in programs, newsletters, and brochures; and on-air acknowledgments of program sponsors are a few of the perks expected today in return for a donation. Fund-raising is no longer as simple as it once was—just sending out a solicitation letter or asking volunteers to make door-to-door calls.

PRIVACY ISSUES

An agreement between American Express and Knowledge-Base, a database marketing firm, angered consumer privacy advocates. Just two months after AmEx arranged to make Knowledge-Base's data on 175 million Americans available to any merchant accepting AmEx cards, the deal had to be scrapped. America Online crafted a new customer privacy policy after an AOL staff member "disclosed confidential customer information about a Navy man to military officials."[20] Pacific Bell decided not to telemarket customers with unpublished phone numbers, and consumer privacy complaints caused the CVS drugstore chain and Giant Food to terminate agreements with a Massachusetts marketing firm.

The Telephone Preference Service of the Direct Marketing Association provides consumers with the option of removing their names from mailing lists. Requests to be on the no-call list are said to have reduced the number of telemarketing calls by 70 percent. This is one way the Direct Marketing Association has responded to rising consumer concerns about privacy. Although the industry offers to regulate itself by agreeing to remove names from lists, 52 percent of the public are unaware of name removal procedures. According to a Harris-Equifax Consumer Privacy Survey, "consumers who are unaware of name removal are more likely to be young and to be African-American, and less likely to be well-educated, to have shopped by mail, and are less likely to be concerned about consumer privacy than consumers who are aware."[21]

A new law also protects consumer rights regarding telemarketing calls. As part of the Telephone Consumer Protection Act of 1991 (effective December 20, 1992), the FCC "among other things, limited residential telemarketing calls to between 8 a.m. and 9 p.m.; prohibited the use of autodialers or pre-recorded messages to emergency and health care facility lines; permitted consumer and state authorities to sue telemarketers in state courts for damages up to $500 per call. Tax-exempt nonprofit organizations were exempted."[22]

BUSINESS-TO-BUSINESS MARKETING

In addition to the growth of direct response consumer marketing, business-to-business direct marketing has also experienced tremendous expansion. In 1995, U.S. businesses spent $51.7 billion on marketing and communications, 37.4 percent of the total U.S. marketing dollars, to sell their products and services to other businesses, according to an OutFront Marketing Research Study.[23] Sales force management was number one with 22.9 percent of the total, advertising was at 21.9 percent, and direct marketing at 12.3 percent. Of the $6.3 billion in total direct marketing spending, 59.9 percent was spent on direct mail.

Direct mail selling, database marketing, telemarketing, print direct response advertising, and other forms of direct marketing provide attractive options for firms that either prefer to avoid the huge expense of a traveling sales force or desire to supplement sales force efforts with supportive marketing communications. The business-to-business area has experienced a trend away from mass market communication to direct marketing that allows for relationship-building two-way communication. Business-to-business marketers are ahead of consumer marketers in advertising and selling goods using online networks, the Internet, CD-ROMs, floppy diskettes, and kiosks. Electronic business-to-business sales are expected to skyrocket by the start of the next century (see Table 15.3).

However, business-to-business advertisers still have a lot to learn from experienced direct marketers, according to a *Marketing News* article. Although business-to-business marketers are buying and merging lists in greater numbers than ever before, these marketers may send out "expensive dimensional" pieces that are too inflexible to "capitalize on the list segmentation advantages computer-based lists offer."[24] Instead, business-to-business advertisers need to do what direct marketers do—be creative in establishing the list, the message, and the offer. For instance, a company offered a modular accounting package at the cost of $149 for five diskettes, then changed the offer to sell one disk for $149 and the other four for a special price of $1 each. The latter offer caused sales to soar. Business-to-business advertisers should follow the same advice often given to consumer marketers in designing their direct response campaigns—"send the right message to the right prospect."

TABLE 15.3. Electronic Business-to-Business Sales Forecast

Year	Electronic Sales of Business-to-Business Products
1997	$800,500,000
1998	$1,130,000,000
1999	$1,580,000,000
2000	$2,200,000,000

Source: Adapted from Karen Burka, "Early Adopters," *Direct*, March 15, 1997, pp. 31-33.

MARKETING WITHOUT BORDERS

Reliable, a $175 million office supplies company, decided to go into international direct marketing when its U.S. growth rates began to decline and the global information superhighway created customer awareness abroad. The strategy included a 1988 to 1990 venture with a United Kingdom contract stationer. Industry background looked favorable: a major competitor, Viking, was already successful in Western Europe, and superstores were not expanding aggressively overseas. Reliable implemented its plan by defining catalog offering and product sources, then cloning its U.S. operational system. Reliable calls this "marketing without borders."[25]

The future of direct marketing depends upon its ability to cross cultures and other borders, whether at home or abroad.

Direct Marketing and Ethnic Communities

Direct marketing is increasingly becoming an effective way to reach the lucrative, $228 billion Hispanic market in the United States. Hispanic consumers might find direct mail appealing for several reasons. Hispanic households receive about 35 pieces of direct mail yearly, compared to 350 for non-Hispanic households, and less volume in the mailbox can translate into better response rates. In addition, Hispanics are now turning to direct marketing, thanks, in part, to unpleasant shopping experiences, according to a study conducted by DraftDirect Worldwide, Chicago. A survey of 750 Hispanics found that about 49 percent of respondents said that they are not treated with respect in stores, and 41 percent said that they buy direct because it is less threatening than in-person shopping. The survey also found that about 94 percent of the respondents said that they receive direct mail, and 66 percent said that they always open and read it. Marketers are increasing their usage of direct mail to the Hispanic market because of improvements in mailing lists and better executions (e.g., the use of a bilingual package—English and Spanish). Marketers can also convey respect in direct mail pieces by featuring Hispanic talent and models and photography that is culturally relevant, placing an emphasis on family in the communication, and using traditional colors (bright, tropical colors such as reds, yellows, and greens).[26]

African Americans surveyed have also shown a positive attitude toward receiving direct mail, especially subscription magazines, personal letters, and catalogs from familiar companies.[27] Younger African Americans reported that receiving such mail reflects their independence and their own perceptions of "where they are in their lives." This younger subset's need to be acknowledged as important in society makes this target receptive to direct mail. Further, urban dwellers are more likely to respond to direct mail offerings than suburbanites because city dwellers are more price sensitive and appreciate the opportunity to fulfill needs quickly in a hectic environment in which control is limited. Since "the little things in life" were most important to African Americans surveyed, direct marketers should pay attention to details in mailings, for instance, accuracy in spelling the target's name.

International Direct Marketing

The Middle East, especially Israel, and Asia, especially Japan, have been international areas with an increasing interest in direct marketing. However, as Japanese marketing growth slowed in 1998, ad spending in China soared. No one can be sure, though, to what extent financial troubles faced by other Asian markets will eventually affect China. The outcome of Asian economic problems is one factor that will shape the future of global direct marketing.[28]

Another factor in the future of international direct marketing involves a single European currency, the euro. The new currency could enable marketers to "offer the same goods at the same price everywhere, eliminating the need to make complex calculations about inter-country exchange rates."[29] The euro may also help offset what some Europeans perceive as the foreignness of non-European marketers. Direct marketers who typically prepare mailings in the customers' native language and tailor offers to specific consumer profiles will be able to also tailor payment options.

On the other hand, the European Union's single market could adversely affect direct marketing practice if a Germanic-Scandinavian faction has its way with tight regulation. Although tensions exist between factions supporting tight regulation and those supporting self-regulation, the current mood is said to be favorable toward direct marketers: it is both attractive and possible to actively trade across Europe.[30] Still, many issues remain unresolved: proposed bans on telemarketing, advertising that requires up-front payments or deposits, advertisements in English in countries where English is not the native language, and a variety of sales promotions, including free premiums.

Interactive marketing abroad has been accelerated by international Internet use, which is growing at a faster rate than in the United States. Increases in European Internet use appear in Table 15.4. In 1997, 5 million households in Asia and the Pacific Rim had Internet access, and that figure is expected to double by the year 2000.[31] Advice for those setting up international electronic direct response advertising includes using the user's language, recognizing cultural differences, offering relevant content, forming

TABLE 15.4. Percentage of Population Using the Internet in Selected European Countries

United Kingdom	30%
Germany	20%
Sweden	9%
Norway	7%
Spain	6%
France	2%
Other countries	16%

Source: Adapted from "European Internet Use," Direct Marketing, March 1998, p. 57.

strategic alliances with international organizations, segmenting the audience (by language, country, or currency, for example), and leveraging both print media and all electronic delivery platforms (telephone, cable, satellite, and digital TV).[32]

The Internet has also become a channel for reaching the Latin American market. Web sites sold $17 million in goods and services in Latin America in 1996, with most customers coming from the upper-middle and upper socioeconomic classes. The number of Internet sites has grown dramatically in some Latin American countries, for example, from 20,113 in Brazil in 1996 to 77,148 in 1997.[33] Internet use in Latin America is projected to quadruple to 34 million by the year 2000, up from 8 million in 1995. Especially interesting to direct marketers is the fact that women have been primarily responsible for new user growth in Latin American countries. In the United States, female consumers have been more likely than males to order via direct mail. Since the Internet poses an alternative channel to direct mail, the rising number of women online in Latin America could be good news for international direct marketers. The North American Free Trade Agreement (NAFTA) and the spread of democracy have also made Latin America an attractive target market for interactive commerce.

As corporations pursue expanding global interests, advertising agencies have begun to strengthen their global direct marketing networks. In February 1998, Tina Cohoe became the new worldwide chief creative officer for New York-based Foote, Cone & Belding Direct, and Stewart Pearson was named FCB's new worldwide chief operating officer. FCB Direct estimated its worldwide billings at $560 million, a figure expected to double by the year 2000. Cohoe, who remains president of FCB's New York office in addition to her new global responsibilities, has expressed her belief in the importance of Integrated Communication skills to global brand management.[34]

Leo Burnett Worldwide acquired Australian direct marketing agency Cartwright Williams, including its database-consulting operations, in May 1998. The Australian agency's clients include Microsoft, Ciba-Geigy, and Cigna Insurance. The acquisition included plans to open Leo Burnett Cartwright Williams Direct in Singapore.[35]

Leo Burnett Direct, one of a number of new direct marketing agencies, seeks to strengthen corporate brands nationally as well as internationally through direct marketing activities. The agency creates the *McMoms* newsletter for its client, McDonald's. The newsletter includes restaurant coupons and tips for busy mothers on topics discovered to be of interest through frequent focus groups conducted with *McMoms* readers. The agency foresees an exciting future for such projects. Leo Burnett Media projects that interactive media penetration of U.S. households will soar by the year 2005. Direct mail is expected to reach 95 million-plus households, digital mail, 65 million-plus, and interactive television, 20 million-plus.[36]

SUMMARY

Whether you call it direct marketing, direct response advertising, interactive marketing, relationship marketing, or database marketing, this industry has reached individual customers directly and personally for centuries—from its roots in door-to-door peddling to its beginning in catalog advertising and sales to its current international, technological thrust. The field of direct marketing now accounts for over half of U.S. advertising expenditures. Direct response mechanisms allow for the two-way communication required for today's trend toward relationship marketing and company-consumer dialogue. Although the future still holds the challenges of communicating across cultures and other borders, the direct marketing industry has been proactive in crossing these borders, all the while pioneering the use of new electronic media.

* * *

THE GLOBAL PERSPECTIVE: EUROPEAN PROBLEMS WITH TECHNOLOGY

- Electronic print ads defray the high costs of paper and postage.
- Teleshopping is a fast-growing marketing tool.
- Database management enables better individual targeting.

Yet, although new media and technologies have already changed European direct marketing practices in the ways listed, they are not expected to replace such traditional channels as direct mail and television for direct response advertising, even by the year 2005.

This was the conclusion drawn from a FEDIM (Federation of European Direct Marketing) overview of European direct marketing responses to technological changes. The overview reflected responses to its survey of members in Belgium, Denmark, Finland, France, Germany, Ireland, Italy, Netherlands, Sweden, Switzerland, and the United Kingdom.

Most respondents to the mid-1990s survey were already interactive, providing home pages and other Internet services. Reasons given by respondents for their opinion that new media will not overtake traditional channels, even by the year 2005, were as follows:

Problem Mentioned	Percentage of Respondents
1. Technical problems	20
2. Lack of training/education	18
3. Regulatory controls	11
4. Cost per individual connection	11

Although 56 percent believed that electronic home shopping would become a global marketplace by 2005, obstacles to be surmounted were assessed as follows:

5. Fulfillment problems	20
6. Privacy/protection rules	20
7. Differing national regulations	20

All respondents believed that consumer education would be key to the development of new media channels for direct marketing. Other factors mentioned included the liberalization of the European telecommunications sector and changes in national and European Union legislation.

Source: FEDIM, "Direct Marketing in Europe: How European Advertising and Media Companies and Agencies See Direct Marketing," *International Journal of Advertising*, 1996, Vol. 15, pp. 314-324.

* * *

ETHICS TRACK: OUT-OF-HOUSE, OUT-OF-COUNTRY TELEMARKETING

An ad for Jamaica Digiport International (JDI) in the Fall 1997 issue of the *DMA Insider* promised a business-environment paradise: "day and night life, sea, sand, sun . . . and absolutely no snow." If that were not enough, the ad detailed generous incentives, a strategic geographic location, and an advanced telecommunications facility in a modern office park.

All this, and "affordable labor."

Although telemarketing agents in the United States earn about $10 per hour, JDI pays "well-educated, English-speaking" Jamaicans as little as $2 per hour (in U.S. dollars). This and Jamaica's "free zones" (100 percent "tax holiday on profits," no import licensing requirement, and duty-free capital and consumer goods importation) enhance the image of JDI as a call-center solution made in heaven.

Or hell?

What ethics issues are raised when corporations export call centers from the United States to Jamaica or other locations around the globe? Find out how the cost of living varies between the United States and Jamaica. Is $2 an hour (U.S.) a fair wage? What problems might a domestic company encounter in placing its inbound or outbound call center in a non-English-speaking country? Assess the advisability of such a venture in light of such concepts as relationship marketing.

Chapter 16

Sales Promotion

McDonald's initial Ty Teenie Beanie Baby giveaway in 1997 was too successful. When customers had depleted the supply of 80 million babies offered free with children's Happy Meals in a special promotion, McDonald's heard distressing stories of disgruntled customers "throwing away Happy Meals they had bought just for the toys."[1] Since the first Teenie Beanie promotion, the inexpensive toy (it costs less than 60 cents to manufacture) has become a collector's item. A full set of twelve has sold for as much as $500 at charity auctions. McDonald's repeated the Teenie Beanie premium offer in spring 1998, armed with 160 million babies this time. The company also modified the offer so that in addition to coming free with a Happy Meal, the critters—ranging from a worm to a hippopotamus—could be purchased outright with any other food item. Most franchises sold them at the suggested retail price of $1.59. Results were impressive: some franchises reported sales increases of more than 30 percent over the previous year. The fast food burger chain is planning another Teenie Beanie promotion in 1999. Although it is difficult to know in advance what will trigger this kind of response, McDonald's Teenie Beanie success speaks to the power of sales promotion.

Marketers and suppliers aim to stand out from the crowd and open new interactive opportunities with unconventional formats and sophisticated back-end capabilities. The Rolling Stones' *Bridges to Babylon* tour was promoted through the issuing of ten-minute prepaid calling cards. The tour's sponsors distributed the calling cards, bearing the concert's red lips and tongue logo, as a pledge premium for viewers who contributed to PBS stations in the United States in 1998. The medium has superseded the message, as marketers devise new ways to utilize America's hottest premium incentive: prepaid phone cards. At one time, only a minority of Americans were acquainted with the credit card-sized phone cards, let alone knew how to use them. However, the trend has gained momentum, and consumers view free phone time as a desirable premium.

However, phone cards do not even need to be phone cards anymore. St. Petersburg, Florida-based Catalina Marketing teamed up with Innova-

ILLUSTRATION 16.1. Creating Relationships

A continuity program encourages continued purchases by offering the consumer a benefit or reward. The Hallmark Gold Crown Card Program rewards its members with cash certificates, newsletters, special gifts, and special offers. Cash certificate rewards are based on points earned for every dollar spent at Hallmark Gold Crown Card Stores. Hallmark sent this holiday postcard to its Gold Crown Card Program members to encourage holiday shopping. The offer was a 100-point bonus on purchases made the weekend after Thanksgiving.

tive Telecom to offer 120 million shoppers the opportunity to earn free long distance phone time at the supermarket checkout line. In return for specific purchases made at grocery stores, consumers received certificates that included a toll-free number and a unique PIN (personal identification number). Since the program's inception in 1995, Catalina has run more than fifteen promotions for such brands as Reynolds Wrap, Gerber baby foods, Carefree chewing gum, and Campbell's Soup.[2]

Sales promotions can effectively appeal to consumers. But, what exactly is sales promotion? The objective of this chapter is to provide an introduction to the role of sales promotion in marketing, to explain the relationships among sales promotion, product publicity, and advertising, and to introduce sales promotion types.

THE ROLE OF SALES PROMOTION IN MARKETING

As mentioned in an earlier chapter, the marketing mix consists of four major components: product, place, promotion, and price. A primary goal of a marketing manager is to create and maintain a marketing mix that satisfies consumers' needs for a general product type. As part of this mix, promotion involves informing individuals, groups, or organizations about an organization's products or services and persuading them to accept these products or services. The promotional mix refers to the communication aspects of marketing: advertising, personal selling, sales promotion, and public relations. Marketers strive for the right promotional mix to make sure that a product is well received. Sales promotion is an activity or material (or both) that acts as a direct inducement, offering added value or incentive to purchase the product, to resellers, salespersons, or consumers (e.g., see Illustrations 16.1 and 16.2).[3]

SALES PROMOTION, PUBLICITY, AND ADVERTISING

The purpose of all marketing communications is to help the company achieve its marketing objectives. Typical marketing objectives include

- introducing new products;
- inducing present customers to buy more;
- maintaining sales in off-seasons;
- obtaining greater shelf space; and
- combating competition.

ILLUSTRATION 16.2. Added Incentive

Arline Thoms designed this newspaper advertisement to promote Lafayette Interior Fashions' holiday sale. In addition to the 25 percent discount, the store offers free in-home consultation and free installation.

The marketing strategy the company uses to achieve these objectives may include the marketing mix—product, place, promotion, and price. Some consider sales promotion supplementary to advertising and personal selling because it binds the two together, making both more effective by increasing sales. In reality, however, sales promotion is far more than supplementary. For example, many companies (e.g., Ralph Lauren) distribute more than 500,000 free samples in Daytona Beach each spring break to get college students to try a new product.

Product publicity is similar to public relations in that both seek to create and maintain relationships between prospective buyers. Product publicity relays new information about products through the media, although it is not considered traditional advertising because it is not paid publicity. Product publicity can generate high-level introductory sales by making consumers aware of the product. Many of the techniques of product publicity will be detailed in the section Consumer-Oriented Sales Promotion in this chapter.

Ben Cohen and Jerry Greenfield, cofounders of Ben & Jerry's Homemade, Incorporated, have become famous as innovators of product publicity techniques. They personally distributed samples of their superpremium ice cream as they drove a converted motor home, dubbed the "Cowmobile," across the country in 1986. As a company that did not purchase traditional advertising until the mid-1990s, Ben & Jerry's employed a variety of product publicity techniques throughout the 1980s, such as tours of the factory in Waterbury, Vermont, where they also staged festivals and other special events. In 1998, Ben & Jerry's teamed up with United Airlines to promote a new flavor, "Dilbert's World-Totally Nuts." On April Fool's Day, Ben & Jerry's awarded business commuters checks for the average ticket price of their United Airlines flights and dished out free samples of the new flavor at the gate.

Starbucks Coffee Company has also made innovative use of product publicity. Before opening a new store, Starbucks engages "local ambassadors," families and friends of local employees, to spread the word of the opening throughout the community and to share free-drink coupons with friends. Starbucks also employs a continuity program with *passports*, punch cards entitling customers to a free half pound of coffee once a *world tour* has been taken by buying Starbucks coffee beans from a variety of countries.[4] Product publicity may also involve the company in environmental preservation or other causes. Starbucks' CARE promotion mug benefits both the Worldwide Relief and Development Foundation and the customer, who receives a discount on coffee refills when the mug is presented. A Starbucks store in Amherst, Massachusetts, awards a discount to the customer who brings back a coffee bag to be refilled, thus encouraging recycling.

Effective sales promotion maximizes sales volume. For that reason, advertising, sales promotion, and product publicity work well together. Advertising helps develop and reinforce quality, differentiate brand reputation, and build market volume. Sales promotion also helps build market volume. Product publicity helps build long-term company-consumer relationships.

TYPES OF SALES PROMOTION

Sales promotion refers to the use of any incentive by a manufacturer or service provider to induce trade businesses (wholesalers and retailers) and/or consumers to buy a brand and to encourage the sales force to aggressively sell that product. Most sales promotion methods can be grouped into trade sales promotion and consumer sales promotion. Manufacturers who market through normal channels must secure the cooperation of wholesalers and retailers. Consequently, their push strategies include trade promotion tactics, such as advertising allowances and slotting allowances. Consumer sales promotion methods encourage or stimulate consumers to patronize specific retail stores or to try particular products. Major manufacturers reach their customers through a pull strategy, such as coupons, sweepstakes, and in-store advertising.

Trade-Oriented Sales Promotion

To encourage resellers, especially retailers, to carry their products and promote them effectively, producers use trade-oriented sales promotion methods. The following are various types of trade-oriented sales promotion techniques.

Trade Allowances

Off-invoice allowances. The most frequently used allowance is an off-invoice allowance, deals offered periodically to trade businesses that permit them to deduct a fixed amount from the invoice.
Buy-back allowances. When introducing a new product, manufacturers sometimes offer retailers a buy-back allowance for the old product that has not been sold.
Bill-back allowances. Retailers receive allowances for featuring the manufacturer's brand in advertisements (bill-back advertisement allowances) or for providing special displays (bill-back display allowances).
Slotting allowances. In response to the glut of new products, some retailers charge manufacturers slotting allowances for the privilege of obtaining

shelf or floor space for a new product. Some retailers have even begun charging an exit fee to remove unsuccessful new products from their distribution centers. These exit fees could just as well be called deslotting allowances.

Advertising allowances. An advertising allowance is a common technique employed primarily in the consumer products area: the manufacturer pays the wholesaler or retailer a certain amount of money for advertising the manufacturer's product. Cooperative advertising (co-op advertising) involves a contractual arrangement between manufacturer and reseller whereby the manufacturer agrees to pay a part or all of the advertising expenses incurred by the resellers. Special co-op deals are used to introduce new products, advertise certain lines, or combat competitors. Unlike advertising allowances, co-op programs typically require the resellers to submit proof of the advertising (tear sheets from the newspaper or affidavits of performance from radio or TV stations), along with invoices from the media.

Display allowances. More stores now charge manufacturers display allowances—fees to make room for and set up displays. In-store displays include counter stands, shelf signs, and special racks.

Push Money or Spiffs

This is additional compensation provided to retail salespeople by the manufacturer to push a line of goods. This method often helps manufacturers obtain commitment from the sales force, but it can be very expensive.

Point-of-Purchase Displays

A point-of-purchase (POP) display is designed by the manufacturer and distributed to retailers to promote a particular brand or group of products (e.g., see Illustration 16.3). Marketers use a variety of items in point-of-purchase communications. These include various types of signs, mobiles, plaques, banners, shelf talkers, full-line merchandisers, wall posters, and numerous other materials. POP advertising is a multibillion-dollar industry.

Trade Incentives and Contests

To get retail dealers and salespeople to reach specific sales goals or to stock a certain product, manufacturers may offer special prizes and gifts. A trade contest typically is directed at store-level or department managers. Whereas contests are typically related to meeting sales goals, trade incentives are given to retail managers and salespeople for performing certain

ILLUSTRATION 16.3. Related Products Display

The point-of-purchase display may promote one brand or a group of related products. Here a POP display for a brand-name film is flanked by cameras. © Dana Hanefeld.

tasks. As an incentive to encourage retailer participation in their special promotional programs aimed at the final consumers, the manufacturer gives the promotional items to the store manager when the sales promotion is completed. Bigger prizes in the form of vacations and other high-ticket items are sometimes used as incentives.

Count and Recount

The count-and-recount promotion method is based on payment of a specific amount of money for each product unit moved from a reseller's warehouse in a given time period. Units of a product are counted at the start of the promotion and again at the end to determine how many units have moved through the warehouse.

Consumer-Oriented Sales Promotion

Consumer-oriented sales promotions are directed at the ultimate user of the good or service. The primary strengths of consumer-oriented sales promotions are their variety and flexibility. Because retailers today "know more about the manufacturer's product and its performance in their stores than ever before," sales promotions at the retail level are particularly powerful.[5] The advent of the Universal Product Code (UPC) and the use of information technology, such as the scanner and the computer, allow the retailer to more efficiently determine which items should be ordered and stocked.

As noted earlier through examples from Ben & Jerry's and Starbucks, a number of techniques can be combined to meet almost any objective of the sales promotion planner. Pepsi-Cola Company's Mountain Dew "Do the Dew" sweepstakes promotion let consumers use a store-issued free swipe card to activate kiosks located in grocery stores. Consumers then selected coupons and entered the sweepstakes automatically. This sweepstakes promotion was supported by a radio and television advertising campaign.[6]

Coupons

A coupon is a certificate with a stated value that is presented to the retail store for a price reduction on a specified item during a specified time period. Marketers use coupons to attract new users to their products, to encourage repeat purchases, and to maintain user loyalty. The four main vehicles for distributing coupons are mass media (newspapers and magazines), direct mail, packages (in and on packages), and in-store. Most (68 percent), however, reach consumers through colorful, preprinted advertisements—called freestanding inserts (FSIs)—in newspapers.[7] The FSI is said to reach eight to ten times more targeted consumers than in-store vehicles at one-tenth of the cost.[8] Coupons are clipped and saved by nearly 90 percent of American adults, according to Decision Analyst, Incorporated, Arlington, Texas. U.S. consumers eighteen to forty-four years old tend to redeem more than eight coupons a week. Those forty-five and older redeem about seven a week.[9]

Statistics show a relationship between a decrease in the specified coupon duration time and falling redemption rates since 1990; that is, if longer expiration dates were used, the redemption rate would be expected to be higher (see Table 16.1). Of coupons redeemed, as many as 25 percent are misredemptions. U.S. manufacturers lose about $250 million annually on fraudulent coupon submissions. Sometimes consumers present expired

TABLE 16.1. Redemption Rates Compared to Coupon Duration

Year	Distribution	Redemption	Average Duration
1990	279.4 billion	7.09 billion	4.9 months
1991	292.0	7.45	4.4
1992	310.0	7.71	4.0
1993	298.5	6.80	3.1
1994	309.7	6.24	3.4
1995	291.9	5.80	3.0
1996	268.5	5.30	3.0

Source: Adapted from "Measuring Your Coupon Vehicle's Performance," *PROMO: The Magazine of Promotion Marketing,* Vol. XI, No. 8, July 1998, p. s38.

coupons, coupons for items not purchased, or coupons for a smaller-sized product than that specified by the coupon. Surprisingly, nonprofit coupon fraud has become a $500 million-a-year criminal activity. Religious, charitable, and civic groups have found clipping and selling coupons to be a profitable fund-raising enterprise, with charities a major player in misredeemed coupons. When grocers and coupon clearinghouses submit these coupons to manufacturers, it is the consumer who pays the price through higher prices.[10]

Although coupons remain a mainstay of sales promotion, inherent problems with the mechanics of couponing remain to be solved. For instance, millions of consumers who flocked to Fantastic Sam's for a free or reduced-price haircut in 1993 were turned away. General Mills had distributed the coupons on cereal boxes, but the coupons were honored at only 25 percent of Fantastic Sam's nationwide outlets. The premium's value was too high for its vehicle—for the cost of a $3 box of cereal, the consumer could get a haircut worth $7 to $10. Among other problems, some of Fantastic Sam's franchisees refused to honor the coupon. The franchisees had not been involved in the decision to offer the promotion, yet the promotion's cost came from their cash drawers.[11]

Refunds and Rebates

The terms *refund* and *rebate* both refer to the practice whereby manufacturers give cash discounts or reimbursements to consumers who submit proofs of purchase. Though often used interchangeably, a refund typically refers to cash reimbursement for packaged goods (such as those given on Centrum multivitamins or Kodak film), whereas a rebate more often refers to reimbursements for durable goods (cars or household appliances). Rebates have enjoyed on-and-off popularity since they originated in the 1960s, but in 1998, rebate offers popped up everywhere, on everything from dishwashers to paper shredders. For example, money-back offers included $75 for a Nikon camera 180 lens, $50 for a Commax image scanner, $20 for a Whirlpool washing machine, and $5 for a Cosco child seat. Rebate fraud that plagued the 1980s and early 1990s has been controlled by the Postal Service, and—even though rebates stimulate sales—only 5 to 10 percent of consumers bother to redeem them, which means a low payoff risk for the manufacturer. In some cases, successful rebate programs have even enabled manufacturers to cut consumer prices. When Sharp Electronics offered a $500 rebate on a $4,695 TV, sales increased dramatically, and unexpectedly. As a result, Sharp permanently lowered the TV's price to $3,995. Companies such as Pepsico, Incorporated, Nestlé SA, and OfficeMax send out 30 million rebate checks a year.[12]

Sweepstakes

On Memorial Day 1998, Philip Morris launched a sweepstakes for those who would like to visit mythic "Marlboro country"—the top prize was a five-day stay at an Arizona or Montana ranch. The prize was appropriate for the tobacco company's most macho brand. The $40 million campaign also included outdoor, magazine, and direct mail advertising, as well as retail promotions—cents-off coupons and a merchandise incentive program.[13]

A sweepstake offers prizes based on a chance drawing of entrants' names and cannot require a proof of purchase as a condition for entry. If an advertiser requires a proof of purchase, it becomes a lottery, which is illegal in some states. Therefore, sweepstakes require only that the entrant submit his or her name for consideration in the drawing or selection of the prize or prizes.

Two of the titans of magazine sweepstakes—American Family Enterprises and Publishers Clearing House—became enmeshed in legal difficulties in 1998. Both American Family and Publishers Clearing House sell magazines at discount prices, although only 10 to 25 percent of the money actually goes to the magazine publishers, who profit, primarily, from renewals.

The Florida attorney general investigated an American Family mailing in February 1998 when about twenty contestants, many of them senior citizens, flew to Tampa to claim what they believed was their $11 million jackpot. None of them had won, although the wording of the mailing—declaring, "We have reserved an $11,000,000.00 sum in your name"—suggested that they had.[14] In March, the company agreed to voluntary compliance in modifying its promotional messages, but it still had forty lawsuits pending, one of which paid 12,000 New Yorkers $60 each for magazine subscriptions they purchased from American Family. By July, American Family was looking for an agency to help overhaul its damaged image. As a result of lawsuits filed by forty-three states, American Family was expected to lose at least $30 million in 1999, the first loss in the company's twenty-five-year history[15]

Publishers Clearing House had already reached a settlement with fourteen states over alleged deceptive sales practices in 1994. The settlement banned the company from using the word "finalist" and required that the words "no purchase necessary to participate" appear clearly on mailings. In 1998, three states began investigations into the company's compliance with this agreement.[16]

A game is a type of sweepstake but is conducted over a longer time. It requires customers to make repeat visits to the dealers to continue playing. Baskin-Robbins thirty-one ice cream stores ran a *Wheel of Fortune* game in 1996. Customers needed to scratch off the game piece to win a 1996 Ford Mustang GT Convertible, a Caribbean cruise, or ice cream prizes.

Contests

A contest offers prizes based on the skill or ability of the entrants (e.g., solving a puzzle), and entrants may be required to submit proofs of purchase. Contests are multiplying fast in the competitive, sports-oriented culture of the United States. Since state lotteries are now offering extremely large cash prizes, companies have been challenged to come up with more substantial prizes. Pepsi-Cola, Coca-Cola, Hershey Foods, and General Motors upped the ante with big prizes for recent contests. For throwing a football ten yards into a thirty-inch circular target, a forty-one-year-old construction worker won the $1 million Gillette football challenge at the Orange Bowl in January 1998.[17]

Companies sponsoring big-prize contests are facing new problems. The probability that someone will be able to perform the feat to receive the prize must be determined. Once the risk has been assessed, companies are asking underwriters to insure them to defray the actual cost to the company in awarding the prize. For instance, by paying a 2 percent premium to an underwriter, a company might pay only $20,000 to award a $1 million prize. SCA Promotions, Incorporated insured only nine contest-type events with million-dollar prizes in 1990, but more than 100 in 1997.

National Hole-in-One Association, another contest underwriter, insured eighty promotions with million-dollar prizes in 1990, which rose to 500 such promotions in 1997.[18]

Insurance coverage is not a cure-all for contest woes, however. Sometimes the fine print in contest rules leads to problems with consumers who litigate to claim their prizes. For example, Randy Giunto shot a puck into a target at a Florida Panthers hockey game to win a $1 million prize, but was disqualified when the puck bounced out. A civil court jury awarded Giunto the prize, but the sponsors—the Florida Panthers and Coca-Cola—have appealed. Publicity about such disputes defeats the manufacturers' intended purpose—product awareness and goodwill.

Premiums

A premium is an item offered free or at a bargain price to encourage the consumer to buy an advertised product. A good premium should have strong appeal and value and should be useful or unusual. There are several types of premiums. In- and on-package premiums offer a premium item inside or attached to a package or make the package itself the premium item. Near-pack premiums provide the retail trade with specially displayed premium pieces that retailers then give to consumers who purchase the promoted product. Free in-the-mail premiums are a type of sales promotion in which consumers receive a premium item from the sponsoring manufacturer in return for submitting a required number of proofs of purchase, with or without postage costs. A self-liquidating premium is one that requires the consumer to mail in a number of proofs of purchase along with sufficient money to cover the manufacturer's purchasing, shipping, and handling costs of the premium item.

Sampling

Allowing the consumer to experience the product or service free of charge or for a small fee is called sampling. It is one of the most effective ways to introduce a new product. However, it is also the most costly of all sales promotions. Samples can be distributed to consumers by mail, door to door, on or in packages, or personally through a representative in the retail store. Samples are often distributed to target markets, for example, giving baby diapers to mothers of newborn infants. Several firms provide specialized sample distribution services, such as Giftpax.

Ben Cohen and Jerry Greenfield, co-founders of Ben and Jerry's Homemade, could not afford traditional advertising when they started their super-premium ice cream business, so, as mentioned earlier, they took to the road in their Cowmobile to personally scoop ice cream samples across the country. Ben & Jerry's continues to use product sampling with good results, although not all companies have been as lucky. Problems with the use of sampling do exist, including mishandling by the postal service, misuse by consumers, and sample distribution that misses the target market.

Recently, Procter & Gamble turned to sampling techniques in its attempt to overcome negative publicity and consumer skepticism about olestra, an ingredient in P&G's new Fat-Free Pringles. Thousands of samples were distributed in twenty major cities in the summer of 1998. Manhattan office workers, Minneapolis mall-walkers, and Atlanta partygoers were among the 30 million samplers in the six-week-long marketing blitz. Internet users were able to order samples simply by clicking on Fat-Free Pringles' ads. An ad campaign that appeared concurrently complemented the sampling effort with its tag line "Tasting is believing."[19]

Continuity Program (Frequent-User Incentives)

A continuity program requires the consumer to continue purchasing the product to receive the benefit or reward. For example, most major airlines offer frequent flier programs through which customers who have flown a specified number of miles are awarded free tickets for additional travel or ticket-class upgrades. Other service providers have joined the airlines in these programs by offering frequent flier miles for their purchase of products or services. For instance, American Airlines Advantage miles may be earned by ordering flowers from FTD, staying at participating hotel chains, or using MCI phone service.

Hallmark Cards' Gold Crown Card loyalty program rewards consumers for purchases in its Gold Crown Card stores with coupons for dollars off retail merchandise. The value of the coupons is based on accumulated purchase points. The program keeps in touch with its members via direct mailings. In 1998, Hallmark traced $1.5 billion in sales to purchases of the program's 16 million members.[20]

An older frequent user incentive, trading stamps, has lost its popularity. Trading stamps are dispensed in proportion to the amount of a consumer's purchase and can be accumulated and redeemed for goods. However, their use as a sales promotion method has declined. A new frequent user incentive may have an even shorter life: In Hong Kong, tobacco companies are encouraging people to smoke their brands by offering a cigarette package trade-in. Thousands of smokers have lined up to trade their empty Marlboro boxes for gifts. RJR Nabisco Holdings recently offered an autographed videodisc of local pop singer Leon Lai in exchange for empty packs of Salem cigarettes. These programs will end in 1999 when Hong Kong bans all tobacco company giveaway programs.[21]

SUMMARY

Marketers have shifted more marketing dollars from advertising to sales promotion in recent years. A variety of factors (e.g., reduced brand loyalty and emphasis on product price) account for this shift in budgetary allocations. However, advertisers need to look into this issue more carefully. Sales promotion complements advertising and personal selling by stimulating or accelerating sales. Product publicity helps introduce new products or businesses and fosters long-term customer relationships. Sales promotion cannot do the job alone.

* * *

THE GLOBAL PERSPECTIVE: PUCCINI ATTRACTS INTERNATIONAL SPONSORS TO CHINA

Was it, as it was billed, China's biggest cultural event in decades? Probably. Colorful costumes, an outdoor setting, three-time Academy Award nominee Zhang Yimou directing a $15 million production—Puccini's *Turandot*, an opera set in Beijing's Forbidden City, was performed there by a cast of 1,000 in September 1998. Guess who sponsored the event? Among others, Pizza Hut, KFC, and Time Incorporated.

Last-minute sponsors flocked to ride the growing trend to link "cultural interests with global business." Better yet, the extravaganza with equally extravagant ticket prices (from $150 to $1,500) took place in a country described as "the No. 1 hot spot for international business." U.S. accounting firms, that have "a big stake in getting associated with Chinese businesses," showed special interest in corporate hospitality tickets for their clients and guests.

International advertising involves decisions in media strategy and selection. Target audience characteristics, campaign objectives, and the budget form the basis for the choice of media vehicles. In addition, consideration of governmental regulations, the target market's technical capabilities, and literacy rates also influence international advertising channel choices. To make it more complicated, not all media are available in all countries. In China's restrictive advertising environment, sponsorship of an event that attracted 20,000 people provided a way for Western marketers to reach a mass audience.

Source: Kate Fitzgerald, "China's International Culture Club," *Advertising Age*, August 3, 1998, pp. 22-23.

* * *

ETHICS TRACK: SELLING YOUR NAME— THE PTA PROFITS WITH OFFICE DEPOT

The Harper Valley PTA is not the only chapter of the Parent-Teacher Association (PTA) that has rocked the public boat. And the latest case—in summer 1998—is not fiction. When Office Depot offered special coupons only available to members of the PTA and sponsored a $250,000 sweepstakes contest that would benefit forty schools nationally, the Center for Commercial Free Public Education wanted to know why. The center's spokesperson pointed to the possibility that the PTA was endorsing Office Depot's products.

The American Medical Association (AMA) ran into a similar problem when it endorsed Sunbeam Corporation products in summer 1997. In this case, doctors and consumer groups forced the AMA to withdraw from the deal.

The PTA, however, is standing by its one-year agreement with Office Depot, which includes the use of the PTA name and logo in "back-to-school" radio and television spots. Although a PTA spokesperson argued that the organization's 6.5 million members were not being asked to "support the company or its products," a former national PTA president felt the agreement overstepped ethical lines.

Should such organizations allow their names and logos to be used for commercial profit—their own and the advertiser's? Do the $5,000 shopping sprees offered as prizes to forty schools in the sweepstakes support the appearance that the organization is selling its image, or do the prizes suggest that the organization wants to use its image to help children in schools?

Source: Tamara Henry, "PTA Getting a Lecture After Office Depot Deal," *USA Today*, September 2, 1998, p. A1.

Lee & Johnson
:60 Spot
"Olympic Sponsorship Ambushed"

The need for companies to financially support the Olympic Games dates back to 1826. The fund-raising efforts of the first three Olympiads in Athens, Paris, and St. Louis were poorly run. As the games grew, so did the costs, and financial burdens escalated. The 1976 games in Montreal raised $4.18 million, leaving Quebec with a debt estimated as high as $1 billion. At this rate, cities would have no incentive to host the games and the Olympians would have nowhere to compete.

To establish incentive, The Olympic Programme (TOP) was created in 1985. Under TOP, companies pay an entrance fee and in turn receive certain rights, entitlements, and privileges to which other companies do not have access. Over the past century, the Olympic Games have become a popular worldwide event, and the companies that advertise in association with them reach a significantly large, diverse audience. According to the Atlanta Committee for the Olympic Games, corporate sponsorship was its single greatest benefactor, providing about $628 million—40 percent of the money needed.

For these reasons, sponsorship has become advantageous. The many nonsponsors who do not choose to invest still see advantages in associating themselves with the games and use every possible technique to do so. These ambush advertisers, though they do not possess any sponsorship rights, still referred to Olympic themes in their advertisements during the 1996 Centennial Games. Some of the ambushers who played significant roles in the Atlanta Olympic Games were Reebok, Nike, Honda, and Lucent Technologies.

The goal of both official sponsors and ambushers was to associate themselves with the positive themes of the Olympics, and each used different tactics to do so. Official sponsors tied themselves to the games by using their rights and showing the games' logos—the rings, torch, and so on. Ambushers also suggested Olympic themes in a variety of ways and were permitted to do so as long as they knew their limits. In essence, ambushers used Olympic-related imagery to sell their product without using the word Olympic and saved $40 million—the price tag worn by official sponsors. In lieu of making a connection through sponsorship, ambushers used other associating techniques to draw similar end results. These techniques included the use of Olympians and their events; Olympic symbols that denote a myriad of Olympic-related themes, such as internationalism, pride, equality, peace, perfection, utopia, and excellence;

selective terminology; and strategic placement of the spots during the airing of the games.

Most ambush companies used Olympians (or athletes who represented Olympians) and sporting events in their advertising. Reebok chose non-Olympian Emmitt Smith of the Dallas Cowboys to portray an Olympic hopeful. Another method of association exploited the wide spectrum of Olympic-related sporting events. Nike used this strategy and created its own sixty-second mini-Olympiad, blending events such as boxing, pole vaulting, discus, swimming, and more into a single spot, "Nike Medley." Soccer is the most popular international sport, with more than 300 million people playing worldwide. Nike took advantage of this event's global popularity and featured the sport in two spots, "Nike Medley" and "Women's Soccer."

Ambushers also associated themselves with the Olympics through the use of various symbols. Reebok's logo consists of two horizontal lines and a third line dissecting them. Reebok cleverly flipped the position of the logo from horizontal to vertical, and a flame appeared at the top. Obviously, Reebok turned the logo into their own version of the Olympic torch, a meaningful symbol that dates back to the ancient origins of the games. One Nike ad featured a female soccer player with interlocking rings on her uniform. Ambushers also used easily identifiable symbols such as the awards platform and gold medals to denote Olympic themes such as excellence, winning, and competition.

Another tactic ambushers used to suggest Olympic imagery was terminology, an extremely powerful strategy. Lucent Technologies, a communication company, mentioned previous host cities of the games. The spot showed a letter being typed on a computer screen from Lucent Technologies to the next host city, Nagano. The voice-over read, "Dear Nagano (Japan), Heard you're hosting next Games. Would like to build your communication network. Have experience. For references, call Atlanta (or Barcelona, Albertville, Lillehammer)." Reebok and Honda incorporated event-related words in their spots. For instance, the Smith campaign used such phrases as "an official event" and "U.S. Football Hopeful" (as opposed to "U.S. *Olympic* Hopeful"). In addition, Honda's spot saluted "all the athletes who have traveled so far to reach their goal," successfully avoiding the word Olympians.

Finally, ambushers strategically aired their ads between coverage of Olympic events to further enhance the association between the spot and the games. Nike's "Slow Motion Swimmer" and "Women's Soccer" were ordinary commercials that could be aired at any time, but were strategically placed to make Olympic associations. When viewers saw a commercial such as "Slow Motion Swimmer" immediately after Janet Evans swam her last Olympic event, the connection could not have been more obvious.

Unlike ambushers, sponsors receive the advantage of owning the rights to all Olympic slogans and logos. Ambush advertisers do not pay millions of dollars for advertising rights, but instead use techniques of association to link their products with the Olympic image. However, not even ambushers may be interested in such a link with the 2002 Salt Lake City Games. As of May 1999, Olympic officials were coming up short in their quest for legitimate corporate sponsorships. It was not the prospect of ambushing that created this dilemma—it was, instead, the scandal surrounding the Olympic Committee's acceptance of gifts and bribes from Salt Lake City promoters who were too eager to ensure that the city would be selected for the 2002 games. According to Bruce Horovitz in his *USA Today* article "Ads to Help Polish Image, USOC Says," the United States Olympic Committee announced plans for its first-ever ad campaign "to burnish its image in the wake of a $300 million fund-raising shortfall" (May 2, 1999, p. A1). Until the Olympic Games have recovered a positive image, ambush advertising may be the least of potential sponsors' worries.

Cynthia L. Dietz
Assistant Account Executive
BBDO Chicago
Chicago, Illinois

Chapter 17

Public Relations, Publicity, and Corporate Advertising

When Queen Elizabeth called 1992 her *annus horribilus*, she had no idea that 1997 would bring even greater crisis management problems than the 1992 fire at Windsor Castle and the much-criticized public behavior and imminent divorces of her children. In September 1997, a *Daily Mail* poll showed that 70 percent of the British public felt that the Queen should consider abdication, perceived as she was by the public as cold and unfeeling following Princess Diana's tragic death. Diana's claims of ill treatment by the Royal Family, even the Queen herself, seemed to place blame for the death of the popular "people's princess" on the royal doorstep. What insiders refer to as the "Family Firm" was in deep trouble, for—as with any "firm"—it depends upon public goodwill and financial support for its existence.

Although Queen Elizabeth, similar to her father George VI, initially enjoyed the cooperation of the media in depicting the Royal Family in "touching, homey little stories" that showed an ideal family "waving to the crowds, taking tea in a garden, feeding the ducks in St. James's Park, taking a picnic lunch at Windsor,"[1] the relationship between the "Family Firm" and the media turned sour in the 1990s. Increasing media exposure of the private lives of members of the Royal Family, especially Charles and Diana's "kiss and tell" public relations war waged in the British press, combined with other factors to bring an end to the family's hard-won positive public image. And one of the tenets of public relations is that a positive image takes decades to build and only seconds to lose.

On August 18, 1998, in an interview on CNN, Watergate reporter Carl Bernstein said that thirst for information drives the news cycle today, that we live in "a tabloid time." Early in 1998, Queen Elizabeth struggled to re-create a positive public image despite tabloid-driven media competition that eroded the traditional respect the monarchy had been afforded. On the other side of the Atlantic, President Clinton entered into his own public

ILLUSTRATION 17.1. Under Fire

Since President Andrew Jackson named Amos Kendall the first White House press secretary in the early nineteenth century, most U.S. presidents have relied on their public relations specialists to maintain positive media relations. President William Jefferson Clinton, pictured here, and his press secretaries have discovered that media relations presents an unprecedented challenge in the Information Age.

relations crisis, as allegations that he had had an affair with White House intern Monica Lewinsky became entangled in the ongoing Whitewater investigation (see Illustration 17.1). White House Press Secretary Mike McCurry fielded press questions in a media frenzy fed by almost daily information leaks and rampant rumors.

Dow Corning Corporation filed for Chapter 11 bankruptcy as a result of thousands of lawsuits fueled by a December 10, 1990, television show, *Face to Face with Connie Chung*. A number of women who appeared on the show claimed to suffer serious autoimmune and connective tissue diseases they said were caused by Dow Corning breast implants. Despite the fact that several studies, including a Mayo Clinic study, have not shown conclusively that breast implants cause these diseases, as of 1998, Dow has recovered neither its image nor its financial losses. The relationship between the media and the governments and institutions they cover in the Information Age has made the expertise of public relations professionals a necessity for corporations and other societal institutions, as well as for individual public figures.

Although numerous and various definitions for public relations exist, simply defined, public relations practitioners act as mediators between an organization and its various publics. These various publics include customers, company employees, suppliers, stockholders, governments, labor groups, citizen action groups, and the general population of consumers. Every company must develop and maintain goodwill with most, if not all, of its publics. If it fails to do so, the company risks losing its customers and revenues, inviting lawsuits, and damaging its reputation. This chapter examines the field of public relations; its subset, publicity; and the related topic of corporate advertising.

PUBLIC RELATIONS

Whereas advertising involves controlled communication in paid-for media time and space, public relations involves nonpaid publicity that is often difficult to attain and, once attained, extremely difficult to control. Nevertheless, public relations represents a crucial part of the promotional mix. The most extravagant advertising blitz cannot substitute for positive public image and goodwill. Crisis management, public relations writing, mediating relations with an organization's various publics, and public relations campaign management are among the most important public relations activities.

Crisis Management

The classic crisis management case occurred in 1982 when seven people in the Chicago area died after taking Johnson & Johnson's pain reliever, Tylenol. Someone had maliciously mixed bottles of Tylenol with cyanide and put them back onto retail shelves. Johnson & Johnson's handling of this tragedy was brilliant. The company quickly removed Tylenol from retail shelves. Spokespersons appeared on television and cautioned consumers not to take Tylenol capsules. Tylenol designed and produced a new tamper-proof package, prompting other pharmaceutical companies to follow suit. The company also offered consumers free replacements for products they had purchased before this tragedy happened. Many analysts were surprised at how quickly Tylenol regained its market share and the public's confidence, since lost reputations are generally difficult to recover.[2]

Advertising is sometimes used to respond to a public relations crisis. In July 1998, it was discovered that, three years earlier, two baby girls had apparently been switched shortly after their births at the University of Virginia Medical Center in Charlottesville, Virginia. The UVa Medical Center was quick to respond, undertaking a thorough records search and, through a spokesperson, informing the nation of the security practices in its maternity unit. To reach its specific Virginia-based target market, UVa turned to newspaper advertisements. These ads publicly apologized for the switch and, referring to the families involved, said, "We share their grief." In the past, other companies had also used advertising to reassure the public following tragic mishaps. For example:

- When one of its planes crashed, USAir ran full-page ads in national newspapers to accept responsibility and to assure the public that safety procedures were being reviewed.
- In the aftermath of the cyanide poisonings, Tylenol ran full-page ads explaining—in the company's own words—what had happened, what they would do to prevent further criminal tampering, and how customers could replace their Tylenol capsules with Tylenol caplets at the company's expense.
- In 1993, Pepsi published a full-page advertisement in national newspapers to inform the public that a claim that a syringe had been found in a Diet Pepsi can was a hoax; the ad's headline read, "Pepsi is pleased to announce . . . nothing." The ad also announced price-saving special offers for the Fourth of July weekend.

Sensitivity to the public mood is crucial in handling a crisis. Whereas USAir communicated with the public through advertisements following the crash of one of its airplanes, TWA pulled its advertising immediately following the tragic explosion of its Flight 800 in July 1996. A company must have guidelines in place to handle a crisis before an emergency situation arises, and TWA had already devised a communications strategy for just such an unexpected situation. Minutes after the explosion, TWA executives were already meeting and making careful plans. The crisis team turned to the Internet as the most efficient medium to "carry its message and control rumors that were spreading with the speed of light."[3] The Internet allowed the team to respond quickly and to deliver direct, unfiltered messages to a number of publics, including the media and the airlines' stakeholders.

Although the airline subsequently rolled out a national advertising campaign it had been planning for months, it changed one advertisement in response to the Flight 800 disaster—a television commercial featuring airline employees unloading cargo bound for a football celebration.[4] Nevertheless, TWA did not escape criticism for its handling of the crisis. The airline failed to come up with a passenger list for days, leaving the families of victims without the financial support needed to gather at the site of the crash. When Swissair Flight 111 crashed in the waters near Halifax, Nova Scotia, in early September 1998, the airline contrasted TWA's behavior with a swift and sensitive response to the needs of the victims' families—transportation to the crash site, cash payments, and even police protection to ensure that the grieving families would have privacy.

Public Relations Writing

Since Edward L. Bernays taught the first public relations course in 1923 at New York University, over 200 schools of journalism and departments of communication have offered programs in concentrated public relations study. Although the practice of public relations takes place largely in the business or corporate world, the public relations practitioner must thoroughly understand the media and be able "to interview, gather and synthesize large amounts of information, write in a journalistic style," and produce copy on deadline.[5] Writing remains the primary entry-level skill for the profession. A main goal of public relations is to secure third-party endorsement through the dissemination of press releases, fact sheets, backgrounders, feature stories, pitch letters, and press kits that consolidate key documents regarding the organization. For instance, a press release that presents factual, positive information about a company may appear in a respected media outlet. Unlike an advertising message, which the public understands to be biased information from the company who has paid for it, information that appears in an objective news story tends to be viewed as credible.

The *news release* (or press release) is the single most important public relations document (see Illustrations 17.2 and 17.3). Information about the organization is released to the media ready to publish as is. Releases must be newsworthy, that is, significant, timely, and of interest to the public. For example, announcement releases inform about new products, acquisitions and mergers, or key personnel changes and appointments. Since the goal is to have the release printed exactly as it is written, the release should be in inverted pyramid style, with the five Ws (who, what, when, where, and why) addressed in the first paragraph (lead). The release should also be concisely written according to the guidelines of the Associated Press or United Press International stylebooks. Release headlines are written to gain the interest of the media editor and let the editor know what the release is about.

Releases are typed and double-spaced, with one-inch margins, on the organization's letterhead (some companies have special letterheads for releases, with the words "NEWS" or "NEWS RELEASE" printed prominently near the company name and logo). The double-spacing and wide margins allow room for editing marks. A contact name and phone number also prominently appear on the release so that an editor may easily reach the right person to answer questions, verify details, or offer further information.

Public service announcements (PSAs) are news releases intended for the broadcast media. These documents are released in a ready-to-air format for radio and in a combination of script and storyboard form for television. The PSA must announce an event, give information about an organization, or provide other information that benefits the public.

In the past, news releases were mailed or personally delivered to the media. Today, news releases are frequently delivered via fax or computer. Overnight delivery services may be used when other materials, such as press kits or photographs, are to accompany the release. Increasingly, though, publicity photographs can be scanned into the computer and electronically delivered.

Fact sheets are usually just one page in length and allow the reporter to quickly reference key details about an organization, product, or event (see Illustration 17.4). *Backgrounders* also provide key details about an organization, product, or event, but do so more extensively, in greater length and depth (see Illustration 17.5). Although backgrounders are strictly factual, they resemble feature stories in style, often written with anecdotes (short human interest stories) and quotes. A *feature* article is a longer manuscript

Public Relations, Publicity, and Corporate Advertising 283

ILLUSTRATION 17.2. The Single Most Important Document

GATX

NEWS RELEASE

FOR FURTHER INFORMATION CONTACT:
Aaron H. Hoffman
GATX Corporation
312-621-6493

FOR RELEASE: IMMEDIATELY

GATX CENTENNIAL WEB CONTEST TEACHES KIDS TO HELP THOSE IN NEED

CHICAGO, October 13--GATX has been celebrating its Centennial with a lot of kids' play this year. Employees have built two playgrounds in neglected neighborhoods near GATX facilities in Buffalo and Chicago, and will soon build another near GATX's facility in Hearne, Texas. Now the company is focusing its celebration on another arena where kids love to play: the world wide web. GATX is sponsoring a unique web-based contest in which the winners receive, well, nothing. Or, to be more accurate, what they win they have to give away to families in need of assistance. But GATX hopes that what they get to keep for life is the experience of helping out the less fortunate.

The idea for GATX's web contest grew out of another Centennial program, "Tanksgiving," a year-long nationwide food drive conducted in partnership with Second Harvest, a national food bank network, and held at two dozen GATX facilities across the country. To publicize the drive, the financial services and supply chain management company ran a brightly painted GATX tank car around the country, including an appearance on September 10 on Wall Street in front of the New York Stock Exchange, tracks and all. The web contest centers on a "virtual" tank car as it travels to and from major GATX sites over a six-week period. Each week, a new question is introduced, related to the area of the country that the tank car crosses. Three winners are selected each week; one for each eligible grade level, third through fifth. And as frosting on the GATX birthday cake, the grand prize winning class will receive a computer for its classroom.

Each winning class receives $200, but they don't get to keep it. Instead, guided by their teachers and a local food bank, the class must spend the money buying food for the hungry. Therefore, playing and winning the contest begins with learning about history, geography, and math, and ends with economics, nutrition, and helping others.

The contest begins October 19 and ends Thanksgiving week. The colorful contest web page may be accessed through GATX's home page: www.gatx.com.

This GATX news release represents the qualities of effective copy; the contest the company sponsors is timely and of interest to the public, as it informs the community about GATX's good citizenship. The contest also represents an integrated public relations campaign, including a publicity event featuring the appearance of a brightly painted GATX tank car on Wall Street, the building of playgrounds in neglected neighborhoods, the dissemination of the press release to the traditional media, and the colorful contest Web page on the Internet.

ILLUSTRATION 17.3. A Credible Format

MEDIA RELEASE

PLAYS ABOUT THE
BEGINNING OF THE
MODERN WORLD

SHAW FESTIVAL

10 QUEEN'S PARADE
POST OFFICE BOX 774
NIAGARA-ON-THE-LAKE
ONTARIO, CANADA L0S 1J0

(905) 468-2153
DIRECT FROM TORONTO
(416) 690-7301
FAX (905) 468-5438

Shaw Festival Tops $11 Million in 1998 as it Announces 1999 Season
presented by Royal Bank Financial Group

Press Release #1

Niagara-on-the-Lake, Ontario, November 4, 1998 . . .The Shaw Festival once again produced record breaking box office results, topping the $11 million dollar mark ($11.75) for the second consecutive season. Paid attendance reached 321,000 or 81.2% of capacity for The Shaw's 765 performances.

The Shaw Festival's Artistic Director, **Christopher Newton** today announced the 1999 season. A total of 12 productions will be running in repertory from April 9th to October 31st in The Shaw's three theatres. The 1999 mystery, **Rebecca**, will run until November 28th. In making the announcement Mr. Newton commented, "wit, ideas, love and a number of explosions - what more could one ask of a season that connects an imaginary past with present-day realities."

The flagship play for the 1999 season will be Bernard Shaw's profound classic **Heartbreak House** directed by Polish actor and director *Tadeusz Bradecki*. Due to its overwhelming success in 1998, Kaufman and Hart's hilarious comedy **You Can't Take It With You**, directed by Shaw resident director *Neil Munro*, returns to the Festival Theatre in 1999 for a limited engagement. Also presented in the Festival Theatre in recognition of his centenary, is Noel Coward's humorous attack on social pretensions, **Easy Virtue**, directed by *Christopher Newton*. Arthur Miller's **All My Sons**, also directed by *Mr. Munro*, is a gripping drama about guilt and responsibility that establishes one code of ethics for private life and another for business.

The Court House Theatre will feature four plays including Bernard Shaw's **Getting Married**, a witty exposé on love and marriage, directed by *Jim Mezon*. **S.S. Tenacity**, a wistful French comedy by Charles Vildrac, will be directed by *Dennis Garnhum*. Sharing the Court House stage is one of Anton Chekhov's great plays, **Uncle Vanya**, directed by *Ian Prinsloo*. The Shaw will stage the sixth production in its Granville Barker series, **The Madras House**, directed by *Neil Munro*.

-more-

This Shaw Festival release illustrates the expected format—a headline with a present tense verb; a dateline with city, state or province, and date; double spacing within paragraphs and quad-spacing between; –more– at the bottom of the page to indicate another page follows. Many companies, as does the Shaw Festival, use letterhead printed with *News release, Press release, Media release*, or simply *News* to label the purpose of the communication. Shaw also numbers its releases, this being the first release for the 1999 season.

Public Relations, Publicity, and Corporate Advertising 285

ILLUSTRATION 17.4. Quick Reference

Clifton Gunderson L.L.C.'s fact sheet features factual information that constitutes the *Firm Profile*. As this one does, many fact sheets use bullets to set off paragraphs that cover specific aspects of the featured information. In the interest of integration—"one sight, one sound"—this fact sheet also employs the distinctive font, used in the firm's other promotional materials and its advertising, for the headline *Firm Profile* and the tag line, *Exploring a unique partnership*. Visuals are also used to enhance reader interest.

ILLUSTRATION 17.5. A Factual Feature

SMUCKER'S

FOR IMMEDIATE RELEASE

CONTACT: Nicole Oppolo
219-277-3114
oppo3456@saintmarys.edu

THE SMUCKER STORY

In the early 19th century, John Chapman, or "Johnny Appleseed," wandered the Ohio countryside, sowing apple seeds and securing a place in American legend.

It was from the fruit of Johnny Appleseed's trees that Orrville, Ohio resident Jerome M. Smucker first pressed cider at a mill he opened in 1897. Later, he prepared apple butter too, which he offered in crocks that bore a hand-signed seal—his personal guarantee. Before long, J.M. Smucker's name became well-known in its own right, as residents throughout the region—and eventually the nation—came to associate it with wholesome, flavorful fruit products.

HISTORY

The J.M. Smucker Co., the leading manufacturer of jams, jellies and preserves, celebrated its 100th anniversary in Dec. 1997. What began with Jerome M. Smucker selling his apple butter door-to-door from the back of his horse-drawn wagon, has grown into a $5.42 million organization employing approximately 2,000 people with products available in more than 60 countries.

The foodservice division of Smucker's was created in the 1950s in response to an ever increasing demand for high quality, convenient products for use outside the home. As America began to eat out regularly, Smucker's wished to follow its consumers to the restaurants. Today the list of restaurants, hotels, and other foodservice institutions that serve their customers Smucker's products is in the tens of thousands nationwide.

- more -

The backgrounder often provides information about a company and its history in storytelling style. Student Nicole Oppolo was assigned to write a backgrounder for an established company, so she researched the history of Smucker's and wrote this creative copy. Notice that a feature-type lead generally precedes subsectioned body copy. Nicole's subsections include History, Growth, Independence, and Today.

prepared for a specific publication, usually a magazine, news magazine, or special section of a newspaper. Features generally profile people—for example a company employee with an unusual or significant accomplishment—or detail the history of a company or product. For example, an organization that represents the Florida orange growers might send a feature about the history of the cultivation and use of the orange to newspaper food section editors. *Pitch letters* propose, or pitch, story ideas to newspaper editors with the hope that a reporter will be assigned to write an article. Essential facts and details about the story must be conveyed in such an attention-getting, interesting way that editors will see the attraction such a story might have for their readers. *Press (or media) kits* bring together a variety of documents that might be useful to a reporter writing about an organization. Usually placed in a pocketed folder, material may include news releases, fact sheets, backgrounders, company brochures and/or annual reports, and publicity photos.

Other public relations documents may be targeted toward nonmedia audiences, especially employees and investors. *Newsletters* became a popular public relations tool during World War II to enhance employee morale and company loyalty, thus increasing production efficiency. Newsletters continue to be important in informing employees about company policies and events and in improving relations between the employer and its employees. All publicly traded companies are required by the Securities and Exchange Commission to issue an *annual report* to stockholders. Since the required financial information may not be particularly engaging to all stockholders, annual reports typically seek to gain interest through human interest stories, a letter—usually a sort of "pep talk"—from the CEO or president of the company, four-color graphics and photographs, glossy pages, and attractive covers. The public relations value of the annual report may extend beyond the stockholder through dissemination to potential investors, employees, and potential employees. Annual reports may also be released to the media or included in press kits.

Many clients and employers call upon public relations professionals to write public addresses for them. *Speechwriting* requires special attention to the speaker's public address skills, personality, objectives, and time constraints. Some public relations professionals are employed exclusively as speechwriters.

Relations with Various Publics

Public relations professionals deal with various publics in matters involving company decisions, policies, or actions. The company has to maintain a level of goodwill with its suppliers, as well as its customers. It also has to demonstrate to community members that the organization is a good citizen. It has to provide stockholders and investors with financial information regarding the firm and deal with governments in matters of public policy. Media relations occupies a great deal of many practitioners' time. In the course of mediating between the organization and its publics, the public relations professional has frequent occasion to speak with, and to, these publics, from daily telephone contacts to hosting special events (see Illustration 17.6). This requires interpersonal and public communication skills.

Public Relations Campaigns

Before the public relations professional decides how and what to communicate to a specific public, the situation and the audience must be researched and analyzed. A public relations campaign is usually conducted using the R-A-C-E formula (research, analyze, create, and evaluate). At the research stage, a public relations team might conduct polls and surveys to determine the audience's existing attitude toward a company, product, or problem. Once that attitude is understood, a campaign will be planned to carry out the organization's objectives.

For instance, a community college decides to ask for a millage increase. Surveys show that people in the community are opposed to the millage because they do not understand what the college does for them. The objective of the public relations campaign will be to create awareness of existing community service programs. At the creation stage of the campaign, news releases might be disseminated to inform the public about special scholarships for members of the immediate community. A feature story, tied in with media coverage of Earth Day, might detail the experiences of students who recently cleaned up a waste site. Engagements might be booked for college officials to speak to various community clubs and organizations regarding college services. Awareness of issues involved in the millage request might be attained by staging a public debate. A press conference could be scheduled so that the media could ask questions the public might have about the reasons for the millage increase.

Evaluation of success has become one of the thorniest areas in public relations. Corporations in the 1990s have demanded measurable results for their advertising expenditures, but they are also looking for quantifiable results from their public relations programs, agencies, and campaigns. Traditionally, public relations activity has been evaluated in terms of gross impressions, percentage of favorable content, media placement, press clippings produced, message fidelity (the printed message corresponds to the intended message), and cost per impression.[6] Problems with these evaluation methods

ILLUSTRATION 17.6. Relations with Various Publics

> Does your business have the right retirement plan?
>
> Having the wrong retirement plan, or even worse, having no plan at all, can cost you and your business thousands of unnecessary dollars.
>
> Don't worry.....
>
> There are an increasing number of retirement plan options available to you. We have developed a seminar to help you determine which plan best fits your business.
>
> When: Tuesday, November 24th
> Where: Champaign Country Club
> 1211 S. Prospect Avenue
> Time: 4:00 – 5:00 p.m.
> Cocktails and hors d'oeuvres will follow.
>
> Please RSVP to (217) 351-7400 by November 20th.
>
> **Clifton Gunderson L.L.C.**
> Certified Public Accountants & Consultants

Public relations professionals are often called upon to plan, organize, and host special events. Clifton Gunderson held a retirement plan seminar as a public service to its clients. This postcard served as the invitation to what sounds like an elegant party, as well as a problem-solving session.

sometimes arise. For instance, the community college in the previous example may have numerous clippings to show extensive and positive press coverage, but if the millage does not pass, can the campaign be said to be successful? How can a list of appearances arranged for the CEO on popular TV talk shows substitute for the first-quarter sales increase that was the campaign's objective? Public relations professionals must deal with increasing demands for accountability. In public relations today, it is not enough to have the requisite communication skills. The public relations practitioner must also understand and speak the language of finance, sales, and business operations and objectives.

Public Relations—Challenges of Change

Public relations is not a new profession. Public relations tactics were central in the founding of the United States, from Thomas Jefferson's position paper (the *Declaration of Independence*) to a special event known as the Boston Tea Party. As a profession, public relations has suffered its own public relations problems. Hucksters such as P. T. Barnum were early contributors to negative public perceptions of public relations as the practice of publicity stunts and the purveyor of propagandistic messages. The attachment of the words spin and spin doctors to the profession has been a recent setback. The Public Relations Society of America (PRSA) has worked diligently to maintain respect for the profession.

Changes in technology have greatly impacted the field in the last decade. The computer has made some aspects of public relations practice easier. For example, desktop publishing has dramatically cut the production time and cost of creating brochures and other public relations documents. Options for delivery of releases and other documents have increased the speed of message dissemination. However, the speed with which information is delivered today has created unprecedented challenges for public relations professionals and the organizations they represent.

The pitfalls of lightning-fast message dissemination were made clear during the 1996 presidential campaign. Faxes literally flew from the desks of the media directors of both the Bush and Clinton campaigns to the press, many of them disseminating charges of the opponent's incompetence or corruption. President Clinton's handlers assembled in what they dubbed "the war room" to monitor print and broadcast coverage by the minute so that responses and corrections could be fired out instantaneously. The longer negative information is out there undisputed in the public forum, the more likely a person's or organization's image will be damaged.

The speed of information flow has also affected the media and, thus, public relations, since the relationship between the two fields is so intimate.

The mainstream press, now in competition with the tabloids, has been accused of losing journalistic integrity by printing—or broadcasting—unconfirmed rumors or improperly, sometimes even fraudulently, investigated stories. *USA Today* columnist DeWayne Wickham wrote, in July 1998, that "the line between hard news and the voyeurism of supermarket tabloids has been trampled."[7] For instance, the *Cincinnati Enquirer* ran a story accusing Chiquita Brands International, Incorporated, of exposing people to dangerous pesticides. When Chiquita denied the charges, which had been based on stolen information, the newspaper agreed to a $10 million out-of-court settlement and to run a three-day, front-page apology.

A rash of exposures of fabricated quotes and stories in 1998 makes some critics wonder whether reporters may have difficulty maintaining accuracy and ethical standards when they are under pressure to bring stories to print in extremely short periods of time. The ability of Web site publishers to get stories out faster than print or television has also increased pressure on the mainstream press. A CNN-Time story, "Valley of Death," aired on June 7, 1998, was retracted when it was discovered that, although producer April Oliver had not fabricated the story about U.S. military misuse of sarin gas during the Vietnam War, her information was taken from a photocopy that was "badly smudged."[8] Such exposures of faulty reporting have created public cynicism about journalism. A *Newsweek* poll conducted in the wake of the sarin gas story revealed that only 11 percent of those polled believe almost all of what they see, hear, or read in the news media (42 percent believe "only some" of it), and that 53 percent believe news organizations are often inaccurate in their reporting.[9] This is an uncomfortable situation for public relations practitioners who depend upon the media for fair and accurate coverage. Also, the organizations who receive negative press coverage—whether fairly or unfairly—increasingly require public relations assistance with image recovery.

Today, the importance of public relations to those who must create and maintain positive relationships with various publics remains unquestioned. When a sample of the top 1,000 U.S. advertisers was asked to rank thirteen advertising and marketing subjects in terms of time and attention given these areas in the past year, public relations was named as one of the most important areas by both consumer and business marketers.[10] If effectively integrated with advertising, personal selling, and sales promotions (the other components of the promotional mix), public relations is capable of accomplishing objectives beyond goodwill. It can create or re-create a positive image, increase brand awareness, build favorable attitudes toward a company and its products, and encourage purchase behavior.

PUBLICITY

Because publicity frequently results from various public relations efforts, it is often viewed as part of public relations. Taco Bell spent $400,000 on a handful of newspaper advertisements for a 1996 April Fools' hoax in which it declared that it was buying the Liberty Bell. In May 1998, two dramatic introductions occurred within an hour and a few hundred feet of each other in New York City. To introduce Virgin Cola, intended to be a new contender in the cola wars, the British billionaire founder of the Virgin Group perched atop a tank as it crashed through a wall of Virgin Cola cans in Times Square.[11] An hour after Branson's publicity event, at a restaurant just blocks away, Tara Lipinski was introduced as the spokesperson for Snapple Refreshers. In these cases, publicity was generated intentionally to increase product awareness.

However, sometimes publicity arises unintentionally, and sometimes this publicity is bad rather than good. The Johnson & Johnson's Tylenol case demonstrates the impact of unwanted publicity. News of unintended acceleration in its cars started a sales slide in 1986 for Audi of America, but three years later, U.S. federal officials cleared Audi, blaming the consumer complaints on driver error. The recovery from bad publicity took Audi a decade.[12]

Publicity can also intentionally or unintentionally contribute to product scarcity. During the 1996 holiday season, publicity about the shortage of Tickle Me Elmo dolls sent consumers fleeing to stores where they even more thoroughly depleted supplies of the dolls. Although shortages frustrate consumers and retailers, the perception of scarcity benefits toy marketers. A similar situation occurred in 1998 when publicity about the scarcity of Beanie Babies created a similar consumer mania. Consumers are now willing to spend as much as $100 for Beanie Babies, which are intended to retail for about $5.

Several major differences between public relations and publicity exist. First, public relations is a program extending over a period of time. Publicity is typically a short-term strategy. Second, public relations is designed to provide positive information about the organization and usually is controlled by the company or its agent. Publicity, on the other hand, is not always positive and is not always solicited by the firm. Typically, publicity—both positive and negative—originates from sources other than the company.

CORPORATE ADVERTISING

Corporate advertising is an extension of the public relations function designed to promote the firm overall—by either enhancing its image (corporate image advertising) or by communicating the firm's position on a social issue or cause (issue or advocacy advertising). Although the goal of corporate advertising is improved relations with its publics, corporate advertising differs from public relations in that it involves the purchase of media time or space.

Image Advertising

Corporate image advertising attempts to increase a firm's name recognition and establish goodwill for the company and its products. According to Wilcox and colleagues, in *Public Relations Strategies and Tactics*, "Image-building advertising is intended primarily to strengthen a company's identity in the eyes of the public and/or financial community."[13] For example, in May 1998, office copier underdog Savin launched a $9 million image advertising campaign "aimed at recreating the old David vs. Goliath imagery."[14] To position itself as producing office copiers that are faster, more responsive, and easier to work with than its giant competitor, Savin reworded its longtime tag line, "We're going to win you over," to read, "We've got what it takes to win you over." Although Savin was still ranked number eleven out of fourteen office copier brands, its new digital copiers brought its sales figures up 20 percent.

When its own company research showed that only "46 percent of any guys on the street" had heard of them, Acer America Corporation, part of Taiwanese electronics power Acer Group, began its first-ever TV campaign in August 12, 1996, intended to make Acer a household name.[15]

Sponsorship marketing is a form of corporate image advertising accomplished by corporate support of television programs, or "specials." Hallmark's longtime sponsorship of the *Hallmark Hall of Fame* specials has promoted the company as a good citizen. By associating itself with high-quality, educational programming, the firm hopes for a carryover effect that benefits its own image. Noting the opportunity to reach an enormous and influential group of upscale decision makers, many companies choose to sponsor such special programming as coverage of the Olympic games. However, the value of sponsorship marketing has been called into question. In May 1998, Coca-Cola decided to pay only $4 million to $5 million for its right to be the NFL's national soft drink sponsor, just a fraction of its previous $15 million-a-year contract. It appears that, in an era of sponsor overload, the value of being the official drink, car, or burger may be eroding.[16] Further, with the new emphasis on more specific audience targeting, some marketers are sponsoring low-profile sports events—"unsung sponsorships"—rather than the flashy, professional pastimes.[17] For instance, Anheuser-Busch has given its largest sponsorship—$15 million over three years—to bowling.

Since 55 percent of the 54 million who bowl each year are women, this allows Busch to reach a demographic not reached by some higher profile sports.[18]

Advocacy or Issue Advertising

A company uses advocacy or issue advertising to communicate its views on social issues to make a political or social statement. Although seeking to portray a "good citizen" image for the company or organization, advocacy or issue advertising builds image in an indirect manner, by adopting a position on a particular issue rather than promoting the organization itself. For example, Allstate Insurance Company has run an advertisement that communicates its commitment to enacting tougher drunk driving laws through organizations such as MADD and the National Commission Against Drunk Driving. This advertisement performs a community service with its "Don't drink and drive" message. Although these advertisements consume only a small part of a corporation's advertising budget, they may "touch sensibilities" and, therefore, receive much positive attention.[19]

SUMMARY

What are the differences between public relations and advertising? Both use the media to create awareness or to influence markets. However, they are not the same. Advertising reaches its market through media for which the advertiser pays. Also, advertisers control the messages they deliver to their audiences. Hence, the public views advertisements with some skepticism. The media receives public relations communications in such forms as news releases, feature articles, press kits, or press conferences. Since the public thinks such messages are coming from the medium rather than a company, it accepts and trusts them more readily. Certain communications about individuals and organizations (e.g., bad publicity) are neither solicited nor paid for. Such publicity, especially when negative, must be dealt with through crisis management strategies.

* * *

THE GLOBAL PERSPECTIVE: INTERNATIONAL PUBLIC RELATIONS FIRMS

High-tech. Full-service. Offices in over thirty countries. A "virtual practice" that links agency and client through a global network.

Could this be what catapulted Burson-Marsteller from the number two public relations firm (in fee income) in 1994 to number one by 1996?

As clients with global interests clamor for high-tech services and overseas offices, Burson-Marsteller has answered the call. NutraSweet and Gatorade are among B-M's clients for Internet services, which include issue monitoring, information distribution, training and consultation, World Wide Web counseling, and design and construction.[a]

In addition to its "new media" programs and Web expertise, B-M's client services include corporate counseling, investor and government relations, special events marketing, and technology and telecommunications (which boasts such clients as Hitachi and Kodak).

In 1996, public relations firms enjoyed their "most successful year ever" with fees exceeding $1.5 billion.[b] The chart below documents the major firms' phenomenal growth from 1994 to 1997. Fraser P. Seitel, a senior counselor at Burson-Marsteller, believes that, due to major world political shifts toward democracy, new technology, and regional trading alliances, no emerging trend will be more important than globalization for the field of public relations in the next century.

Top PR Firms by Fee Income—1994 to 1997

	1997 Net Fee Income	Percent Change from 1996	1996 Net Fee Income	1994 Net Fee Income
1. Burson-Marsteller	$264,545,502	+13.5	$233,344,022	$13,440,000
2. Shandwick	158,673,000	+6.9	190,700,000	37,713,000
3. Porter Noveli International	148,106,661	+22.0	121,178,280	Unranked
4. Fleishman-Hillard	134,950,000	+25.0	107,494,000	9,047,000
5. Edelman Public Relations	133,625,098	+19.7	111,680,350	12,063,448
6. Ketchum Public Relations	96,623,000	+29.0	74,836,000	5,500,000
7. Manning, Selvage & Lee	63,523,000	+32.5	47,925,000	6,511,000
8. GCI Group	62,037,966	+18.6	52,293,330	5,598,097
9. BSMG Group	61,565,000	+40.2	Unranked	Unranked
10. Weber PR Worldwide	61,971,000	New entity		

Source: Adapted from *O'Dwyer's Directory of Public Relations Firms*, Jack O'Dwyer, editor, New York: J. R. O'Dwyer Company, 1998, p. A7.

[a] "Profiles of high-tech PR firms," *O'Dwyer's PR Services Report*, Vol. 9, No. 11, November 1995, p. 27.
[b] Fraser P. Seitel, *The Practice of Public Relations*, Upper Saddle River, NJ: Prentice-Hall, 1998, pp. 473, 478-479.

ANOTHER GLOBAL PERSPECTIVE: HOW TO OVERCOME INTERNATIONAL COMMUNICATION BARRIERS

Your press release is picked up on the Internet by an Italian reporter. He telephones for an interview, but speaks very little English. Another release went out on the news wires. A French reporter calls to clarify some of the details in the story, but you have difficulty explaining due to language differences. A public relations nightmare? More often than not, this is today's public relations reality.

Public relations professionals face new challenges as more and more companies become global marketers, and international communication barriers may be one of the most frustrating. *Ragan's Media Relations Report* gives the following tips:

1. If your company does business in Europe, consider posting press releases on the Internet in French, German, and Spanish (Japanese and Chinese for the Pacific Rim).
2. Hire a multilingual public relations assistant.
3. Realize that what might be a hot story at home (e.g., food safety and the salmonella problem, for instance) may pale in comparison to what is a hot topic (e.g., typhoid) in another country.
4. Network with public relations peers at other companies within your industry to learn what they know about marketing differences among countries.
5. Call commercial attachés at embassies—"larger ones may have attachés for specific industries, such as agriculture or farming."
6. Call the State Department (202-647-4000) or the press department of the country's embassy in Washington to find out the way the media operate in a targeted country.
7. Read Keyser's newsletter (www.prninternational.com/newsletter.html).
8. Do not assume that you can send your press release electronically. The targeted country's media may not have the equipment to receive your messages, or that equipment may not be working. Find out about hand delivery options.
9. Read *The Economist* and the *Financial Times*.

Source: Adapted from "Going Global: Get Ready for Press Calls from Paris," *Ragan's Media Relations Report*, Vol. 2, No. 16, June 1, 1998, pp. 1-2.

* * *

ETHICS TRACK: TEXACO— CALLING BASIC VALUES INTO QUESTION

Motorists blocked Texaco pumps, and the company received a telephoned threat to blow up a Los Angeles Texaco station. But had Texaco executives really referred to black employees as "black Jelly Beans"?

It is difficult enough to deal with questions about safety procedures (as some airlines have had to do following crashes) or about product flaws (as, for example, some toy companies have had to do when children choked on toy parts). But when an organization's basic values are called to question, the public relations damage can take much longer to repair. Coors Brewing learned this when racial slurs were attributed to its chairman in *The Rocky Mountain News* in 1984. Even though the newspaper subsequently ran a retraction, it still took Coors years of effort, at a price tag in the millions, to recover its damaged image.

Texaco faced a dire crisis in 1996 when 1,500 black employees filed a $520 million discrimination lawsuit. A laid-off employee turned over to the court an audiotape he had recorded in which Texaco executives supposedly referred to African-American employees in derogatory terms. Though digital and other analysis of the tape revealed that it was not as racist as originally reported, Texaco was presumed guilty in the court of public opinion—and by its own managers, who gave interviews in which they offered personal, anecdotal evidence against the company.

Texaco acted quickly in responding to the public—forming a special diversity panel to overhaul company programs and launching an advertising campaign headlined "Where we go from here . . ." However, the possibility exists that the company acted *too* quickly, assuming responsibility before all the facts were in. Further, damage done to Texaco's credibility with its publics—including its own employees—is among the most difficult to repair. The company's ethics were the focus of initial attention, but the "whistleblower" who secretly recorded the company meeting later faced his own legal problems. Discuss the ethics issues involved in an employee's secret taping of company officials and in the other employees' willingness to make negative statements about Texaco to the media.

Source: Fraser P. Seitel, *The Practice of Public Relations*, Upper Saddle River, NJ: Prentice-Hall, 1998, pp. 15-18.

Lee & Johnson
:60 Spot
"Defining Public Relations: What's Your Function?"

Most people do not know that public relations has been a communication function since the time of ancient Greece; in America, the function dates back to the seventeenth century. Public relations has shaped America through some of its most important documents and events, such as the *Declaration of Independence*, the midnight ride of Paul Revere, and the Constitutional Convention. These employed such public relations tools as writing, public speaking, special events, and strategic planning. Our forefathers practiced public relations by informing the public and shaping public opinion. Despite the historical examples of good public relations, a few bad examples have given the industry a negative reputation.

It wasn't Thomas Paine, Thomas Jefferson, or George Washington who put public relations on the map. It was George Creel, Ivy Ledbetter Lee, and Watergate. First, Secretary of War George Creel and the Office of War Information were accused of luring the United States into World War I with a major publicity campaign. After the war, the public felt U.S. involvement in the war was unnecessary. Then Ivy Ledbetter Lee, the father of public relations, was convicted of "un-American" activities. Prior to the eruption of World War II, Lee advised Hitler and other German officials on public relations matters. Lee practiced business with Hitler before knowing the truth about Hitler and his plans. Finally, the largest detriment to the industry's reputation was not public relations at all. As a result of the Watergate scandal, the public developed "an attitude that anything was OK, so long as it could be masked by a good façade," said Harold Burson, chairman of Burson-Marsteller, in his speech titled "Beyond 'PR': Redefining the Roles of Public Relations." He added that the industry was most hurt when "President Richard Nixon was quoted as using the term 'to P-R' a situation." One of the worst scandals in American history gave public relations a negative connotation because of the association with Nixon and Watergate.

The core of public relations is public opinion. Our forefathers did not label the function public relations until 1803 when Thomas Jefferson used the word in a speech, Burson acknowledged. They realized that informing the public through the communications media of the day (e.g., by publishing essays such as the Federalist Papers in newspapers) would enhance their fight for freedom.

In 1998, people are still asking how much of public relations is a mask. The function of public relations is lost in its negative reputation. According to Burson, the function of public relations is "creating an opinion, where there is none; reinforcing an opinion that already exists; or changing an existing opinion." This does not mean creating a façade but rather informing the public. Public relations mediates between the company or product and its publics. Another public relations expert, Fraser P. Seitel, mentions in *The Practice of Public Relations*, "Ethics, truth, credibility—these values are what good public relations is all about. Coverup, distortion, and subterfuge are the antithesis of good public relations."

Catherine A. Narbone
Assistant Account Executive
Golin/Harris Communications, Inc.
Chicago

Chapter 18

Internet Advertising

In 1996, America Online opened the last uncommercialized window in cyberspace by making its public chat rooms available to advertisers. Ads rotate every minute, appearing at the top right-hand corner of the screen.[1] Since then, consumer Internet advertising reached 1997 revenue totals of $544.8 million for banner ads, interstitials, and sponsorships, a 147.1 percent increase over the previous year. This figure, from InterMedia Advertising Solutions, does not include revenue from listings, online directories, and space on malls, which, when added to the total, bring 1997 revenues to $906.5 million. Table 18.1 shows the biggest advertising spenders on the Internet during that year.

In an Ernst & Young survey, almost half the retailers who responded said that they expected Internet-generated sales to increase by as much as 10 percent by the year 2000. According to *Fortune* magazine, as more businesses discover the Internet, the Web is starting to resemble a mall.[2] Movie star Robert Redford's mail-order company, Sundance, encourages prospective customers to request catalogs online. Wal-Mart offers a full range of products, from toothpaste to lawn chairs, which customers can

TABLE 18.1. Top Advertisers on the Internet—January to September 1998

Rank	Spender	Total Spent in Millions	1997 Twelve-Month Rank
1	Microsoft	$25.5	1
2	IBM	21.0	2
3	Excite	8.8	3
4	General Motors Corp.	8.2	9
5	Infoseek	7.0	6

Source: Adapted from Kate Maddox, "IAB: Internet Advertising Will Near $2 Billion for 1998," *Advertising Age,* February 15, 1999, p. 34.

302   PRINCIPLES OF ADVERTISING: A GLOBAL PERSPECTIVE

ILLUSTRATION 18.1. The Information Superhighway

The view from the highway of the future is nothing but Net, literally, as a highway billboard proclaims, OPEN YOUR EYES TO THE WORLD. © Dana Hanefeld.

order via computer. General Motors' Web site, which scored more than 300,000 hits in its first twenty-four hours online, allows customers to choose option packages and price a new car. In April 1997, Bell Atlantic Electronic introduced its Interactive Yellow Pages to enable companies to reach Internet-savvy consumers who are ready to buy.[3] Using the same tag line, "Keds Feel Good," Keds extended its traditional television campaign to electronic postcards and e-mail stores in May 1998.[4]

Welcome to the world of cyberspace marketing and communication. The traditional marketplace faces new challenges from what has been called the "new market space."

THE INTERNET

The Internet, also referred to as cyberspace or the information superhighway (see Illustration 18.1), permits the electronic transfer of information. It is a global network of interconnected computers whereby an individual connected to one network can speak to any of thousands of other computers if the network is linked to other networks. Geographical boundaries are irrelevant. Regardless of the operating system of the network or PC (personal computer), the Internet offers several modes of information exchange:

- E-mail—still the dominant source of traffic and a versatile delivery vehicle
- World Wide Web (WWW)—the first multimedia platform
- Gopher—first menu-driven browsing tool
- Usenet Groups—groups who use internet chat rooms to discuss areas of mutual interest
- IRC (Internet relay chat)—real-time, text-based, chat talk
- Finger—a way to share personal information about oneself
- TELNET (remote log-in)—allows use of remote PC and its programs regardless of distance

The Internet began as a U.S. Department of Defense project in the 1960s as a tool to guarantee communications during nuclear attack. It grew into an information-sharing vehicle for universities in the 1970s and 1980s for research projects. Key tools for using the Internet, such as Gopher, Usenet, and Mosaic, all developed as freeware. The Internet opened to commercial vendors in 1991, with growth soaring at a rate of 300 percent by 1994. It took only three years after the introduction of commercial activity on the Internet for commercial hosts to pass the once dominant educational hosts.[5]

The 1990s have seen the birth of the World Wide Web (WWW), hypertext markup language (html), and graphical browsers such as Netscape. The Web, hypertext, and graphical browsers have made cyberspace a very friendly place and spawned the rush to get connected. One common misconception is that the Web and the Internet are one and the same. They are not. The term Internet refers to the physical infrastructure of an interconnected global computer network. The Web refers to just one of many modes of data storage and transfer commonly used on the Internet. E-mail is one example. Every Internet connection goes through an Internet service provider (ISP).

One of the most common sources of confusion with respect to the Internet is the unique position occupied by major commercial online services such as America Online, CompuServe, and Prodigy (these three companies handle 90 percent of online subscribers). Many newcomers to the information superhighway assume that these services are synonymous with the Internet. They are not. These networks are independent systems offering a wide variety of informational, entertainment, commercial, and other resources, only one of which is access to the wider, global system we call the Internet (including the Web). It is important to understand this distinction when considering the Internet, more specifically the Web, as a marketing medium.

Internet Regulation

On July 1, 1997, the Clinton administration released "A Framework for Global Electronic Commerce," a paper that "asserts that the world is poised on the cusp of an economic and cultural shift as dramatic as that of the Industrial Revolution." Today, a marketer can set up "a virtual storefront on the Web and instantly gain access to the global market," according to *Newsweek*'s Steven Levy.[6] The U.S. government, which initiated the computer communication system known as the Internet, now seems poised to take a hands-off position on Internet regulation. The Clinton position paper states that where government intervention is needed, "its aim should be to support and enforce a predictable minimalist, consistent and legal environment for commerce." Although the government's current position is to "act aggressively and globally" to nurture digital commerce through improving security and protection of free speech, the paper assures that cyberspace will be a tax- and tariff-free zone. President Bill Clinton and Vice President Al Gore have already used their influence to encourage China and Singapore not to censor the Internet. However, it will be up to the U.S. private sector to set online standards and to discourage foreign governments from regulating or censoring the Internet.

Nonetheless, public concerns are growing about the availability to children of pornographic Web site content, as well as advertising. The House and Senate have proposed legislation that would require federally funded schools and libraries to protect children from indecent material on the Internet by installing filtering software. The Senate Commerce Committee has already passed Senator John McCain's filtering bill (S. 1619).[7]

Another concern regards so-called spam, the Internet counterpart to "junk mail." This will be discussed in "Disadvantages of Web Advertising" in this chapter.

WEB ADVERTISING

Thousands of marketers have turned to the Internet as a prospective medium for promoting their brands and transacting sales. In July 1998, Unilever, the world's second-largest consumer products manufacturer, announced "three-year, multimillion-dollar advertising deals with America Online and Microsoft" that will produce over 1 billion impressions (or views) over that period.[8] The campaign, largely centered on advertising such Unilever brands as Lipton tea, Dove soap, Vaseline, and Good Humor ice cream bars, may also include online consumer purchase options. Online sales tripled from $707 million in 1996 to $2.6 billion in 1997 and are expected to reach $15.6 billion by the year 2000.[9]

Procter & Gamble, which spends $3 billion a year on advertising, spent $12 million on Internet marketing in 1998. P&G showed signs of taking the Internet very seriously when it hosted an invitation-only Internet summit for marketers and Internet "techies" on August 20 to 21, 1998. The company even invited rival Unilever to the conference. Business writer Bruce Horovitz has noted that P&G "helped turn radio—then TV—into the two most powerful mediums," and now may "do the same with the Internet." Although radio and television still boast larger audiences, consumer product giants such as Unilever and P&G realize that the Internet not only allows for direct communication with consumers but also "gives consumers the chance to respond to ads immediately without picking up a phone or mailing a check."[10]

Hundreds of companies have rushed to display Web sites, also known as home pages. Most of these offer advertisements for the company's products or services. Home pages are also used to disseminate promotional materials, such as press releases, backgrounds (company histories), newsletters, and consumer education materials.[11] To facilitate online traffic, Snap! Online,

Excite, and Compaq offer software "agents," called "shopbots," that allow consumers to compare products and prices from a "virtual database" of available products on a potentially huge variety of Web sites.[12] Although considered experimental at the present time, "shopbot" technology is expected to be fine-tuned by Christmas 1999.

In addition, companies now use the Internet for product promotions and other incentives. For instance, users can earn $2 by applying for a Cyber-Gold Visa card or earn 500 frequent flier miles by subscribing online to *The Red Herring* magazine. BonusMail and ClickRewards sites provide incentive points programs to encourage orders from 1-800-FLOWERS and other participating Web sites.[13]

Advantages of Web Advertising

In 1994, the Internet as a whole doubled in size, as it had done every year since 1988. According to a writer in *The Economist*, "The growth of the Net is not a fluke or a fad, but the consequence of unleashing the power of individual creativity," fostering "openness and interactivity, making it a combination of community and marketplace."[14] The home is now the hottest computer market. Compaq, Gateway, Acer, Apple, and Hewlett-Packard all brought out new home computer gadgets in 1996. As prices come down, the home is becoming the fastest-growing marketplace. In the future, *Fortune* magazine predicts that American homes will have a network hooked up in various rooms, including the kitchen.[15] Internet popularity continues to grow, with Relevant Knowledge reporting that U.S. users twelve and older spent eight hours and forty-eight minutes each week on the Web in July 1998, compared to seven hours in February 1998 and eight hours and six minutes in June 1998.[16]

In addition to its growing accessibility, the Internet has the advantage of being an interactive medium especially suited to audience targeting. In 1995, the demographics of online subscribers ranged from 60 to 94 percent male, depending on the server. Most subscribers were thirty-nine to forty-two years old, over half were college educated, married, and had household income of over $60,000.[17] More recent demographics place 38 percent of Web users in the eighteen to thirty-four age bracket, 36 percent at thirty-five to forty-nine, 15 percent at ages fifty and over, and 11 percent at twelve to seventeen.[18] In addition, 80 percent of college students were online by 1998, ensuring that an educated user population of both genders will be online in the future. That younger users are already key in Internet commerce is clear from an August 1998 Media Metrix report (see Table 18.2) that shows that trendy storefronts popular with Generation X and younger baby boomers show the healthiest growth rates.

TABLE 18.2. Some Top Internet Storefronts

E-merchant	May 1997	May 1998	Change
Amazon	2.7%	6.3%	+133%
CDnow	1.1	2.4	+118
Barnes and Noble	0.4	2.2	+450
Music Boulevard	0.4	2.0	+400
BMG Music	1.3	1.7	+31

Source: Adapted from Media Metrix, Inc., August 1998. Reach definition: The percentage of Web-active individuals who visited a site once in the given month. Individual visits are unduplicated. If a site has a 2 percent reach, then 2 percent of these individuals visited that site in a given month.

According to Simba Information, Incorporated, "Perhaps the most promising demographic statistic for all marketers and advertisers entering the electronic marketplace is the affluence of new media users. Consumers with more discretionary income tend to make more purchases that are not necessities." Ogilvy & Mather Direct has dubbed this person the "technology-savvy consumer." Fifty-four percent of the company's clients have a household income of $100,000 plus. Prodigy subscribers surpass the national average in measures of affluence, activity, and influence, with 75 percent having attended or graduated from college—compared to the average U.S. household, which has only 33 percent college graduates.

Although ad banners (e.g., see Illustration 18.2) remain the predominant advertising vehicle on the Web, local advertising and classified advertising are becoming a growing presence. According to the Internet Advertising Bureau's (IAB) third-quarter report in 1997, approximately 12 percent of total Internet advertising revenues came from local advertisers, up from less than 5 percent in the previous quarter.[19] Furthermore, online advertising has been viewed as a superior vehicle for building customer relationships and brand awareness. IAB writer Tom Hyland views the Internet as "the only medium where users can view ads, request and receive specialized product information, make an instant purchase and save time and expense."[20]

In addition, electronic communication has been "a blessing" for business managers.[21] More than 45 percent of 400 managers polled by the American Management Association and Ernst & Young reported using e-mail more than any other communication tool. Electronic communication is especially

ILLUSTRATION 18.2. Twinkle, Twinkle

Blinking banner ads for Children's Memorial Hospital urge Internet users to *Brighten the life of a child*, a message that transforms into a specific call to action in the blink of an eye: *Buy our corporate holiday cards*. Banner ads remain the predominant advertising vehicle on the World Wide Web.

beneficial for global marketing. It is a powerful tool for overcoming time zone problems. Some U.S. companies communicate almost entirely with a foreign market via the Internet or fax.[22] Stephen H. Haeckel, director of strategic studies at IBM's Advanced Business Institute, believes that "low-cost global digital networks give us the potential to collaborate with one another in a new medium, on a scale unprecedented in human history."[23] He also cautions that "learning to exploit these potentials might require the development of substantially different cognitive processes." This brings us to the arena of new problems created by the Internet.

Disadvantages of Web Advertising

Although Hormel Foods Corporation officials have objected to the generic use of its trademark name for a canned meat product, "Spam," the word has become part of the vocabulary of Internet users. "Spam" is "slang for the practice of sending commercial e-mail in bulk."[24] Steve Case, chairman of America Online, reports that junk e-mail is the number one complaint of its subscribers. Unsolicited electronic messages hawking a wide range of products are sent to millions of Americans each day. For some small businesses with a limited advertising budget, "Spam mail" is considered a "free" way to get a message out. For example, by hitting one computer key, Rick Miles, vice president of Idea Concepts, sent a message extolling the benefits of Liquid Oxygen, an oxygen-rich dietary supplement, to over 50,000 e-mail addresses. This sort of advertising, "junk e-mailing," uses lists of addresses acquired through special computer software or from surfing the Internet.[25]

Two bills were introduced in Congress in May 1997 to deal with the continuing problem of "Spam" messages. One bill would outlaw sending any unsolicited commercial e-mail (UCE). The other would require those sending out advertisements over the Internet to label them as such and set up a mechanism that would prevent their intended recipients from ever having to see them if they so chose. In June 1998, the Senate's Telephone Anti-Slamming Amendments Act addressed junk e-mail issues. However, users disagree on whether the problem is serious enough to warrant government intervention. Some feel that, so far, efforts to curb spam "haven't stopped a flood of unwanted messages from clogging electronic mailboxes" with everything from advertising to pornography. Those determined to "spam" electronic mailboxes find ways to get around new legal standards since none of the legislation bans spam outright.[26] Another option to control spam is being addressed by Internet service providers. To differentiate their services from those of competitors, some ISPs offer such special services as on-request spam filtering. The ISP can even selectively filter for those who do not want all domains blocked.[27]

Spam defenders believe that bulk e-mail will eventually be an accepted part of the Internet and become a valuable tool for the public to keep up with new ideas and products.

Another challenge to Internet advertisers has been the possibility of Internet intrusions. Credit card buying and selling via the Internet has been slowed by the challenge of protecting customers from cyberthieves who steal credit card numbers. A company's home page may be vandalized, with information and graphics changed to embarrass the company or to impede the flow of business. Some companies are now protected from Internet intrusions by "firewalls." A "firewall," or "bastion," is a system that protects one network from another.

Another major concern is the lack of product diversity among Internet ads. Although the Web ad business has skyrocketed, and online shopping revenues have grown substantially (see Table 18.3), as much as 67 percent of the Internet-generated revenue has been attributed to either Web-based companies, telecommunications, or computer companies—all of which have nothing to lose and everything to gain by promoting a networked, computer-based medium.[28] Of the $1.1 billion online shopping revenue estimated for 1997, only 3 percent of purchases were estimated for entertainment/recreation and just 2 percent for financial services. The number of big marketers (companies in categories such as financial services, travel, health care, and entertainment) participating online obviously needs to increase.

Many Web publishers have recognized this problem and have tried to promote the Web's value as a marketing medium. Cox Enterprises, Incorporated has formed Cox Interactive Media to build new brands and audiences on the Internet to serve local advertisers in several of its markets.[29]

Disadvantages of Internet advertising and marketing are more complex than represented here, of course. Robert Kuttner, author of *The End of Laissez-Faire*, addressed some of these issues in *Business Week*: "The Internet is a nearly perfect market because information is instantaneous and

TABLE 18.3. Online Shopping Revenue Estimates (in Billions)

Year	Revenue
1997	$1.1
1998	2.4
1999	4.0
2000	6.6

Source: Adapted from "On-Line Shopping Splurge," *USA Today*, August 29, 1997, p. B4.

buyers can compare the offerings of sellers worldwide," he wrote.[30] On the other hand, fierce competition quickly undercuts cyberspace profits—the Amazon/Barnes and Noble price wars in 1998 led to Barnes and Noble selectively underpricing the "upstart" Amazon. Although profits are being made on the Internet, Kuttner warns that the Internet also "produces speedy imitation and thin margins." As another example, "consumer sovereignty" in price haggling on the Internet has wreaked "consumer revenge on industries such as airlines that have restored profitability by counting on consumer ignorance to sell the same product at different prices."

Whether it is a "perfect" market space or not, the Internet must be recognized as a major player to be dealt with among advertising media.

INTERNET DIRECTORY ADVERTISING

A weighty debate has been staged over the future of traditional mass media as computer platforms prove their ability to deliver more information, in more depth, and in less time than their nonelectronic competitors. An ad placed by *The Wall Street Journal* in the July 17, 1996 edition of *The New York Times*, posed this question: "Will content delivery on the World Wide Web spell the death knell for traditional newspapers and magazines?" The conclusion drawn in this advertisement is that print and electronic publications can complement each other.

How will electronic publishing affect the field of advertising?

The Yellow Pages industry has already begun the journey from print publication to electronic publishing. Yellow Pages directories are making a relatively smooth transition into Internet advertising. According to Harvey Leong, a consultant to the YPPA (Yellow Pages Publishers' Association), the early adopters of electronic shopping services are also heavy users of Yellow Pages, so offering electronic Yellow Pages makes a lot of sense.[31]

The scope of electronic Yellow Pages is broad, ranging from community to international. Local electronic directories, such as the Banana Pages in Seattle, include traditional Yellow Pages content in select special interest categories, information on communities in the regional territory served, yet link the user to national Yellow Pages listings. Although most regional directories still have limited special interest categories, compared to the print Pages, listings are constantly being expanded and enhanced. Users searching the regional directories will be linked to Big Yellow, with additional links back to the regional directory.[32] Yellow Pages offers consumers a number of electronic platform choices:

- CD-ROM is an integral part of home computing. Half of the computers shipped today have CD-ROM players. Some electronic directories, such as BellSouth Raleigh, offer multimedia CD-ROM, with audio tips and maps, free to consumers.
- Audio Text allows consumers to call a telephone number to access free information. Yellow Pages takes this service beyond the standard time and weather—consumers are prompted to push buttons to access general Yellow Pages information, consumer tips (ranging from tips on etiquette to theater reviews), and talking ads. Audio text advertising is packaged with print Yellow Pages purchases.
- Online services have experienced "spectacular growth to date," according to Leong. In addition to business listings and advertisements, electronic Yellow Pages offer hyperlinks to other Web pages and search engines and enable consumers to conduct business transactions, such as orders for merchandise, restaurant reservations, or service requests.

Thus far, no usage erosion of print Yellow Pages has occurred as a result of alternative shopping technologies. Although electronic growth for Yellow Pages has been fairly flat, dramatic growth is expected between 2000 and 2010. An Associated Press study, "Newspapers 2000 and Beyond," also shows movement toward electronic publishing growth.[33]

INTERNET CUSTOMER SERVICE

Commerce Clearing House (CCH), a business-to-business subscription publisher in Riverwoods, Illinois, faced a decrease in net income from $53 million in 1987 to $31 million in 1991. The advent of alternative media, such as CD-format products, online information services, and other nonprint products, was causing this print publisher to lose market share and profitability quickly. The company began to offer its publications in nonprint formats. It also radically downsized, cutting from its payroll 1,200 of its 7,000 employees.[34] The sales force was cut by nearly two-thirds. Prior to reengineering, CCH's sales force developed and maintained one-on-one customer relationships. CCH turned to the Internet for the crucial two-way communication that had been lost with the downsizing of the sales force. CCH's Web home page provides its customers with corporate and product press releases, new product information, basic subscription information on each product, a full books catalog, and corporate information. CCH customer service representatives are now easier to reach via an 800 number staffed from 6 a.m. to 6 p.m. The Internet and other interactive technology "has allowed CCH to tailor the level of service to client needs and wants."[35] Since the reengineering effort reflected the commitment of CCH's president and CEO, Oakleigh Thorne, to the principles of Integrated Marketing Communication, the ability to focus on customer needs and wants was especially important.

As the CCH case illustrates, the Internet offers more than the opportunity to advertise and sell products. It also makes customer service more immediately and constantly available. A company may provide new product introduction via the Internet, including product demonstrations that may be downloaded by the customer. Trade show and seminar schedules may be disseminated to customers online. Some companies currently use electronic tracking systems provided by UPS and Federal Express to provide the status of shipments via these carriers to online customers. Internet users who send online inquiries to customer service departments generally receive responses via the Internet.

SUMMARY

The Internet has become the hot new market space. Although corporations and organizations of all types are flocking to the Internet, profit margins remain slim. Most see an Internet presence as building for the future. Advertising on the World Wide Web has its advantages and disadvantages. What is clear is that advertisers can no longer ignore this medium. Online shopping revenues are expected to climb to $6.6 billion by the year 2000. Electronic publishing, including Internet directory advertising, has been growing at dramatic rates. Finally, electronic communication allows those in the business world to more easily exchange ideas and general knowledge with colleagues, customers, consumers, and vendors all over the world.

* * *

THE GLOBAL PERSPECTIVE: ENGLISH LANGUAGE IN THE CYBERFUTURE

The combined populations of China and India represent one-third of the world's population, and now they also represent the fastest-growing Internet market. By the year 2000, the World Watch Institute projects that 5.5 million Chinese and Indian users will be online.

Analysts say this raises new questions about the way the Internet will be used globally in the future. Many Indians speak English, yet prefer to communicate in their native tongue, as do many others around the world for whom English is not their native language. According to Michael Marriott in "The Web

Reflects a Wider World," this means that the way "commerce, news, research and entertainment are presented on the Internet will have to be rethought."

Since its beginnings, the Internet "has been dominated by the English language and North American culture," Marriott said. All this is changing. Non-U.S. users may already outnumber U.S. users on the Web.

What will the cyberfuture look like? Marriott makes these predictions:

- More major search engines will offer services in languages other than English. Netscape has already partnered with the leading Latin American service, Star Media Network, to create a Spanish and Portuguese Internet guide.
- International users may see U.S. sites offered in their own languages, much as American television networks now provide popular programming, such as *Seinfeld,* in a variety of languages for airing abroad.
- The "global village" may become a reality, as a wider range of goods and ideas are exchanged in cyberspace.

Nevertheless, English is expected to remain "the common language of commerce." Its current dominance on the Internet could "deepen its hold on the world," influencing global culture in much the way American film, television, music, and lifestyles have done. Even the French, "famously fastidious about guarding their language against dilution by foreign words and phrases," have no other word for Internet.

Source: Michael Marriott, "The Web Reflects a Wider World," *The New York Times*, June 18, 1998, pp. D1, D7.

* * *

ETHICS TRACK:
THE DIRTY LITTLE SEARCH ENGINE SECRET

When is Mickey Mouse not safe for the viewing of children? When children use the Infoseek search engine, 43 percent of which is owned by Disney.[a]

Despite the scrutiny of media watchdogs, Infoseek, Yahoo!, Excite, and HotBot all accepted pornography ads in 1998. AltaVista and Lycos sold out all their illicit key words through 1999. Children searching a key word such as "CHEERLEADER" are likely to turn up banner ads with pornographic pictures and messages. Clicking on these ads may turn up even more salacious material, such as porn sites with live sex shows. Yahoo! has tried to circumvent this problem by requiring "that all porn ads have a jump page, directing all under-18 users off the site."[b] Lycos provides SafetyNet software to prevent children from accessing pornographic key words, but this software must be requested and installed by the parent.

The role of advertising is controversial. In the advertising industry, people know that sex sells. Now pornography ads have become commonplace on Internet search engine sites, and groups such as the Center of Media Education have become concerned. Another media center concern is the blending of interactive and ad content on children's sites. For instance, television guidelines "force a clear separation between content and advertising on television" and "a ban on characters, real or animated, acting both as content and pitchmen."[c] These guidelines do not apply to the Internet. Agencies such as Saatchi & Saatchi use Web sites such as Kid Connection to conduct marketing research. Kidscom.com, an advertising-supported site, has offered children points toward free merchandise for answering marketing questions.

The Internet is here to stay as a powerful societal force. Internet advertising revenues reached $491 million during the third quarter of 1998, a 116 percent increase over the third quarter of 1997.[d] The Internet Advertising Bureau predicts that Internet advertising revenues will reach $2 billion in 1999, outpacing outdoor advertising revenues and equaling cable television's current 20 percent of the advertising revenue pie. When the Internet is compared to these more mature media, its phenomenal growth may seem overwhelming.

Lobbyist groups, such as the Center for Media Education, are calling for commercial-free Web areas for children, similar to public playgrounds, and pressuring Congress for Internet regulation. However, America Online and other companies that do Internet business want Congress to move more slowly on regulation.[e] Businesses feel that self-regulation and public education are better ways to deal with issues raised by this young, complicated, and quickly changing medium. Will bridge pages, such as the Yahoo! jump pages, resolve some of the problems of children confronting pornographic material? What are the problems with such innovations as SafetyNet software? What might be the long-term effects of exposing children to the Internet's content/advertising blends? Is regulation the answer, or will self-regulation and public education be adequate in protecting children?

Answers to these questions continue to be debated, but the events that transpired in Littleton, Colorado, on April 20, 1999, exposed the issue of children and the Internet to its most dramatic public scrutiny yet. Alleged shooter Eric Harris' hate-filled Web site, in which he detailed his plan to kill people and even named certain intended victims, and his obsession with violent computer games, left the country with no choice but to wonder about the new medium's power to influence.

[a] Jason McCabe Calacanis, "Are Portal Sites Promoting Porn?" *Silicon Alley Reporter,* Iss. 17, September 1998, p. 47.
[b] Patricia Riedman, "Risky Business: Selling Web Porn Ads Stirs Debate," *Advertising Age,* November 3, 1997, Vol. 68, Iss. 44, p. 50.
[c] Ian Austen, "But First, Another Word from Our Sponsor," *The New York Times on the Web,* February 18, 1999, <http://www.nytimes.com>.
[d] Lisa Napoli, "Quarterly Internet Ad Revenues Double," *The New York Times on the Web,* February 10, 1999, <http://www.nytimes.com>.
[e] Cassandra Burrell, "Internet Companies Push to Slow Regulation," *The South Bend Tribune,* April 26, 1999, p. C6.

Notes

Chapter 1

1. Chuck Ross, "Coke Readies Team of 70 Television Ads for Games," *Advertising Age*, April 29, 1996, p. 3.
2. Don E. Schultz, "The Evolving Nature of Integrated Communications," *Journal of Integrated Communications*, Vol. VIII, 1997-1998, p. 15.
3. Don E. Schultz, "Integration Helps You Plan Communication from Outside-In," *The Marketing News,* March 15, 1993, p. 12.
4. Don E. Schultz, "The IMC Process," in Ron Kaatz (Ed.), *Integrated Marketing Symposium,* Lincolnwood, IL: NTC Business Books, 1995, pp. 6-13.
5. Kim Cleland, "Rep Firms Stake out Web Territory," *Advertising Age*, February 19, 1996, p. 36.
6. Michael Diamond, "Advertising Spending May Hit Record $200B This Year," *USA Today*, June 24, 1998, p. 6B.
7. "Magazines and TV Spar over Drug Ads," *The Wall Street Journal*, October 16, 1997, p. B8; and Melanie Wells, "First Prozac TV Ads Air on Cable," *USA Today*, September 15, 1998, p. B2.
8. Michael Diamond and Julie Schmit, "Buyers flock to Apple's iMac," *USA Today*, August 19, 1998, p. B3.
9. "Republican Candidate Using Clinton Affair in TV Ad," *The South Bend Tribune*, August 18, 1998, p. A3.
10. Gary Fields and Carrie Hedges, "Drug Ads Blitz: A Wake-up Call," *USA Today*, July 10, 1998, p. A1.
11. Daniel McGinn, "Chiat's New Day," *Newsweek*, August 3, 1998, pp. 40, 41.
12. Sally Goll Beatty, "Miller's Flagship Brew Sets Sail on a 'Sea Change' of Attitudes," *The Wall Street Journal*, February 1, 1996, p. B5.
13. "Can It Regain Its Golden Touch?" *Business Week*, March 4, 1998, p. 70; "Nielsen's Top TV Advertisers," *USA Today*, August 10, 1998, p. B6.
14. Miriam Jordan, "In Rural India, Video Vans Sell Toothpaste and Shampoo," *The Wall Street Journal*, January 10, 1996, p. B1.
15. AMA Board of Directors, "AMA Board Approves New Marketing Definition," *Marketing News*, March 1, 1985, p. 1.
16. Stephen Fox, *The Mirror Makers*, New York: William Morrow, 1984; James Playsted Wood, *The Story of Advertising*, New York: Ronald Press, 1958; William Leiss, Stephen Kline, and Sut Jhally, *Social Communication in Advertising: Persons, Products, and Images of Well-Being*, New York: Routledge, 1990;

Frank Presbrey, *The History and Development of Advertising*, Garden City, NY: Doubleday, Doran, 1929.

17. Bob Schulber, *Radio Advertising: The Authoritative Handbook*, Lincolnwood, IL: NTC Business Books, 1989.

18. Sherilyn K. Zeigler and Herbert H. Howard, *Broadcast Advertising*, Third Edition, Ames, IA: Iowa State University Press, 1991.

19. Roland Marchand, "The Parable of the Democracy of Goods," in Sonia Maasik and Jack Solomon (Eds.), *Signs of Life in the USA*, Boston: Bedford Books, 1994, pp. 110, 115.

20. Gary C. Woodward and Robert E. Denton Jr., *Persuasion and Influence in American Life*, Prospect Heights, IL: Waveland Press, 1996, pp. 228-291.

21. Jack Solomon, "Masters of Desire: The Culture of American Advertising." in Gary Colombo, Robert Cullen, and Bonnie Lisle (Eds.), *Rereading America*, Boston: Bedford Books, 1995, p. 490.

22. Ibid., p. 493.

23. Ibid., p. 499.

24. Ibid., p. 495.

25. Sonia Maasik and Jack Solomon, "Brought to You B(u)y," in Sonia Maasik and Jack Solomon (Eds.), *Signs of Life in the USA*, Boston: Bedford Books, 1994, p. 107.

26. Schultz, "The Evolving Nature of Integrated Communications," pp. 11-18. All the direct quotes in this section are from this article.

Chapter 2

1. Leah Haran, "Mobil Fuels Minority Ads," *Advertising Age*, April 15, 1996, p. 8.

2. Melanie Wells, "Ethnic Agencies Create One World," *USA Today,* November 17, 1997, p. B6.

3. Mark Landler, "What Happened to Advertising?" *Business Week*, September 23, 1991, pp. 66-71.

4. Courtney Crandall, "It Pays to Advertise," *New England Business*, May 1991, p. 35; Horst Stipp, "Crisis in Advertising?" *Marketing Research*, March 1992, pp. 39-45.

5. Robert J. Samuelson, "The End of Advertising?" *Newsweek*, August 19, 1991, p. 40; Neil H. Borden, *The Economic Effects of Advertising*, Chicago: Richard D. Irwin, 1942, pp. 734-735; Mark Landler, "Fear of Flying in Ad Land," *Business Week*, November 19, 1990, pp. 100-105.

6. David Rynecki, "Latin America Crisis Could Tame U.S. Bull," *USA Today*, August 25, 1998, p. B1.

7. Courtland L. Bovee, John Thill, George P. Dovel, and Marian Burk Wood, *Advertising Excellence*, New York: McGraw-Hill, Inc., 1995, pp. 56-58; George E. Belch and Michael A. Belch, *Introduction to Advertising and Promotion*, Homewood, IL: Irwin, 1993, pp. 828-830.

8. Kirk Davidson, "Look for Abundance of Opposition to Television Liquor Advertisements," *Marketing News,* January 6, 1997, pp. 4, 30.

9. Yumiko Ono, "Sometimes Ad Agencies Mangle English Deliberately," *The Wall Street Journal,* reprinted in *The South Bend Tribune,* November 9, 1997, p. B5.

10. Kathleen Hall Jamieson and Karlyn Kohrs Campbell, *The Interplay of Influence: News, Advertising, Politics, and the Mass Media,* Third Edition, Belmont, CA: Wadsworth, 1992, pp. 173-174.

11. Martha T. Moore, "Study: Ads Improve Little in Diversity," *USA Today,* August 29, 1992, p. B1.

12. Ernest F. Cooke and Monle Lee, "Advertising Follows, Not Leads the Culture: The Example of Women in Liquor Advertisements," *Marketing: Moving Toward the 21st Century,* edited by Elnora W. Stuart, David J. Ortinau, and Ellen M. Moore, Proceedings of the Annual Meeting of the Southern Marketing Association, New Orleans, LA: Southern Marketing Association, 1996, pp. 327-331.

13. Jim Kirk, "Deal with It: Women Are Sick of Stereotypical Advertising," *The Chicago Tribune,* February 22, 1998, p. C1.

14. David Goodman, "For New Kellogg Ads, Thin No Longer Is 'in,'" *The South Bend Tribune,* February 9, 1998, p. C7.

15. "Survey Time," *USA Today,* December 18, 1996, p. D3.

16. Ellen McCracken, *Decoding Women's Magazines,* New York: St. Martin's Press, 1993, p. 279.

17. John W. Ellis IV, "Web TV, Cable Reasonable Content, Ads with Client Base," *Advertising Age,* April 12, 1999, p. S12.

18. Debra Aho Williamson, "Web Ads Mark 2nd Birthday with Decisive Issues Ahead," *Advertising Age,* October 21, 1996, pp. 1, 43.

19. Elizabeth Weise, "Net Use Doubling Every 100 Days," *USA Today,* April 16, 1998, p. A1.

20. Sally Beatty, "Forecast Is Boosted for '98 U.S. Ad Budgets," *The Wall Street Journal,* June 24, 1998, p. B5.

21. Robert Risse, "Is the Price Right?" *Silicon Alley Reporter,* March 1998, p. 6.

22. Debra Aho Williamson, "Outlook '97: Will Web Ads Go Mainstream?" *Advertising Age,* October, 26, 1996, p. 38.

23. Skip Wollenberg, "KFC Ads to Use Animated Colonel," *The South Bend Tribune,* September 8, 1998, p. C8.

24. Jolie Solomon and Arlyn Tobias Gajilan, "A Tale of a Tail," *Newsweek,* November 11, 1996, pp. 58-59.

25. Jonathan Karp, "Medium and Message," *Far Eastern Economic Review,* February 25, 1993, pp. 50-52.

Chapter 3

1. Todd Pruzan and Chuck Ross, "Absolut Considers Breaking TV Ad Ban," *Advertising Age,* March 11, 1996, pp. 1, 33.

2. David E. Rosenbaum, "Senate Drops Tobacco Bill with '98 Revival Unlikely; Clinton Lashes out at G.O.P.," *The New York Times,* June 18, 1998, p. A1.

3. Barbara Martinez, "Gap Is Named in Infringement Suit over Eyewear Included in an Ad," *The Wall Street Journal,* January 6, 1998, p. B4.

4. Wendy Bounds, "Polo Magazine Gets a Whipping from Lauren in Trademark Case," *The Wall Street Journal*, July 7, 1998, p. B6.

5. *Coca-Cola v. Tropicana*, 690 F2d 312 (1982).

6. Federal Trade Commission Act, section 5(a)(1).

7. William Wells, John Burnett, and Sandra Moriarty, *Advertising: Principles & Practice*, Upper Saddle River, NJ: Prentice-Hall, 1998, p. 48; Pat Sloan and Jennifer DeCoursey, "Gov't Hot on Trail of Calvin Klein Ads," *Advertising Age*, September 1, 1995, pp. 1, 8; Michele Ingrassia, "Calvin's World," *Newsweek*, September 11, 1995, pp. 60-66.

8. Nick Catoggio, "Inn-Discretion," *Entertainment Weekly*, August 21, 1998, www.epnet.com.

9. Sally Goll Beatty and Richard Gibson, "Taste-Test Wars Heat up Among Rivals," *The Wall Street Journal*, March 30, 1998, p. B8; Louise Kramer, "Papa John's Blasts Rival Pizza Hut's Ad Imagery," *Advertising Age*, January 25, 1999, p. 4.

10. Sally Goll Beatty, "Campbell to Alter Soup Ad," *The Wall Street Journal*, October 29, 1997, p. B10.

11. Antoaneta Bezlova, "China Subjects U.S. Direct Marketers to Party Line," *USA Today*, April 29, 1998, p. B2.

12. "Main Chinese Channel Bars Spirits Spots from Prime Time," *Advertising Age International*, November 1997, p. 23.

13. "Some Regulations on Experimental Advertising Agency Systems," *China Advertising*, Iss. 51, p. 3.

14. Louisa Ha, "Concerns About Advertising Practices in a Developing Country: An Examination of China's New Advertising Regulations," *International Journal of Advertising*, 1996, Iss. 15, pp. 91-102.

15. Michael H. Anderson, *Madison Avenue in Asia: Politics and Transnational Advertising*, Cranbury, NJ: Associated University Presses, 1983.

16. "Japanese Clear Smoke out of Some Media," *Advertising Age International*, November 1997, p. 23.

17. Rochelle Burbury, "International Special Report," *Advertising Age International*, October 1996, p. 113.

18. Fair Trade Law. Taiwan, Republic of China: Preparatory Office of the Fair Trade Commission, 1991, p. 9.

19. *Selling Dreams: How Advertising Misleads Us*, Penang, Malaysia: Consumers' Association of Penang, 1986.

20. Anderson, *Madison Avenue in Asia*.

21. Burbury, "International Special Report," p. 113.

22. Ibid.

23. "Gov't. Regulations Sting U.K. Outdoor Biz," *Adweek Western Advertising News*, May 23, 1994, Vol. 44, No. 21, p. 14.

24. Barbara Sundberg Baudot, *International Advertising Handbook*, Lexington, MA: Lexington Books, 1989.

25. Burbury, "International Special Report," p. 113.

26. Jeffery D. Zbar, "Latin America Cracking Down," *Advertising Age International*, October 1996, p. 116.

27. Ibid.

28. Portions of text in this chapter were derived from the following book and booklets: Adnan Hashim, *Advertising in Malaysia*, Malaysia: Pelanduk Publications (M) Sdn. Bhd, 1994; The Indonesian Association of Advertising Agencies, *Media Scene Indonesia*, Indonesian, 1989/1990; Consumers' Association of Penang, *Selling Dreams: How Advertising Misleads Us*, Malaysia, 1986; Ramesh Shrestha, editor and publisher, *The Advertising Book: A Guide to the Advertising Industry in Thailand*, Thailand: AB Publications, 1984; Antonio V. Concepcio and Nimia G. Yumol, *Profile of the Philippine Advertising Industry*, Phillipines: Advertising Board of the Phillipines, 1989; and other materials collected by the Institute of Southeast Asian Studies, Republic of Singapore.

Chapter 4

1. Rachel Kaplan, "Ad Agencies Take on the World," *International Management*, April 1994, pp. 50-52.

2. Ibid., p. 52.

3. "'94 Advertising Agencies Report," *Advertising Age*, Chinese Edition, May 1995, p. 62.

4. Frederick R. Gamble, *What Advertising Agencies Are—What They Do and How They Do It*, Seventh Edition, New York: American Association of Advertising Agencies, 1970, p. 4.

5. R. Craig Endicott, "World's Top 25 Agency Brands," *Advertising Age*, April 19, 1999, p. S16.

6. Judann Pollack, "McDonald's to Aim Its Arch at Grown-Ups," *Advertising Age*, April 8, 1996, p. 3; Judann Pollack and Pat Sloan, "McDonald's Looking Beyond Core Agencies," *Advertising Age*, May 13, 1996, p. 52.

7. "Adweek's Marketing," *Adweek*, March 12, 1990, p. RC27; Mark Gleason, "McCann to Buy Health Agency," *Advertising Age*, June 3, 1996, pp. 1, 53.

8. Keith J. Kelly and Jeffery D. Zbar, "Spanish Magazines Capture Attention with 3 New Entries," *Advertising Age*, June 3, 1996, p. 44.

9. Jeffery D. Zbar, "Honda U.S. Hispanic Shop Widens Reach," *Advertising Age*, January 29, 1996, p. 30.

10. Melanie Wells, "Procter & Gamble Tells Ad Agencies to Diversify," *USA Today*, April 26, 1996, p. B2.

11. Sally Beatty, "'Integration Fees' of TV Networks Draw Ire of Ad-Group President," *The Wall Street Journal*, April 3, 1998, p. B7.

12. "For the Record," *Advertising Age*, February 22, 1999, p. 64; Judann Pollack and Beth Snyder, "Kellogg Shifts Two JWT Brands to Burnett in Rift," *Advertising Age*, February 1, 1999, p. 3.

13. Yumiko Ono, "Miller Brewing Gives Boot to 2 Agencies," *The Wall Street Journal*, December 13, 1996, p. B12; Melanie Wells, "Recreating Advertising," *USA Today*, November 30, 1998, p. B1.

14. Melanie Wells, "Ad Agency, Nabisco End Long Relationship," *USA Today*, June 18, 1997, p. B2.
15. James B. Arndorfer and Laura Petrecca, "Seagram Shuffles Agencies on Two Top-Selling Brands," *Advertising Age*, April 27, 1998, p. 4.
16. Beatty, "'Integration Fees' of TV Networks Draw Ire of Ad-Group President," p. B5.
17. Stuart Elliott, "A Group is Making a Multiyear Effort to Show the Importance of Ads to Marketers and Consumers," *The New York Times*, June 18, 1998, p. C6.
18. Kate Fitzgerald, "Beyond Advertising," *Advertising Age*, August 3, 1998, p. 1.
19. Dottie Enrico, "Leadership Problems, Bad Decisions Devastate Ad Agency," *USA Today*, March 6, 1998, p. B1.
20. Sally Beatty, "Merger Boom Expected in Ad Industry," *The Wall Street Journal*, May 21, 1998, p. B10.
21. Sally Beatty, "Citigroup May Need to Trim Brand Names," *The Wall Street Journal*, April 7, 1998, p. B10.
22. Sally Beatty, "Agencies Get Creative with Shops to Dodge Conflict Issue for Clients," *The Wall Street Journal*, November 14, 1997, p. B6.
23. "Minishops at Leo Burnett," *The Wall Street Journal*, November 14, 1997, p. B6.
24. Sally Beatty and Patrick McGeehan, "Merrill May Get Something Extra When It Chooses New Ad Agency," *The Wall Street Journal*, May 29, 1998, p. B8.

Chapter 5

1. Robert Frank, "Potato Chips to Go Global—Or So Pepsi Bets," *The Wall Street Journal*, November 30, 1995, pp. B3, B10.
2. William M. Pride and O.C. Ferrell, *Marketing*, Ninth Edition, Boston: Houghton Mifflin, 1995.
3. Tara Parker-Pope, "Ford Puts Blacks in Whiteface, Turns Red," *The Wall Street Journal*, February 22, 1996, p. B8.
4. Keith J. Kelly, "Kids Magazines Learn to Multiply," *Advertising Age*, December 2, 1996, p. 6.
5. Michael Wilke, "ABC Debuts Radio Disney AM Outlets," *Advertising Age*, December 2, 1996, p. 6.
6. Alicia Lasek, "Radio Ad Boom Sweet Music to Station Owners," *Advertising Age*, March 18, 1996, p. 30.
7. Hugh Pope, "Plying Ex-Soviet Asia with Pepsi, Barbie, and Barf," *The Wall Street Journal*, May 6, 1998, p. B1.
8. Bruce Horovitz, "New Ads Go After Kids," *USA Today*, May 19, 1997, p. B1.
9. Wendy Bounds, "Meredith Introduces 'more' for Women," *The Wall Street Journal*, June 19, 1998, p. B4.
10. Barbara Martinez, "Dog Food, Toothpaste and Oreos Star on Popular Hispanic Television Program," *The Wall Street Journal*, March 25, 1997, pp. B1, B7.
11. Sally Beatty, "Some Great Ads You'll Probably Never See," *The Wall Street Journal*, June 2, 1998, p. B12.

12. Joshua Wolf Shenk, "The New Anti-Ad," *U.S. News and World Report*, October 20, 1997, p. 80.

13. Dottie Enrico, "Admakers Narrow Focus to Zero in on Income Groups," *USA Today*, June 29, 1998, p. B5.

14. Dottie Enrico, "Popular Ad Campaigns Can Bridge Generation Gap," *USA Today*, June 22, 1998, p. B6.

15. William M. Pride and O.C. Ferrell, *Marketing,* Tenth Edition, Boston: Houghton Mifflin, 1997.

16. Jeff Jensen, "Chief Auto Steers for Quality Positioning," *Advertising Age*, April 1, 1996, p. 8.

17. Nikhil Deogun, "'The Exorcist' Meets 'Goodfellas' in New Pepsi Ad Challenging Coke," *The Wall Street Journal*, July 9, 1998, p. B12.

18. A. Jerome Jewler, *Creative Strategy in Advertising*, Fourth Edition, Belmont, CA: Wadsworth, 1992, p. 69.

Chapter 6

1. Norihiko Shirouzu, "Flouting 'Rules' Sells GE Fridges in Japan," *The Wall Street Journal*, October 31, 1995, p. B1.

2. Paul Sherlock, *Rethinking Business to Business Marketing*, New York: Free Press, 1991, pp. 19-22.

3. Courtland L. Bovee, John V. Thill, George P. Dovel, and Marian Burk Wood, *Advertising Excellence*, New York: McGraw-Hill, Inc., 1995, pp. 108-109.

4. L. W. Turley and Scott W. Kelley, "A Comparison of Advertising Content: Business to Business versus Consumer Services," *Journal of Advertising,* Vol. XXVI, No. 4, Winter 1997, p. 40.

5. Turley and Kelley, "A Comparison of Advertising Content," p. 47.

6. Kevin Goldman, "Women Endorsers More Credible Than Men, a Survey Suggests," *The Wall Street Journal*, October 12, 1997, p. B1.

7. Gary C. Woodward and Robert E. Denton Jr., *Persuasion and Influence in American Life*, Prospect Heights, IL: Waveland Press, 1992, pp. 227-228.

8. Bill McDowell, "New DDB Needham Report: Consumers Want It All," *Advertising Age*, November 18, 1996, p. 32.

9. Melanie Wells, "Marketers Can't Get Old Tunes Out of Their Heads," *USA Today*, June 2, 1997, p. B1.

10. Rebecca Piirto, "Beyond Mind Games," *American Demographics*, December 1991, pp. 52-57.

11. Ernest Beck, "Soap Makers Aim Laundry Tablets at Europe's Young and Harried," *The Wall Street Journal*, May 27, 1998, p. B8.

12. Wayne Weiten, *Psychology Applied to Modern Life*, Second Edition, Belmont, CA: Brooks/Cole, 1986, p. 19.

13. Marco R. della Cava, "Luxury-Car Makers Happily Cater to Any Whim," *USA Today*, February 16, 1998, p. B3.

14. Peter Francese, "America at Mid-Decade," Market Report, *American Demographics*, 1995, p. 1.

15. Lisa-Fortini Campbell, *Hitting the Sweet Spot: How Consumer Insights Can Inspire Better Marketing and Advertising*, Chicago: The Copy Workshop, 1992, p. 176.

Chapter 7

1. Michael Diamond, "Networks Take Step to Replace Nielsens," *USA Today*, August 4, 1998, p. B2.
2. Joe Mandese, "Groups Propose Television Rating Changes," *Advertising Age*, September 9, 1991, p. 33; Chuck Ross, "Nielsen Explores Switch to Continuous Measurement," *Advertising Age*, April 8, 1996, p. 10.
3. Lisa Bernhard, "Ad Climate: Sunny," *TV Guide*, May 2, 1998, p. 34.
4. Ibid.
5. Jack Honomichl, "Research Revenues Rise 9 Percent for Industry's Top 50 Firms," *Marketing News*, June 8, 1998, pp. H1-H32.
6. Jack Honomichl, "Top 25 Global Firms Earn $5.6 Billion in Revenue," *Marketing News*, Vol. 30, No. 20, September 23, 1996, p. H2.
7. Jack Honomichl, "Research Revenues Rise 9 Percent for Industry's Top 50 Firms."
8. Ibid.
9. Fara Warner, "France's Sofres Overtakes Nielsen for China's Television Ratings Service," *The Wall Street Journal*, February 21, 1996, p. B6.
10. Jack Honomichl, "Research Revenues Rise 9 Percent for Industry's Top 50 Firms."
11. Terence A. Shimp, *Advertising, Promotion, and Supplemental Aspects of Integrated Marketing Communications*, Fourth Edition, Fort Worth, TX: The Dryden Press, 1997.
12. Jack Honomichl, "Research Revenues Rise 9 Percent for Industry's Top 50 Firms."
13. Joe Schwartz, "Back to the Source," *American Demographics*, January 1989, pp. 22-26.
14. Jack Honomichl, "Research Revenues Rise 9 Percent for Industry's Top 50 Firms."
15. Leslie Kaufman, "Enough Talk," *Newsweek*, August 18, 1997, p. 48.
16. Ibid., p. 49.
17. Dr. Joseph Plummer, "Foreword," in Lisa Fortini-Campbell *Hitting the Sweet Spot: How Consumer Insights Can Inspire Better Marketing and Advertising*, The Copy Workshop, 1992, p. 7.

Chapter 8

1. Jeff Jensen, "Marketer of the Year," *Advertising Age*, December 16, 1996, pp. 1, 16.
2. Bill Richards, "Nike Had $67.7 Million 4th-Period Loss, First in over 10 Years, Amid Asia Woes," *The Wall Street Journal*, July 1, 1998, p. B12.

3. Dottie Enrico and Melanie Wells, "Lee, Levi's Design New Ad Approach," *USA Today*, May 5, 1998, p. B2.
4. Ibid.
5. Wendy Bounds, "Levi's Simply Say Its Rivals Wore Them," *The Wall Street Journal*, May 5, 1998, p. B6.
6. Nikhil Deogun, "Pepsi Has Had Its Fill of Pizza, Tacos, Chicken," *The Wall Street Journal*, January 24, 1997, p. B1.
7. Kate Fitzgerald, "Bank's Magazines Target Customers," *Advertising Age*, November 18, 1996, p. 30.
8. Ibid.
9. Anne R. Carey and Marcy E. Mullins, "Where Big Spenders Advertise," *USA Today*, July 10, 1997, p. B1.
10. Melanie Wells, "Ad Nauseum: A Dizzying Barrage of Commercials," *USA Today*, June 15, 1998, p. B1.
11. Sally Beatty, "Iridium Hopes to Ring up Global Sales," *The Wall Street Journal*, June 22, 1998, p. B8.
12. Don E. Schultz and Beth E. Barnes, *Strategic Advertising Campaigns*, Fourth Edition, Lincolnwood, IL: NTC Business Books, 1995, pp. 54-57.
13. Chad Rubel, "Mustache Ads Change Attitude Toward Milk," *Marketing News*, August 26, 1996, p. 10.
14. Charles H. Patti and Vincent J. Blasko, "Budgeting Practices of Big Advertisers," *Journal of Advertising Research* Vol. 21, December 1981, pp. 23-29.
15. Denis Higgins, *The Art of Advertising: Conversations with Masters of the Craft*, Lincolnwood, IL: NTC Business Books, 1989, p. 92.
16. Melanie Wells, "R. J. Reynolds Tries Smoke-Screen Ad Approach," *USA Today*, June 8, 1998, p. B5.

Chapter 9

1. Dottie Enrico and Melanie Wells, "Pros: Ads-Travaganza Was Short on Creativity," *USA Today*, May 15, 1998, p. B3.
2. Bob Lamons, "Research Won't Yield the Big Idea," *Advertising Age*, November 18, 1996, p. 18.
3. Don E. Schultz and Beth E. Barnes, *Strategic Advertising Campaigns*, Fourth Edition, Lincolnwood, IL: NTC Business Books, 1995, pp. 172, 174.
4. Jolie Solomon and Arlyn Tobias Gajilan, "A Tale of a Tail," *Newsweek*, November 11, 1996, pp. 58-59.
5. James Webb Young, *A Technique for Producing Ideas*, Lincolnwood, IL: NTC Business Books, 1975, pp. 53-54, cited in Schultz and Barnes, *Strategic Advertising Campaigns*, pp. 177-178.
6. Arthur Miller, "Introduction to the *Collected Plays*," In Robert A. Martin (Ed.), *The Theatre Essays of Arthur Miller*, New York: Penguin, 1978, pp. 141-143.
7. Edward deBono, *Lateral Thinking for Management,* New York: American Management Association, 1971, cited in Schultz and Barnes, *Strategic Advertising Campaigns,* pp. 179-182.

8. Dottie Enrico, "Kellogg's Generic Ads: Thinking Outside the Box," *USA Today*, February 9, 1998, p. B1.

9. Dottie Enrico, "Automakers Switch Gears on Ads," *USA Today*, October 1, 1997, p. B3.

10. Anthony Vagnoni, "They Might Be Giants," *Advertising Age*, April 27, 1998, p. 24.

11. Bradley Johnson, "Levi's Boos 'Box' Thinking," *Advertising Age*, May 11, 1998, p. 8.

12. Dottie Enrico, "Automakers Switch Gears on Ads."

13. David A. Aaker and John G. Myers, *Advertising Management*, Third Edition, Englewood Cliffs, NJ: Prentice-Hall, 1987, p. 350.

14. Charles F. Frazer, "Creative Strategy: A Management Perspective," *Journal of Advertising*, Vol. 12, No. 4, 1983, pp. 36-41, cited in A. Jerome Jewler, *Creative Strategy in Advertising*, Fourth Edition, Belmont, CA: Wadsworth, 1992, p. 69.

15. Dottie Enrico, "Soft-Drink Maker Pours on Humor in Super Ads," *USA Today*, January 27, 1998, p. B1.

16. Melanie Wells and Dottie Enrico, "Humor Pays Off When Toying with Emotions," *USA Today*, December 9, 1996, pp. A1, A2, B3; Dottie Enrico, "Humorous Touch Resonates with Consumers," *USA Today*, May 13, 1996, p. B3; "Snickers Ad Wins Award," *USA Today*, June 4, 1998, p. B1.

17. David Ogilvy, *Ogilvy on Advertising*, New York: Random House, 1985, pp. 103-113.

18. Ogilvy, *Ogilvy on Advertising*, pp. 113-116; Bob Weinstein, "Radio Is a Riot," *Madison Avenue*, June 1985, pp. 70-74.

19. William F. Arens and Courtland L. Bovee, *Contemporary Advertising*, Fifth Edition, Burr Ridge, IL: Irwin, 1994.

Chapter 10

1. "Online Shopping Gets Even Easier," *Newsweek*, May 11, 1998, p. 90.

2. Sally Goll Beatty, "Latest Ads Star a Clean, Modern Face," *The Wall Street Journal*, October 3, 1996, pp. B1, B11.

3. Ibid.

4. Tom Lichty, *Design Principles for Desktop Publishers*, Second Edition, Belmont, CA: Wadsworth, 1994, p. 34.

5. "Landmarks," *Advertising Age*, October 21, 1996, p. 62.

6. Judann Pollack, "Pop Tarts Packs More Pastry for Same Price," *Advertising Age*, August 5, 1996, p. 6.

7. N.Y. Times News Service, in *Simon & Schuster College Newslink*, August 3, 1998, www.penahll.com.

8. Ibid.

Chapter 11

1. Sally Goll Beatty, "Motorola's Image Campaign Set to Fly," *The Wall Street Journal*, April 16, 1998, p. B14.

2. Michael Diamond, "Advertising Spending May Hit Record $200B This Year," *USA Today*, June 24, 1998, p. B6.

3. Kevin Goldman, "Study Finds Ads Induce Few People to Buy," *The Wall Street Journal*, October 17, 1996, p. B10.

4. Ed Papazian, "CPM: Friend or Foe?" *Marketing & Media Decisions*, June 1990, pp. 53-54; Karen Ritchie, "Media Accountability: An Innovative Idea," *Marketing & Media Decisions*, March 1990, pp. 81-82.

5. Goldman, "Study Finds Ads Induce Few People to Buy," p. B10.

6. Pat Slogan, "Colgate Readies $32 Million Launch," *Advertising Age*, October 28, 1996, p. 3.

7. Elys A. McLean, "Comparing 30-Second Ad Costs," *USA Today*, January 22, 1998, p. B1.

8. Melanie Wells, "Media Firms Lure Young Ad Buyers' Business with Pleasure," *USA Today*, August 10, 1998, p. B6.

9. Skip Wollenberg, "Seinfeld Ads Aren't About Nothing," *South Bend Tribune*, (AP Business Writer, New York), May 6, 1998, p. D3; Sally Goll Beatty, "NBC Looks to Cash in on 'Seinfeld' Finale," *The Wall Street Journal*, March 4, 1998, p. B11; Dottie Enrico, "Advertisers Pick Spots for 'Seinfeld' Finale," *USA Today*, May 11, 1998, p. B4.

10. Melanie Wells, "Networks Face Hard Sell for Next Season's Ads," *USA Today*, April 10, 1998, p. B1.

11. John D. Leckenby and Jongpil Hong, "Reach/Frequency and the Web," *Journal of Advertising Research*, January/February 1998, p. 9.

12. Ibid., p. 11.

13. Ibid., p. 10.

14. Ibid., p. 12.

15. Leslie Wood, "Internet Ad Buys—What Reach and Frequency Do They Deliver?" *Journal of Advertising Research*, January/February 1998, pp. 21-28.

Chapter 12

1. Judann Pollack, "Magazines Reap Thanksgiving Harvest of Ads," *Advertising Age*, November 4, 1996, p. 28.

2. Ann Marie Kerwin, "Magazines Report Gains Despite Some Soft Spots," *Advertising Age,* April 19, 1999, p. 46.

3. Alicia Lasek, "No Backing Out Now for Custom Publishing," *Advertising Age*, November 6, 1995, p. s14.

4. These and the 1997 paid circulation figures that follow are from R. Craig Endicott, "Ad Age 300/The Annual Countdown," *Advertising Age*, June 15, 1998, pp. s1, s22.

5. Andrew Zipern, "After Year of Floundering, a Magazine Monolith Finds Its Market," *Silicon Alley Reporter,* Iss. 19, Vol. 2, No. 11, November 1998, p. 57.

6. Keith J. Kelly, "Magazine Circulation Takes a Dive," *Advertising Age*, February 19, 1996, pp. 29, 34.

7. Press Release, "New Study Finds Online Magazines Delivering More Promotion Than Profit," New York: Ernst & Young, March 21, 1997.

8. "Comments from Selected Speakers," *Special Report: Magazines and New Media,* Magazine Publishers of America Web site, June 6, 1998, <http://www.magazine.org>.

9. David Lieberman, "Newspapers Tout Clout with Consumers," *USA Today,* April 15, 1998, p. B1.

10. Ibid.

11. Keith J. Kelly, "Kids Magazines Learn to Multiply," *Advertising Age,* December 2, 1996, p. 6.

12. Patrick Reilly, "Advertisers Bristle over Big Rate Increase," *The Wall Street Journal,* November 6, 1995, p. B9.

13. Jane Hodges, "Newspapers Plug Along in Quest for Web Answer," *Advertising Age,* April 29, 1996, p. s6.

Chapter 13

1. Skip Wollenburg, "At Least the Ads Will Be Super," *The South Bend Tribune,* January 26, 1996, pp. 1-2; Dottie Enrico, "Firms Pivot to Super Bowl," *USA Today,* August 12, 1996, p. B4.

2. Dottie Enrico, "Costly TV Ads Seen As Big Image Builders," *USA Today,* June 8, 1998, p. B4.

3. Ibid.

4. Anne R. Carey and Gary Visgaitis, "Free-Time Choices," *USA Today,* September 22, 1997, p. A1.

5. Mike Snider, "Wired Homes Watch 15 Percent Less Television," *USA Today,* August 13, 1998, p. A1.

6. Anne R. Carey and Quin Tian, "Cable Cities," *USA Today,* May 6, 1998, p. B1.

7. Melanie Wells, "Expert's Prediction: Ad Spending Could Hit $186B This Year," *USA Today,* June 18, 1997, p. B2.

8. Charles Waltner, "Cable Nets Covet $500 Mil Shift of the Upfront Pie," *Advertising Age,* May 11, 1998, p. s10.

9. Melanie Wells, "Jean Pool: Wants Less Commercial Clutter on TV," *USA Today,* May 26, 1998, p. B3.

10. "Numbers," *Time,* May 11, 1998, p. 23.

11. Chuck Ross, "Paramount Picks TeleVest to Buy $60 Mil in Spot TV," *Advertising Age,* August 3, 1998, p. 2.

12. Bruce Horovitz, "Olympic Sponsors Run Spending Obstacle Course," *USA Today,* August 10, 1998, p. B1.

13. Wells, "Jean Pool," p. B3.

14. Anthony DeBarros, "Amid Consolidation, Fear of Less Diversity, Choice," *USA Today,* July 7, 1998, p. A2.

15. Ibid., p. A1.

16. Ibid., p. A2.

17. Kathy Clay-Little, "An Unclear Future: Will KSJL-FM Keep Its Community Focus?" *San Antonio Current,* June 11-17, 1998, p. 14.

18. Michael Wilke, "National Spot Radio Prices Hit Double-Digit Increases," *Advertising Age*, April 27, 1998, p. 64.

Chapter 14

1. "Suited to a T," *USA Today*, July 6, 1998, p. D1.
2. "Ad Follies," *Advertising Age*, December 18, 1995, p. 20.
3. "Landmarks: Consumer Pole," *Advertising Age*, April 27, 1998, p. 68; "Give Us a Break," *Newsweek*, March 9, 1998, p. 6.
4. Michael Wilke, "Outdoor Woes: Gannett Could Suffer Layoffs," *Advertising Age*, August 19, 1996, p. 3; Bruce Horovitz, "Greyhound Turns Buses into Rolling Billboards," *USA Today*, July 2, 1997, p. B2.
5. Michael Wilke, "Outdoor Ads Entering Whole New Dimensions," *Advertising Age*, July 29, 1996, p. 20.
6. Information provided by the Institute of Outdoor Advertising, New York, NY, 1991.
7. Michael Wilke, "Outdoor Biz Urged to Join Ad-Limit Fight," *Advertising Age*, November 6, 1996, p. 8; Carol Krol, "Life After Tobacco," *Advertising Age*, April 19, 1999, pp. 1, 48.
8. Lisa Brownlee, "Outdoor-Billboard Companies Are Finding Receptive Markets," *The Wall Street Journal*, September 12, 1996, p. B1.
9. *Preference Building: The Dynamic World of Specialty Advertising*, Irving, TX: Specialty Advertising Association, 1988.
10. Joel J. David, *Understanding Yellow Pages*, Troy, MI: Yellow Pages Publishers Association, 1995.
11. Deborah Branscum, "Online Yellow Pages," *Newsweek*, July 6, 1998, p. 74.
12. "Breaking: Chrysler," *Advertising Age*, July 13, 1998, p. 40.
13. Good Housekeeping Institute Report, "As Seen on Infomercials," *Good Housekeeping*, June 1998, pp. 120-122, 160.
14. A. Jerome Jewler and Bonnie L. Drewniany, *Creative Strategy in Advertising*, Belmont, CA: Wadsworth, 1998, p. 212.
15. Deeann Glamser, "This Class Brought to You by . . . ," *USA Today*, January 3, 1997, p. A1.
16. Carol Marie Cropper, "Fruit to Walls to Floor, Ads Are on the March," *The New York Times*, February 26, 1998, pp. A1, A8.
17. Ibid.
18. James B. Arndorfer, "Miller Lite Promo by 'Dick': Scratch 'n' Sniff Labels," *Advertising Age*, April 27, 1998, p. 8.
19. Joshua Hammer and Corie Brown, "Licensed to Shill," *Newsweek*, December 15, 1997, p. 43.
20. Richard Lorant, "License to Shill?" *The South Bend Tribune*, December 5, 1997, p. B1.
21. "Fruit Became the Ad Medium," *The World Journal*, October 11, 1997, p. B8.
22. "Inquiry: McNonsense," *Time*, May 11, 1998, p. 18.
23. Lorrie Grant, "Vending Machines Offer Movie T-shirts," *USA Today*, April 3, 1998, p. B6.

24. Press Kit, "It's Time to Get Connected," Fort Lee, NJ: MSNBC, 1997.
25. David Lieberman, "In a Snap, NBC Takes on Net Powers," *USA Today*, June 10, 1998, p. B5.

Chapter 15

1. "Japan Mail Order Still Growing," *Dateline: DMA*, Vol. 10, No. 2, p. 7.
2. Rebecca A. Fannin, "Neiman Marcus Is Looking Far East," *Advertising Age*, September 16, 1996, p. 16.
3. Fred Fassman, "Increasing Profits—and Service—in Multi-Channel Direct Marketing," *The DMA Insider*, Fall 1997, p. 16.
4. *Fact Book on Direct Response Marketing*. New York: Direct Marketing Association, 1982.
5. "New Facts and Forecasts Predict Steady Growth for Direct Marketing," *Direct Connection*, Winter 1996-1997, pp. 1, 8.
6. Elizabeth Lee, "Cyber Shopping Could Be a Hit As Stores Open," *The South Bend Tribune*, December 13, 1997, p. C2.
7. Susan Jones, *Creative Strategy in Direct Marketing*. Lincolnwood, IL: NTC Business Books, pp. 9-12, 408.
8. Rob Jackson, "Breaking the Code: Maximizing Customer Value," *Direct*, August 1997, p. 57.
9. Jones, *Creative Strategy in Direct Marketing*, p. 130.
10. Bruce Horovitz, "Retailers Send Catalog Blizzard," *USA Today*, September 19, 1996, p. B1.
11. Rebecca A. Fannin, "Neiman Marcus Is Looking Far East."
12. James Cox, "Catalogers Expand in Asia," *USA Today*, October 18, 1996, p. B4.
13. Direct Marketing Association, *The DMA Environmental Action Kit*, New York: Direct Marketing Association, Winter 1992.
14. Laura Loro, "Direct Mail Thriving Through Better Executions, Lists," *Advertising Age*, March 18, 1996, p. 32.
15. Michael Faulkner, "Address to the DMA's Eighth Annual Nonprofit Washington Conference," *Direct Line Journal*, March 1, 1998, Vol. 15, pp. 1, 3.
16. Philip Kotler and Alan R. Andreasen, *Strategic Marketing for Nonprofit Organizations*, Englewood Cliffs, NJ: Prentice-Hall, pp. 279-280.
17. Jones, *Creative Strategy in Direct Marketing*, p. 214.
18. Ibid., p. 232.
19. Tom Pope, "Direct Merchandising Spurs New Revenues for Nonprofits," *Direct Marketing*, October 1996, pp. 1, 4.
20. Bruce Horovitz, "AmEx Kills Database Deal After Privacy Outrage," *USA Today*, July 15, 1998, p. B1.
21. Maria Rosa Balzaretti, Kimberly Evard, Adam Von Ins, Hugh Williams, and Kevin Young, "African Americans: Lifestyles, Purchase Behaviors and Perceptions of Marketing Communication Tactics," Northwestern University Integrated Marketing Communication Program, February 27, 1995, unpublished.

22. Direct Marketing Association, *Direct Marketing Association's Grassroots Advocacy Guide*, New York: Direct Marketing Association, 1991, p. 71.

23. Char Kosek, "Business-to-Business Grabs $51.7 Billion," *Advertising Age*, June 10, 1996, p. s3.

24. Bob Lamons, "Learning from the Business Mailing Experts," *Marketing News*, March 2, 1998, p. 6.

25. "Direct Marketing Without Borders," Presented at the Direct Marketing Education Foundation's Institute, Chicago, June 1, 1995.

26. Laura Loro, "Mail Favorite Tool in Direct Marketing Circles," *Advertising Age*, June 10, 1996, p. s16.

27. Balzaretti, Evard, Von Ins, Williams, and Young, "African Americans."

28. Laurel Wentz, "Happy New Year? Asia Drops Long Shadow over Forecast," *Advertising Age International*, January 1998, p. 5.

29. David Reed, "DMers Well Placed to Utilize the Euro," *Direct*, February 1998, p. 23.

30. David Reed, "Double Standard," *Direct*, May 1, 1997, pp. 37-38.

31. Henry Heilbrunn, "Interactive Marketing in Europe," *Direct Marketing*, March 1998, p. 56.

32. Ibid., pp. 58-59.

33. Rebecca A. Fannin, "Internet Finds Its Audience Among Elite Latin Americans," *Advertising Age International*, December 1997, p. 9.

34. Carol Krol, "FCB Direct Makes Global Shift," *Advertising Age*, February 16, 1998, p. 12.

35. Suzanne Vranica, "Leo Driving Down Under," *The Wall Street Journal*, May 22, 1998, p. B8.

36. Leo Burnett Media, "The Future of Direct Marketing in the Interactive Age," Presented at the Direct Marketing Education Foundation's Institute, Chicago, June 1, 1995.

Chapter 16

1. Richard Gibson, "At McDonald's, a Case of Mass Beaniemania," *The Wall Street Journal*, June 5, 1998, p. B1.

2. Carolyn Shea, "Breaking out of the Pack," *PROMO: The Magazine of Promotion Marketing*, Vol. IX, No. 4, March 1996, pp. 43-44.

3. John J. Burnett, *Promotion Management*, Boston: Houghton Mifflin, 1993, p. 7.

4. Howard Schultz and Dori Jones Yang, *Pour Your Heart into It*, New York: Hyperion Press, 1997, pp. 255-256.

5. Don E. Schultz and Beth E. Barnes, *Strategic Advertising Campaigns*, Lincolnwood, IL: NTC Business Books, 1994, p. 229.

6. Jane Hodges, "Kiosks' Local Motion," *Advertising Age*, December 16, 1996, p. 18.

7. *Special Release*, "Consumers' Use of Coupons Rose in 1991," Manufacturers Coupon Control Center, 1991.

8. "Measuring Your Coupon Vehicle's Performance," *PROMO: The Magazine of Promotion Marketing*, Vol. XI, No. 8, July 1998, p. s38.

9. "Adults Love Coupons," *Marketing News*, August 26, 1996, Vol. 30, No. 18, p. 1.

10. Martin Sloane, "Coupon Fraud Is a Serious Problem," *The South Bend Tribune*, June 16, 1997, p. D3.

11. Bill Stack, "Cheery Coupon Deal Turns Hairy for Fantastic Sam's," *Marketing News*, October 6, 1993, pp. 1, 9.

12. William M. Bulkeley, "Rebates' Secret Appeal to Manufacturers: Few Consumers Actually Redeem Them," *The Wall Street Journal*, February 10, 1998, pp. B1, B5.

13. Judann Pollack, "PM Readies $40 Mil-Plus Marlboro 'Ranch' Promo," *Advertising Age*, May 11, 1998, p. 8.

14. Greg Jaffe, "Sweepstakes Industry May Not Be a WINNER!" *The Wall Street Journal*, February 18, 1998, pp. B1, B16.

15. Tom Lowry, "New Yorkers, You May Have Won a $60 Legal Settlement," *USA Today*, August 24, 1998, p. A1; Carol Krol, "Image Makeover," *Advertising Age*, July 13, 1998, p. 22; Ann Marie Kerwin, "Sweepstakes Giant Faces Huge Losses," *Advertising Age,* April 26, 1999, p. 1.

16. Tom Lowry, "Second Sweepstakes Firm Under Investigation," *USA Today*, February 5, 1998, p. B1.

17. Axel Threlfall, "As Promotional Contests Rise, Insurers Back up the Marketers," *The Wall Street Journal*, April 27, 1998, p. B2.

18. Michelle Higgins, "Foul! Sports-Feat Contestants Trip over Rules," *The Wall Street Journal*, July 8, 1998, p. B1.

19. Tara Parker-Pope, "P&G Puts Lots of Chips on Plan to Give Away Fat-Free Pringles," *The Wall Street Journal,* June 23, 1998, p. B6.

20. Carol Krol, "Hallmark Uses Loyalty Effort for Segmenting Customers," *Advertising Age,* February 1, 1999, p. 36.

21. Joanne Lee-Young, "In Hong Kong, Tobacco Promotes Away," *The Wall Street Journal*, June 30, 1998, p. B8.

Chapter 17

1. Donald Spoto, *The Decline and Fall of the House of Windsor*, New York: Simon & Schuster, 1995, p. 298.

2. "Product Survival: Lessons of the Tylenol Terrorism," Washington, DC: Washington Business Information, 1982, pp. 11-17.

3. José Rivera, "The Case of TWA Flight #800: Uncovering New Challenges and Opportunities for Public Relations Practitioners on the Internet," *Journal of Integrated Communications*, Vol. VIII, 1997-1998, p. 56.

4. Lisa Brownlee, "TWA Cautiously Rolls out Campaign," *The Wall Street Journal*, September 6, 1996, p. B2.

5. Dennis L. Wilcox, Phillip H. Ault, and Warren K. Agee, *Public Relations Strategies and Tactics*, Fifth Edition, New York: Longman, 1998, p. 12.

6. Jennifer Nedeff, "The Bottom Line Beckons: Quantifying Measurement in Public Relations," *Journal of Corporate Public Relations*, Vol. VII, 1996-1997, p. 36.

7. DeWayne Wickham, "More Professionalism Would Improve News," *USA Today*, July 7, 1998, p. A13.

8. Evan Thomas and Gregory Vistica, "A 'Bombshell' That Went off Wrong," *Newsweek*, July 13, 1998, p. 65.

9. Evan Thomas and Gregory L. Vistica, "Fallout from a Media Fiasco," *Newsweek*, July 20, 1998, p. 25.

10. David N. McArthur and Tom Griffin, "A Marketing Management View of Integrated Marketing Communications," *Journal of Advertising Research*, October 1997, p. 22.

11. Skip Wollenberg, "New General Ready for Battle in Cola Wars," *The South Bend Tribune*, May 13, 1998, p. C8.

12. Jean Halliday, "Audi's A4 Sedan Helps Propel Revival a Decade After Bad PR," *Advertising Age*, July 29, 1996, p. 3.

13. Wilcox, Ault, and Agee, *Public Relations Strategies and Tactics*, p. 490.

14. Raju Narisetti, "Savin Hopes Campaign Will Boost Image," *The Wall Street Journal*, May 19, 1998, p. B8.

15. Bradley Johnson and Alice Z. Cuneo, "Acer Gets Branding Campaign," *Advertising Age*, July 29, 1996, p. 1.

16. Stefan Fatsis, "Coke Wins Matchup With NFL in a Changed Sponsorship Game," *The Wall Street Journal*, May 22, 1998, p. B10.

17. Melanie Wells, "Companies' Unsung Sponsorships Hit Targets," *USA Today*, August 8, 1997, p. B3.

18. Ibid.

19. Wilcox, Ault, and Agee, *Public Relations Strategies and Tactics*, p. 492.

Chapter 18

1. Bruce Horovitz, "AOL's Chat Rooms Opened to Advertisers," *USA Today*, 1996, p. B1.

2. David Kirkpatrick, "Riding the Real Trends in Technology," *Fortune*, February 19, 1996, p. 58.

3. "Link Up," *Link*, Vol. 2, No. 4, April 1997, p. 4.

4. "Networthy: Keds," *Advertising Age*, April 27, 1998, p. 54.

5. Jeffrey H. Kessler, *Internet Task Force Report,* Riverwoods, IL: CCH, 1994. Reprinted with permission.

6. Steven Levy, "Bill and Al Get It Right," *Newsweek*, July 7, 1997, p. 80.

7. Jeffrey D. Neuburger and Jill Westmoreland, "Legal Link," *Silicon Alley Reporter*, September 1998, p. 76.

8. Paul Davidson, "AOL Stock Surges on Internet Ad Deal," *USA Today*, July 2, 1998, p. B1.

9. Elizabeth Weise, "Net Can't Fill All Your Stockings Yet," *USA Today*, December 10, 1997, p. D1.

10. Bruce Horovitz, "Summit Will Be 'Defining Moment' of Net Advertising," *USA Today*, August 17, 1998, pp. B1-2.

11. Bill Barnhart, "Nothing but Net: A Commentary on the Impact of the Internet on Investor Relations," *Journal of Corporate Public Relations*, Vol. VII, 1996-1997, pp. 16-17.

12. Deborah Branscum, "Online Yellow Pages," *Newsweek*, July 6, 1998, p. 74.

13. Deborah Branscum, "Click Your Way to Discounts," *Newsweek*, August 31, 1998, p. 60.

14. "The Accidental Superhighway," *The Economist*, July 1, 1995, pp. 3-4.

15. Kirkpatrick, "Riding the Real Trends in Technology," pp. 54-62.

16. Michael Tchong, "Iconoclast," August 12, 1998, http://www.247media.com/sites.html.

17. "Sizing the Electronic Marketplace. The Electronic Marketplace 1995: Strategies for Connecting Buyers and Sellers." Wilton, CT: Simba Information, Inc., 1995, p. 37.

18. Thomas E. Weber, "Who, What, Where: Putting the Internet in Perspective," *The Wall Street Journal*, April 16, 1998, p. B12.

19. Tom Hyland, "A Year of Growth," *IAB Online Advertising Guide*, Spring 1998, p. A20.

20. Ibid., p. A66.

21. Stephanie Armour, "E-mail 'a Blessing' for Business," *USA Today*, July 2, 1998, A1.

22. "Global PR Effort Can Help Start-Ups Survive,' *O'Dwyer's PR Services Report*, November 1995, p. 45.

23. "About the Nature and Future of Interactive Marketing," *Journal of Interactive Marketing*, Vol. 12, No. 1, Winter 1998, p. 68.

24. "E-mail Company Asked Not to Use the Word 'Spam,'" *The South Bend Tribune*, July 6, 1997, p. B3.

25. Natalie Hopkinson, "'Spam' Mail No Treat for Internet Users," *The South Bend Tribune*, January 7, 1997, p. C7.

26. Don Porter, "Reaction Mixed to Proposals on E-mail Ads," *The South Bend Tribune*, May 29, 1997, p. A12; Deborah Branscum, "The Big Spam Debate," *Newsweek*, June 22, 1998, p. 84.

27. "Value-Added Services," *Austin/San Antonio Computer Currents*, June 1998, p. 20.

28. "The Accidental Superhighway," pp. 3-18.

29. Davie E. Easterly, "Ad Venture on the Net," *Marketing News*, August 12, 1996, Vol. 30, No. 17, p. 1.

30. "The Net: A Market Too Perfect for Profits," *Business Week*, May 11, 1998, p. 20.

31. Harvey Leong, "Expanding Beyond the Core Product," YPPA Educators' Seminar, Denver, August 1996.

32. "Bell Atlantic Launches Internet Yellow Pages," *Link*, Vol. 2, No. 4, April 1997, p. 4.

33. Cited by Harvey Leong in his speech "Expanding Beyond the Core Product," August 6, 1996, at the YPPA Educators' Seminar, Denver, Colorado.

34. Carla Johnson and Tony Hughes, "The Customer-Focus Challenges of Integrated Marketing Communication at CCH," in Kenneth L. Bernhardt and Thomas C. Kinner (Eds.), *Cases in Marketing Management*, Chicago: McGraw-Hill, 1997, pp. 395-396.

35. Ibid., pp. 406-407.

Index

Page numbers followed by the letter "i" indicate illustrations.

ABC
    Audit Bureau of Circulation, 199-200
    TV network, 9, 71, 121
Absolut vodka, 121
Accountability, 17, 28, 288-290
Accounting industry, 96-97
Account planners, 93
Acer, 293, 306
AdMedia, 62
Adopt-a-Car program, 221
Advertisers
    competing, 62
    on the Internet, 310
    local, 164
    and pre-production approval, 161
    selecting agencies, 63
Advertising
    basic tasks, 52-54
    billings, 52
    business-to-business, 5, 88, 236
    classifications, 4-8
    common criticisms, 25-27, 32
    creative strategy, 123-124
    definition, 3
    and economic forces, 23-24
    evaluation, 125
    evolution, 13-16
    functions, 8-9
    future trends, 60-63
    and the Internet, 3, 27-29
    and marketing strategy, 121
    objectives, 33-34, 123, 138
    by professionals, 5

Advertising (*continued*)
    and public relations crises, 280
    reactions to environment, 23
    for services, 88
    and special effects, 29-30
    spending data, 3-4, 9, 23-24
        by medium, 124, 175
        on World Wide Web, 28
    subliminal, 89
    versus public relations, 294
Advertising agencies
    cable television billings, 210
    and consumer information, 92-93
    definition, 55
    direct marketing, 57
    ethnic, 21, 57-58, 61
    full-service versus in-house, 60-61
    income sources, 58-60
    international, 127-128
    and Internet ads, 165
    network television billings, 209
    and prospective clients, 63
    specialized versus full-service, 56-58
    top ten United States, 55
    top ten worldwide, 52
Advertising allowances, 263
Advertising plan, 122-125
Advertising research, 104-108
Advertising Research Services (ARS), 107-108
Advertorials, 202
Advocacy advertising, 8, 292-293, 294

337

African Americans, 72i
  agency ownership, 57-58
  and direct marketing, 250-251
  and name removal, 248
  radio station ownership, 215
Age factor, 74, 77, 180. *See also*
    Generational target marketing
Agee, Warren, 293
Agriculture Department, 40
Airline industry
  advertising regulation, 40
  continuity programs, 270
  crisis management, 280-281
Alcohol, Tobacco, and Firearms
    Bureau, 39-40
Alcoholic beverage industry
  and Alcohol, Tobacco, and
      Firearms Bureau, 39-40
  ethical considerations, 50
  and hard liquor television ads,
      19, 25-26, 35, 41
    in Asia, 42, 46
  and sponsorship, 294
  and StarTV, 30
Alden, Dana, 169-170
Allowances, 262-263
Allstate Insurance Co., 294
AltaVista, 314
Amazon.com, 311
American Express, 79, 158, 248
American Family Enterprises,
    267-268
America Online, 248, 301, 304, 315
Anheuser-Busch, 19, 64, 77, 293
Animal rights, 80-81
Animals, 131, 143
Announcer, 162-163
Annual reports, 287
Anticommercial, 15, 77
Anti-Defamation League, 159, 160i
Apple Computer, 5, 25, 306
Arbitron, 105
Arm & Hammer, 157
Arndorfer, James, 63

Asia. *See also specific countries*
  and coatings industry, 67-69
  and direct marketing, 251
  mail-order, 233, 243
  and market segmentation, 71
  pan-Asian TV, 30
  political and legal environment,
      37, 42-46
  snack foods, 69
Asian Americans, 58, 215
Athletes, 89
"Attitude," 40
Attitudes, 90
Audi of America, 292
Ault, Phillip, 293
Australia, 47
Auto-by-Tel, 205
Automobile industry, 92, 109
Avid system, 172
Avis Rent-A-Car, 79, 137, 228
Avon, 201

Baby-boomers, 33
Back-end marketing, 245
Backgrounders, 282, 286i
Bait and switch, 39
Banana Republic, 242
Banner ads, 151, 165, 307, 308i
Barnes, Beth, 121-122, 131
Barnes and Noble, 311
Bars and tone, 172
Baskin-Robbins, 268
Ted Bates Agency, 137
BBDO Agency
  computer-generated ad, 29
  and controversial ad, 94
  and Ernst and Young, 63
  income ranking, 55
  Pepsi ad, 79
Beanie Babies, 257, 292
Behavioral segmentation, 73, 122
Belch, George, 212
Belch, Michael, 212
Benetton, 170

Ben & Jerry's, 261, 269-270
Beta tape, 172
Big Idea, 131-133, 170
Bill-back allowances, 262
Billboards, 223-225, 228
Blitz advertising, 121
BMW, 71, 229
The Body Shop, 94
Boston Market, 73
Bovee, Courtland, 212
Bozell and Jacobs, 8
Bozell International, 51
Brand agencies, 55
Brand loyalty, 33, 238
Brand rankings, 55
Branding
 of fiberoptic company, 116i, 129-130, 132i
 generic, 137
 global, 18
 image establishment, 137
 and the Internet, 307
 in marketing mix, 12
 regulation of names, 37
Braniff Airlines, 131
Brann Worldwide, 55
Braun, Neil, 183
Bravo, 35
Brazil, 48
British Commonwealth, 47. *See also* United Kingdom
Broadcast media. *See* Radio advertising; Television advertising
Bruce, Gary, 7i
Budget, 54, 125-126, 161, 177
Burger King, 83
Burke's day-after recall (DAR), 106-107
Burnett, John, 201
Burnett, Leo. *See* Leo Burnett
Burrell, Cassandra, 314-315
Burrell Advertising, 57-58
Burson, Harold, 298-299
Burson-Marsteller, 295, 296

Business magazines, 190
Business review, 122
Business-to-business advertising, 5, 88, 236
Business-to-business marketing, 244-245, 248-249. *See also* Industrial market
Buy-back allowances, 262
Buy one, get one free, 39

Cable networks, 35
Calacanis, Jason, 314-315
Calvin Klein, 40
Camera shots, 157-159
Campbell Soup Company, 28-29, 41
Canada, 47, 94
Canon USA, 60
Careers, 65-66, 171-172, 180, 203-204
Carey, Anne, 77, 78, 110-111, 124
Carlisle Cereal, 228
Carlson, Brandee, 112-114
Carson, David, 154
Case, Steve, 309
Catalogs, 233, 241-246, 301. *See also* Electronic commerce
CBS Radio, 217
CD-ROM, 312
Celebrities
 and ad results, 173
 camera shots, 158
 in combination appeal ad, 143
 ethics of endorsements, 218-219
 and infomercials, 227
 local, 228
 in milk ads, 112
 and non-profit organizations, 246-247
 and product perception, 78-79
CFC International, 67-69
Chancellor Media Corp., 217
Chanel, 12
Character generators, 163
Chase and Sanborn Coffee, 14

Chemical industry, 67-69
Chiat, Jay, 93
Chief Auto Parts, 78
Children
    and drinking ads, 19
    hospital ad, 100i
    and the Internet, 314-315
    and jeans, 117
    and market segmentation, 71
China, 42-43, 69, 105, 271
Chiquita Brands International, 291
Chisholm-Mingo Group, 61
Chrysler Corp., 227
Circulation
    of magazines, 192
    of newspapers, 199
Citrus Express, 227
Classified advertising, 198
Clear Channel Communications, 215
Clients. *See* Advertisers
Clifton Gunderson L.L.C., 2i, 120i, 285i, 289i
Clinton, William, 277-279
Close-up (CU), 158
Clothing industry. *See also* Shoe industry
    and brand perception, 78-79
    jeans, 83, 115-117, 134-135, 186i
    T-shirts, 221, 229-230
Clow, Lee, 136
CNN, 291
Coca-Cola
    in Central Asia, 71
    and foreign economic crises, 24
    and Generation X, 77
    as IMC example, 1, 16
    product positioning, 79
    and sponsorship, 293
    and subliminal messages, 89
    versus Tropicana, 38
Cohoe, Tina, 252
Colgate-Palmolive Co., 10, 75, 76i, 179
Combination appeals, 143-145
Commerce Clearing House, 312-313

Community service, 206i
Compaq, 306
Comparative advertising, 49, 79
Competitive parity method, 126
Complaints, 41, 44, 46
Computer industry, 74, 306
Computer magazines, 191
Computers. *See also* Software
    Internet ad production, 165-169
    in print production, 155-156, 157
    in television production, 163
ConAgra, 185
Concept, 123-124, 157
Consulting industry, 96
Consumer cynicism, 15, 19, 77
Consumer information, 1, 17
Consumer magazines, 188-190
Consumer response, 6-7
Consumer-centric approach, 181
Consumers
    ad reactions, 106-108, 178-179
    buying decisions, 85-87, 88-92
    environmental concerns, 183-184, 231-232
    and fear appeals, 138-143
    and individualized products, 92-93
    information about, 17, 92-93, 121-122, 238
    and involvement matrix, 143-145
    lifestyle, 73, 90-91
    need satisfaction, 85-86, 92-93
    postpurchase behavior, 87-88
    and product differentiation, 78-79
    reaction to ads, 106-108
    technology-savvy, 307
    and telemarketing, 246
Consumer watchdog groups, 110-111
Contests, 263-264, 268-269, 283i
Continuity programs, 177, 257-259, 258i, 270
Cooperative advertising, 166, 213, 263
Coordination, 54
Coors Brewing Co., 297

Copy
  in catalogs, 244
  and language, 25
  print, 146
  public relations, 281-288
  radio, 147-148
  television, 146
Copy platform, 138, 150
Copyright violations, 37
Corporate advertising, 5, 116i, 121, 129-130, 292-293
Cost-per-thousand (CPM), 177-178, 212
Count-and-recount promotion, 264
Coupons, 13, 173, 261, 265-266
Covert advertising, 202, 219. *See also* Infomercials
Cox Interactive Media, 310
CPM, 177-178, 212
Creative boutiques, 56
Creative brief, 138, 150
Creative tasks, 54
Creative thrust, 121
Creativity
  appeal types, 138-145
  Big Idea, 131-133
  in direct marketing, 249
  execution style, 145-146
  idea-producing techniques, 133-136
  strategy development, 136-138
Credibility, 239, 281-282, 291
Crisis management, 280-281, 292
Cross promotions, 229-230
Cub Foods, 228
Culture
  and Big Idea, 170
  and buying decisions, 91
  and event sponsorship, 271
  and humor, 80
  and infant formula ads, 48
  information sources, 110
  and international direct marketing, 251-252
  and offensive ads, 31, 217-218

Culture (*continued*)
  and product lines, 67-69
  and sex, 94
  and targeted advertising, 135-136
Culture Jam, 170
Currency, 251
Custom Foot, 83
Customer focus, 20
Customer service, 312-313
Customization, 83, 92
Cut, 162
CVS drugstores, 248

Database marketing, 238, 248
Davidson, Kirk, 219
DDB Needham Worldwide
  and IMC, 56
  lifestyle study, 73, 90
  media cross-training, 231
  and storyboard shopping, 64
deBono, Edward, 134, 135
Deceptive advertising, 38-39, 46
Decision Analyst, Incorporated, 265
Decision-making process
  of individual consumers, 85-87, 88-92
  of industrial purchasers, 87-88
Dell Computer Corp., 231
Delta Airlines, 61
Demand, 85-86. *See also* Derived demand
Demographics
  age factor, 74, 77, 180
  and buying behavior, 88-89
  ethic groups, 21, 23, 33, 57-58
  and magazine ads, 187, 188, 190, 191
  and market segmentation, 71
  and media selection, 180
  of new media users, 307
  of online subscribers, 306-307
  and target marketing, 33, 74-75
Demonstrations, 146, 313
Denton, Robert, 15

Dentsu, 52, 55
Derived demand, 87-88
Desktop publishing, 155-156
Dietz, Cynthia, 274-275
Differentiation, 78-79
Digital video effects (DVE), 29, 163
Digitizing, 172
Direct mail, 239-241, 246-247
Direct marketing. *See also* Catalogs; Direct response advertising; Telemarketing
　background, 237-238
　and creativity, 249
　environmental concerns, 244
　and ethnic communities, 250-251
　international, 251-253
　and non-profit organizations, 246-248
　technology advances, 235-236
Direct marketing agencies, 57
Direct Marketing Association, 235-236, 244, 248
Direct response advertising, 6-8, 235-236, 253
Directory advertising, 6
Disconnecteds, 178-179
Display advertising, 198
Display allowances, 263
Dissolve, 162
Distribution channels, 1, 12, 16, 119-121
DMB&B, 109
Dolls, 292
Domino's pizza, 91
Dooner, John, 51
Douglas, S., 218
Dow Corning Corp., 279
DraftDirect Worldwide, 250
Drunk driving, 294

Earth Day, 288
Eastern Europe, 69
Eastman Kodak, 58, 61
Economic forces, 23-24

Eddie Bauer, 151
Edelman Public Relations Worldwide, 82
Editing, 162-163, 171-172
Editing terms, 162
Effie Awards, 144-145
800 phone numbers, 227, 240
Electronic commerce, 28, 233-235, 237-238, 310-313
Electronic tracking, 1, 313
Elizabeth, Queen of England, 277
E-mail, 307-309
Emotional appeal, 139, 140i, 143-145
Emotional response, 107
Endicott, R. Craig, 52, 55
Energizer bunny, 15, 30
Enrico, Dottie, 94, 169-170
Environmental concerns
　and direct marketing, 244
　green marketing, 183-184
　product containers, 231-232, 261
　and public relations, 261, 288
Ernst & Young, 63
Ethics
　of ad parodies, 170
　and alcoholic beverages, 19
　of celebrity endorsements, 218-219
　consumer watchdog groups, 110-111
　content versus advertising separation, 315
　covert advertising, 201-202, 219
　and environmental concerns, 231-232
　and green marketing, 183-184
　Internet pornography, 314-315
　Jamaican telemarketers, 254-255
　racial slurs, 296-297
　and standardization, 217-218
　storyboard shopping, 64
　subliminal messages, 95
　and targeted advertising, 149-150
　and targeting middlemen, 80-81

Ethics (continued)
    tobacco industry, 49-50, 95, 128-129
    Wal-Mart example, 19
Ethnic agencies, 21, 57-58, 61
Ethnic audiences. *See also specific groups*
    demographics, 23, 33
    and direct marketing, 250-251
    ethical implications, 149-150
Etzel, Michael, 183
Europe
    Internet use, 252, 253-254
    lifestyle, 90-91
    senior population, 77
European Union
    currency, 251
    regulatory environment, 46-47, 251
Event planning, 82
Events, 16, 34, 261, 271, 289i. *See also* Sponsorship
Excite, 301, 305-306
Extreme close-up (ECU), 157-158

Fact sheets, 282, 285i
Fade under, 164
Fallon McElligott, 60, 108-109
False advertising, 38-39, 46
Family values, 94
Fantastic Sam's, 266
Fantasy, 146
Farm magazines, 190-191
Fear appeals, 15, 139-143
Feature articles, 282-287
Federal Bureau of Investigation (FBI), 40
Federal Trade Commission Act, 39
FedEx, 1, 17, 313
Fees. *See* Payment, to agencies
Feminine hygiene products, 49
Fifty-plus market, 33
Film production, 161
Financial services industry, 3, 236

Fitzgerald, Kate, 18, 231, 271
Flighting, 177
Focus groups, 101, 108-109
Food and Drug Administration (FDA), 40, 50
Food industry, 67, 69-70, 185. *See also* Pizza
Foote, Cone & Belding, 55, 131, 143-145, 252
Ford Motor Co., 136
Fortini-Campbell, Lisa, 93
Fox, 229
Freestanding inserts, 265
Frequency, 176
Frequent flyer miles, 270
Fretts, Bruce, 169-170
FTP, 169
Fulfillment, 254
Full showing, 225
Full-service agencies, 56, 60-61
Fund-raising, 236, 246-248, 266, 272-272

Games, 268
Gannett Outdoor, 224
The Gap, 137, 158
Gardenburger, 205
Gateway, 306
GATX, 283i
Gay market, 33
General Electric, 83, 85
General Mills, 266
General Motors, 24, 268, 301-303
General Nutrition Centers, 92
Generation Xers, 75-77
Generational target marketing, 77, 117. *See also* Age factor
Generic brand, 137
Geographic segmentation, 71, 73, 188-190, 228
Giant Food, 248
Gifts
    premiums, 247, 257, 269
    unsolicited, 247
Gillette, 268

Global advertising
  audience characteristics, 169-170
  Avon example, 201
  and direct marketing, 251-253, 253-254
  local differences, 49, 217-218, 231
  in underdeveloped countries, 231
Global public relations, 294-295, 296
Goodby, Jeff, 136
Grant, Diane, 82
Greece, 49
Green marketing, 183-184
Greeting cards, 242
Grey Advertising, 52, 55, 60, 61
Group identification, 15
GRPs, 177
Guilt, 15, 139
Guy, Pat, 49

Haeckel, Stephen, 309
Hallmark, 138, 210, 240i, 258i, 270, 293
Hard sell, 138, 143-145, 148-149
Harris-Equifax, 248
Havas Advertising, 52
Health care industry, 56-57, 100i
Hendrickson, Paula, 209
Hennessy, 30
Henry, Tamara, 272
Hepatitis Foundation, 139-140
Hewlett Packard, 230, 306
Hispanic agencies, 57
Hispanic Americans
  and direct marketing, 250
  and market segmentation, 71
  and radio ads, 215
  and target marketing, 50, 75, 76i
Hoffman, Aaron, 20
Holiday Inn, 40
Home pages. *See* Web sites
Home surveillance, 109
Homeshopping networks, 227
Honda, 109
Hong Kong, 30, 43, 270

Hormel Foods, 309
Horovitz, Bruce, 305
HotBot, 314
Hoyer, Wayne, 170
HTML, 166
Humor, 80, 139, 141i, 142i, 169-170
Hyland, Tom, 307

IBM, 210, 301, 309
Iconography, 18
Idea Concepts, 309
Image
  brand, 78-79, 137
  corporate, 116i, 121, 151, 293-294, 296-297
  history, 15
  IMC campaign, 141i-142i
IMC. *See* Integrated marketing communication
Impressions, 177
Incentives
  for consumers, 260i, 270
  Internet role, 306
  for trade, 263-264
Independent production companies, 162
India, 10, 31, 49
Indonesia, 46, 48
Industrial market, 12, 13, 119-121. *See also* Business-to-business marketing
Industrial organizations
  classification, 74
  purchasing behavior, 87-88
Infant formula, 48
Infomercials, 226-227
Information
  about consumers, 17, 92-93, 121-122, 238
  international research, 110
  for marketing research, 102-104
Information Resource, Incorporated (IRI), 108
Informational appeal, 138, 143-145
Infoseek, 301, 314

Inner City Broadcasting, 215
Innovative Telecom, 257-259
In-package premiums, 269
Insurance, 268-269
Integrated marketing communication
 and agencies, 57, 61-62
 and business education, 20
 examples, 1-3, 312-313
 global tobacco campaign, 18
 and media selection, 182
 phases, 16-17
 planning approach, 121-122
Interfacers, 179
International advertising. *See* Global advertising
Internet. *See also* Web advertising
 advertising revenues, 315
 agencies, 165
 audience measurement, 106
 content versus advertising separation, 315
 and crisis management, 281
 in cross-promotions, 230
 and customer service, 312-313
 directory advertising, 311-312
 E-mail, 307-309
 in Europe, 252, 253-254
 growth, 27-29
 and incentives, 306
 information exchange modes, 303
 and international direct marketing, 251-252
 for international research, 110
 and languages, 314
 and newspapers, 200
 online magazines, 191, 194
 pornography, 314-315
 product demonstrations, 313
 production, 166-169
 reach/frequency measures, 181-181
 regulation, 304-305, 309, 315
 sales transactions, 151
 shopbots, 226
 top advertisers, 301

Internet (*continued*)
 versus World Wide Web, 304
 Web site guidelines, 166
Internet Advertising Bureau, 307
Internet magazines, 191
Interpublic Group of Cos., 52
Involvement, high versus low, 143-144
IPSOS-ASI, 107
Iridium, 121, 139
Israel, 31, 80, 251
Issue advertising, 8, 292-293, 294
IXL, 165

Jamaica Digiport International (JDI), 254-255
Japan
 distribution channels, 12
 hard sell versus soft sell, 148
 mail-order business, 233, 243
 product adaptations, 83-85, 91
 regulation, 43
 television advertising, 148-149
JCPenney, 242
Jeans, 83, 115-117, 134-135, 186i. *See also* Lee Jeans; Levi Strauss
Johnson & Johnson, 90, 281, 292
Jones, Susan, 237
Junk mail, 239-241
 on the Internet, 309-310
Jupiter Communications, 226
Justice, Department of, 40
J. Walter Thompson, 14, 55, 61, 91
 Dell Computer campaign, 231
 Japanese mail-order, 233

Kane, Jane, 183-184
Kaplan, Rachel, 169-170
Karp, Jonathan, 49
Kaufman, Leslie, 201
Keds, 303
Kelley, Scott, 88

Kellogg's
  agency change, 60
  computer-generated ads, 157
  generic brand, 137
  and lateral thinking, 134
  sex appeals, 139
  and women, 26
KeyCorp, 119
Keyser's newsletter, 296
KFC fast food chain, 29
Kimberly-Clark, 71
Knowledge-Base, 248
Kodak, 31
Krull, Tara, 129-130
Kruse Farm Supply, 147
Kuntz, Mary, 170
Kuttner, Robert, 310-311

Labor-based fees, 59
Language, 25, 250, 251, 313-314
Lanham Trademark Act, 37, 39
Lateral thinking, 134, 135
Latin America, 24, 47-48, 252
Laundry products, 91, 131-133
Lawrence, Mary Wells, 62
Layout and design, 153, 174i
Lee, Chol, 169-170
Lee, Ivy Ledbetter, 298
Lee Jeans, 115-117, 118
Legal factors. *See* Regulation
L'eggs, 231-232
Leo Burnett
  creativity example, 134, 137
  decentralization, 62-63
  in Hong Kong, 43
  income rank, 52, 55
  international direct marketing, 253
  media buying division, 180
  and Miller Brewing Co., 60
  production example, 157
Leong, Harvey, 311, 312
Letters, 239-241

Levi Strauss
  and creative advertising, 134, 136
  customized product, 83
  target marketing, 117, 118
Levy, Steven, 304
Lichty, Tom, 154
Lifestyle, 73, 90-91
Live production, 161
L.L. Bean, 242-243
Local advertising, 164, 165, 307
Lochner, Ken, 189
Logos, 18, 115, 273
Lois, George, 131
Long shot (LS), 158
Lotteries. *See* Sweepstakes
Lowe & Partners/SMS, 60-61
Loyalty. *See* Brand loyalty
Lucent Technologies, 274
Lucky Strike cigarettes, 18
Lycos, 314

Madden, Normandy, 127-128, 217-218
Maddox, Kate, 301
Magazine advertising. *See also* Newspaper magazines
  advantages and disadvantages, 192-193
  audience measurement, 105-106
  circulation types, 192
  covert advertising, 202
  and food industry, 185
  history, 14
  media buying, 193-194
  and sales results, 173
  and target marketing, 74-75
  types of magazines, 187-191, 194, 195-196
Mailing lists, 239, 248, 249
Mail-order, 233, 301. *See also* Electronic commerce
Malaysia, 44-45, 49
Mandese, Joe, 208
Market Facts, Incorporated, 107
Market segmentation, 69-74

Marketing
  business-to-business, 244-245, 248-249
  definitions, 10-11, 69, 96
  objectives, 118, 259
  strategy development, 119-121
  targeted, 74-78, 96, 119, 120i
Marketing communication. *See* Integrated marketing communication
Marketing director, 203-204
Marketing mix, 11-13, 122
Marketing plan, 117-122
Marketing research, 101-104
Markups, 59-60
Marlboro cigarettes, 137
Marriott, Michael, 313-314
Master control, 172
Maynard, Michael, 148-149
McCann-Erickson Worldwide, 51, 55, 56, 57, 90
McCracken, Ellen, 27, 201-202
McDonald's
  corporate advertising, 5
  and creative boutique, 56
  cross-promotions, 229
  and cultural differences, 31
  and reminder function, 9
  sales promotion, 257
  styrofoam containers, 232
  and targeted ads, 15
McLean, Elys, 77
Meat industry, 80-81
Media. *See also specific media*
  costs
    evaluation, 177-178, 179
    magazines, 193-194
    newspaper, 198-200
    radio, 215, 216-217
    television, 59, 179, 208, 211-213
  cross-promotions, 229-230
  direct marketing, 235
  and ethics, 26, 32
  movies, 228-229

Media (*continued*)
  and objective, 176-178
  out-of-home, 223-225, 228
  packaging, 228
  planning factors, 175-178
  and product publicity, 261
  public schools, 227-228
  specialty merchandise, 225-226
  spending data, 124, 175
  and strategy, 121, 124
  vehicle selection, 178-179, 180
  yellow pages, 226
Media commission, 58-59
Media kits, 287
Media Metrix, 106, 306, 307
Media research, 99-101, 104-106
Media Research, Incorporated (MRI), 106
Medium shot (MS), 158
Meijer, 5
Men
  and athletes, 89
  and food ads, 185-187
  and jeans, 117
  in laundry ad, 133, 134
  purchasing behavior, 89
Merchandise-for-pledge, 247-248
Meredith Corp., 74-75
Mergers, 62-63
Message, 106-108, 124, 138, 249
Message weight, 176-177
Microsoft, 301
Miles, Rick, 309
Milk advertisements, 90, 112-114, 136
Miller Brewing Company, 9, 60, 228
Minorities. *See* Ethnic audiences
M&M/Mars, 29, 145
Mobil Oil, 58
Mock-ups, 39
Montgomery Ward, 242
Moriarty, Sandra, 201
Moslem countries, 31, 49
Motivation, 89-90
Motorola, 173

Movies, 135-136, 147, 228-229
Ms. magazine, 27
MSNBC, 230
Mullins, Marcy, 110-111, 124
Muse Cordero Chen, 58
Music, 157, 164
Music in, music out, 164

Name-removal option, 248
Napoli, Lisa, 314-315
Narbone, Catherine, 65-66, 298-299
Narrative Communications, 151
Native Americans, 215
NBC network, 180-181. *See also* MSNBC
Near-pack premiums, 269
Need recognition, 85-86, 92-93
Negative advertising, 6, 7i
Neiman Marcus, 233, 243
Neo-bytes, 178
Nestlé, 48, 267
Networkers, 178, 179
New Zealand, 47
News releases, 282, 283i, 284i
Newsletters, 287
Newspaper advertising
  advantages and disadvantages, 196-197
  costs, 198-200
  and the Internet, 200
  top ten newspapers, 195
  types of ads, 198
  types of newspapers, 195-196
Newspaper magazines, 195-196
Nextel, 139
A. C. Nielsen
  international research, 103, 110
  sales response measurement, 108
  TV audience measurement, 99-101, 104-105
Nike
  ad agency, 136
  athletic sponsorship, 274-275
  marketing formula, 115

Nike (*continued*)
  niche programming, 75
  and typography, 151
  typography use, 151
Non-profit organizations, 236, 246-248, 266, 271-272
Nudity, 40, 49
Number 100 showing, 225

Objective and task method, 126
Objectives
  advertising, 33-34, 123, 138
  marketing, 118, 259
  media selection, 176-178
  public relations, 281, 288
O'Dwyer, Jack, 295
Office Depot, 271-272
Off-invoice allowances, 262
Ogilvy, David, 15, 137
Ogilvy & Mather, 43, 55, 137, 307
Ohler, Steve, 154
Olympic Games, 210, 273-275
Omnicom Group, 52, 62, 79, 165
1-800-FLOWERS, 306
One World Communications, 21
Online magazines, 191, 194
Oppolo, Nicole, 286
Optimizer software, 183
Orci & Associates, La Agencia de, 57
Order forms, 233, 244
Outdoor advertising, 222i, 223-225
Outdoor Systems, 224
Out-of-home advertising, 221, 223-225

Packaging, 228
  environmental concerns, 231-232
  in marketing mix, 12
  and premiums, 269
Page, Dan, 6
Painted bulletins, 224
Palk, Vicki, 171-172
Pan, 158
Papa John's Pizza, 41

Parodies, 170
Payment, to agencies, 58-60
Pearson, Stewart, 252
People-meters, 99, 105
PepsiCo
   combination appeal ad, 143
   crisis management, 280
   local ad adaptations, 49
   market segmentation, 67, 69
   product positioning, 79
   rebates, 267
   situation analysis results, 118
Percentage of sales, 125-126
Perception, 78-79, 89
Peres, Judy, 31
Personal hygiene products, 49
Personal selling, 13, 119, 245. *See also* Telemarketing
Personalized mailings, 239
Persuasion measurement, 107-108
Petrecca, Laura, 63, 201
Pharmaceutical industry, 3, 56-57, 62, 218
Philip Morris, 60, 70, 267
Phone cards, 257-259
Physiological arousal, 107
Picture window format, 174i
Pitch letters, 287
Pizza, 41, 91, 185
Planning, 53
Plans
   advertising, 122-125
   marketing, 117-122
   media selection, 175-179
Plants (billboards), 224
PLATINUM Technology, 141i, 234i
Pledge premiums, 247, 257
Plummer, Joseph, 109
Point-of-purchase displays, 18, 263, 264i
Political advertising, 5-6, 7i
Pollack, Judann, 95
Polo Magazine, 37
Pornography, 40, 314-315
Positioning, 137

Poster panels, 223-224, 225-227
Postpurchase behavior, 86-87
Postscripts, 239-241
Premiums, 247, 257, 269
Preprinted inserts, 198
Press, 291
Press kits, 287
Press releases, 282, 283i, 284i
Price
   in marketing mix, 12
   suggested retail, 44
Price factor, 85
Pride & Ferrel, 69
Prime time, 211
Print advertising. *See also* Magazine advertising; Newspaper advertising
   and ad results, 173
   basic components, 146
   production, 153-156
Privacy issues, 248, 254
Problem-solution, 146
Procter & Gamble
   and ethnic market, 58
   geographic segmentation, 71
   in India, 49
   Internet marketing, 305
   in Japan, 148-149
   sampling, 270
Prodigy, 307
Product
   and consumer needs, 83
   in creative brief, 150
   in marketing mix, 11-12
   packaging, 228
   usage, and market segments, 74
Product adaptations, 67, 83-85, 91, 92
Product advertising, 4-5
Product concept, 123-124
Product differentiation, 78-79
Product placement, 228-229
Product positioning, 78-80
Product publicity, 261
Product shortages, 292

Production
    Internet advertising, 166-169
    print advertising, 153-156
    radio advertising, 163-165
    television advertising, 156-163
    typical day, 171-172
Professional services, 5, 96-97
Promotion. *See* Sales promotion
Psychographic segmentation, 73
Public notices, 198
Public relations
    audience characteristics, 287-288
    campaigns, 288-290
    career success factors, 65-66
    crisis management, 280-281
    definition, 13
    description, 298-299
    document types, 281-288
    evaluation, 288-290
    examples, 112-114, 277-279
    international, 294-295, 296
    and product shortages, 292
    technology impact, 290, 295
    term origin, 298
    versus advertising, 294
    versus corporate advertising, 293
    versus mainstream press, 291
    versus publicity, 13, 292
Public service, 8, 282
Public television, 247, 257
Publicis, 52
Publicity, 261, 292
Publishers Clearing House, 268
Publishing industry, 311, 312-313
Puffery, 202
Pulsing, 177
Pupillometrics, 107
Push money, 263
Pytka, Joe, 143

QVC, 227
Qwest Communications, 116i,
    129-130, 132i

R-A-C-E formula, 288
Racial slurs, 296-297
Radio advertising
    advantages and disadvantages,
        214-216
    audience measurement, 105
    buying time, 216-217
    community service, 206i
    copy, 147-148
    and ethnic groups, 215
    history, 14
    and market segmentation, 71
    pan-regional stations, 231
    production, 163-165
    station ownership, 215, 216
    time categories, 212
Radio station fund-raising, 247
Radzievsky, Yuri, 21
Ralph Lauren, 261
Ralston Purina, 15, 30, 90
Randolph, Amy, 96-97
Rapp Collins Worldwide
    combination appeal, 100i, 145i
    creative brief, 150
    direct marketing role, 57
    emotional appeal, 140i
    ethnic advertising, 72i
    humor, 141i
    image coordination, 142i
    mail examples, 241i, 242i
    Web site map, 167i
Rating services, 99-101
Rational appeal, 138
Raw materials industry, 74
Reach, 176, 224, 307
Rebates, 266-267
Recall measurement, 106-107
Recognition measurement, 106-107
The Red Herring, 306
Reebok, 274
Reese's Pieces, 229
Reeves, Rosser, 137
Reference groups, 86, 91-92
Referrals, 244
Refunds, 266-267

Regulation
  in Asia, 42-46, 49
  of brand names, 37
  in British Commonwealth, 47
  comparative ads, 49
  in European Union, 46-47, 251
  of the Internet, 304-305, 309, 315
  Latin America, 47-48
  opponents, 128
  pornography, 40
  and privacy issues, 248
  self-regulation, 40-41, 45, 46
  in United Kingdom, 46-47
  in United States, 38-40
Relationship marketing, 57, 237, 249
Relevant Knowledge, 306
Reliable office supplies, 250
Religion, 31, 49
Research
  international, 110
  marketing, 101-104
  media, 99-101, 104-106
  message, 106-108
  trends, 108-109
Resonance, 137-138
Response
  in advertising plan, 125
  and directory ads, 6
  and Internet ads, 28
  to telemarketing, 245-246
Results, 173, 235
Retail Advertising, 5
Retailers, 12, 16
Retroactives, 178
Reverses, 152i
Revis, Glenna, 206i
Riedman, Patricia, 314-315
Ries, Al, 137
R. J. Reynolds, 95, 128
RJR Nabisco, 58, 270
Rosenberg, Daniel, 80-81
Royalty fees, 164
Rubin v. Coors, 39-40
Run of paper (ROP) rates, 199

Saatchi & Saatchi, 26, 57
Sales call, 245
Sales promotion
  consumer-oriented, 265-270
  Lucky Strike campaign, 18
  in marketing mix, 12-13
  promotional mix, 259
  trade-oriented, 262-264
Sales response, 108
Sampling, 13, 173, 261, 269-270.
  See also Coupons
Sarin gas, 291
Savin Co., 293
SCANTRACK, 108
Schedule evaluation, 183
Schools, advertising in, 227-228
Schreiber, Alfred, 149-150
Schultz, Don E., 3, 16-17
Seagram's, 35, 41, 61
Sears Roebuck, 33, 75, 237-238, 242
Segue, 164
Seitel, Fraser, 295, 296-297
SelfCare catalog, 243
Self-liquidating premiums, 269
Self-regulation, 40-41, 45, 46, 48, 315
Service concept, 123-124
Services
  advertising, 5, 88
  marketing, 96-97
Sex, 94, 139, 314-315
SFX, 164
Shamrock Net Design, 165, 166
Sharp Electronics, 267
Shaw Festival, 284i
Shi, J. Stephen, 183-184
Shidler, Jon, 33-34
Shoe industry, 83, 274. *See also* Nike
Shopbots, 226, 305-306
Shortages, 292
SIC codes, 74
Silverstein, Rich, 136
Simba Information, 307

Simmons Market Research Bureau (SMRB), 105-106
Simmons-Scarbough, 200
Simpson, Harold, 200
Singapore, 45
Site-centric measurement, 181
Situation analysis, 117-118, 123
Slice-of-life, 146
Slogans, 146
Slotting allowances, 262-263
Smucker's, 286
Snap! Online, 305-306
Social status, 92
Soft sell, 139, 143-145, 148-149
Software
  desktop publishing, 155-156
  for Internet sales, 151
  nonlinear editing, 172
  optimizer, 183
  pornography-filtering, 314, 315
  shopbots, 226
  for Web sites, 169
Solomon, Jack, 15
South America, 47-48
South Korea, 217-218
Special effects, 29-30
Specialized agencies, 56-58
Specialty advertising, 221, 225-226
Speechwriting, 287
Spiegel's, 242-243
Spiffs, 263
Sponsorship, 210, 273-275, 293
Spot announcements, 210-211
Stacey, Julie, 78
Standard Rate and Data Service (SRDS), 211-212
Stanford Research Institute, 73
Stanton, William, 183-184
Starbucks Coffee Co., 127, 261
Starch INRA Hooper, 106
StarTV, 30, 49
Statistical programs, 103
Status, 92
Stereotyping, 25-26, 32
Storyboard, 159-161, 160i

Storyboard shopping, 64
Storytelling, 134-135
Strategy
  creative, 136-148
  marketing, 119-121
  media, 176-178
  sales promotion, 261, 262
Stratford Festival, 84i
Subliminal advertising, 89, 95
Sundance, 301
Super Bowl, 205
Super(imposition), 162
Superstores, 5, 16
Supplier selection, 88
Survey Research Group (SRG), 105, 110
Suzuki, 18
Sweepstakes, 267-268
Syndicated programs, 211

Taco Bell
  camera shots, 158
  "informative" advertising, 8-9
  popularity, 77
  publicity, 292
  specialty advertising, 221, 226
Tactics, 122
Tag line, 146, 163, 164
Taiwan, 43-44
Target groups, 176
Target marketing, 74-77, 96, 119, 120i
Targeted advertising. *See also* Direct marketing
  audience characteristics, 33, 123, 137-138, 150, 178-179
  background, 15
  and cultural interests, 135-136
  and ethics, 149-150
  to ethnic market segments, 21, 33, 50, 250-251
  generational, 77, 117
  for jeans, 115-117, 158

Targeted advertising (*continued*)
  and magazine ads, 188-190, 195-196
  and media selection, 176
  message selection, 249
  to middlemen, 80-81
  to other countries, 49, 169-170
  and radio, 215
TBWA Chiat/Day
  Apple Computer campaign, 5
  blitz advertising, 121
  and creativity, 136
  focus groups, 101
  "informative" advertising, 8-9
  jeans campaign, 118
  liquor TV advertising, 35
Technology, 17, 27-30
Teenagers, 227-228
Teinowitz, Ira, 195
Telecommunications industry, 129-130, 132i
Telemarketing, 244-246, 248, 254-255
Television advertising. *See also* Public television
  and ad results, 173
  advantages and disadvantages, 208-209
  and alcoholic beverage ads, 35, 41
  audience measurement, 99-101, 104-105
  content versus advertising separation, 315
  copy, 146-147
  costs, 59, 179, 208, 211-213
  GRPs, 177
  history, 14
  home shopping networks, 227
  infomercials, 226-227
  in Japan, 148-149
  media buying, 180-181, 210-211
  network versus cable, 207-208, 209, 210
  options, 210-211
  production, 156-163

Television advertising (*continued*)
  recall evaluation, 106-107
  "specials," 293
  time categories, 211, 212
  WebTV, 213-214
Terminal posters, 225
Terminology, 274
Testimonials, 14, 146
Texaco Co., 296-297
Thailand, 46
Thompson, Christian, 50
Thompson, J. Walter. *See* J. Walter Thompson
Thoms, Arline, 260i
Tickle Me Elmo dolls, 292
Time Incorporated, 71
Time magazine, 8, 26
Time zones, 307-309
Tobacco industry
  advertising restrictions, 35, 36i
  in Asia, 42, 43, 46
  and billboards, 224-225
  continuity program, 270
  and ethics, 49-50, 95, 128-129
  and FDA, 40, 50
  global IMC campaign, 18
  Marlboro ads, 137
  sweepstakes, 267
  in United Kingdom, 46-47
Tocci, Angela, 112-114
Toll-free phone numbers, 227, 240
Toyota, 109
TRACE, 107
Trade allowances, 262-263
Trademarks, 37
Trading stamps, 270
Transit advertising, 225
Transportation, Department of, 40
Trends
  ad spending, 52
  consumer behavior, 92-93
  consumer information, 1, 17
  demographics, 33, 57-58
  full-service versus in-house agencies, 60-61

Trends (*continued*)
  on-line advertising, 3
  in research, 108-109
  typography use, 152
Tricon Global Restaurants, 41
Tropicana, 38-39
Trout, Jack, 137
True North Communications, 52, 149
T-shirts, 221, 229-230
Turley, L. W., 88
TWA, 281
Two for the price of one, 39
Tylenol scare, 280, 292
Typography, 151-152, 153-155

Unilever, 30, 62, 91, 305
Unique selling proposition (USP), 137
United Airlines, 108-109, 261
United Distillers, 30
United Kingdom, 46-47, 277
United States
  consumer motivation, 90
  political and legal environment, 38-41
  and sexually explicit ads, 94
Universal, 225
University of Virginia Medical Center, 280
Uniworld, 58
Unsolicited gifts, 247
UPS, 313
U.S. Gypsum, 231
USAir, 280-281
USA Today, 13
U S Web, 165
Utumpom, Pichayaporn, 31

Value and Lifestyle Program (VALS), 73
Values, 297
Vaughn, Richard, 143
Vending machines, 229-230

Venezuela, 47
Victoria's Secret, 243
Videotape, 161, 172, 239
Vietnam, 46
Virgin Group, 292
Voice-over, 162
Volvo, 78

Walker, Bruce, 183-184
Wal-Mart, 16, 19, 301-303
Watchdog groups, 110-111
Web advertising. *See also* Internet
  ad types, 307
  and credit cards, 310
  demographics, 306-307
  industries, 310
  reach, 307
  spam, 309
  spending data, 28
Web sites. *See also* Shopbots
  agencies, 165
  examples, 167i, 168i
  intrusions, 310
  in print ad, 174
  site creation, 166
WebTV, 213-214
Weight, 176-177
Wells, Melanie, 94
Wells, William, 201
Wells BDDP, 62
Wheeler-Lea Act, 39
White balance, 172
Wholesalers, 12
Wickham, DeWayne, 291
Wieden, Dan, 136
Wieden & Kennedy, 136
Wilcox, Dennis, 293
Wilke, Michael, 218-219
Wilson, Craig, 94
Wilson, Judeanne, 203-204
Wind, Yoram, 218
Winicur, Paula, 174i, 186i
Wisner, Kathy Evans, 138, 150

Women
- in alcoholic beverage ads, 26
- and bowling, 294
- and jeans, 117
- and magazine ads, 74-75
- and milk ads, 114
- in Moslem countries, 49
- purchasing behavior, 89
- and sexist ads, 26, 27, 32

Wood, Leslie, 181
Woodward, Gary, 15
WPP Group, 52, 91

Yahoo!, 314
Yates, Ronald, 110
Yellow Pages, 6, 62, 226
- electronic, 303, 311-312

Young, James Webb, 133
Young & Rubicam, 52
Y&R Advertising, 55

Zoom, 158

Order Your Own Copy of This Important Book for Your Personal Library!

PRINCIPLES OF ADVERTISING
A Global Perspective

_____ in hardbound at $69.95 (ISBN: 0-7890-0615-4)

COST OF BOOKS_____

OUTSIDE USA/CANADA/
MEXICO: ADD 20%_____

POSTAGE & HANDLING_____
(US: $3.00 for first book & $1.25
for each additional book)
Outside US: $4.75 for first book
& $1.75 for each additional book)

SUBTOTAL_____

IN CANADA: ADD 7% GST_____

STATE TAX_____
(NY, OH & MN residents, please
add appropriate local sales tax)

FINAL TOTAL_____
(If paying in Canadian funds,
convert using the current
exchange rate. UNESCO
coupons welcome.)

☐ **BILL ME LATER:** ($5 service charge will be added)
(Bill-me option is good on US/Canada/Mexico orders only;
not good to jobbers, wholesalers, or subscription agencies.)

☐ Check here if billing address is different from
shipping address and attach purchase order and
billing address information.

Signature _____

☐ **PAYMENT ENCLOSED:** $_____

☐ **PLEASE CHARGE TO MY CREDIT CARD.**

☐ Visa   ☐ MasterCard   ☐ AmEx   ☐ Discover
         ☐ Diner's Club

Account # _____

Exp. Date _____

Signature _____

Prices in US dollars and subject to change without notice.

NAME _____

INSTITUTION _____

ADDRESS _____

CITY _____

STATE/ZIP _____

COUNTRY _____ COUNTY (NY residents only) _____

TEL _____ FAX _____

E-MAIL_____
May we use your e-mail address for confirmations and other types of information? ☐ Yes   ☐ No

Order From Your Local Bookstore or Directly From
The Haworth Press, Inc.
10 Alice Street, Binghamton, New York 13904-1580 • USA
TELEPHONE: 1-800-HAWORTH (1-800-429-6784) / Outside US/Canada: (607) 722-5857
FAX: 1-800-895-0582 / Outside US/Canada: (607) 772-6362
E-mail: getinfo@haworthpressinc.com
PLEASE PHOTOCOPY THIS FORM FOR YOUR PERSONAL USE.

BOF96